THE COLORED
CONVENTIONS
MOVEMENT

THE JOHN HOPE FRANKLIN SERIES IN
AFRICAN AMERICAN HISTORY AND CULTURE

———

Waldo E. Martin Jr. and Patricia Sullivan, editors

THE COLORED CONVENTIONS MOVEMENT

BLACK ORGANIZING IN THE NINETEENTH CENTURY

EDITED BY

P. Gabrielle Foreman,
Jim Casey, and
Sarah Lynn Patterson

THE UNIVERSITY OF NORTH CAROLINA PRESS
CHAPEL HILL

Manufactured in the United States of America

Designed by April Leidig
Set in Arnhem by Copperline Book Services, Inc.

The University of North Carolina Press has been a member
of the Green Press Initiative since 2003.

Cover illustration: *The National Colored Convention in Session at Washington, D.C.*,
sketch by Theo. R. Davis, 1869. Courtesy of the Library of Congress.

Library of Congress Cataloging-in-Publication Data
Names: Foreman, P. Gabrielle (Pier Gabrielle), editor. |
Casey, Jim, 1985– editor. | Patterson, Sarah Lynn, editor.
Title: The colored conventions movement : black organizing in the nineteenth
century / edited by P. Gabrielle Foreman, Jim Casey, and Sarah Lynn Patterson.
Other titles: John Hope Franklin series in African American history and culture.
Description: Chapel Hill : The University of North Carolina Press, [2021] |
Series: The John Hope Franklin series in African American history
and culture | Includes bibliographical references and index.
Identifiers: LCCN 2020038655 | ISBN 9781469654256 (cloth) |
ISBN 9781469654263 (paperback) | ISBN 9781469654270 (ebook)
Subjects: LCSH: African Americans—Civil rights—Congresses—
History—19th century. | Congresses and conventions—
United States—History—19th century.
Classification: LCC E185.18 .C64 2021 | DDC 323.1196/07309034—dc23
LC record available at https://lccn.loc.gov/2020038655

To the tens of thousands of participants in the Colored Conventions,

to the lions of activism whose names we know,

to those whose generosity has been ignored and genius erased.

We are in your debt.

CONTENTS

FIGURES AND TABLES

TABLES

ACKNOWLEDGMENTS

It is one of the principles of the Colored Conventions Project (CCP) to joyfully acknowledge the labor of all those who contribute to the project's ongoing work. It is a pleasure to do that here. This book emerges from that collective work. The project itself began in a graduate class taught by P. Gabrielle Foreman at the University of Delaware (UD) when Jim Casey and Sarah Patterson suggested we extend a class assignment and posed questions that continue to inform the CCP. We want to thank the members of that class. In addition to this volume's coeditors, they include Clay Colmon, Jessica Conrad, Olivia Meunier, Holden O'Brian, Danya Pilgrim, Dia Samuel, Lara Southgate, Sametta Taylor, and Arline Wilson. Clay Colmon, now associate director of instructional design at the University of Pennsylvania, has stayed connected to the CCP from its inception and served as its first Grants Committee chair. Jessica Conrad, now assistant professor of English at Kent State University, was also a long-term project member and an Exhibits Committee cochair. Danya Pilgrim, now assistant professor at Temple University, and Olivia Meunier, who is now working to support our society's underserved and underresourced, were also early and important CCP members.

This book is accompanied by an extensive website filled with digital collections and interpretive exhibits. The collections and exhibits are veritable book series unto themselves; they have grown with the community and with North American teaching partnerships that mirror the distributed nature of the conventions themselves. These intertwined initiatives have been created and expanded by the many dedicated members of the Colored Conventions Project over the past eight years and counting.

A number of collaborators contributed to the early foundations of the CCP. Professor Colette Gaiter, her design student Cassy Galon, and Audrey Hamelers, then digital humanities and web services librarian at UD, helped upgrade the design and interface of the CCP's first website. Their contributions enabled a growing project to proudly share its collections online. Ben Mearns also guided early technical development. Meg Meiman helped create a pipeline structure for our undergraduate researchers.

Librarians have been at the heart of the project since its start, providing intellectual leadership, mentorship, and so much more. They have helped the project hold steady and keep growing. Curtis Small has long brought joy and an uncommon thoughtfulness to the work of archival recovery on the CCP and beyond. It has been a true delight to work and learn alongside Dr. Small and to have him represent the project in person and in scholarship across multiple eras in the project's growth. Linda Stein created the first LibGuides for related classes at UD and then, with Carol Rudisell, the research guides that quickly became vital parts of our North American teaching partner network and curriculum. Carol has been an important thinker, leader, and presence in the CCP community. Her indispensable spirit and insightful questions have added inestimably to our understanding of the conventions, teaching us a great deal about the intersections of libraries, research, and communities. For just a small sample of her thoughtful approach to the complex questions surrounding our work, we refer readers to her award-winning *Common-Place* article, "Liberating History: Reflections on Rights, Rituals and the Colored Conventions Project."

Also in the library, Keith Jones may have thought we were just a little crazy at times, which makes his patience, generosity, and help with all things technical all the more remarkable over his many years on the project. Thank you, Keith, for everything. When Maisha Carey joined us, she brought a new level of professional energy, expertise, and deep dedication to our collective. Her contributions and presence have made all of us richer in the execution and spirit of our work. Having Aimee Gee's eyes on emerging work and educational swag made us all breathe easier. Kaitlyn Tanis joined our website team, helping Lauren Cooper, Michelle Byrnes, Jim Casey, Kelli Coles, and Caleb Trotter reach the finish line of a massively complex website migration, including by proofreading a huge swath of the digital exhibits.

In addition to those named above, the editors would like to thank the leadership, librarians, and IT specialists at the UD library, including Trevor Dawes, vice provost for libraries and museums and May Morris university librarian, his predecessor Susan Brynteson, as well as Gregg Silvis, Monica McCormick, Mark Grabowski, and Katie Fortney. Gregg Silvis joined Gabrielle Foreman to negotiate the project's first licensing agreements with ProQuest, Gale (a Cengage Company), and Accessible Archives, with Sarah Patterson copiloting. Molly Olney-Zide joined Jordan Howell in one of the great leaps forward for our digital collections, way back in the adolescence of the CCP. Several other people lifted up the work of the CCP over years, including Tracy Jentzsch and John Jungck.

The essays in this volume were first presented as papers at a 2015 symposium with support from the UD College of Arts and Sciences and the Delaware Humanities Forum. The symposium was made possible not only by the authors whose work appears in this volume but also by the tireless efforts of a planning team that included this volume's coeditors. Michele Blum and Charlotte Marshall, the CCP symposium coordinators, helped Sarah Patterson, Gabrielle Foreman, and Jessica Conrad with conference organizing, registration, and evaluation efforts. We also thank Dr. A. Sheree Brown, then head curator of the Center for African American Heritage at the Delaware Historical Society, where part of the conference was held. In addition to the presentations by contributors included in the volume, the symposium was also enriched by presentations from Margarita Simon Guillory and A. Nevell Owens, not to mention the august and generous lineup of moderators and respondents, which included Erica Armstrong Dunbar, Anne Boylan, John Ernest, and Richard Newman. Several extraordinary undergraduate students from UD and Penn State Brandywine also presented research posters, including CCP members Monica Lindsay, Nathan Nikolic, and Caleb Trotter, along with Penn State students Heather Sinkinson and Haleigh Swansen under the direction of CCP teaching partner Kimberly Blockett. We were honored to include among these speakers the dynamic and inspiring Pamela F. Tilley, historiographer for the Connectional Lay Organization of the African Methodist Episcopal (AME) Church. Joycelyn Moody, scholar, editor, and coach extraordinaire, spent a whole day directly after the symposium meeting with junior contributors about turning their conference papers into the essays that appear here.

The results of that symposium grew into this volume through the generosity and intellectual engagement of many people. Members of P. Gabrielle Foreman's 2016 graduate class read and wrote reader reports for draft essays that some volume contributors graciously made available, while the coeditors responded to the rest. Class members include Jake Alspaugh, Jenn Briggs, Eric Brown, Denise Burgher, Samantha de Vera, Harrison Graves, Rosalie Hooper, Carolyne King, Anna E. Lacy, Harry Lewis, Labanya Mookerjee, Eileen Moscoso, and Amos Tarley. They were joined by CCP project librarians Curtis Small and Carol Rudisell. Labanya Mookerjee's final assignment was the basis for the piece she and Gabrielle Foreman coauthored for *Always Already Computational: Library Collections as Data National Forum Position Statements*, titled "Computing in the Dark: Spreadsheets, Data Collection and DH's Racist Inheritance." The other students in the course adapted some of the essays in this volume into digital exhibits. Their exhibits significantly expand the project and extend the arguments of the essays, alongside exhibits created from scratch. We heartily recommend consulting the exhibits to browse a bounty of visual materials on the long history of Black organizing. These exhibits are described in depth in the open-access "How to Use This Book" piece that begins this volume. They were all designed to be taught in college and high school classrooms as accessible introductions to the broader landscape of nineteenth-century Black activism.

As the book neared its completion, more people lent a hand to get us over the finish line. We thank Scott Mangieri, director of corporate and foundation relations at UD, for his endless good work and good humor with the CCP over the years and for his efforts to complete an unusual contract that directed proceeds back to the project. We thank the indefatigable Scott Bennett, associate dean for research and graduate studies in the College of the Liberal Arts, for stewarding that process at Penn State University with the Office of the General Counsel. For expert proofreading and feedback on the "How to Use This Book" section, we are indebted to Curtis Small and

Lynn Foreman. The coeditors also thank Darlea Dominelli for serving as the manuscript coordinator as we submitted the final manuscript.

At the University of North Carolina Press, we would like to express our strongest appreciation to Chuck Grench for his enthusiastic shepherding of this project and, when Chuck retired, to Debbie Gershenowitz for her equally appreciated dedication and attention, along with Mark Simpson-Vos, Dylan White, and Cate Hodorowicz, who helped with this volume's many moving parts. We thank Mary Caviness for help managing the project's final stages, and Iza Wojciechowska for copyediting that greatly improved the final shape of the volume. We are particularly thankful to our two reviewers, professors Erica Armstrong Dunbar and Sharla Fett, whose own prize-winning books have deeply inspired our collective scholarship. This volume is so much richer for their enthusiasm, incisive suggestions, and leadership in the field of early African American history.

Members of the Colored Conventions Project have helped bring this longer history of Black activism to new digital life in many ways. It has been an honor and privilege for the coeditors to work at UD alongside dedicated long-term project members and leaders, including Alyssa Ashley, Michele Blum, Eric Brown, Denise Burgher, Michelle Byrnes, Maisha Carey, Kelli Coles, Clay Colmon, Jessica Conrad, Lauren Cooper, Rashida Davis, Samantha de Vera, Emily Gessmann, datejie cheko green, Keith Jones, David Kim, Anna E. Lacy, Brandi Locke, Kira Lyle, Gwen Meredith, Labanya Mookerjee, Eileen Moscoso, Nate Nikolic, Briana Richardson, Marie Riemerschmid, Carol Rudisell, Curtis Small, Caleb Trotter, and Ariana Woodson. These CCP leaders helped create and grow our digital archive, curriculum, teaching partner network, exhibits, public partnerships, outreach, scholarly communications, and website platforms and design. Though we can't delineate the extraordinary work each of them did or continues to do, each has contributed talents, energy, and expertise that not only advanced the project but also enriched the CCP community.

We also appreciate the collective work of those who have been with us as team members or team leaders, if for a shorter time. These members include Ayo Adeoti, Simone Austin, Melissa Benbow, Morgan Brownell, Mali Collins-White, Amanda Cooper-Ponte, Portia Flowers, Cassy Galon, Aimee Gee, Jenny Goldsmith, Harrison Graves, Vanessa Hatton, Quader'a Henry, Jordan Howell, Lovely Lacey, Paul Lesica, Monica Lindsay, Jourdan Lobban, Natalia Lopez, Hans Louis-Charles, Liselle Malenchek, Charlotte Marshall, Kayla Martin, Adam McNeil, Kelsey Mellow, Olivia Mendes, Lizbeth Mora-Martinez, Amani Morrison, Rachel Nelson, Molly Olney-Zide, Caleb Owens, Danya Pilgrim, Allison Robinson, Marissa Ross, Ethan Scott Barnett, Elizabeth Sobel, Kaitlyn Tanis, Amos Tarley, Allegra Taylor, Brett Tielman-Fenelus, Monet Timmons, Arline Wilson, Gerti Wilson, Kevin Winstead, Darby Witek, and James Wohr. This volume and the broader rediscovery of the Colored Conventions stand on their collective shoulders.

Additionally, we have continued to learn and gain new perspectives on the history of the conventions through the contributions of external collaborators. In our early years, we had the good fortune of welcoming Joycelyn Moody and Kimberly Blockett as our first North American teaching partners. Their intellectual generosity and pedagogical expertise helped show us the broader and exciting potential of our now robust teaching partners network. We are also indebted to the makers of Omeka and Scripto, at George Mason University's Center for History and New Media, along with the staff at Reclaim Hosting for creating and maintaining the infrastructure and tools driving the online components of our project. A major turning point in this collective work came with the start of Transcribe Minutes, our initiative to crowdsource the transcription of digitized primary sources from the convention movement. Transcribe Minutes grew to include more than 1,400 people, who deserve full thanks and recognition as coauthors of a new digital archive. The outreach to a distributed community around Transcribe Minutes succeeded beyond our wildest hopes thanks directly to the leadership of two people: Denise Burgher and Pamela F. Tilley. Brought on board to engage Black church communities, Denise shepherded the Transcribe Minutes initiative into AME communities across North America, many of which had once hosted state and national conventions. It was our good fortune to welcome Denise subsequently to UD as the chair of the CCP Community and Historic Church Outreach Committee.

The addition of project leaders and partners has greatly enriched our work. Lauren Cooper became the CCP project manager in fall 2018, coming to us from the Zinn Education Project with experience that further professionalized the project. Her ability to bring long-term goals to completion is appreciated more than she can ever know. Lauren Cooper picked up from David Kim, the CCP's first project manager, who stepped into a moment of turbulence in our project. As the CCP began arts partnerships in 2018, Lynnette Overby built on her long-term collaboration with Gabrielle. Lynnette's Sharing Our Legacy theater group designed and choreographed arts research projects and ensemble performances highlighting the Colored Conventions movement. As our first official arts partner, Sharing Our Legacy then created a full-length piece on one of the most important female convention delegates, *Mary Ann Shadd Cary: Her Life and Legacy*. In 2019, Professor Kim Gallon joined the project as a low-residency fellow. She and Denise Burgher developed the Curriculum Committee, forging new partnerships to share these re-remembered histories with elementary and secondary school classes in the School District of Philadelphia. That year we were also grateful to add two Council on Library and Information Resources postdoctoral fellows in Data Curation for African American and African Studies, who added new dimensions and knowledge to the CCP. We appreciate you, Amani Morrison and Kevin Winstead.

We would be remiss not to thank the larger body of students, librarians, archivists, and faculty who preceded us in the study of African American literature and history. The project that spawned this volume began in 2012, mere weeks after the passing of Howard Holman Bell, whose early reprint volumes, journal articles, and dissertation stood for decades as some of the precious few guides to the vast history of the Colored Conventions. We also continue to build on the foundational reprint volumes of the state and national conventions edited by Philip Foner and George Walker. As we added hundreds of conventions to our archive, Laura and Elizabeth Foner kindly granted us permission to digitally reproduce the notes and documents from those foundational volumes.

The progress of research on the Colored Conventions has accelerated at particular junctures thanks to sources of invaluable encouragement and support. In 2014, Jennifer Serventi welcomed us to a meeting at the National Endowment for the Humanities (NEH), happily hosting our director and our growing team of librarians and graduate students. Those discussions were pivotal as we began to plot a course forward for the project and its research agendas, eventually resulting in an NEH Office of Digital Humanities Start-Up Grant. The coeditors are grateful to Jen and the rest of the NEH Office of Digital Humanities leadership, including Perry Collins and Brett Bobley. We take this opportunity to proclaim the importance of the NEH, which provides so much more than funding; it is the lifeblood of the humanities, how we preserve and share our cultures and histories in this country. The Andrew W. Mellon Foundation helped propel the work into many new areas. The coeditors would like to thank then president of the Mellon Foundation, Earl Lewis, Elizabeth Alexander, and Patricia Hswe for their sage advice and their investment in the progress of this work. We also deeply appreciate the support of the leadership from UD's College of Arts and Sciences. Thank you to Ann Ardis, John Pelesko, Robin G. Schulze, and George Watson. We would also like to thank UD president Dennis Assanis for inviting the founding faculty director to speak about this project at the president's inauguration, to the board of trustees, and to alumni across the country.

John Ernest has played an essential role in the recovery of the Colored Conventions. As both a leading literary historian of the period and chair of UD's Department of English, John helped pave our way. His scholarship and unstinting administrative advocacy made the CCP's work possible in more ways than we can begin to enumerate. As we can join others in testifying, not only is John one of the most respected scholars in the field; he is deeply committed to promoting others' work.

The coeditors would also like to acknowledge our debts to the places and people who invited us to present earlier iterations of this work, including at the Franklin Humanities Institute Conference at North Carolina Central University and Duke University; the German Historical Institute; the Gilder Lehrman Center at Yale University; the Harry Ransom Center at the University of Texas at Austin; Northeastern University; Oberlin College;

the Price Lab for Digital Humanities at the University of Pennsylvania; the Roy Rosenzweig Center for History and New Media at George Mason University; Tulane University; the University of California, Santa Barbara; the University of Iowa; Vanderbilt University; Washington University; the Winterthur Museum; and Yale University. We extend additional thanks for invitations to present or participate in the Anna Julia Cooper Symposium at Howard University's Moorland Spingarn Research Center; the Black Bibliography Project Conference and Think Tank; the Collections as Data group; the "Frederick Douglass Across and Against Times, Places, and Disciplines" conference in Paris; a "Humanities Data Viz" gathering at Georgia Tech; the NEH summer institute "Space and Place in Africana/Black Studies: On Spatial Humanities Theories, Methods and Practice"; the Schomburg Center for Research in Black Culture; and the Race, Memory, and Digital Humanities Symposium at the College of William and Mary. We have learned a great deal from the many conference panels our team members have joined. In addition to the three coeditors, the cadre of graduate student team leaders who have represented the project as keynote and conference presenters includes the indefatigable and dedicated expert current cochairs of the Digital Archives Committee, Anna E. Lacy and Brandi Locke; the chair of the Community and Historic Church Outreach Committee and cochair of the CCP's Curriculum Committee, Denise Burgher; Exhibits Committee cochair Kelli Coles and former cochair Samantha de Vera; datejie cheko green; and former project photographer Harrison Graves. Associate librarian in Special Collections Curtis Small and CCP project manager Lauren Cooper have also taken up the call to represent the team as keynote speakers, conference presenters, and invited workshop participants. We are grateful for opportunities to think with and present in various community forums, podcasts, videos, and radio shows in groups that included Denise Burgher, Brandi Locke, and Curtis Small as well as Gabrielle Foreman and Jim Casey. We've also had an opportunity to present in art forums, particularly with our stalwart partner Lynnette Overby. We are also thankful for the opportunity to join with the Frances Ellen Watkins Harper Think Tank and Lenwood Sloan in Philadelphia and across Pennsylvania. Anna Mae Duane kindly invited a group of us to publish early findings of this work in the online journal *Common-Place*.

We want to thank those who nominated and elected us for awards from the Modern Language Association, the American Studies Association, and the Popular Culture Association. Thanks to Rafia Zafar, Carla Peterson, and other, anonymous nominators and supporters. We are particularly humbled by the selection of the CCP as one of approximately fifty NEH Essentials; to be recognized in such illustrious company is an extraordinary and unexpected honor.

—P. Gabrielle Foreman, Jim Casey, and Sarah Lynn Patterson

It has been a pleasure to work on this volume. I am indebted to a multitude of African American progenitors whose fiery spirits ignited a grassroots platform committed to upholding values of equality and unity against daunting odds. From discovering Black census records to studying incredible orators such as John Mercer Langston and Sarah Woodson Early, my time with Colored Conventions continues to evoke wide-eyed appreciation and edification. I thank my colleagues, librarians, and friends for thoughtfully responding to drafts and expanding my professional network.

I am immensely grateful for the intellectual energy and acts of teaching and learning that undergird our collective understanding of African American literary history and social change movements. I especially thank the scholars featured in this book for illuminating Black convention cultures for readers around the world. Each participant in the birth and lifespan of ColoredConventions.org receives my praise. Lastly, I owe my thanks to the historical societies, digital collections, and funding avenues that have sustained my scholarship, including the NEH, the Massachusetts Historical Society, and the Ohio Historical Society.

—Sarah Patterson

I would like to reiterate my thanks to the many people directly and indirectly responsible for this volume. Scores of names already appear in these acknowledgments; like the conventions, this volume is a by-product of many collectives past and present. I would like to extend my first personal thanks to my coeditors. It has been the privilege of a career. As this volume goes to press, Gabrielle Foreman and I are going into our ninth year (and counting) of collaborating. Perhaps more than anyone, I can attest that Gabrielle has raised the work of building communities, supporting people, and forging partnerships to the level of an art form. I'm more grateful than I can express, both for all of our time together, writing, thinking, and strategizing, and for all of her countless efforts—all the million emails, texts, meetings, group calls, and walks—that most people may never see, even as those efforts have touched so many lives. Her insanely hard work and radical generosity, along with her scholarship, create the kind of debts that one spends an entire career trying to repay and relay. When we began this project, I was a graduate student at UD, where I had the great fortune of having John Ernest supervise my dissertation, encourage my digital extracurriculars, and teach me so much about the conventions, the field, and our profession. I'm deeply thankful for John's support and wisdom and always look forward to more of our conversations. At UD, the larger CCP crew was also a constant, sustaining source of personal support, community, and endless inspiration. I am more grateful than I can say for the opportunity to work with such an uncommonly creative and generous group of people over the past three years at the Center for Digital Humanities at Princeton University, including Meredith Martin, Natalia Ermolaev, Rebecca Munson, Nick Budak, Rebecca Sutton Koeser, Ben Hicks, Jean Bauer, Elizabeth Samios, Gissoo Doroudian, Mana Winters, and Nora Benedict.

I want to thank my family—Art and Mary Casey, plus Laura, Derek, Meghan, Pierce, and Erin—for all of the love, support, and enthusiasm over the years. It is entirely possible that my parents have told more people about the CCP than anyone else in this volume. Finally, my greatest thanks to Natalie Smith for being there through it all.

—Jim Casey

The underlying principles and structures of the CCP seek to build on lessons learned from community-based organizing. I'm continually humbled and inspired by the organizers and activists of the movement that this book documents and to the activists and community partners who have shared their wisdom with me more directly along the way. William L. Andrews provided an example of publishing with graduate students long before I had the opportunity to imagine how much I would grow and learn alongside them. Earlier inspirations still include teachers who opened doors for me to imagine living an expansive academic life devoted to radical Black/feminist principles of intellectual care or community. To Laura Wexler, David Wills, and Julius Lester, my undergraduate years wouldn't have been intellectually rich or thick or interesting—they wouldn't, actually, have been possible— without you. To Earl Lewis, whose leadership, scholarship, and generosity is a boundless example, thank you. Barbara Christian's joyful and vibrant scholarly, cultural, and political engagement shaped me more than I had thought possible. We miss you. My cofounders of the Action for Social Change and Youth Empowerment collective (AScHAYE) laid the groundwork for the CCP. Hoang, Kianna, Mia, and Noemi, *besitos* and hot sauce.

I thank my sister scholars at UD: Erica Armstrong Dunbar, Tanisha Ford, Colette Gaiter, Tiffany Gill, Carol Henderson, Lynnette Young Overby, and Carol Rudisell. Y'all know. The Sharing Our Legacy theater, all the dancers and arts researchers, my poet/sister Glenis Redmond, and my composer/ brother Ralph Russell managed to get me dancing, and that's no small thing. It's been a great honor to have you extend my research to the stage and to be able to be a witness and participant in that work. Thanks to my writing group: Daina Ramey Berry, Jackie Goldsby, Maurice Wallace, Andrea Williams, and Psyche Williams-Forson. My writing buddy Kimberly Blockett is likewise a much-appreciated source of inspiration and accountability. Thanks to Denise Burgher, John Ernest, my mom Lynn Foreman, datejie cheko green, and Carla Peterson, whose comments on draft versions of my chapter in this volume made it stronger. Shout-outs to Bill Andrews, Daphne Brooks, DoVeanna Fulton, Charlene Gilbert, Alex Juhasz, Joycelyn Moody, Carla Peterson, Julie Segre, Laura Wexler, Cynthia Young, and Rafia

Zafar for letters, nominations, and love. Shirley Moody Turner and I have been trying to work together for almost a decade now. I'm so excited that the CCP will join the Black Women's Organizing Archive as a project of the Center for Black Digital Research that we get to codirect. Thanks, Shirley, for the future you've helped to make possible.

Rarely does one get to work with someone whose work is so closely aligned as mine and John Ernest's. John's ability to keep writing brilliant books and essays, to elevate *everyone*, and to do so with a calm and grace that makes it all seem easy is a gift to everyone lucky enough to be in his expansive orbit. Curtis Small, Colette Gaiter, and I began the social club Black Arts Quarterly, and I've learned more from—and had more fun with—them than they probably know.

I was confused beyond measure when Barbara Christian thanked me after my qualifying exams. Now I understand what it means to know that the field you've given so much to is in good hands. It's been an honor to work with Jim Casey and Sarah Patterson. Their commitment as cofounders and early project coordinators was both a true labor of love and a demonstration of organizational brilliance that they offered long before the enhanced stipends, professional development funds, and secure summer funding that the super-talented and hardworking CCP graduate student leaders enjoy today. Seeds Sarah Patterson planted, from our unrelenting focus on Black women, despite their absence in convention records, to the project's exhibits and many of the project's early structures, continued to blossom long after she left for UMass Amherst and started her own career. I'm not sure where to start or stop when it comes to Jim Casey's endless commitment to the scholarly, digital, and project-building work that infuses this project's shared leadership. I'm humbled by the collaborative visioning, laid-back problem solving, perfect turns of phrasing, countless hours, and ever-growing expertise, networks, and knowledge he brings to our ongoing work. His commitment continued uninterrupted even during his three years at Princeton's Center for Digital Humanities. Jim has an uncanny talent for getting me into all sorts of "good trouble," to quote John Lewis. When he put together an image of a book called "The Colored Conventions in the Digital Age" for the PowerPoint in one of our very first on-campus presentations, none of us realized we were taking baby steps on the long path to creating the first edited collection on the earliest sustained movement for Black civil rights. Other graduate students deserve thank-yous in the spirit of Barbara Christian's gracious praise. In their dedication, as experts in digital archive building, and as mentors of graduate students and undergraduate researchers alike, Anna Lacy and Brandi Locke continue to make me proud. Team building, place making, and community care for a group this diverse and complex is no easy thing. In that, in addition to her official and substantial roles as the chair of multiple committees, Denise Burgher has been a quiet copilot. I can't express how lucky I am that Jim, Denise, Anna, Brandi, and our only undergraduate committee chair, Michelle Byrnes, are slated to come with us to the Center for Black Digital Research.

I thank my husband, Jeffrey L. Richardson, for his unflagging commitment to the communities and causes that spurred convention leaders to action centuries ago. My mom flags every reference to nineteenth-century conventions she sees. She goes to my colleagues' talks and reads their books with glee and pleasure. What a gift. Thanks to my uncle Reggie, who always asks me, "Did you take that five minutes?" I'm getting there.

—Gabrielle Foreman

As a collective, we don't only fear but know that we have omitted or failed to significantly highlight people and work that we value a great deal. Please charge it to our heads and not our hearts. This volume has been a collective endeavor, with missing and misspelled names and contributions like the convention records themselves.

THE COLORED
CONVENTIONS
MOVEMENT

HOW TO USE THIS BOOK
AND ITS DIGITAL COMPANIONS

Approaches to and Afterlives
of the Colored Conventions

Jim Casey, P. Gabrielle Foreman,
and Sarah Lynn Patterson

This is the very first collection of essays to examine the seven-decade history of Colored Conventions. As such, it is also an invitation for future scholarship that revises, corrects, annotates, refigures, and reframes not only what is presented here but also many of the assumptions scholars and the public hold about nineteenth-century Black organizing, abolition, slavery, and "freedom." Our humility comes from the knowledge that many of these essays are contained in a form too small for them; they could grow into books unto themselves. Some essays have already inspired visually rich online exhibits featured at ColoredConventions.org that are created by faculty and students working with the Colored Conventions Project (CCP). As that project is interdisciplinary in its makeup and approaches, so, too, is this volume. Contributors hail from departments of African American studies and American studies, from English, history, and communications. Its writers include religious studies scholars and archeologists as well as emerging leaders in digital humanities and seasoned, award-winning authors. *The Colored Conventions Movement* has much to offer. Readers who are deeply acquainted with aspects of these early Black political gatherings and those who had never heard of them will read these essays and find themselves thinking, "Why didn't I know about this?"

Chapter Summaries

Critical Conventions, Methods, and Interventions

This volume begins with an essay by the CCP's founding faculty director, P. Gabrielle Foreman, which serves as both an introduction to the movement and an argument that studying early Black convention organizing reorients the very questions scholars and the public can pose about Black organizing, agency, and authorship. She notes that the inaugural Colored Conventions meeting predates the establishment of the American Anti-Slavery Society by a full three years and that the Massachusetts Anti-Slavery Society (1831), the New England Anti-Slavery Society (1832), and the American Anti-Slavery Society (1833) were all founded after the convention movement's first convening. Foreman asks how a commitment to what she calls a Black "parallel politics" that took place over seven decades revises Black genealogies of reform and networks of influence. Centering conventions disrupts perceptions that for too long have orbited around interracial relationships that have eclipsed Black circuits of exchange, mentorship, and development. Foreman makes a case that the writing practices that emerge from the convention movement provide as powerful a model as the Black writing that came out of the abolition movement. If slave narratives chart individual journeys toward freedom and literacy, she argues, Colored Conventions offer a paradigm of Black being and belonging centered not in individual rights and singular authorship but in collective writing and organizing. In their commitment to community efforts and collective models, convention organizers—and conventions as a structure of organizing—highlight the committee alongside the singular author, preacher, or heroic protagonist. Foreman's essay offers an important reframing of this long history of Black organizing around parallel politics and communal expression.

The volume continues with a group of essays that offer critical methods for approaching the historical records that document the Colored Conventions. As contributors Eric Gardner, Psyche Williams-Forson, and Carla Peterson contend, where one looks may be as significant as what one finds. These scholars suggest ways to account for gaps and omissions in convention minutes by offering correctives to traditional definitions of both convention leadership and convention events themselves. "Where does a convention—and what we know about it—both start and stop?" These scholars ask that we pay close attention to gender and class as well as to how news of conventions traveled. By offering methodologies that expand the lens through which we view and analyze conventions, they attune scholars, students, and general readers to dynamics that aren't always obvious to readers of convention proceedings. These authors' essays begin the book because their calls to refine methods of consideration and analysis shift the scope, spaces, and documents that will shape emerging scholarship on early Black organizing and the convention movement.

Reading the convention documents themselves leaves the impression that women were barely involved in this movement for Black educational, labor, and legal rights. Frances E. W. Harper and Edmonia Highgate gave speeches at the 1864 national Colored Convention in Syracuse, New York; yet the published minutes minimize their presence and give little clue to what either might have said. In his essay, literary historian Eric Gardner demonstrates the value of looking beyond the officially sanctioned minutes as he reconstructs what both speakers likely presented by consulting coverage of speeches they gave at other venues in the months leading to and just after the convention. Gardner draws clues from a wide range of nineteenth-century newspapers (including the *Liberator*, the *National Anti-Slavery Standard*, and the *Weekly Anglo-African*) as a method of accounting for women's ideas and activism that are otherwise excised from what Gardner calls the "the work of the convention."

Psyche Williams-Forson shares Gardner's focus on print culture through her research on nineteenth-century boardinghouses and the advertisements they placed in papers as a means of attracting convention attendees. Extending her work as a leading critic in Black foodways, she examines Black women's entrepreneurial contributions to conventions and asks readers to consider food presentation and menus in relationship to "definitions of home, domesticity, and respectability." Williams-Forson's essay reveals the extent to which "domestic labor was radicalized as a source of female empowerment." Her method widens our historical lens; instead of zooming in on the podium from which delegates spoke, she pans out past the seats and pews to focus on boardinghouses, where critical conversations and planning no doubt took place. Williams-Forson offers us a method that expands the spatial and temporal definition of a "convention" to include spaces beyond the convention sites named in proceedings. In doing so, she is able to locate and center more examples of Black women's activist contributions.

While tracing James McCune Smith's efforts to establish a permanent convention body, Carla Peterson argues for sequential readings of convention minutes. Adopting this method in her essay, she shows how Smith's efforts to redesign convention infrastructure spilled into newspaper columns in a heated debate that placed him in stark opposition to famed editor Frederick Douglass before the convention even took place. Peterson argues that we must read conventions and coverage sequentially "in order to get a fuller picture of Black Americans' intellectual work and social activism and of the leaders who stood at their vanguard." Pre- and postconvention materials provide insight into the linkages between debates at state and national conventions, Peterson asserts.

The essays in this section not only examine conventions and their contexts but also advance methodological imperatives to consult greater networks of source materials and to expand both the focus and the archive used to understand the Colored Conventions movement.

Antebellum Debates: Citizenship Practices, Print Culture, and Women's Activism

The essays in this section address a number of the most prominent, if understudied, debates and political rituals that characterize the first thirty years of the Colored Conventions movement. Popular assumptions about campaigns for Black freedom in antebellum America often center white-led abolition advocacy and emancipation efforts. Conventions took up these subjects but were also deeply invested in how educational, labor, and legal rights in the expanding United States impacted ostensibly "free" African

Americans. Scholars Derrick Spires, Erica Ball, Joan Bryant, and Jewon Woo consider how Black convention activists advanced their claims to individual citizenship rights and freedom while advancing collective action and inclusion in the body politic.

Derrick Spires's essay traces several "divergent editions" of Rev. Henry Highland Garnet's fiery "Address to the Slaves of the United States of America." Garnet first gave the speech at the famous 1843 convention where he and Douglass made their debut in national meetings. Often taught outside of its convention contexts, the speech was first meant to emerge from a committee as a collectively written and sanctioned convention "address" to be distributed all over the United States. Garnet's performance during the ensuing debate enraptured his audience and has since become foundational to scholarship on early Black activism, Spires argues. He reads Garnet's original speech and its subsequent iterations as "performative texts." Spires demonstrates that the address "was collaborative from the start and each printing was deeply engaged with the events of the moment." Spires's essay reveals how reading convention speeches and addresses outside of their organizational contexts obscures the process of their composition and mutes the fullness of the political objectives that inspired them.

Black communities assembled in antebellum conventions to assert their claims to a social and political contract that included them as individuals and as a larger collective. In her contribution, historian Erica Ball disputes the perception of early U.S. political conventions as spaces dominated by a "democratic, white male prerogative." To support her claim, she situates Colored Conventions as parallel gatherings that officially represented "the wishes of their constituents." There, delegates honed their political abilities and articulated their own agendas. Starting as early as 1837, Ohio was a hotbed of antebellum activism, hosting more conventions than any other state. Ball's readings of the 1849 and 1856 Ohio state conventions highlight the way convention goers responded from the audience; she charts the dynamic participatory activism of a public that included Black women. Ball also shifts readers' focus from debates and addresses to the various "procedures, customs, and rhetorical strategies" that shaped convention debates. She argues that paying attention to these "conventions of the conventions" reveals strategies Black communities used to try to gain access to American citizenship.

Joan Bryant, a scholar of African American religious history, examines the political debates that caused organizational fissures between some who had served as early Colored Conventions delegates and those who formed the American Moral Reform Society in the mid-1830s. The society's founder, the well-known William Whipper, was a regular convention delegate who developed his integrationist goals for moral reform "squarely within colored reform arenas." The founding of the American Moral Reform Society instigated an eight-year national convention hiatus, which stretched from 1835 to 1843. At the 1834 convention, Whipper successfully proposed the new organization's formation, which, along with denouncing slavery, would eschew the use of color or racial terminology and reject the Black-led, Black-community approaches to movements for equal rights. Bryant's work helps readers apprehend the competing strains and strategies that are evident throughout decades of convention organizing and that threatened a Black-led convention movement in its very first decade of existence.

At the 1849 Ohio state convention, a woman named Jane Merritt moved to be seated as a delegate. Her male peers initially refused. As Jewon Woo shares in her essay, such assertions of presence and power by Merritt and other women ruffled the male-only standard of leadership in Black conventions. As Woo puts it, national and state conventions for Ohio African Americans in the mid-nineteenth century widened the debate about Black women's participation in racial and political leadership. Woo points out that Ohio's 1848 convention came on the heels of women's conventions in Seneca Falls and Rochester, New York, prompting Frederick Douglass to introduce a white woman speaker at the 1848 Colored National Convention in Cleveland, Ohio. One year later, the 1849 Ohio state convention saw Black women revolt against their exclusion from the previously all-male proceedings. Woo's essay also raises questions about how historical documents are created at the time of the events themselves and how such practices impact both the public's and scholars' ability to envision Black women as central players in activist histories.

Out of Abolition's Shadow: Print, Education, and the Underground Railroad

Many public narratives about nineteenth-century racial resistance persist in heralding white leaders of the Underground Railroad and the antislavery movement. Until recently, little scholarly or public attention recognized the adjacent history of the Colored Conventions. Essays in this section, by Benjamin Fagan, Sarah Patterson, Kabria Baumgartner, and Cheryl LaRoche, track Black-led and Black-community-directed efforts to build political power and institutions through early Black newspapers, statistical reports, and schools and as Black agents on the Underground Railroad. These essays show how conventions were used as spaces for concrete planning, coordination, and advocacy for equal justice and freedom through collective efforts. Essays in this section also challenge assumptions that early Black organizing was merely reactive to circumstances. As delegates worked to start newspapers, census surveys, and schools, they affirmed the power of building an infrastructure for Black progress.

Benjamin Fagan reads "the minutes of Colored Conventions and the pages of Black newspapers together," as he puts it, "exploring how these two crucial institutions of antebellum Black life and activism understood and imagined each other." In both forums, leaders saw that local solutions alone would not be enough to counter increasingly virulent anti-Black laws, disenfranchisement, and racial violence as the nation inched closer to the Civil War. As he traces delegates' affirmations of the importance of the Black press in the earliest conventions, Fagan examines how specific press committees at national conventions over the 1840s and 1850s created new plans for national, centralized, Black newspapers. Rather than focus on papers edited by white abolitionists, Fagan focuses on the columns of such Black-edited papers as *Freedom's Journal*, the *Colored American*, the *North Star*, *Frederick Douglass' Paper*, and the *Provincial Freeman*. Calling the Black press and Black conventions "two of the primary institutions of antebellum Black activism," Fagan places the robust debates about the role of the press held at conventions into conversation with the lively discussions about national authority held in the pages of Black newspapers.

Conventions sought to achieve some control over their collective representations through the press as well as through the growing international use of statistics and data. Sarah Patterson's essay unpacks the use of what she calls "Black demography" in the conventions between 1830 and 1843. Patterson shows that delegates created what amounted to a shadow census as part of their agenda for self-governance. Committees at each of the 1830s conventions outlined ways to collect information about Black Americans in surveys that sought to measure economic, political, and "moral" progress. Challenging census records that misrepresented Black economic and mental health, these self-generated statistical reports spoke loudly to refute ideas of Black inferiority. Patterson argues that conventions' collections of statistical and other data amount to the creation and circulation of numerical portraits of African Americans.

Kabria Baumgartner attends to a central, recurring focus in the conventions: educational access and equality. Noting that in their earliest years, conventions advocated for educational opportunities and institutions for Black boys and men, Baumgartner examines women's roles in the evolution of antebellum advocacy for African American higher education. Although Black women were absent from many of the published convention proceedings and Black girls often were not the intended students in the Black schools proposed at conventions, Baumgartner argues that Black women's participation pushed the discussions of African American education to be more gender inclusive. In her essay, Baumgartner reveals how Black women conventioneers and delegates vigorously recast and redefined Black education as not just gender inclusive but "empowering."

While some convention proceedings featured debates about the Black press, statistical measures of Black achievement, and equal schooling, other topics required discretion and intentional silence. Across more than sixty antebellum conventions' minutes, none record debates about the Underground Railroad. Few even mention it by name. Cheryl LaRoche's essay explains that loud absence as indicative of two worlds that Black activists navigated simultaneously: one in which they created visible public platforms at the conventions while, in the second, they hid their efforts to aid those emancipating themselves. LaRoche joins other volume contributors in observing that many aspects of the conventions were never recorded in the minutes themselves. Organizers often came to antebellum state and national conventions with what LaRoche calls "hidden agendas," or plans to discuss illegal, by-any-means operations to assist self-liberating runaways. LaRoche offers a small sample of delegates who were also underground conductors, revealing that the list of those involved in both efforts includes a pantheon of Black family leadership: Bishop Richard and Sarah Allen, Austin and Patience Steward, Harriet and William Whipper, David Ruggles, Julia and Henry Highland Garnet, and Sarah Mapps and Frederick Douglass, among others.[1] Studying the Underground Railroad and the convention movement in isolation, LaRoche argues, fails to adequately establish critical connections. Naming those interconnected circuits allows scholars and the public to document overlapping networks and hidden strategies of resistance to slavery and quasi freedom.

Locating Conventions: Black Activism's Wide Reach and Unexpected Places

This first collection of essays on the Colored Conventions is an invitation to relearn, or at least reframe, much of nineteenth-century Black history. As essays by Jim Casey, Selena Sanderfer, Andre Johnson, Jean Pfaelzer, and Daina Ramey Berry and Jermaine Thibodeaux display, conventions occurred in a dizzying number of locales. Local Black histories matter. Even as national conventions addressed different contexts, state conventions offer details about their communities' local circumstances and larger concerns. Many of the essays in this section examine conventions in the South and expanding West, regions that have largely been understudied because collections of minutes focused on antebellum meetings often held in the Northeast and in what is now the Midwest; likewise, earlier scholarship tended to build out from studies on antislavery activism in New England and the northeastern United States. With the robust and growing collection of postbellum and lesser-known convention meeting records now available at ColoredConventions .org, scholars and others interested in early Black advocacy and politics can appreciate a much fuller range of early Black political organizing all over North America.[2] The essays in this section illuminate the process of activating Black communities to collective action across seemingly distant places. They form just a small sample of opportunities to learn more about how Blacks came together to advocate for their rights in what Eric Gardner calls unexpected places.

In the first essay of this section, Jim Casey maps the social networks of antebellum Colored Conventions. Casey contends with the massive scale of the antebellum conventions even before they increased exponentially in the South after the Civil War. His research shows that nearly 2,000 delegates attended at least forty-eight conventions between 1830 and 1864. Casey maps the delegates and their locations using tools of social network analysis and data visualization to show how and where communities formed across the conventions year after year. Joining other scholars who never assume that historical records—in this case convention minutes—are objective records of the facts, Casey argues that we should understand the documents published by conventions as "collective self-expressions." Using a critical digital method, Casey observes patterns by examining who attended conventions together (what's called co-attendance). Casey's network analysis offers new insights into some familiar networks in Pennsylvania and the Northeast. His work also trains our gaze on conventions held in border states and California, on transnational conventions, and on the only antebellum convention held in a slave state. Casey compares these groups in the Colored Conventions movement to nineteenth-century data on antislavery and Underground Railroad groups. Thinking critically about data collection and visualization, he shows how these organizational histories—how dated and racially freighted data—raise more questions than answers. As Casey points out, across so many different communities, the Colored Conventions "resist neat narratives."

The rancorous and recurring debates over emigration to the Caribbean and West Africa particularly resist neat narratives and trajectories. Selena Sanderfer's essay shows the importance of formerly enslaved people's desire for independence as expressed through landownership and, eventually, through emigration. She shows how, as racialized violence in the South surged and the prospects of landownership diminished, Black southerners retreated from racial conciliation and turned to emigration in increasing numbers. Black leadership followed their lead, she shows, gradually condoning leaving the country as a viable resistance and uplift strategy—a means to achieve Black independence. Sanderfer brings our attention to how these debates played out in state conventions held in South Carolina, Virginia, Tennessee, and Alabama. She shows how, when elite Black leaders from northern cities hesitated to consider emigration, it was the intellectual leadership of formerly enslaved Black men and women in the South that fostered these evolving conversations. Their leadership testifies to the number of intellectual tributaries that flow into and from the Colored Conventions.

Andre Johnson brings to readers' attention one of the most dynamic leaders to emerge from the postwar South, Henry McNeal Turner. Turner would become bishop of the African Methodist Episcopal (AME) Church and one of the most important, if overlooked, leaders of the entire convention movement. Johnson traces how Turner's work as a newspaper editor and activist AME bishop informs his service as president of many state, regional, and national Colored Conventions. Starting in 1865, and continuing for almost thirty years, Turner led state conventions in Georgia and had prominent roles in other state and national conventions. In response to violent white removal of Black elected officials in his home state, Turner spoke before the U.S. Congress. Turner's testimony details how Colored Conventions used statistics to enter white violence and "outrages" into the congressional record. These reports—excised from official proceedings to avoid further state-

sanctioned violence, record the 1,500 Black men, women, and children murdered by whites in Georgia over just three years (1868–71). Turner reveals that
across the South, not "less than twenty thousand" were targeted and killed.
Delegates and attendees protested such atrocities in convention after convention, including during a major regional gathering in 1871 in Columbia,
South Carolina, and at a national convention in 1893. Often called "Turner's
Convention," the 1893 meeting attracted more than 700 delegates as well as
daily press coverage across the entire country and beyond. Held not in the
South but in southern Ohio, it displays Turner's extensive influence within
the convention movement. Indeed, Turner's Convention took place in Cincinnati, the city where white mob violence prompted the very first national
convention in 1830; the momentous 1893 national Colored Conventions is
one of the very last to claim that title.

Focusing on named delegates and charismatic leaders such as Douglass
and Turner can make it easy to forget those who were neither granted delegate status nor featured in the proceedings. Daina Ramey Berry and Jermaine Thibodeaux examine how "Black male delegates at the Austin Colored Men's Convention [in 1883] believed it both practical and justifiable to
address a host of issues that affected *all* Black Texans, yet at the same time
they excluded Black women." Berry and Thibodeaux detail how the all-male
delegation harnessed collective organizing principles to present a five-point
list of grievances that, while overlapping with other efforts to secure Black
rights across the South, left Black women without an official voice on issues
that impacted them directly. Texas conventions protested unfair miscegenation statutes, unequal school funding, the state's use of convict labor,
segregated public accommodations, and the exclusion of Blacks from jury
service—issues that impacted Black families and communities, not just the
Black men who claimed exclusive leadership of those communities in conventions. The authors show that while male delegates sought to speak for
everyone, they did little to invite the participation of such Texans as Milly
Anderson, who sued the railroads in federal court in 1877 for denying her
equal access to a seat in train cars reserved for white women. Instead, Black
male delegates depended on the politics of respectability to advance a collective argument. In Berry and Thibodeaux's reading, "This group of Black men
had their women under control and therefore were equally worthy patriarchs
in a state and region where rigid gender, like racial, conventions also mattered." As the Black communities shaped by the Texas state meetings laid
the foundations for future movements, Texas women were neither invited
nor welcomed.

Detailing Black state conventions even farther west, Jean Pfaelzer provides
a compelling history of earlier civil rights movements through her analysis
of California state Colored Conventions in the 1850s. California had abol-
ished slavery under Mexican rule in 1829. Once under U.S. rule, however, the
influence of state-sanctioned racism and discrimination grew. Black leaders

such as Mifflin W. Gibbs and Peter Lester, among others, had attended northeastern conventions and knew well the power of organized, collective dissent. A series of racist decisions in California, including a state supreme court decision robbing Black citizens of their right to testify in court, prompted Black communities to hold state conventions. There, they considered a wide array of ideas and gathered more than 8,000 signatures to send to the state government. The stakes of the California state Colored Conventions were crystallized in 1858 with the case of Archy Lee, a narrative Pfaelzer offers as a convention victory that ended the ban on Black court testimony and the free rein of chattel slavery in the Golden State. The conventions helped form new Black communities in the West and helped shape new political possibilities for freedom and full civil rights.

Online Companion Exhibits

This collection emerges from the collective work of an award-winning digital project. Since 2012, the CCP has developed an online archive, major transcription events, and interpretive exhibits to bring the Colored Conventions movement to digital life. This book springs from what very well may be the first symposium held on the Black convention movement; the symposium deliberately included scholars from a wide array of areas: religion, literature, and food studies, for example, as well as nineteenth-century history, culture, and politics. Along with freely accessible digitized records of hundreds of Colored Conventions, many of the website's online exhibits are adapted from essays included in this volume. Other exhibits examine additional aspects of convention history and culture: Black women's entrepreneurial enterprise in Philadelphia in the 1830s (Samantha de Vera); the launch of the movement itself (Eric Brown); Black mobility and national conventions in the 1850s (Jessica Conrad, Samantha de Vera, et al.); and Black women in the Ohio conventions (Christine Anderson and Nancy Yerian).[3] Often adopted in high school and college classrooms, the digital exhibits are now available alongside the essays that inspired them. We intend for the exhibits to expand upon the essays featured here, thereby offering more interactive, visual, and exploratory stories of the collective lives and issues connected to the Colored Conventions.

Of the sixteen essays featured in this volume, half are complemented by exhibits:

- Kabria Baumgartner's essay, with an exhibit created by Occidental College students in Sharla Fett's class with David Kim: Gabriel Barrett-Jackson, Emma Cones, Christina Delany, Lindsay Drapkin, Lila Gyory, Sydney Hemmindinger, Rosa Pleasant, Reilly Torres, Victoria Walker, and Daniel Waruingi.[4]
- Benjamin Fagan's essay, complemented by an exhibit on debates about a national Black newspaper. This exhibit was created by

Auburn University graduate students—Melanie Berry, Christy Hutcheson, Eli Jones, and Morgan Shaffer—in a class Fagan taught.

- Andre Johnson's exhibit on Bishop Henry McNeal Turner's leadership of southern postbellum conventions, created by Denise Burgher, University of Delaware (UD) graduate student in English and chair of the CCP's Community and Historic Church Outreach Committee, in a class taught by Gabrielle Foreman.
- Sarah Lynn Patterson's essay, accompanied by an exhibit she curated. Instead of the speeches at the famous 1843 convention, Patterson highlights the understudied statistics about Black communities that delegates gathered for that convention. Patterson, a CCP cofounder, created this pilot exhibit while she was chair of the CCP Exhibits Committee and a UD graduate student in English.[5]
- Derrick Spires's work on Henry Highland Garnet's famous "Address to the Slaves of the United States of America," given at the 1843 convention Patterson also discusses. This exhibit was cocurated by Harrison Graves and Jake Alspaugh, then English graduate students at UD, in a class taught by Gabrielle Foreman.
- Selena Sanderfer's essay on postbellum conventions and southern interest in land and emigration, made into a digital exhibit by Eileen Moscoso and Rosalie Hooper, graduate students in English and art history, in a class taught by Foreman.
- Psyche Williams-Forson's essay on where delegates stayed and what they ate at these multiday meetings; the exhibit was created by Anna Lacy—who went on to become the cochair of the CCP's Digital Archives Committee and a project leader—and Jenn Briggs, both UD history students who cocurated the exhibit in a class taught by Foreman.
- Readers interested in California and Jean Pfaelzer's essay might visit the exhibit cocreated by historian Sharla Fett, David Kim, and their students Gabriel Barrett-Jackson, Emma Cones, Christina Delany, Lindsay Drapkin, Lila Gyory, Sydney Hemmindinger, Rosa Pleasant, Reilly Torres, Victoria Walker, and Daniel Waruingi at Occidental College in Los Angeles.

Visitors to the exhibits at ColoredConventions.org are able to zoom in on maps, trace the routes delegates journeyed to conventions, examine the neighborhoods where attendees stayed, look at the blueprints of homes where they slept, and flip through an interactive menu featuring recipes from two nineteenth-century African American cookbooks. Interactive maps display the proximity between local eateries, boardinghouses, and the halls and churches where morning and evening sessions were held. The procedural rule books delegates used are showcased in the exhibit based on Erica Ball's essay, along with the mastheads and convention coverage from the newspapers delegates founded. Online exhibits not only add interactive and visual elements to some of this volume's essays, but they also feature biographies, including fascinating stories about a wide array of women associated with delegates and the conventions.

Indeed, project guidelines require those who create exhibits to include Black women, whose energy and expertise were key to these multiday meetings, even though historical records encourage researchers to focus almost solely on the men whose names appear in the proceedings. North American teaching partners who adopt the CCP curriculum and generate exhibits sign a memo of understanding affirming that they will create biographies of women associated with convention places and people that appear in the convention records (fig. 1.1). For example, viewers of the exhibit about Henry McNeal Turner, which accompanies Andre Johnson's essay, will discover stories of AME women preachers. Curator Denise Burgher presents previously unknown information about Sarah Hughes, the first Black woman officially ordained as an AME pastor—by Bishop Tuner himself—even though her authority and ordination were later revoked, despite Turner's hopes and intentions.[6] Harrison Graves and Jake Alspaugh's exhibit includes a tab on Julia Williams Garnet, the activist Henry Highland Garnet married, that includes evidence of her contribution to his "Address to the Slaves," which is widely regarded as one of the most important Black speeches of the century.[7] And Sarah Patterson's 1843 exhibit includes a wealth of biographies of women closely associated with delegates and the institutions that hosted conventions, including information on Elizabeth Gloucester.[8] Gloucester directed the Colored Orphan Asylum and was one of the wealthiest Black women of her time, but only her husband's name appears in convention records. Dr. Sarah Marinda Loguen-Fraser, child of the fearless self-emancipated activist and convention goer Jermain Wesley Loguen, is said to be the first woman to earn an MD from Syracuse University. After moving to the Dominican Republic, she became one of the first female doctors and pharmacists on the island.[9] Including women in exhibits, then, not only is an ethical imperative to fully examine archival silences that do not represent historical absences, but it also allows researchers to begin to assemble pieces of convention history and to apprehend the reach and scope of activist convention cultures.

Those who pair this volume with the CCP's online exhibits will have a wealth of historical documents and images at their fingertips: advertisements for convention housing, photos of the churches and halls where the meetings were held, excerpts from nineteenth-century papers, and interactive maps that show the locations of newspapers that covered these gatherings across North America. The exhibit on Henry Highland Garnet features images from an article on Garnet's "Address" in *Ebony* magazine in September 1964 and visualizes, in striking detail, the political contexts of civil rights protest that made Garnet of such interest to readers in 1964. Readers will encounter liberty songs performed at conventions. "I Am a Friend of Liberty" was sung at the 1843 Michigan state convention and "Freedom's Gathering" and "I Dream of All Things Free" at the 1849 Ohio convention. The words of

THE COLORED CONVENTIONS PROJECT
Teaching Partner Memo of Understanding

The Colored Conventions Project attends to issues of race and gender equity
and bias, historical and present-day. We ask all instructors to commit to confronting
the under-representation of women in the convention minutes and to articulating
their substantial contributions to reform and organizational movements of the
nineteenth century.

☑ I agree.

I will assign a connected Black woman such as a wife, daughter, sister, fellow
church member, etc., along with every male convention delegate. This is our shared
commitment to recovering a convention movement that includes women's activism
and presence–even though it's largely written out of the minutes themselves.

☑ I agree.

Excerpt from Colored Conventions Project's original MOU, http://coloredconventions.org/memo-of-understanding

FIGURE 1.1. Teacher Memo of Understanding
on ColoredConventions.org.

"Liberia Is Not a Place for Me" rang out at the 1851 Ohio state convention, and William Wells Brown, the author and historian, wrote and performed a liberty song at the 1859 New England convention.[10] Clearly, "freedom" meant more than the end of slavery—postbellum conventions document the continuation of this tradition. From song lyrics to convention advertisements, from menus to frontispieces of the books attendees authored, this collection and its online companions allow readers to encounter well-known and less remembered figures and communities. The online resources complement this volume with visually engaging pathways into the movement's histories. Exhibits and book chapters encourage readers to explore the figures, sites, print materials, and Black thought that fueled massive efforts across time and geographical locales. In partnership, the essays and exhibits convey the depth and scope of nineteenth-century Black culture, travel, print, and political organizing.

Digital Companions and Resources for Expanding Study of the Colored Conventions

Readers of these essays may be inspired to dive into the exhibits and other materials housed on the website of the CCP. To help put this digital collection to good use for academic and other researchers, we have developed a number of free resources. In addition to the still-growing archive of convention minutes, we have generated an index of convention delegates' names.[11] Recognizing that using the names listed in the records reproduces the almost all-male focus of the minutes themselves, our index also contains every mention of women in the conventions, even those who were not delegates. The list of these women attendees numbers over 160 names. Using the name index on our website, visitors to ColoredConventions.org can search to find all of the conventions attended by figures such as editor Mary Ann Shadd Cary or writer Frances Ellen Watkins Harper, alongside thousands of their famous or since-forgotten male and female co-conventioneers. These historical records along with the index and exhibits create vast new opportunities for teaching, learning, and researching the long history of Black activism in the United States.

Transcribe Minutes was the CCP's initial crowdsourcing initiative. It involved thousands of volunteers who helped make digital copies of these historical records both free and easily searchable on the web for the very first time. The records that now exist online far exceed those of the twelve national conventions once found in the rare and expensive collection of antebellum minutes edited by Howard Holman Bell and published in 1969 and the forty-five state conventions published in the volumes edited by Philip Foner and George Walker in the 1980s. The online archive includes minutes found in scores of repositories and databases, and the number of proceedings featured online continues to grow. Scattered archives, however, do not readily lend themselves to the digitization efforts necessary for easy online access and searchability.[12] Following our project principles, this became an opportunity for the CCP to mirror the organizing efforts of the Colored Conventions themselves, involving thousands of volunteers spread out over North America. These volunteers have become active participants in an ongoing initiative to preserve this movement for Black rights, much as the conventions' own publication committees once did.[13] To ensure that those whose cultural ancestors organized conventions were likewise involved in the twenty-first-century effort to digitize the proceedings, the Colored Conventions Project reached out to the AME Church. Hundreds of its members transcribed the minutes of conventions that were originally hosted in AME churches up to 190 years ago.[14] These efforts have expanded into live transcription events held at universities, community centers, and historical societies across the country (and beyond) every year on February 14, the day Frederick Douglass chose as his birthday. Fondly called a day of "collective love for Black history," Douglass Day revives an early twentieth-century holiday celebrated by Black communities on his birthday. At Douglass Day celebrations in both centuries, groups gathered to hear some of Douglass's words, to reflect on the past and present together, and to engage in coordinated efforts for commemorating Black history.[15] Mirroring the convention movement's network of geographically dispersed events, our twenty-first-century Douglass Day celebrations give new digital life to these freedom struggles of the past.[16]

The collective labor of Transcribe Minutes has made possible the creation of the CCP Corpus, a collection of plain-text files of convention minutes that will be useful for scholars and researchers who wish to delve deeper into the information these records offer. The CCP Corpus is available to download at no cost. Two features of the Corpus reflect the Colored Conventions' values.

First, the web page where these materials are made available is preceded by a short memo of understanding, a statement asking those who access these materials not to reduce these people's lives and efforts to "data points," as has become increasingly popular in the field known as the digital humanities. Instead, the CCP asks that researchers honor the spirit and humanity of the movement itself by contextualizing and narrating the conditions of the people who appear as "data," naming them whenever possible.[17] Second, the collection is available as a zipped folder that contains all of the transcriptions and metadata. This zipped folder provides an easy way to begin to navigate the vast collection using computational text-analysis and pattern-tracking tools. Contrary to some common assumptions, these tools are not intended to perform analysis for us automatically. Rather, these tools provide a set of instruments for exploring different kinds of questions at varying scales, such as the shifting use of words for race and gender in the Colored Conventions throughout the century.

This volume and its digital companions are early forays into a sustained study of the history and legacy of the Colored Conventions. Appearing in the very first collection that addresses the conventions, and at a moment when the number of known meetings that were held, records that documented them, and petitions and addresses that emerged from them are ever expanding, these essays will be amended and corrected, evaluated and extended. That continual reassessment, reinvigoration, and recommitment mirrors the ongoing struggle for Black rights themselves. May that struggle continue.

NOTES

1. It's important to note that though men are often the named the "agents" of Underground Railroad activity, reformers and convention activists were often away from their families. Those who ran their homes—often wives, older children, and other family members—facilitated the journeys of those who took their emancipation into their own hands and feet. Austin Steward's daughter Barbara Ann, for example, was both active in New York state conventions and commended for her advocacy on behalf of fugitives. Likewise, the Whippers raised a nephew, James Whipper Purnell, who became a convention delegate and was also active in the Underground Railroad. See "Barbara Ann Steward," in *Working for Higher Education: Advancing Black Women's Rights in the 1850s*, by Sharla Fett and David Kim, digital exhibit, Colored Conventions Project, https://coloredconventions.org/women-higher-education/biographies/barbara-ann-steward. This exhibit accompanies Kabria Baumgartner's essay in this volume.

2. While Philip S. Foner and George E. Walker, eds., *Proceedings of the Black State Conventions, 1840–1865*, 2 vols. (Philadelphia: Temple University Press, 1979); Howard Holman Bell, *A Survey of the Negro Convention Movement, 1830–1861* (New York: Arno, 1969); and Howard Holman Bell, *Minutes of the Proceedings of the National Negro Conventions, 1830–1864* (New York: Arno, 1969), have provided the backbone of all scholarship produced on the convention movement, the periodization communicated in their titles has translated to too little work being done on the postbellum convention that spread and grew after the war and has also occluded state conventions that preceded 1840. Foner and Walker's sole postbellum collection, which only includes

conventions until 1870, has been drastically underutilized. See Philip S. Foner, and George E Walker, eds., *Proceedings of the Black National and State Conventions, 1865-1900* (Philadelphia: Temple University Press, 1986). ColoredConventions.org now builds on these editors' fine work and provides searchable convention documents that build on the records the Foner and Walker collections and the Bell volumes made available.

3. The exhibit on Black women in the Ohio conventions was developed with contributions from undergraduate researchers in a Spring 2016 course at Xavier University, taught by Christine Anderson.

4. Readers will note that the names of collectively created exhibits and the labor of those editing student work, for example, are noted here. Though this may seem laborious, it follows from the CCP Principles, one of which reads, "Mirroring the Colored Conventions' focus on labor rights and Black economic health, our project seeks structures and support that honor the work members bring to the project through equitable compensation, acknowledgement, and attribution." See "Colored Convention Project Principles," Colored Conventions Project, accessed July 20, 2020, https://coloredconventions.org/about/principles.

5. As chair of the Exhibits Committee, Patterson guided the initial efforts to create exhibit guidelines used by CCP teaching partners. She was joined by Samantha de Vera, now a PhD candidate in history at the University of California San Diego, who has cochaired the committee, created additional visualizations, and supported the technical development of many of the exhibits that accompany this collection. The current exhibit guide was created by Michelle Byrnes, UD undergraduate student and cochair of the Exhibits Committee, and Jim Casey.

6. Denise Burgher and Linda Stein, a CCP member and UD librarian emerita, worked on the Sarah Hughes research together.

7. This biography was written by Steve Sebzda in English 139, taught by Professor Kimberly D. Blockett, at Pennsylvania State University, Spring 2014, and edited by Sarah Lynn Patterson.

8. This biography was written by Sarah Ottino in English 344, taught by Gabrielle Foreman, at UD, Fall 2014, and edited by Gabrielle Foreman and Sarah Lynn Patterson.

9. This biography was written by Melinda Nanovsky in English 344, taught by Gabrielle Foreman, at UD, Spring 2014, and edited by Gabrielle Foreman and Sarah Lynn Patterson.

10. This information comes from a cultural biography written by Alysia Van Looy, created in English 344, taught by P. Gabrielle Foreman, at UD, Fall 2014. It is included in Sarah Patterson, *Prosperity and Politics: Taking Stock of Black Wealth and the 1843 Convention*, digital exhibit, Colored Conventions Project, https://coloredconventions.org/black-wealth.

11. This name index originated from a two-year individual digital research project by CCP cofounder Jim Casey. It was extended by David Kim, Keith Jones, Morgan Brownell, Michelle Byrnes, Kelli Coles, Anna Lacy, Brandi Locke, Natalia Lopez, Allison Robinson, and Carol Rudisell. Work is ongoing to provide online access to the index of names.

12. In inviting people to join in a collective crowdsourcing effort, founding faculty director Gabrielle Foreman foregrounded the participation from Black communities whose cultural forebearers hosted those conventions. With Jim Casey at the helm of Transcribe Minutes, Foreman recruited Denise Burgher to lead the CCP's partnership as chair of the CCP's Community and Historic Church Outreach Committee. Burgher created and supported partnerships with AME leaders, including Pamela Tilley, who, as the historiographer of the lay, is one of the AME Church's most important preservers of its critical contributions to African American and African diaspora history.

13. "Principle 1: CCP seeks to enact collective organizing principles and values that were modeled by the Colored Conventions Movement." See "Colored Convention Project Principles," https://coloredconventions.org/about/principles.

14. Among the many contributors, top volunteers include Jean W. Voigt, Rev. Caroline D. Shine, Dr. Ethel Bayley Scruggs, and many others we wish we could name here. The number of convention record transcribers, including those who joined through our AME joint effort, totaled over 1,400 people.

15. For more on Douglass Day, see videos and descriptions at "History of Douglass Day," Douglass Day, http://douglassday.org/history-of-douglass-day. The CCP's first Douglass Day, in 2017, brought together approximately 275 people at nine colleges and universities to work on Transcribe Minutes. In 2018, Douglass Day grew through a partnership with the National Museum of African American History and Culture and the Smithsonian Transcription Center. Together we organized gatherings of more than 1,600 people at nearly 100 locations across the United States, Canada, and Europe. Douglass Day 2019 featured a partnership with the African American Museum of Philadelphia, with a focus on Anna Murray Douglass. Douglass Day 2020 transcribed the records of Anna Julia Cooper through a partnership with Shirley Moody Turner and the Moorland Spingarn Research Center.

16. The focus in 2018 was the records of the Freedmen's Bureau, the federal agency charged with helping formerly enslaved Black men and women transition to freedom. In the future, Douglass Day events will focus both on convention records and on Black women's archives, honoring Douglass's own commitment to women's rights and addressing the ways in which Black women's voices and archives have been particularly buried.

17. For more on this, see P. Gabrielle Foreman and Labanya Mookerjee, "Computing in the Dark: Spreadsheets, Data Collection and DH's Racist Inheritance," in *Always Already Computational: Library Collections as Data; National Forum Position Statements*, March 2017, https://collectionsasdata.github.io/aac_positionstatements.pdf.

PART 1

CRITICAL CONVENTIONS, METHODS, AND INTERVENTIONS

BLACK ORGANIZING, PRINT ADVOCACY, AND COLLECTIVE AUTHORSHIP

The Long History of the
Colored Conventions Movement

P. Gabrielle Foreman

In Cincinnati's "riot of 1829," white anger crescendoed throughout three days as white thugs vented their outrage about rising numbers of Black residents, holding "sway in the city" as "the police were unable or unwilling to restore order."[1] The white mob gave sharp teeth to previously unenforced racial exclusionary laws. Expressed through legal hostility and physical violence, the laws abridged "the liberties and privileges of the Free People of Colour" especially in Ohio, as the minutes of the inaugural national Black convention the next year decried, "subjecting them to a series of privations and sufferings, by denying them a right of residence, a course altogether incompatible with the principles of civil and religious liberty."[2] In need of a "place of refuge" and "obliged to leave their homes," more than 1,000 of Cincinnati's Black residents became forced migrants in Canada after being dragged through the streets of the city then known as "the Queen of the West."[3] Outrage spread as they fled, and Black leaders from the country's free states gathered in Philadelphia to protest and plan. That meeting would become the first of hundreds of national and state Colored Conventions held in almost every state in the United States and in Canada, from Schenectady, New York, to Sacramento, California, from Chatham, Ontario, to Cleveland, Ohio, from Little Rock, Arkansas, to New Orleans, Louisiana. In response to white violence and state apathy that ran rampant not only in the storied South but also in the North and West, from 1830 through the end of the century, Black communities in North America organized political conventions that articulated Black people's refusal to accept their place as people who were not really, not fully, citizens even when they were said to be "free."

Why is such a continuous history of Black organizing and protest, one that featured the most prominent writers, newspaper editors, speakers, church leaders, educators, and entrepreneurs in the canon of early African American leadership, known to so few?[4] Self-emancipated writers and orators such as

Frederick Douglass and Henry Highland Garnet attended scores of conventions over four decades. They served on committees with the wealthiest Black entrepreneurs and activists of the era—George Downing, Charles Remond, and Robert Purvis—as well as editors such as Samuel Cornish, Charles Ray, Frederick Douglass, and Mary Ann Shadd Cary. Those who would become the century's most important Black authors—William Wells Brown, Martin Delany, and Frances E. W. Harper—for example, were speakers and committee members at multiple Colored Conventions. As young unknowns and later as wizened activists, the giants of the nineteenth century joined new generations participating in this movement, coming together to offer complex and often contested ideas about strategies and tactics. As heterogeneous as they were in their thinking, they remained unified in their demands and desires for civil and human rights. Tens of thousands participated. Many who contributed their energy, vision, and labor remain unsung and unknown. Others form the pantheon of Black "abolitionists": the writers, clergy, editors, and entrepreneurs whom scholars study and whose stories are known. How could a movement that challenged slavery not as its most important, but as its most basic, demand, one that focused on Black voting, legal rights, and educational equality and access, remain in obscurity for so long? How could more than half a century of formal protest and strategizing to counter labor discrimination and unequal pay and to challenge anti-Black state violence and state apathy be known to so few when it speaks so directly to the issues of our own time?

This is the first edited volume to examine the Black-led Colored Conventions movement; it is the first essay collection to address the many facets of the long history of Black nineteenth-century activism, organizing, and advocacy that the Convention movement launched.[5] The movement included activists who led churches and newspapers, those who were both nameless and well known, those whose travels took them to Canada, the Caribbean, Africa, and Europe, those whose lives bridged the eighteenth and nineteenth centuries, and those who only became active well after the Civil War. This volume also seeks to address—or redress—the exclusion and erasure from convention proceedings of Black women who were partners in this organizing history. The volume's editors and the project from which this book emerges embrace methodologies and conceptual frameworks that center Black women's intellectual and infrastructure-building labor in convention organizing, even as the written proceedings and records too often marginalize and anonymize them. The scholarship in this volume does not replicate those silences.

This essay opens by outlining the genealogy and importance of a long-term and Black-led movement whose energetic organizing and activism has faded from public, if not scholarly, memory and view. It then highlights the hundreds of postbellum conventions that have received even less critical and public attention, multiday gatherings that took place across the South and Southwest when millions of formerly enslaved people were able to join the free, freed, and fugitive peers who began the movement. It goes on to pose questions about how to define these conventions in relation to space and time. Should our scholarly attention be trained on the podium and the almost exclusively male delegates and speakers who spoke at the halls and churches where they gathered, or should it pan out to include—to focus on—the participants in the pews? Should convention contours start at the doors of buildings where they "took place" or include the boardinghouses and neighborhoods where delegates and participants—including women and children—stayed? Do conventions start and end on the dates printed in the proceedings? The issues announced in the calls and also debated in coverage afterward were likewise read from pulpits and were the subjects of conversations in reading rooms and societies. Black conventions' strategic and structured use of print (and pulpit) exponentially extended their participatory, geographic, and gendered base.

Black newspapers and convention proceedings, I argue, also offer an important paradigm of collective authorship that has been underconsidered, especially in relation to the slave narratives that often emerged from the context of organized antebellum abolition. After considering the implications of how nineteenth-century antislavery movements have both illuminated and overshadowed the Black-led Convention movement, I turn to the contemporary and collective effort to create a digital archive and public site, ColoredConventions.org, that illustrates this movement's centrality to interdisciplinary scholarship and to Black organizing histories. This essay closes by arguing that digital-archive- and community-making efforts can be structured to mirror the collective, geographically expansive, and distributed structures and ethos of the Convention movement itself. Indeed, it proposes that Black digital projects work best when they are inclusive and collective and when they name and empower those who work on them—not only scholars but library, archivist, student, and community leaders and participants. This piece seeks to emphasize that those engaging in this work should build capacity and community and that we should acknowledge, rather than erase or sideline, the labor and leadership of the Black people and communities we choose as our subjects.

This essay makes several important arguments and interventions that complicate and challenge narratives and scholarship about nineteenth-century Black agency and Black-led activism and subjectivity, as well as about white leadership, racial heroism, and antebellum abolition. We have not yet taken full account of Black-led organizational efforts such as the Colored Conventions, even as scholars are now excavating and highlighting Black leadership within the interracial antebellum abolition movement. How does a decades-long commitment to what I call a Black "parallel politics" revise genealogies of racial activism and networks of influence and exchange? I also argue that the Convention movement is as foundational a literary and organizing model as the slave narrative has been. Convention records provide a collective (and also masculinist) articulation of Black subjectivity and the assertion of Black worth, ambition, and belonging in North America with which scholars have yet to fully grapple. If slave narratives chart individual journeys toward freedom and literacy, Colored Conventions offer a paradigm of Black being and belonging grounded not in individual rights and singular authorship but in collective writing and organizing.

When readers consider the processes, performances, and publications that conventions modeled and created, we can reframe the ways in which we understand early Black print culture, Black organizing, and Black authorship. Convention organizers—and conventions as a structure of organizing—highlight the committee alongside the singular figure: the eloquent preacher, lecturer, or editor, the exceptional author, or the heroic protagonist. Conventions provided spaces in which to hammer out (or hammer in) differences in perspective, strategy, and ideology, even as they modeled the fact that part of recognizing Black humanity was understanding complexity rather than reaching consensus and prioritizing intellectual heterogeneity over unanimity of thought. The conventions advanced collectivity as a way of militating for rights and actualizing community within a nation that consistently communicated Black lack and alien/nation. What does this model offer to thinkers, scholars, and organizers today?

Colored Conventions: Genealogies and Legacies

From their inauguration in 1830 through the decades after the Civil War, conventions spread across North America. Tens of thousands of once captive, already free, and recently freed Blacks traveled from their homes, churches, and communities to participate as official delegates or attendees. From the podium and in the pews, in the meeting halls where they met and the boardinghouses where they stayed, attendees strategized about how to secure citizenship and civil liberties. Representatives considered resolutions to advance educational and labor rights, increase voting and jury representation, and extend the reach of the Black press. They debated the utility of jobs in (the) service (sector), the power of owning one's own land and business, and ways to best support the self-emancipated, the still enslaved, and the newly freed. They gathered and disseminated data about Black occupations, property, wealth, and institutional affiliations.

After the war, they encouraged each other in landownership, educational attainment, and government participation during the short era when they thought opportunities would last and the doors to citizenship might stay open. They gathered to gird each other as they strategized and petitioned for protection, as the dreams that Reconstruction kindled first began to smolder and then went up in flames, as those dreams began to stink and sag. They challenged so-called friends and outright foes who threatened or

"offered" to expatriate them. And they denounced the American Colonization Society while also considering emigration to places—Haiti, Canada, and
West Africa—where they might face less virulent forms of legal, educational,
and physical violence. Earnestly, and often angrily, they questioned whether
this country would—or could—ever deliver on its democratic rhetoric when
it came to a people its national founders and founding documents disparaged and degraded. What options were there in the form of advocacy and
emigration, they debated over and again, if that answer were no.

The organized Black response to white physical and civic violence—to
the refusal to extend full citizenship rights to the United States' Black inhabitants—begins almost eighty years before the National Association for
the Advancement of Colored People (NAACP). "The nation's oldest, largest
and most widely recognized grassroots-based civil rights organization," to
quote its website, was founded in 1909.[6] Even the event that precipitated the
NAACP's founding eerily echoes its predecessor's genesis. Once more, white
mob violence erupted in what is now the Midwest; nearly eight decades after
the first convention met in 1830, another throng of enraged whites ran rough-
shod, this time in Lincoln's Springfield, Illinois, leaving Black businesses
and families in ruins and again running upward of 2,000 Black community
members out of town.[7] Though it is often understood to mark an "early"
phase in Black movements for civil rights, the NAACP is an extension of well
over half a century of organized state and national conventions and legal
advocacy. It also builds on many of the late nineteenth-century organizations scholars now recognize as its direct predecessors: the Afro-American
League (1887–93), the National Association of Colored Women (1896–present),
and the Niagara Movement (1905–9). The convention movement, as historian Eddie Glaude contends, was "the first national forum for civic activity"
among free Blacks in the United States and Canada.[8] "The public and democratic debate and exchange the conventions formalized," he asserts, "became the principal agency for black activism from 1830 up to the Civil War."[9]
When considering the numbers of Colored Conventions and attendees in
the postwar period as well, it becomes even clearer that if groups such as the
Afro-American League have recently been situated as the country's "first national civil rights organization," Colored Conventions highlight for just how
long Blacks in North America have advocated for full citizenship, articulated
those appeals in print, petitions, and legal cases, and been largely ignored.[10]

As the United States unfurled its dominion, claim, and geographical reach
throughout the nineteenth century, Black inhabitants protested the racial violence and exclusion that likewise expanded with force and fervor. During these
conventions' first thirty-five years, from 1830 through the Civil War, Blacks "of
the North, East, and West" became accustomed to meeting together, as Henry
Highland Garnet made clear in his opening of "An Address to the Slaves of the
United States of America," the most famous speech to emerge from the conventions.[11] Free, freed, and self-emancipated Black people organized in the

face of tightly constricting legal and voting rights, responding to shrinking job opportunities as white immigrant populations spread and as "universal" manhood suffrage expanded unevenly and for whites only.

From their inception, Colored Conventions extended both the assumptions and the questions David Walker had posed just a year before the inaugural 1830 meeting: "The greatest riches in all America have arisen from our blood and tears:—and will they drive us from our property and homes, which we have earned with our *blood*?"[12] This was no mere rhetoric, it was a prophetic articulation of economic and ethical facts as they cohered. By 1860, America's wealth in the Blacks it enslaved was worth more than all the manufacturing wealth, all the transportation wealth, all the railways and trains, and all the banking wealth in the country combined. Those who were considered chattel property—Black people who were owned and assessed— were valued at more than all real property: all state buildings, all schools, and all personal and commercial real estate added together. As Black collectives organized for civil rights, participants both imagined and tried to build bridges—or even tunnels—from a bastardized republic, fathered by those who tightly clung to their racial entitlement as the nation's only right holders, to an actualized democracy that was "strewn with blood all the way along—and not only with blood," as E. C. Jackson of Xenia, Ohio, declared, looking back as he addressed the state's Colored Convention in 1871, "but with the bones of thousands of our brethren."[13] This volume examines their collective assertions of freedom. It elucidates their collective will to make real the self-evident: that Black education, Black employment, and Black claims to equal rights mattered, even when so-called friends as well as stalwart foes insisted they did not.

Black organizers were deeply cognizant of the symbolism that undergirded their strategic efforts. They held the 1830 inaugural meeting in Philadelphia, a city whose history of organizing for democratic rights against entrenched colonial and political power was resonant and emblematic. Mindful that the Declaration of Independence had been penned and adopted in Philadelphia, that the city had hosted the nation's constitutional conventions, and that the United States' founding documents had been ratified there, Black delegates from seven of the young nation's twenty-four states gathered there. They met at Bishop Richard Allen's invitation—one he had wrested from others who had also vied to host this first meeting—in his historic church, Mother Bethel, the center of the ever-growing independent African Methodist Episcopal (AME) denomination, in the last year of its founder's life.[14] There, the delegates vowed to continue their meetings while laying claims to a constitutional and religious legacy and warning, prophetically, that America's democratic fruits would turn rancid and rank if not shared.

It's worth asking if there are any other occasions in the nineteenth century when so much Black intellectual and activist manpower gathered in one place as at the Colored Conventions that occurred year after year, decade after decade. Scholars have yet to fully consider how convention culture not only impacted the generations of those who participated but also influenced those who were children as their elders organized, hosted, and traveled to such multiday political meetings in various states and towns, where they gathered in the churches these children called their own and ate and slept in bedrooms even closer to home. In 1847 Othello Burghardt headed from Great Barrington, Massachusetts, to Troy, New York, as a delegate to the national convention, where a proposal for a national Black press was hotly debated by authors such as Frederick Douglass and William Wells Brown, the first Black novelist; William Allen, one of the very first African American professors; and a virtual who's who of activist, editorial, and other luminaries, including Charles Ray, Alexander Crummell, William Cooper Nell, Lewis Hayden, James Pennington, and Dr. James McCune Smith. Though Burghardt was unknown compared to the luminaries who also served as delegates, his grandson W. E. B. Du Bois, who lived with him as an infant, is a giant among twentieth-century intellectuals, a founder of the NAACP and of modern sociology.[15] Charles Langston, whose grandson Langston Hughes is one of the most beloved U.S. poets and cultural figures of all time, attended more than twenty state and national conventions over nearly twenty-five years. Charles and his younger brother, John Mercer Langston, were steeped in a convention culture that watered the work they did over decades. Together, the two Langston brothers served as delegates more than thirty-four times over twenty-five years, according to numbers that new accountings already reveal to be an undercount.[16] John Mercer Langston would become the first dean of the Howard University School of Law, the president of Virginia State University, and one of five nineteenth-century African Americans to serve in the U.S. House of Representatives.[17] During Langston's tenure at Howard, Charlotte Ray, the daughter of committed convention goer and newspaper editor Charles Ray, became the first woman graduate of Howard's law school, attending alongside Mary Ann Shadd Cary, another trailblazing child of a regular convention goer.

Children of the attendees of the early conventions seeded future generations of activism. Charlotte Ray, said to be the first Black woman lawyer in the United States, went on to be active in the conventions held by the National Association of Colored Women. Mary Ann Shadd Cary's father, Abraham Shadd, stands out as one of the most consistent participants and leaders of the early national movement. He participated in five of the first six national meetings between 1830 and 1835 and served as president of "the Third annual Convention, for the Improvement of the Free People of Colour in these United States" (1833), to which Black delegates from a quarter of the nation's states—and nearly half of its free states—had traveled.[18] Two decades later, Shadd Cary became one of only a handful of officially recognized women delegates in the convention movement as well as the editor of the important *Provincial Freeman*, the first North American newspaper edited by a Black woman. The pantheon of Black leadership and the movement's geographic reach and generational influence beg for a consideration of not only conventions but convention culture.

Though so many of those whose names, work, and writing make up the known world of nineteenth-century Black reform were active in the conventions, tens of thousands of attendees and followers—women as well as men—whose histories went unrecorded nonetheless infused the movement with their ideas, energy, and support. Together they both raised the money for delegates to leave their towns to attend state conventions and also hosted them in their homes. Collectively, they founded newspapers and colleges, filed legislative petitions, and protested new prohibitions on their legal rights. They advocated incessantly for their voices, children, and labor to be respected and valued. Delegates pressed for the right for Blacks to testify in court and advocated for equal schooling. They fought for the end of the state-sanctioned burning of their churches and meetinghouses, the ransacking of their homes and businesses, and the violence meted out all too regularly on their siblings, elders, and friends. Their protests resonate with today's ongoing struggles for racial justice.

Black organizers came together to launch the Colored Conventions movement *before* the formal establishment of the antebellum antislavery movement, the most chronicled and celebrated narrative of nineteenth-century racial justice after the end of the transatlantic slave trade. Radical white abolitionists often followed the organizational lead of antebellum Black reformers, not the other way around. Despite a persistent narrative of white leadership and sponsorship of Black abolitionists, the inaugural Colored Convention meeting predates the American Anti-Slavery Society by a full three years. Black editors founded *Freedom's Journal* in 1827, four years before the start of the *Liberator*; *Freedom's Journal* may have been as influential as Benjamin Lundy's *Genius of Universal Emancipation* on William Lloyd Garrison's radical editorial stands.[19] Blacks joined each other in conventions "to plead [their] own cause," as the editors wrote in *Freedom's Journal*'s first issue. The Massachusetts Anti-Slavery Society (1831), the New England Anti-Slavery Society (1832), and the American Anti-Slavery Society (1833) all were founded *after* the convention movement's first convening. Yet it is antebellum antislavery that looms so large in the public imagination and on library shelves, peopled as it is with heroes whose names Americans are more often taught in high school and college: William Lloyd Garrison and Wendell Phillips, Lydia Maria Child and Lucretia Mott. Chronicling the history of the convention movement upends a genesis story that continually situates radical abolition as the progenitor and sponsor of the nineteenth-century movement for Black freedom.

In the United States, antebellum abolition and the Underground Railroad are the lenses through which many scholars, as well as the public, habitually view nineteenth-century movements for racial freedom. Until important recent scholarly interventions, white reformers were too often framed as organizational pioneers in a courageous struggle for Black rights that was accompanied by a select number of Black abolitionists they sponsored. Additionally, the nineteenth-century antislavery movement and the Underground Railroad formally end with slavery's official demise, so often closing the doors of the institutions and print organs that supported their work as the Civil War waned and the Thirteenth, Fourteenth, and Fifteenth Amendments were passed. Public narratives often repeat these tropes, leaving the impression that whites led the movement against Black oppression or white supremacy—as opposed to advocating for an end to racial slavery. This narrower focus on antislavery serves national narratives of democratic progress; it offers well-known heroes to lionize and proclamations of emancipation to celebrate. Black agency and the intragroup cooperation, complexity, and heterogeneity that the Colored Conventions display across region, status, denomination, decades, and interests rarely take center stage.

Throughout decades of convention organizing, nineteenth-century African Americans enacted an ongoing political practice, a *parallel politics*, actualized in the face of official exclusion, derision, and violence. The first thirty-five years of convention gatherings, much like the final decades that scholars often call the "nadir," occurred at times when Black Americans were often violently excluded from political participation. In 1860, as the Civil War dawned, African American men could vote in a mere five of thirty-three states, that is, in fewer than one of every six states. Yet Black communities refused to be deterred from participating in public and civic life despite virulent political and economic prohibitions. As historian Elsa Barkley Brown has taught us, community members need not be politically recognized to be political agents. She demonstrates how Black women were active in post–Fifteenth Amendment voting despite being legally excluded; "focusing on formal disenfranchisement," she warns, "obscures the larger story."[20] Women did more than use their persuasive powers to influence men in their family circles. Black women advocated for candidates, were active in campaigns, and physically protected their husbands, brothers, and other community members against white violence as they headed to the polls. Though this wasn't direct participation, it was far from political disengagement— or political silence.[21] Likewise, there's much to be gained from a sustained analysis of the conventions alongside other sites of intracommunity organizing.

Convention participation, of course, meant that far from being unprepared to serve in legislatures after the Civil War—as mainstream newspapers, pamphlets, and films such as *Birth of a Nation* relentlessly caricatured them to be—a whole cadre of Black leaders was deeply familiar with, indeed embedded in, the language, issues, parliamentary procedures, and committee structures of state and national service. Yet decades of convention participation, I argue, should not be treated simply as experience that readied African Americans for eventual integration into political structures recognized by the state. This is not simply a pre- or protopolitics, in part because integration in the body politic as fully enfranchised citizens (think the U.S. Senate or governorships) has been perpetually contested and deferred.[22] In the face of that exclusion, Blacks not only lobbied for full civil rights within political structures that continually spurned them but also advocated for parallel developments in Black community, capacity, and institution building within the continental United States and outside of it.

Postbellum Conventions

The antebellum period has largely been the focus of the handful of scholars who substantively include Black conventions in their work.[23] Yet as the Civil War came to an end and 4 million once-enslaved people could move and mobilize in ways that previously had been impossible, conventions spread across the South in the wake of Rebel soldiers' retreat. Meeting numbers swelled, and tens, perhaps hundreds, of thousands participated. The Maryland convention of 1852, "the Free Colored People's Convention," was the only one that had been held in slave territory before the Civil War—and delegates there had faced a violent white mob. As the war drew to a close, almost twenty Colored Conventions convened in 1865 alone: in Tennessee, Louisiana, the Carolinas, Arkansas, Virginia, Georgia, and Texas, as well as in California and all over the Northeast and Midwest. Delegates gathered in Norfolk, Virginia, resolving that "traitors shall not dictate or precscribe [sic] to us the terms or conditions of our citizenship" just days after the last commander of Confederate forces, Gen. Edmund Kirby Smith, formalized his surrender to the Union on June 2.[24] In the largest city of the South, confident Black New Orleanians threw the Union's early occupation of the city in the face of the Confederacy, hosting the inaugural southern convention of the postbellum period in early January 1865, before the war had ended.[25] The Black-owned New Orleans Tribune, the meeting's official organ, reported that at the convention "were seated side by side the rich and the poor, the literate and educated man, and the country laborer, hardly released from bondage, distinguished only by the natural gifts of the mind. There, the rich landowner, the opulent tradesman, seconded motions offered by humble mechanics and freedman. Ministers of the gospel, officers and soldiers of the US Army, men who handle the sword or the pen, merchants and clerks,— all the classes of society were represented, and united in a common thought: the actual liberation from social and political bondage."[26] When the paper proudly announced that "the day of the meeting of this Convention has inaugurated a new era" and underscored that "it was the first political move ever made by the colored people of this State acting in a body," it spoke not only for Louisiana but, in terms of political conventions, for the whole of the South.[27]

Those who participated in postbellum conventions (that is, in the community, state, and national organizing efforts that followed the inaugural New Orleans meeting) were met with white force and violence as well as with Black collective will and mobilization. In September 1865, 150 delegates gathered in Raleigh, North Carolina, some having traveled at night, some having walked long distances "so as to avoid observation," such was "the opposition manifested to the movement."[28] They enumerated their rights: to vote, to testify in court, to serve on juries, and, if they found themselves in court, to be tried before a jury of their peers. These were the rights they met to contend for, they proclaimed; "these are the rights we shall have."[29] Farther west, Blacks likewise gathered in Little Rock to "effect a permanent organization" and to petition state and national legislatures for "equality before the law and the right of suffrage" that was "bought with our blood" and that we "earned and deserve," announced the convention chair.[30] No longer will the "yes sirs" and "no ma'ams" whites were accustomed to, this "seeming respect," fall from the lips of Arkansas Blacks, the minutes proclaim. "We have now thrown off the mask," the delegates averred; hereafter they would do their own talking, they declared. They joined Black Americans in scores of other state conventions to "use all legitimate means to get and to enjoy our political privileges."[31]

Southern Blacks joined their peers in the so-called free states as those in the Northeast and Northwest continued to hold conventions at the war's close. The year 1865 included meetings all over the South—and also in Detroit, Michigan; New Haven, Connecticut; Boston, Massachusetts; Xenia, Ohio; Trenton, New Jersey; and Harrisburg, Pennsylvania. The meetings' demands upended deeply entrenched public and sectional mythologies by laying bare the continuous demands for citizenship rights and inclusion that Blacks clearly and unequivocally lodged both in the North and in the South before and after the Civil War. By making citizenship claims in convention bodies, they replicated the conventions of political conventions, as Erica Ball puts it in her essay in this volume about the political rituals and traditions of conventions.[32] They claimed full citizenship as equal political partners not just through their demands but through the process they used to collectively articulate and circulate them. The resounding echo of Black calls for equal rights, suffrage, and testimony as well as education and labor equality reveal the far reach of a movement that had met, until the war's end, with some regularity in every region of the expanding country with the exception of the South.[33]

Despite growing white violence and the concrete obstacles whites enacted against Black organizing after the Civil War, because nearly 90 percent of African-descended people in the United States by 1860 lived in the South, participation in postbellum conventions grew, often dwarfing the numbers of delegates and attendees at earlier state and national meetings. The 1868 Georgia state convention sent 180 delegates to Macon, where some delegates "had to walk 50 or 60 miles; and one man," as Henry McNeal Turner testified to Congress later that year, "I think, walked 105 miles to get to the convention, owing to the fact that neither he nor his constituents were able to pay his fare there by railroad."[34] The next year, Georgia's convention included an almost 25 percent increase in delegates; they discussed "fair labor practices and equity of pay," as Andre Johnson reveals in his essay in this volume.[35] They adopted resolutions that "declared that capital could only be safe when the laborer is protected," that capital elites and business owners "could have no advantage over united labor," and "that there was no advantages between the two when justice was done."[36] Strategically concerned about getting their message out to ever larger numbers in the struggle for labor rights, delegates named Turner to serve as editor of a newspaper to support the movement.

As Turner became increasingly active and prominent over the next several decades, he helped organize conventions that challenged the labor conditions and unbridled violence which mirrored the anti-Black riots that had initiated conventions in other regions decades earlier. The 1893 "Turner's Convention" demanded substantive reparations both for collective Black labor (valued at more than $40 billion) and for the families of lynching victims. At one of this country's racial nadirs, delegates planned to use reparations for emigration costs, at least for those who believed there could be no future in a nation that continued to violently spurn and violate Black communities. Convention records show that the longevity and force of emigration was a debate that Black communities acted on with their feet, family, and funds for almost a century before Marcus Garvey stepped onto the historical stage. As Denise Burgher's research for her digital exhibit shows, Turner's Convention was widely reported in places as far away in geography (and demography) as Minnesota's *St. Paul Globe*: "Bishop H. M. Turner, of Atlanta, called to order the national colored convention [which] met pursuant to his call issued Sept. 30. To the surprise of all, the list of *delegates* reached over 500, and more are soon to come."[37] The *Voice of Missions* urged Blacks to respond to the "reign of mobs, lynchers, midnight and midday assassins" that continually terrorized them, as Andre Johnson shares in his essay here. Echoing the familiar proclamation for independent representation voiced in the inaugural 1827 issue of *Freedom's Journal* ("We wish to plead our own cause. Too long have others spoken for us."),[38] Turner wrote, "At all events, while other people are saying so much about us and doing so much affecting our destiny, we as a free and distinct race should meet in council and say or do something ourselves."[39] Traveling to Cincinnati almost sixty-five years after the 1830 inaugural meeting in Philadelphia, thousands participated in one of the last national meetings to be called by the same name as those that launched the Colored Conventions movement.

Thirty-five years of antebellum state and national conventions readied a generation of Black-justice advocates who took the helm in U.S.-sanctioned local, state, and national roles that became available, if only for a short time, after the Civil War. The understudied postbellum conventions included not only lifelong southerners but also northerners and Canadian emigrants who moved south after the war. These activists were deeply embedded in circuits of Black community and national organizing; they honored such intergenerational connections most notably through naming their children after the early leaders of the Black Convention movement.[40] Born in Philadelphia, Rev. Jonathan C. Gibbs named his children Thomas Van Renssalaer Gibbs and Julia Pennington Gibbs after well-known convention leaders and Black activist editors and religious leaders. He became one of the most powerful Black officeholders in Reconstruction Florida. Active in antebellum northern state conventions, as the war ended he began his sojourn south, attending the 1865 South Carolina convention held in Charleston, the proceedings of which were published "together with the declaration of rights and wrongs; an address to the people; a petition to the legislature, and a memorial to Congress."[41] Being an experienced convention goer no doubt led to his election to the Florida State Constitutional Convention of 1868 and to his appointment as Florida's secretary of state (1868–73). He also served as superintendent of public instruction, and he introduced legislation that founded the Normal School, which would become one of the country's largest historically Black universities, Florida A&M University; his son would serve as its vice president until his death in 1898. The elder Gibbs's political commitment to Black conventions and to state political leadership is just one example of how antebellum Black parallel politics became transformed into formally recognized roles in the postbellum era. It mirrors, for instance, U.S. Representative John Mercer Langston's even more pronounced involvement in the political arena of Colored Conventions.[42]

The newly freed joined established leaders at the helm of some conventions. William Savery and Thomas Tarrant, for example, traveled 300 miles south to Mobile, Alabama, just months after the war ended their enslavement. There they attended a five-day state convention in 1865 and conceived of the institution that would become Talladega College.[43] Though the American Missionary Association gets much of the credit for founding the college, the idea was born, and in many ways borne out, by attendees of a convention held by the newly free just six months after the Civil War ended. Conventions provided a forum for ongoing engagement with civic advocacy, institution building, and protest—again, a parallel politics—during moments of hope and decades of exclusion. They provide a record of Black organizing and activism that has yet to be fully incorporated into scholarly and public narratives.

Re: Defining Conventions

Defining conventions poses conceptual challenges about what counts. In the movement's earliest years, how do we characterize organizational outgrowths such as the American Moral Reform Society, which held meetings during the national convention hiatus that began in 1836? Joan Bryant poses this question in her essay in this volume.[44] How does one fix a historical terminus for a movement that didn't end as much as it flowed into tributaries that extended into a new century and into changing lexical, gendered, and organizational territories? This collection hopes to spawn scholarly discussions, if not answers, to those and the many other, sometimes simple, questions that call for complicated answers. Are Equal Rights Leagues and their conventions another name for postbellum Colored Conventions, emerging, as they did, directly from the 1864 national convention in Syracuse, adopting the same rules and procedures, and sharing so many of the same delegates? Do the Colored press, education, and labor conventions that so clearly overlap with issues raised in state and national conventions belong in the same archive? Should the well-researched and well-preserved records of the National Association of Colored Women's conventions be grouped with the online archive at ColoredConventions.org? How clear is the through line between the conventions this book addresses and the Afro-American Council and the Afro-American League, which Shawn Alexander calls "the first national civil rights organization"?[45] Alexander differentiates the leagues and councils from the conventions despite their similar state and national structures and regardless of the league's leadership appeal to convention leaders such as John Mercer Langston. Now that the contours of a steadily growing archive of postbellum Black meetings is coming into focus, can we identify and strengthen the ligaments that support and connect them with meetings held under different names?

The shape and scope of discussions about periodization and characterization directly impact archive building. Answers to the above questions govern not only what gets digitized but where and in what contexts such documents land online. The ways in which we characterize and define these aligned convention state and national meetings directly determine what is digitized, transcribed, and uploaded for scholarly and public use. Classifying these convention tributaries thus helps determine what attention is paid to them. Archive-building decisions influence what is included and valued in future scholarship that recenters Black-led organizing in the movements for nineteenth-century racial justice.

The proceedings convention organizers so deliberately published and circulated, in one sense, are lodes of informational gold; the luster of details they give about sessions, debates, and delegates attracts researchers' attention. Yet, if we look beyond the archival gems the minutes provide and focus beyond the delegates who speak from the floor, podium, or pulpit, we might better account for those who were participating from the pews, seats, and benches. When we then ask about what was happening in the parlors, dining rooms, and boardinghouses where thousands of delegates stayed over decades, different questions arise. How do we trace the roles played by the most marginalized or anonymous groups—women and children, for example—in convention proceedings? How did they participate in Black convention culture, not only practiced, to build on Martha Jones's definition of Black public culture between 1830 and 1900, in the communal associations they founded but also encompassed in "a realm of ideas, a community of interpretation and a collective understanding of the issues of the day"?[46] How does this wider angle of vision encourage us to view not only those we might call convention celebrities but also broader (and also more granular) convention cultures, circuits, and collectives?

When we adjust our point of view from an emphasis on delegates to include the many community participants who gathered in hostile and segregated—or at best ambivalent—streets and cities, the scale of these organizing efforts comes into sharper focus. This shifts the conceptualization of conventions from one of officially numbered meetings among credentialed delegates and in recognized civic spaces, in public halls or churches, to one that accounts for the varied sites and places peopled by multiple attendees who converged in a neighborhood or town to debate, discuss, and advocate for political access, inclusion, and justice. When Blacks gathered at state and national conventions, whites in the city asked, "Where are the d——d niggers going?" as Douglass proclaimed at the 1864 national meeting.[47] Conventions not only demanded but embodied Black people's claims to public and civic spaces as deserving citizens. Yet scholar Psyche Williams-Forson pushes us further by focusing on domestic places where convention goers stayed, slept, and ate. In her essay in this volume, she asks what we learn from a recalibration of Black political space. How were Black women's "influence and power enacted in [convention] rituals and practices using food" and lodging arrangements? What kind of work got done over meals, and who was present during those discussions? What did children learn, to extend her questions, when delegates stayed at their homes, displaced them from their beds, and met at the home churches where they went to Sunday school? We know from visual records that children attended conventions. Did they also travel with their own family members who were delegates? What do scholars learn by examining the "intimate associations that African American women [and children and men] had with their boarders and lodgers"—for a brief but critical time?[48]

Multi-use sites such as boardinghouses buzzed with political energy during conventions, serving as reconfigured extensions of the meetings themselves. Regardless of region or decade, in the vast majority of cases, delegates and convention participants weren't allowed unrestricted access to local pub(lic) and civic spaces. Nor were they able to frequent most local eateries. The thousands of meals that existed as announced breaks after morning and afternoon sessions call for readers to literally read between the lines and fill in the proceedings' undocumented hours. Often forced out of the larger public square, convention goers thanked Black boardinghouse hosts and sang their praises in newspaper announcements that are nineteenth-century versions of Airbnb reviews. Williams-Forson and the curators of the digital exhibits her essay has inspired consider the morsels of information served up in the many such advertisements they've located.[49] New work in this volume highlights the relationship between nineteenth-century Black public spheres and Black domestic spaces, situating the gathering sites beyond conventions' recognized meetings as central to Colored Convention politics and cultures.

FIGURE 2.1. 1869 National Colored Convention in Washington, DC.
Sketch by Theo. R. Davis, *Harper's Weekly*, February 6, 1869.
Courtesy of personal collection of Jim Casey.

Consider for a moment the domestic and business infrastructure needed
to coordinate those who lodged, catered, cooked, and transported food to
convention attendees as well as the logistical expertise needed to transport
participants to locales that offered food and board. Attendance at political
events—as opposed to the number of delegates—is no easy thing to report
with certainty, then as now. It's no stretch to say, however, that the number
of Black people (converging in one city, then in one area of town, and then at
the convention site itself) swelled wherever such a gathering was held—be
it Montgomery or New Orleans, Omaha or Brenham, Texas. At the 1879 national convention in Nashville, for example, proceedings report that the gal-
leries in the hilltop state capitol building where it was held "were thronged
until there was not even standing room."[50] Hosting conventions necessitated
"elaborate institutional frameworks," to borrow from Martha Jones.[51] Convening took large-scale funding, planning, preparation, and execution. Community members, female and male, young and old, would need to have—and
would need to develop—a broad set of logistical skills to support and accommodate the meetings held in their cities, neighborhoods, and homes. Regardless of the size or location of the meetings, housing and feeding visitors
meant intimate access to the conversations, debates, and deliberations that
happened in spaces that are recorded as gaps on the proceedings' pages but
that hummed with activity during the meetings themselves. Though wom-
en's and children's participation is obscured in the minutes, viewing these

three- and four-day state and national meetings more broadly reveals that they were active in the larger scope of convention events.

If we define conventions not simply as the sessions that occurred in the physical locations listed in the minutes but rather as the formal and informal activities and organizing that took place from the opening session until they adjourned several days and nights afterward, then we radically redefine a central understanding of convention spaces, gendered participation, and organizational leadership. Taking full measure of the breaks between sessions from start to finish—again, the empty spaces in the print proceedings—suggests a level of community building and infrastructure in host locations that would have been considered threatening by the many who were not interested in Black civic inclusion, access, and equality, the very issues that were at the heart of these meetings for decades. Black communities not only asserted and advocated for their rights over and again but, in doing so, developed and displayed organizational and political capacities that fed these communities long after conventions adjourned.

Though scholarly focus is often trained on the days detailed in the proceedings, expanding the event timeline to account for travel reveals how meeting goers asserted their political equality en route to and from conventions. Travel, as historian Elizabeth Stordeur Pryor puts it, was "a vital mechanism for citizenship."[52] In the antebellum North and in southern states where state-sanctioned patrollers and their scions regulated Black mobility before and after the war, "whites deemed it aggressive and dangerous for free people of color to enter public vehicles as equals."[53] Spurred on by virulently anti-Black travel laws that preceded Jim Crow, as early as 1837 in New Jersey and throughout the 1850s in Indiana, Illinois, and Ohio, for example, whites were encouraged "to scrutinize the travel of Black people."[54] Thus delegates had to chart out routes and places to replenish themselves. They also had to plan what they would say to whites whose ire might ignite into violence were white instigators to discover Black travelers' destinations. In the summer of 1838, a 200-plus-mile trip from New York to Boston took about fourteen hours for Black editor and vigilance committee leader David Ruggles.[55] When a New York City delegate (such as editor Charles Ray) attended the 1843 Buffalo convention, such a trip would be an additional 200 miles, resulting in about twenty-eight hours of one-way travel—and delegates to this national convention came from Chicago, Cleveland, Cincinnati, and Detroit.[56] At any juncture in the journey—on the roads, railways, stagecoaches, or steamships—convention goers could encounter white travelers or conductors whose objection to their presence held more purchase than the tickets they had paid for and whose racism was more valued than Black comfort or safety.

Violently excluded and forcibly removed from first-class or ladies' cars, Black travelers were often mistreated and disrespected wherever they found themselves—and then they took up these issues at conventions. This is precisely what happened in 1848 when long-term convention delegate

Abner Francis traveled from upstate New York to Cleveland "with his lady," Sydna E. R. Francis, president of the Ladies' Literary and Progressive Improvement Society of Buffalo and leader in the city's Dorcas society. After Abner Francis asked for a cabin passage and was refused by the clerk, he and Frederick Douglass proposed a resolution calling out the clerk by name: "That Alexander Bowman of the Steamboat Saratoga and resident of Cleveland, receive the burning reprobation of this Convention, until he repents." Collectively organizing to offer a "unanimous shout against him" at the convention and then in writing afterward, they made certain that "he was fairly ostracized."[57] Almost thirty years later, Louisiana delegate T. Morris Chester ventured that "nearly all the delegates had [been forced to] come" to Cincinnati for the 1875 Convention of Colored Newspaper Men "on the smoking car," as attendees debated the best way to secure travel, lodging rights, and security against anti-Black outrages.[58] Participants often stated their objections to such violence, disrespect, and surveillance not only in the moment but also in newspapers, which spread the word. The travel that bookended convention meetings could itself be an assertion of civic rights; it almost always provided a reminder of the dire need for long-term, strategic, and collective activism that challenged second-class citizenship.

The breadth and scope of the Colored Conventions movement also come into sharper view when we enlarge our vista beyond the print editions that made this scattered archive available before the advent of digital technologies.[59] In 1969 Arno Press reprinted Howard Holman Bell's 1953 dissertation as *A Survey of the Negro Convention Movement, 1830–1861*.[60] It has remained, for at least fifty years since its publication, the only full-length book on Colored Conventions.[61] Long out of print, Bell's important edited volume *Minutes of the Proceedings of the National Negro Conventions, 1830–1864* can cost more than $3,000 when a copy becomes available; it includes only twelve national conventions.[62] Bell's lonely status as the author of the sole monograph devoted to Colored Conventions and his all but exclusive emphasis on northern and antebellum conventions has had an overwhelming influence on the subsequent scholarship that builds on it. The rich work of scholars such as William and Aimee Lee Cheek, John Ernest, Eddie Glaude, Martha Jones, and Derrick Spires, to name a few scholars who have examined conventions in articles or book chapters, have shared Bell's interest, and perhaps his lead, in highlighting northern conventions that occurred before the Civil War. Now, for the first time, scholars can consult an array of easily accessible online records at ColoredConventions.org that have as much to reveal about Black organizing during Reconstruction, after Reconstruction, and during the nadir as the well-mined antebellum proceedings have to say about Black protest and activism in the antebellum North.[63]

Extending the timeline beyond the Civil War and reading the state and national conventions together also weaves a thicker and more complex tapestry of Black organizing, mobility, and advocacy. Philip Foner and George Walker's important two volumes of forty-five state convention proceedings from 1840 to 1865 complement Bell's edition of minutes and proceedings from a dozen antebellum national meetings.[64] Accompanied by meticulous editorial notation, the state proceedings in Foner and Walker's volumes document local tactics, leaders, and advocacy as well as the surprising mobility of Black activists who appear in unexpected places.[65] Scholars often emphasize the eight-year hiatus between the last of the early national meetings in 1835 and the next one, the celebrated 1843 Buffalo convention, where Henry Highland Garnet delivered the fiery "Address to the Slaves," Douglass made his first appearance at a Black convention, and the two took opposite sides in a famously heated debate. Yet the convention movement's hiatus wasn't really one. Focusing on organizing at state and national meetings together reconfigures the timeline completely. Ohio activists launched state conventions as early as 1837, only two years after the last national convention of that decade. Though Foner and Walker list 1843 as the date of the first Ohio state convention, the well-organized Ohio activists assembled almost yearly from as early as 1837 through the Civil War, holding at least twenty-one meetings before the war's end.[66] Black New Yorkers joined Ohioans in 1840, holding a "State Convention of Colored Citizens, Held in Albany," with a focus on "considering their political condition."[67] At these state meetings, many who would become the most stalwart reformers and the intellectual and editorial giants of nineteenth-century Black activism—Charles and John Mercer Langston, William Howard Day, Peter Clark, Henry Highland Garnet, Alexander Crummell, Charles Reason, and Charles Ray, for example—made their debuts.[68]

Building on previous commitments of editorial love and labor, the growing archive at ColoredConventions.org has helped to change the scope and timelines of convention scholarship and public memory. It has more than quadrupled the number of conventions identified in the antebellum Foner and Walker volumes; through its "seeking records" curriculum, satellite partnerships, and growing outreach to historical societies and repositories, it will add thousands of additional records that document these meetings. The digital archive features fully searchable minutes the public has transcribed and, as we've seen, includes proceedings and coverage of postbellum conventions held into the 1890s.[69] As current readers consult the minutes that make up this ever-growing and far-flung archive, we must also enlarge the scope of the records themselves so that the pre- and postconvention calls and coverage that appear in columns of hundreds of nineteenth-century newspapers are included in our records and analyses. In her essay in this volume, Carla Peterson joins Howard Holman Bell, who opens his foundational work by noting that "the pamphlet reports are, of course, the official records, but in many cases, pertinent information is lacking, or becomes clear only when supplemented by newspaper reports," and, one might add, by the convention petitions to be found in archives and in state and national legislative records.[70] Peterson's essay is a call to read proceedings embedded in a large and scattered print context. Her call also serves as both a methodological directive and a time-traveling response to Samuel Ringgold Ward's 1855 contention that "our condition is far from favourable for the furnishing of historical data. Scraps, patches, anecdotes, these are all that bear record of us."[71] Engaging the public and students in research to find these records and make them widely available helps stitch these convention scraps and patches together in ways that print technologies can't facilitate, adding records to a digital archive as they're located over time and place. Curriculum and crowdsourcing initiatives involve the public in the work of collective recovery.

Expanding beyond published convention minutes is critical, in part because proceedings remained highly curated documents. Over decades, "Committees on Printing" and "Committees on Address" determined what was included in—and excluded from—the minutes; these decisions could reflect strategic concerns about public perception, including safety. Testifying to Congress about the 1871 southern states convention held in Columbia, South Carolina, for example, Henry McNeal Turner notes that the convention kept track of white violence and Black fatalities, with delegates from each area reporting to the "Murder and Outrages" Committee. No fewer than 20,000 Blacks had been murdered between 1868 and 1871, according to the committee's records. As Andre Johnson narrates in his essay in this volume, when asked by a congressman if the proceedings were already in print, Turner testified: "They are now in press for publication. I will say, however, that it was thought best not to insert" this estimate in our proceedings. "While it was put in our report, it was stricken out afterward, that that particular feature will not appear when our proceedings come to be published. The report was curtailed to a small document from what it was originally."[72] Today the findings of such Committees of Murder and Outrages are available to a generation of academic and community scholars and organizers, not in the proceedings themselves (as of publication, the Colored Conventions Project is still seeking the minutes that Turner confirms were in print) but in the legislative records that preserved Turner's testimony.

Other examples of the necessity of complementing proceedings with other documents abound, especially when it comes to resituating women's roles in conventions. Mary Ann Shadd Cary's presence at the 1855 national convention in Philadelphia was noted in the proceedings, and the contested vote about recognizing her as a delegate is duly documented. Yet nowhere does the powerful emigration debate between her and fellow delegate J. J. Bias that spilled over into postconvention coverage appear. Though Shadd Cary had left for Canada in the disastrous decade that began with the Fugitive Slave Act and gained force through state exclusionary laws as it barreled toward the *Dred Scott* decision, she remained connected to the region where this convention was held, where she was born, raised, and worked, and where her father had served as a convention leader in meetings held more than twenty years earlier. Her paper, the *Provincial Freeman*, was no doubt named after the *Pennsylvania Freeman*. Now back in Philadelphia as the first Black female editor of a North American newspaper, her presence and emigration positions caused a stir that was more fully captured in newspapers than in the proceedings.[73] In another example, Frances E. W. Harper, by then already one of the most beloved poets and prose writers of her era, was just back from a southern tour among freed people, which resulted in her 1872 *Sketches of Southern Life*, when she gave closing remarks in Dover, Delaware, at one of the few known conventions the state held despite the many born there who lent energy and activism to the movement.[74] The 1873 proceedings are eloquent in their denunciation of educational inequities and unfair taxation without access to equal schools, averring that

> as long as a portion of citizens are thus excluded and restricted in their rights, it is folly to expect that portion to be contented, they must of necessity be a disturbing element, and will not cease to agitate the body politic. Again, it puts upon the State a class of people that must remain poor, and consequently unable to contribute but little to the support of the State and yet which must be the most expensive to govern. Intelligence, it is well known, is much cheaper to the State than ignorance. To foster education then, is the noblest work of the State; to oppose it among any class of citizens is to oppose the State's highest interest.

Harper's role and remarks, however, are truncated; "after adopting the address" written by committee and quoted above, the proceedings end with an almost throwaway line about its most famous participant, then as now: "The convention was entertained by Mrs. F. E. W. Harper, in reading her excellent poem entitled 'Sketches from Southern Life,' after which all joined in singing the Doxology, 'Praise God from whom all Blessings flow,'" and the convention "adjourned sine die."[75]

While Harper is relegated to two clauses in the proceedings, papers such as the *Delaware State Journal* capture the "eloquent colored lectureress's" closing comments and additional lectures. As she brought the convention to a close, she told the crowd that "it had been a question with many . . . as to the best age in which to live. For herself, she preferred to live in this age as the chimes are ringing out the freedom of her race," the *Journal* reported.[76] "Our work is not yet done," she went on. "Other races than the colored had been low, socially," and ours, she proclaimed, would "produce poets, authors and statesmen."[77] That is why the equal educational rights they advocated for at this convention were so needed, she avowed, because "knowledge is power."[78] Denise Burgher's research reveals how Harper's presence and comments bolstered the work of Delaware Black women who were at the forefront of Black educational advocacy. Burgher suggests that "Harper's singular presence represents the lives, labor, and words of [that] entire network" and that "the convention was the turning point for Black public education" in the long struggle for Black education in the state.[79] Practicing the art of signifying deflection in her educational advocacy and as a regional ally, Harper counted herself and her fellow convention speakers as embodiments of those "poets, authors and statesmen" that education would no doubt develop in greater number. In doing so, she artfully included Black women in her declaration. The women organizers in the immediate audience, as well as those in the press's wider reach, must have recognized themselves in her words.

John Ernest notes that convention meetings anonymize women's convention labor, underscoring how women's presence "can be observed more by implication than by design" and displaying how Frances E. W. Harper's voice is also all but erased in multiple conventions. Harper's active engagement also had been muted in the proceedings of the earlier 1858 Ohio convention, where she was the convention's sole female delegate.[80] As Nancy Yerian asserts in the CCP digital exhibit on the 1858 Cincinnati convention, coverage in the *Liberator* and *Anti-Slavery Bugle* establishes Harper as a "principal speaker" in "the lengthy and spirited debate on emigration" that was taking place less than a decade after the Fugitive Slave Act and harsh state exclusion laws alienated Blacks living in "free" states from their birthland and just a year after the *Dred Scott* decision put an exclamation point on Black exclusion. Despite her animated participation, the proceedings note only her male counterparts' input. Still, Harper's ten-dollar contribution to the convention's fundraising efforts was matched only by male leaders who share her stature: John Mercer Langston, editor William Howard Day, and her cousin, writer William Watkins.[81] "Outlines and vague traces are all that one can detect of African American women in the black communal body through these conventions," as literary historian Ernest puts it.[82] Reading the proceedings alongside print coverage allows readers to fill in the canvas of nineteenth-century Black political activism and to examine the design, curation, and brushstrokes of convention minutes from multiple perspectives.

Amassing, consulting, and analyzing the formal reports of the convention movement without also including print sources now available in (often paywalled) databases, as well as those housed, and not yet digitized, in state and university repositories, is inadequate if scholars want to puzzle together existing pieces, the scraps of scattered historical data, that "bear record of us," to borrow again from Ward. This is the argument Howard Holman Bell makes in his monograph and the one Peterson makes most explicitly in this volume. In a digital age where amassing such an online archive is possible and necessary, casting a wide net for convention records (writ large) is a methodological decision, and perhaps a methodological position, also informed by commitments to recentering Black women in their own histories and to making such records freely available, accessible, and fully searchable for twenty-first-century publics as well as scholars.

If postmeeting coverage and reports offer crucial records, preconvention calls that appear in extant print and newly digitized papers also furnish thousands of "patches" of "historical data." Calls announced upcoming state and national meetings, seeking not only to inspire attendance but also to garner interest in the circles and circuits of nineteenth-century print's wider reach. Calls inspired preconvention debates; yet the numbers of such ads and the types of different newspapers in which they appeared, and for how many weeks or months the calls ran, is information that has rarely been considered. These announcements shared when and where an upcoming meeting would be held and also detailed central concerns that would be its focus. They circulated in newspapers, were read from church pulpits, and, one must imagine, were shared in reading rooms and announced at Black literary as well as "moral improvement" society meetings.

Reading rooms and literary societies served to spread the word of conventions; as the two shared both an opening downbeat in the early 1830s and a harmonic development, it's useful to think about how they developed in concert. From the early societies founded in larger centers of Black organizing such as Boston, New York, and Philadelphia, to the Anti-Slavery Office and Reading Room where Harriet Jacobs worked in Rochester (in the building it shared with Douglass's *North Star*), reading rooms no doubt publicized the Black conventions that Black newspapers covered in depth.[83] Early organizations such as the New York Phoenix Society and Boston's Afric-American Female Society expanded not only the number but also the gender of those engaging the conventions' key concerns.

Evidence suggests that the "mental feasts" such societies created and consumed included convention announcements and proceedings; the debates they engendered no doubt found a place at the table.[84] For example, the Phoenix Society, founded in 1833, opened a library and reading room where, according to society member, convention goer, and editor Samuel Cornish, the society chose readers to share passages and news aloud before members retired "to an adjacent room to converse on the subjects together with occurrences of the day."[85] The national convention of that year made these links explicit in a declaration meant to replicate the society throughout the free states; the convention "Resolved, that the Vice-President and Secretaries, appointed in the different States, be requested to use their exertions to form Phoenix Societies, similar to those in the City of New-York."[86] As John Ernest points out, the 1833 convention address to a broader public extended this recommendation, "noting that 'societies for mental improvement, particularly among the females, have been established in several places, and a manifest improvement has marked their progress.'"[87] In alignment with census and statistical work taken up by conventions to rebut misrepresentations in official records, the Phoenix Society likewise divided the community into wards to create a registry seeking to document (and then to raise) Black literacy rates. Their concerns, methods, and members overlapped directly with those of the conventions.

The efforts of reading groups and Black conventions continued to work in concert for decades.[88] The call for the 1868 Iowa convention, for example, invited "you, EN MASSE . . . to assemble in Convention." "All in favor of equal rights come!" it proclaimed. "Strike for freedom whilst it is day! Let all our churches, literary and other societies, be represented."[89] Likewise, many state and national conventions collected information on these very societies and reading rooms as they collated and mapped information on Black community assets at a time when statistical analysis, conferences, and societies were on the rise—and often were being used by whites in the service of diminishing, caricaturing, and ignoring Black intellectual and economic capital and wealth and those who wielded it.[90]

Reading groups were one of the ways Black women claimed civic space in the extended circles of Black public culture. One of their primary objectives, as Elizabeth McHenry outlines in *Forgotten Readers*, was to "give active form and voice to the social and historical contexts in which they lived and to their own burgeoning political perspectives" as they also engaged in collective reading and writing practices.[91] The Afric-American Female Society, formed in 1831, overlapped directly with the early national conventions that held annual meetings until 1835.

Similarly, the Philadelphia Library Company of Colored Persons was cofounded by William Whipper, who attended five of the six national conventions held in the 1830s. Women were excluded from that society as they also were from being named delegates at those conventions.[92] Yet, in the City of Brotherly Love, Black women's groups outnumbered the larger Black men's groups by more than three to two.[93] Indeed, from 1830 to 1850, says McHenry, evidence suggests that Black women's reading societies, though often smaller, outnumbered men's group beyond Philadelphia.[94]

Convention organizers deliberately took up the challenge of expanding audiences and extending the movement's participatory base. Delegate rolls are filled with editors and pastors whose role was, among other things, to quite literally spread the word to the congregations and communities they preached to on Sundays, reached through their newspapers' columns, and represented as delegates. In some conventions in the 1850s, according to Jim Casey's research, nearly a third of the named attendees had been or would become involved in editorship. A veritable who's who of nineteenth-century Black print pioneers served as committee chairs and speakers at meeting after meeting, including Samuel Cornish, Charles Ray, Philip Bell, Martin Delany, Frederick Douglass, Mary Ann Shadd Cary, David Jenkins, William Howard Day, Jonas Townsend, and Henry McNeil Turner, among many others.[95] They were attentive to and deliberate about reaching broader Black reading publics and expanding conventions'—and their newspapers'—base and reach.

Conventions and Black Print Culture

The Black press served not only as a conveyer of information but as a convener of audiences and ideas; such papers not only announced Black literary societies and convention events, but they functioned as a virtual meeting place. The *Colored American* (1837–41) reported on Black reading culture and societies with gusto and dedication, printing their constitutions and the discussions that occurred "as if the reader were a participant," as Elizabeth McHenry points out, "reproducing the experience of being present at a meeting in its pages."[96] These papers both shared conventions' content and happenings and offered another form of and forum for participation. They carried copious coverage of pre- and postconvention activities and featured commentary, critique, and encouragement by and for a much larger audience than those who attended the meetings themselves. In *Frederick Douglass' Paper* alone, at least fifteen convention announcements and editorials appeared in the summer and fall months that preceded the mid-October 1855 national meeting in Philadelphia, as Carla Peterson's essay in this volume reveals. Calls themselves could initiate debates that had a force and life of their own, appearing only in traces in the official proceedings, however robust they may have been in the press's columns. As Peterson points out, though engaged in a vociferous newspaper debate before the convention, frustrated that his point might not carry an argument, James McCune Smith sat out the otherwise star-studded 1855 convention. If scholars consult the proceedings isolated from other materials, they risk muting the very loud debate that sometimes served as convention prelude. The print participants, or print attendees, as we might call them, may not have been in the physical spaces where the meetings took place, but to ignore their role is to diminish an understanding of conventions' wider circuits and circles.

Black convention culture existed in close relation to nineteenth-century Black print culture; indeed, one could argue that conventions were held in the press as much as they took place in the halls, churches, and buildings in which delegates and attendees gathered. Control over the news and the need for a national Black press were on the agenda of multiple convention gatherings. The *Colored American*, *Frederick Douglass' Paper*, the *Christian Recorder*, and the *New Orleans Tribune*, as well as many shorter-lived Black news organs, provided delegates and participants with a way to report on conventions and their concerns. They offered access to Black women and men from cities and hamlets alike. By extending the conventions' geographic and temporal reach exponentially, these convenings were designed to inspire discussions and to spawn—even demand—action beyond the time and place of their occurrence. Organizers were keen to spread the word; as political tacticians, they were attentive to the dissemination and communication of their message and the role of the press in keeping their issues alive.

Attention to print was embedded in committee structures and taken up as a subject during the meetings themselves. Conventions were to include a "Committee on Printing" or a "Publishing Committee" to actualize and formalize strategies for reaching audiences beyond the convention halls over decades.[97] It's useful to take an in-depth look at the Troy, New York, 1847 national convention, where a proposal by the "committee on a National Press" elicited sustained discussion and spirited debate.[98] The details of this meeting are illustrative. When Henry Highland Garnet called the meeting to order and read the convention call, he welcomed seventy-five delegates hailing from nine of the country's twenty-nine states. The delegates filled the seats at Morris Place Hall, joining others for 9:00–1:00 and 2:00–6:00 sessions for four full days.[99] Douglass, now an author just recently returning from England, joined William Cooper Nell, James McCune Smith, William Wells Brown, Alexander Crummell, Charles Ray, William Allen, Charles Remond, James Pennington, Amos Beman, and Thomas Van Rensselaer, among others, while W. E. B. Du Bois's grandfather, Othello Burghardt, a Massachusetts delegate from Great Barrington, as we recall, took in the debate. They elected as the convention's president Nathan Johnson, at whose home Douglass, as a fugitive nearly a decade before, had first begun "to feel a degree of safety" and where Johnson helped him choose the name by which he'd become so well known.[100]

Though the discussion about the ability to launch and sustain a national Black paper in the 1847 convention was spirited, there was little debate about the importance of the Black press in advancing the work of equal justice. Garnet staked the claim that "the most successful means which can be used for the overthrow of Slavery and Caste in this country, would be found in an able and well-conducted Press, solely under the control of the people of color."[101] Establishing such a "National Printing Press would send terror into the ranks of our enemies, and encourage all our friends," he averred.[102] Douglass, on the verge of launching his own paper, spoke in opposition and was joined, as Garnet noted sarcastically, by other "editors, who are, or are to be."[103] After Douglass spoke, James McCune Smith, who had served for a short time as the editor of the *Colored American*, rose to declare that having a national press was necessary to amplify and connect state efforts for political rights.[104] The debate was heated, but by the end of the four-day meeting, "a resolution was adopted recommending" a national press, alongside Black papers that included the "*'Ram's Horn,' 'Nation Watchman,' 'Northern Star,' 'Disfranchised American'* and *'The Mystery,'* as worthy of the encouragement and support of the people."[105] In the records of such debates, not only is the political necessity of a Black press made plain, but networks of Black editors and activists and the existence and contexts of scores of Black newspapers are preserved.

Conventions' decades-long attention to supporting and establishing Black papers and a Black press offers an implicit critique of the insufficiency of white leadership and labor practices (including in the white abolitionist press). The substantive "Report of the Committee on a National Press" included in the 1847 proceedings declares: "Of the means for the advancement of a people placed as we are, none are more available than a Press. We struggle against opinions. Our warfare lies in the field of thought."[106] It went on, "Let there be, then, in these United States, a Printing Press, a copious supply of type, a full and complete establishment, wholly controlled by colored men; let the thinking writingman, the compositors, pressman, printers' help, all, all be men of color;—then let there come from said establishment a weekly periodical and a quarterly periodical, edited as well as printed by colored men."[107] Here they double down on their (indirect) reproach of the white ally-run press through the slant repetition of "wholly controlled by colored men" and "all, all be men of color," making the representational and economic stakes they detail here crystal clear. Like past efforts and future conventions, the 1847 meeting sought to raise Black soldiers: pressmen, editors, compositors, and typesetters to wage the warfare, as they put it, which lies in the field of thought. This was meant to be not a series of local interventions but rather a larger army of ideas and idea makers.

The 1875 Convention of Colored Newspaper Men held in Cincinnati also expresses motifs that appear on the political canvases on which national and state conventions were drawn. This postbellum meeting displays both new leadership and a continued commitment to intergenerational activism and ideas. Convened after a call for a "national organizing of colored editors," this newspaper convention again presented collective planning for a Black press that worked across regions and was also cross-pollinating. Attending alongside the man who had served as the nation's first Black governor, Louisiana's P. B. S. Pinchback, was a formidable array of convention goers, editors, and politicians from all over the country. Those who had attended their first Black conventions in the 1840s served on committees with those who would organize conventions into the 1890s: Mifflin Gibbs, Peter H. Clark, and J. Sella Martin, for example, were joined by Lewis Douglass (Douglass's eldest son, representing California's long-lived newspaper, the *Elevator*), Benjamin W. Arnett, and Henry McNeal Turner. They once again affirmed that "no white man, however friendly, can feel our wrongs as acutely, or express our wants as fully as a colored man can" and highlighted the link between ownership and opportunities that are only "grudgingly given by the conductors of white men's newspapers."[108] As in previous decades, they underscored the role of Black religious activism: "For [pastors] can do more than any other class to induce the colored people to become readers of newspaper." And they called for economic power as well as a say in public policy.[109] Well before the short-lived national Afro-American League and Councils were formed by Black pressmen such as T. Thomas Fortune and John Bruce in the late 1880s, conventions continually underscored the interconnected role the Black press played in Black justice struggles.

It's hard to overstate the importance of the connection between the Black press and the convention movement; as Jim Casey puts it, "Colored Conventions helped found many Black newspapers and Black newspapers helped organize many Colored Conventions."[110] Black editors took advantage of the opportunity to come together and practice their usually more private, more local "craft in public, revising language, assembling patchwork texts, and speaking in collective voices," as Casey points out.[111] Papers and editors emerged from the conventions. California's *Mirror of the Times* was a direct outgrowth of the 1855 First State Convention of Colored Citizens of the State of California. Philip Bell—who was instrumental in the founding of the influential *Colored American* (New York, 1837–41, with Charles Ray and Samuel

Cornish), the *Pacific Appeal* (California, 1862–80, with Jonas Townsend and Mifflin Gibbs), and the *Elevator* (California, 1865–98)—participated in conventions that discussed the importance of founding and supporting a vibrant Black press. As Benjamin Fagan displays in *The Black Newspaper and the Chosen Nation* and the exhibit *The Early Case for a National Black Press*, seeds planted at conventions were—and were meant to be—carried for miles.[112] One example is "the outline of the *Repository* printed in the minutes of the 1854 National Emigration Convention," which holds, Fagan points out, striking similarities to "the *Anglo-African Magazine* that appeared five years later again [suggesting] that . . . the deliberations of such bodies [as the Colored Conventions] deeply shaped the contours of the Black press."[113] Tracing the interconnections and influences between Black papers and conventions reveals direct links and connections disrupted by time and place.

Collective Address and Authorship

An emphasis on individual expression and an often hagiographic focus on the singular, exceptional personality are so deeply embedded in academic and American narratives that they obscure foundational commitments to Black collective authorship and address. Departing from, or at least augmenting, the model of singular authorship to encompass the editing/ production practices of both the conventions and newspaper culture, then, offers a new perspective on what has been called the plagiarism, or "inspired borrowing" practices, of writers such as William Wells Brown, "Hannah Crafts," and Pauline Hopkins. Black nineteenth-century writing was so embedded in practices of broader print culture that these "problem cases" may be fruitfully read in relation to a culture of writing that valued collaboration, incorporation, and reach—rather than singular authorship.[114]

Collective—not individual—action, expression, and even writing is at the center of Black liberation cosmology and historiography, to extend from John Ernest's seminal work and recent calls.[115] To borrow from Stephen Hall, "African Americans have always imagined and constructed history as a communal act."[116] One of the earliest African American publications, the *Narrative of the Proceedings of the Black People* (1794), was jointly written by two men many call Black founders, Absalom Jones and Richard Allen, the latter of whom established the AME Church, and who would, in the last year of his life, host the first meeting of what would become the Colored Conventions movement. Theirs is a "Narrative of the Proceedings of the *Black People*" (emphasis mine), a coauthored narrative about a plural collective and community. Though it's often referred to as the "narrative," following its typeset emphasis, the authors pair that with the term "proceedings," that is, both the actions—the way Philadelphia Blacks *proceeded* during the calamity—and the *records* that frame and preserve those actions. In this early, collectively authored foundational text, the Black literary tradition that will blossom into the slave narrative—"I" witness stories that have been

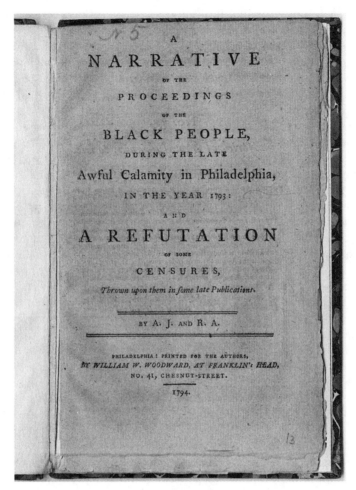

FIGURE 2.2. Title page of *A Narrative of the Proceedings of the Black People, during the Late Awful Calamity in Philadelphia, in the Year 1793*. Courtesy of the Library Company of Philadelphia.

valorized as the seed of *the* African American literary tradition—are found side by side with the representation of collective "proceedings" that are the cornerstone of the Colored Conventions archive. This difference of both degree and kind challenges narratives of (Black) American individualism and exceptionalism; individual Black orators, editors, and writers organized not only for themselves but for the larger community. And they often did so, in print as in oral culture, using collective forums and structures.

Centering the Colored Conventions movement's role in reform, print culture, and Black community development offers compelling reconfigurations of nineteenth-century authorship and political address. Collective address was, in fact, a conventional form of Black nineteenth-century expressive culture. The Black press, Black conventions, and the churches that so often hosted conventions created independent spaces for Black leadership, stewardship, and collective action with an eye on state and national policy. New York's 1840 state convention serves as both example and precursor. There, Garnet worked with editor Rev. Charles Ray and Rev. Theodore Wright on the Committee on the Address; together they used their substantial shared experience and rhetorical force to craft the convention's addresses.[117] The 1848 national convention had a committee of five "appointed to prepare an Address to the Colored People of the United States," which was then to "report to" the delegates whose votes were needed to approve it.[118] Twenty years later in Iowa, in another example, "the committee on address, through their chairman, Alex. Clark, presented and read the address *as prepared by the committee*; which was unanimously adopted."[119] Countless national and state conventions authored addresses in committee. When it came to the reach of Black political expression organized by and for Black people, the giants of the age cut their teeth at Black conventions and on such committees.

Collective practices of Black print and the writing of addresses in committee offer new models of authorship. While Douglass's "What to the Slave is the 4th of July" and Garnet's "Address to the Slaves" are often understood to be among the most powerful rhetorical addresses to emerge from Black antebellum pens, the latter was "never meant to be Henry Highland Garnet's 'Address to the Slaves,'" as Derrick Spires asserts in his essay here.[120] Indeed, it follows the model set by the "Appeal of Forty Thousand Citizens, Threatened with Disfranchisement, to the People of Pennsylvania" of 1838, most often attributed to Robert Purvis, though there's every reason to believe it was composed collectively as suggested by the fact that it is signed "in [sic] behalf of the Committee, Robert Purvis, Chairman."[121] Its closing echoes its collective title; its rhetorical force, as with the ending declaration of the "Address to the Slaves," is dependent on its claim to the collective force of the citizenry it represents, one, in this case, 40,000 strong. "Firm upon *our* old Pennsylvania BILL OF RIGHTS, and trusting in a God of Truth and Justice, *we*," it proclaims, "lay our claim before you, with the warning that no amendments of the present Constitution can compensate for the loss of its foundation principle of equal rights."[122] Likewise, "An Address to the Slaves" was meant to be a collective public assertion, "part manifesto, part historical assessment of abolitionism, and part vehicle for creating and sustaining a national Black movement," Spires contends.[123] The fiery address was penned by the Business Committee of the famous 1843 national Buffalo convention and put up for a vote again, and again defeated, at the national convention in 1847.[124]

That Garnet chose to create a publication provenance grounded in collective action even after the address was narrowly voted down at two national conventions is made clear by his choice *not* to put out the work as a freestanding pamphlet even after these rebuffs. It's useful, then, to situate the address iteratively rather than individually. When it was finally published in 1848, Garnet paired it with a second edition of the other most famous—and radical—political appeal of the antebellum period, David Walker's *Appeal*. And that bundled publication was recognized by the Ohio state convention, which "recommend that five hundred copies of Walker's Appeal, and Henry H. Garnet's Address to the Slaves, be obtained *in the name of the Convention*, and gratuitously circulated."[125] The five-year delay between the famous 1843 debate and the 1848 publication can't simply be read as an example of Garnet's own ideological point of view, expressive eloquence, and rhetorical mastery. Rather, it is one of many foundational instances of early Black expression and political address that illustrate alternative and collective models of authorship that have been transmogrified into a celebration of a single, and supposedly singular, Black figure.

Antislavery Shadows

Situating both the collective genesis and the communal arc of the Colored Conventions as central to Black freedom struggles upends long-embedded assumptions carried in the very language found in scholarly tomes and public commentary alike. The most famous individual antebellum slave narratives often emerge from the context of abolition.[126] Advocacy for Black collective rights was more often the provenance of nineteenth-century Black conventions and newspapers. What does it mean, then, to call so many nineteenth-century Black activist editors, religious leaders, and entrepreneurs "abolitionists" when they continued to organize and advocate for Black justice for decades after the Civil War's close, many well into the 1890s? How does the nearly ubiquitous moniker of "abolitionist" subsume and make secondary antebellum—much less postbellum—Black institution building, civic participation, and protest? How does it obscure convention goer Mary Ann Shadd Cary's postwar return to the United States from Canada (where she had been North America's first Black woman editor) to become the country's first Black woman law student when she enrolled at Howard University, where John Mercer Langston was the law school's founding dean, before he was elected as Virginia's first U.S. congressman and then appointed, following Douglass, as the U.S. minister to Haiti, the same position Garnet served in for Liberia, dying in West Africa as Du Bois would eight decades later? That last sentence goes on and on—just like these "abolitionists'" postbellum careers and activism. Though their association with antislavery activism is what has made these reformers (more or less) famous, critics' and the public's dependence on the term "abolitionist" reduces and truncates their work, commitment, and advocacy in ways that impact the historiographies, arcs, and trajectories of nineteenth-century Black organizing and association.

Abolition's historical dominance overshadows, or overpowers, nineteenth-century Black institutions and personas. Why do we almost exclusively label not only people but the many newspapers of such active convention goers as

Samuel Cornish, Charles Ray, David Jenkins, Mary Ann Shadd Cary, and others "abolitionist" when, from its inception, the Black press advocated for and against so much more: for suffrage and the right to testify in court, for jury and legal rights well beyond the South, for educational access and equity for Black children, and against anti-Black and anti-immigration provisions that were built into the constitutions of Illinois, Indiana, and Oregon—all issues that were rarely given a solo in white abolitionist papers though they were among the most frequent songs to be sung in the Black press. Papers edited by convention leaders also claimed, as they did in 1827, that "useful knowledge of every kind . . . shall find a ready admission into our columns" (*Freedom's Journal*, issue 1); they covered "foreign news" with alacrity and published prose and poetry that had—and also had nothing—to do with transnational slavery. These papers asserted the full and global citizenship of Black peoples—and did so often in contrast to organized antislavery efforts led by the most recognized names of (white) abolition.

In addition to the convention movement's collective power, number of participants, and longevity, it's again important to stress that its advocacy for Black freedom, livelihood, and political inclusion both precedes and outlives the antebellum antislavery movement. As scholars from Benjamin Quarles to Manisha Sinha affirm, the "story of abolition must begin with the struggles of the enslaved."[127] Yes. And we must also underscore that the story of Black convention and print activism begins not only with Black resistance against slavery but also with sustained organizing to make real an enlivened notion of Black freedom's relationship to participatory democracy embodied in collective, as much as individual, Black agency and rights. Such assertions of Black rights and belonging run counter not only to the ideology and efforts of the American Colonization Society but also to the advocacy of the vast majority of eighteenth-century and pre-antebellum abolition efforts. Much of the scholarship on nineteenth-century racial history, both abolition and Reconstruction, until recently has been governed by "something of a liberal internationalist framework," one that doesn't fully envision enslaved, self-emancipated, or freeborn Black people "as political beings."[128] These scholarly arguments and presumptions, as Steven Hahn argues, see Black mobilization through the lens of inclusion and the pursuit of individual rights rather than community development and demands for collective rights.[129] The difficulty of seeing African Americans—and particularly African American institutions and collectives—as political equals and actors, rather than as historical exceptions, adjuncts, or beneficiaries, explains why, whether it's being denounced or lauded, abolition (like white Radical Reconstruction) has always occupied a significant place in discussions about American race and politics. It also explains why, despite its importance, longevity, and continued resonance with ongoing struggles, the convention movement has not been well enough remembered as the progenitor of the long civil rights movement. Indeed, in large part it has been disremembered as the cradle of collective organizing for Black rights because of the shadows antislavery casts, that is, because of abolition's historiographical centrality.

Though white antebellum antislavery activists were long dismissed as unhinged members of a radical fringe, since the modern civil rights movement, abolition has been in critical vogue. Hundreds of scholarly tomes, edited collections, and biographies have been published. The work of the Colored Conventions Project builds on the histories of activists once called "Black abolitionists" as they are being increasingly untethered from the white sponsors and associates whose papers, records, and stories have been better preserved. If reams of paper have been spent considering, for example, Douglass's relationships with whites such as William Lloyd Garrison, Julia Griffiths, and Ottilie Assing, how much, in comparison, do we know about Black networks of exchange, influence, and community that include James McCune Smith, Charles Lenox Remond (for whom Douglass named a son), Lewis Hayden, Austin Steward (Douglass's elder and Rochester neighbor), or Jermain Wesley Loguen, whose daughter Amelia married Douglass's son Lewis at the Loguens' home?[130] Douglass is but the most obvious node in the most obvious of social networks. Such a network could be mapped using Mary Ann Shadd Cary as its subject, or Mifflin Gibbs, the long-lived John Mercer Langston, or many of the other Black convention advocates for full citizenship rights. In other words, building on the work of historians who center Black agency and activism as the ground on which they plant their inquiries, the convention movement allows us to ask new questions about networks and circuits of Black influence, debate, and community in all of their complexity, heterogeneity, and power.

Colored Conventions in the Digital Age

Digital platforms facilitate collective approaches that are engaging thousands of participants in assembling and analyzing the scattered and discarded records of a convention movement that itself was characterized by collective organizational and committee structures, a broad geographic reach, and an approach to engaging Black communities beyond the halls where meetings were held. Digitization and transcription have made available millions of newspaper pages, pamphlets, and other materials; materials that once were available only in archives and library special collections departments, as well as records once made accessible on microfilm machines, can now be searched online from anywhere and by anyone with computer and institutional access. These make it possible for the CCP to include thousands of students in original research through a network of North American teaching partners and research librarians who adopt the Colored Convention Project's "seeking records" curriculum and research guides. Collectives make it possible to reconceptualize the process and terms of Black historical "recovery" even though "our condition is far from favourable for the furnishing of historical data," to again recall the words of Samuel Ring-gold Ward. When married to community organizing principles, digital platforms can facilitate the online gathering and sharing of the "scraps, patches, anecdotes . . . that bear record of us."[131]

Furthering its reach as the conventions so deliberately did, the CCP engages graduate students and undergraduate researchers from various geographic sites through inter/national teaching partners' classes. Students create digital exhibits—many based on essays in this volume—that are assigned in college and high school classrooms and that anyone can peruse. Unearthing coverage and historical images and amassing data they transform into visualizations, these exhibits bring convention debates, delegates' travels, and neighborhoods where conventions took place to life, offer biographies of delegates and associated women, present timelines and charts from the data the conventions themselves collected, share social network visualizations that trace conventioneers' relations to each other, and unearth boardinghouse ads aimed at Black convention goers. Online visitors can trace the routes and streets convention goers took, clicking on markers and information about Black boardinghouses, churches, schools, and literary societies. Licensing agreements with private database firms such as Gale Cengage and Accessible Archives allow the CCP to showcase (otherwise paywalled) images that raise new research questions based on an expansive visual archive that would have been much too expensive to present in a print volume.[132] The thousands of students and scores of far-flung teaching partners approximate the distributed structure of the conventions themselves as they unearth the sources and narrate the stories of this Black organizing movement.

The CCP's transcribing efforts involve an even wider public in a deliberate attempt to enlarge the circle of those actively reclaiming a history that's been disremembered, much as the conventions used print technologies to engage those who could not find the time and resources to attend. The CCP's Douglass Day transcribe-a-thons and read-a-thons transform Douglass's chosen birthday, February 14, into what we call a "day of collective love for Black history." Today's Douglass Day yearly events resurrect the celebrations of Douglass's birthday that started after his death and were popularized by Mary Church Terrell before spreading across the nation and being covered in newspapers from "Boston to Pittsburgh, from Iowa to Oregon."[133] Though largely lost to historical memory, Black History Month grew from Carter G. Woodson's Black History Week, which itself was built around Douglass's chosen birthday on February 14. Like Douglass Days 100 years ago, the contemporary day of "collective love for Black history" is a day of commemoration in action. It involves hundreds of hosts and thousands of "volun-peers" who gather to help make documents (such as convention records or Freedmen's Bureau records) fully available and searchable and to learn more about their contexts and importance.[134] Such gatherings not only involve participants across the globe in preserving Black records, but they also shift the scale, cost structure, and time frame of such public history efforts.

If conventions were keen on elevating Black papers to engage their communities in the larger debates that impacted their lives, the effort to reintroduce the long history of Black organizing deliberately engages the movement's cultural and institutional descendants. One example is the CCP's Community and Historic Church Outreach Committee's partnership with the AME Church. Working with AME lay historiographer Pamela Tilley and CCP leaders Denise Burgher and Jim Casey, scores of AME members transcribed hundreds of pages of proceedings from Colored Conventions originally held at AME churches. Again, mirroring the tactics modeled by conventions themselves in archive assembly and digital engagement, this complex work of restorative history is broad based, publicly engaged, and collaborative.

Archivists and interested independent researchers can also serve as critical partners in efforts to locate scattered records and reunite them with their long-lost historical kin. Those working in historical societies and at collections are familiar with the records that exist in the many historical cul-de-sacs into which there aren't yet digital inroads. The Colored Convention Project's objective to make new convention records available elicited rare minutes such as those of the 1873 Delaware state convention, which features Frances E. W. Harper and Levi Coppin. Not accounted for in the scholarship on Harper, Coppin, or the convention movement, these proceedings are one example of newly located records now included at ColoredConventions.org because a curator, Constance Cooper, shared them when the Colored Conventions Project's faculty director visited the Delaware Historical Society to ask them to cosponsor the symposium out of which this collection arose.[135] A series of 1880s Illinois conventions have been identified by the director of the Illinois State Archives, Dave Joens.[136] An independent scholar, Sebastian Page, sent in a previously uncatalogued proceeding record of an 1851 Indiana convention from the National Archives at Kew—setting up a tripod with his own camera to get quality images.[137] The CCP's first satellite partners in Iowa found at least eight previously unlisted conventions held in Iowa. These conventions were led by Alexander Clark, a national figure whose family integrated the University of Iowa law school; Alexander Clark and his son became the University of Iowa's first and second Black graduates.[138] When housed in conventional local, state, and inter/national repositories and church archives, records of these conventions, though not technically out of place, haven't been exactly at home either, finding themselves sitting, like (homemade) macaroni and cheese, greens, or peach cobbler, on a table set for those who prefer the taste of Yorkshire pudding and green bean amandine. Once unknown, uncatalogued, or simply isolated, these records now reside together in a cohesive online archive.

Though these collective recovery methods are meant to mirror the structures and processes of the movement itself, the CCP has also chosen to deliberately depart from some convention practices, most notably, again, by reinfusing the importance, centrality, and labor of Black women into convention histories. In alignment with and indebted to scholarship and activism that centers Black women who traditionally have been relegated to the margins, the project out of which this volume emerges is attentive to creating "friendly accountability" by crafting scholarly structures and guidelines for its digital archives and collections. The CCP memos of understanding, calls for proposals, and leadership protocols make visible the influence, participation, and power of Black women that are so often erased and disremembered in records of movement making then and now.[139] Those creating online research exhibits in classes that form part of the CCP's broad network of teaching partners sign a memorandum of understanding that encourages them to embrace a gender-inclusive methodology that broadens their historical focus and asks research questions that direct students to seek out the presence and influence of women in a movement that could not have taken place without them. (See fig. 1.1.)

The call for proposals for the symposium that was the basis for this volume encouraged papers that highlight the organizational work of Black women who have been largely erased from convention minutes. This collection seeks to account for the crucial work done by women in the broader social networks that made these conventions possible.[140] Indeed, the resulting essays so deeply center women's labor and involvement that readers of this volume who have not yet delved into the proceedings themselves might be surprised at how absent women are in the overwhelming majority of convention minutes.

Creating collectives and structures that disrupt traditional academic hierarchies is also a project principle that stems from the conventions themselves. As "the rich landowner, the opulent tradesman, seconded motions offered by" those with less conventionally recognized power, such as "mechanics and freedmen," faculty and national codirectors often second the ideas of undergraduate researchers and graduate student leaders whose vision, ideas, and expertise so often drive the project. Following the UCLA Center for Digital Humanities' "Student Collaborators' Bill of Rights" and other articles and statements that set out objectives for equitable project relations, research exhibits cite student researchers, including CCP Exhibits Committee members who edit, fact check, and create additional data visualizations.[141]

The welcome turn to digital and distributed approaches, as well as to microattribution and project-based work, mirrors the ways in which conventions not only were organized collectively but also, in the minutes, acknowledged collective labor. Likewise, visualizations that emerge from data sets collected by geographically connected or networked classes offer opportunities both to model the larger work of collaborative archive assembly and to disrupt conventional models of individual knowledge production and scholarship. In these ways, again, digital platforms married to organizing principles allow us to extend convention working principles as we also preserve and present them online. Questions about how to unearth a buried history and about the tools we use, the protocols we implement, and the ways we categorize, value, and frame records that have been preserved between then and now—these are also questions about whose lives matter. Documents are not "history," after all; they are artifacts created by those who seek to preserve historical events, to enter them into the record embedded with the values and assumptions they seek to pass on. Historical silencing "is due to uneven power in the production of sources, archives and narratives," as Michel-Rolph Trouillot puts it.[142] Directives that encourage us to look for hidden labor and influence both in conventions themselves and in the online site where their records and narratives are housed raise critical questions not only about convention infrastructure but about the production of history that this volume and the Colored Conventions Project consider.

Conventions were—and were meant to incite—collective action. And the determination, eloquence, organizational commitment, and community building this history provides offer inspiration for those who continue to address the issues the conventions raised. Unlike the most celebrated movements against racial tyranny in the nineteenth century, Colored Conventions speak directly to the ongoing issues Black people face as disenfranchised denizens of the United States and as global, diasporic, citizens of the world. Far from being centuries removed from the pressing concerns of today's Black organizers, parents, community leaders, and laborers, the scenes and scenarios discussed at these conventions speak directly to the value of Black lives and to the continuously insistent assertion that they do, in fact, matter, then as now. Yet the history of the Colored Conventions also chronicles the equally long and committed refusal of this country to respond to the peaceful petitioning and the demonstrations of cultural, economic, and political worth and wealth that nineteenth-century Black Americans documented and displayed. It is a record of state denunciation of racial equality and democracy in the face of our most able and eloquent advocates. The Colored Conventions movement mirrors its future (our present) and the causes so many Black organizers over time have cared about: jury and voting rights, a living wage and jobs outside of domestic service and the service sector, educational access and good schools no matter the district or skin in which we live, and an end to state apathy in the face of white violence against our parents, siblings, classmates, caretakers, neighbors, and community.

Incorporating the Colored Conventions into the long civil rights movement documents a history of the cold shoulder, the blind eye, the "talk to the hand"—the unmistakable, far-from-metaphorical turning away of the entire body politic to the legitimacy of continuous Black claims to equal rights before the law. It amplifies the repeated refrain of a legal and political system that continues to reiterate that it was not meant to serve or protect everyone equally, and, if you're Black in history or at this moment (the one of my writing or the one of your reading), not meant to serve or protect you at all. How many years, how much service and sacrifice, how much unpaid and underpaid labor, how much organizing and movement building will it take for Blacks on this continent to be recognized as members of society as worthy of the promises of justice, domestic tranquility, and general welfare, to quote the U.S. Constitution? This history raises deeply unsettling questions—then as now, north and south, from Missouri to Michigan, from Cincinnati to Charleston, from New York to New Orleans—about this country's desire and ability to move from the founding assumptions of Black worth and place, as chattel property and noncitizens, to full recognition of African Americans who have been residents of this country for more than four centuries. Like the story of any well-burnished movement that passes from one generation to another without the luxury of forming a patina of the past, this is a history that reflects exclusion and rejection as well as inspiration and motivation. Black organizing in America provides a history of the continuous denial as well as the unmitigated assertion of Black rights. It offers a legacy of community, institution building, and self-sufficiency as well as advocacy and outreach. It is a movement still in the making.

NOTES

1. Carter G. Woodson, "The Negroes of Cincinnati Prior to the Civil War," *Journal of Negro History* 1, no. 1 (1916): 6–7, as quoted in "Emergency in Cincinnati," in *The Meeting that Launched a Movement: The First National Convention*, by Eric Brown, digital exhibit, Colored Conventions Project, https://coloredconventions.org/first -convention/origins-1830-convention/emergency-in-cincinnati.

2. "As much anxiety has prevailed on account of the enactment of laws in several States of the Union, especially that of Ohio, abridging the liberties and privileges of the Free People or Colour, and subjecting them to a series of privations and sufferings, by denying them a right of residence, unless they comply with certain requisitions not exacted of the Whites, a course altogether incompatible with the principles of civil and religious liberty." Convention of the People of Color, First Annual (1831: Philadelphia, PA), *Minutes and Proceedings of the First Annual Convention of the People of Colour, Held by Adjournments in the City of Philadelphia, from the Sixth to the Eleventh of June, Inclusive, 1831*, Colored Conventions Project, coloredconventions.org /items/show/72.

3. The 1831 convention proceedings number members of these families at 2,000. Convention of the People of Color, First Annual (1831), *Minutes and Proceedings*.

4. Language from the jointly written copy on ColoredConventions.org by Gabrielle Foreman, Sarah Patterson, and Jim Casey.

5. Howard Holman Bell's monograph, based without revision on his 1953 dissertation, has remained the only full-length book to take up the conventions as its subject until the publication of this volume. His book covers the national conventions until the Civil War. See Howard H. Bell, *A Survey of the Negro Convention Movement, 1830–1861* (New York: Arno Press, 1969). Philip Foner and George Walker's two-volume edition of state conventions (Philip S. Foner and George E. Walker, eds., *Proceedings of the Black State Conventions: 1840–1865*, 2 vols. [Philadelphia: Temple University Press, 1979]) has made many of the antebellum state conventions available. Foner and Walker's later postbellum collection has been less frequently cited and incorporated into historical scholarship. Their editorial work and Bell's scholarship have been deeply influential in subsequent discussions of the convention movement.

6. The NAACP notes that it is the "oldest and the boldest" throughout its website and this phrase appears on many of its state chapters' websites as well. The language here is also taken from its website. This phrase was once found at "Oldest and Boldest," NAACP (website), accessed September 18, 2017, http://www.naacp.org /oldest-and-boldest/.

7. The NAACP was founded in 1909. Like the first Colored Convention, it was a response in part to an anti-Black race riot in the Midwest, this time in 1908 in Springfield, Illinois. "Appalled at the violence that was committed against blacks, a group of white liberals . . . issued a call for a meeting to discuss racial justice. Some 60 people, seven of whom were African American (including W. E. B. Du Bois, Ida B. Wells-Barnett and Mary Church Terrell), signed the call." Echoing "the focus of Du Bois' Niagara Movement [which] began in 1905, the NAACP's stated goal was to secure for all people the rights guaranteed in the 13th, 14th, and 15th Amendments to the United States Constitution, which promised an end to slavery, the equal protection of the law, and universal adult male suffrage, respectively." The NAACP's mission, says its website, "is to ensure the political, educational, social and economic equality of minority group citizens of United States and eliminate race prejudice." "Oldest and Boldest."

8. Eddie S. Glaude Jr., *Exodus! Religion, Race, and Nation in Early Nineteenth-Century Black America* (Chicago: University of Chicago Press, 2000), 113.

9. Glaude, 114.

10. See Shawn Leigh Alexander, *An Army of Lions: The Civil Rights Struggle before the NAACP* (Philadelphia: University of Pennsylvania Press, 2013), xi. Alexander's preface doesn't mention Colored Conventions, though they were still being held when the Afro-American League was launched and are an example of the continuous organizing that he notes the shorter-lived league and subsequent Afro-American Council did not enact (xiv). He suggests that after the anti-Black Danville riot in 1883, editors and other Black leaders decided "organization was needed—and in a form in which the community had no prior experience." They would protest "lynch law, mob violence, segregation, the penal system and the inequitable distribution of school funds" (7). In doing so they directly extended issues taken up by convention after convention—though, as Alexander notes, T. Thomas Fortune didn't think the convention movement did so effectively (8). It's worth noting that before the online archive gathered scattered state and national records together, it was difficult to reconstruct the scope of the movement.

11. Henry Highland Garnet declared this in the opening paragraph of "An Address to the Slaves of the United States of America," which is widely available online and in anthologies. The speech itself, as Derrick Spires points out in his essay in this volume, is not the address he gave at the national 1843 Colored Convention in Buffalo, New York, and different versions circulate with almost no distinction made.

12. David Walker, "Appeal to the Coloured Citizens of the World," David Walker's Appeal, accessed July 20, 2018, http://utc.iath.virginia.edu/abolitn/abesdwa3t.html.

13. Ohio Colored Men's Convention (1871: Columbus, OH), *Proceedings of the Ohio State Convention of Colored Men*, Colored Conventions Project, http://coloredconventions .org/items/show/541.

14. The first meeting has a complicated and competitive lead-up that includes Hezekiah Grice, a New York contingent of Black leaders, and Bishop Allen. For more, see Eric Brown, *The Meeting that Launched a Movement: The First National Convention*, digital exhibit, Colored Conventions Project, https://coloredconventions.org/first -convention/origins-1830-convention.

15. The 1847 minutes list Du Bois's grandfather's name as Othelo Burghard, while W. E. B. Du Bois spells it Othello Burghardt in his autobiography. The minutes are replete with misspellings of delegates' names. I use the spelling Du Bois himself used when writing about his family genealogy. For "Othelo Burghard" see National

Convention of Colored People and Their Friends (1847: Troy, NY), *Proceedings of the National Convention of Colored People and Their Friends; Held in Troy, NY; On the 6th, 7th, 8th, and 9th of October, 1847*, Colored Conventions Project, https://omeka.colored conventions.org/items/show/279. For Du Bois's spelling, Othello Burghardt, see *The Autobiography of W. E. B. Du Bois* (New York: International, 1968), 64.

16. The Langston brothers may have attended more conventions than any other delegates. According to the Colored Conventions data set that Jim Casey and Colored Conventions Project members have compiled, John Mercer Langston attended at least twenty-one conventions between 1849 and 1873; this would tie him with Douglass as the attendee of the most conventions in the entire century. His older brother, Charles Langston, helped organize and served in leadership or as a delegate at thirteen or more conventions from 1848 to 1872. Yet we now know that this undercounts their leadership and activity. Ohio conventions started in as early as 1837, launching the state movement at least three years before the 1840 New York meeting that is often cited in scholarship as the first state convention (following Foner and Walker, *Proceedings of the Black State Conventions*). Indeed, Foner and Walker first list an Ohio convention in 1849, twelve years after the almost annual meetings began in that state. Ohio had a strong state organizing committee that counted Charles as an early key member, and William and Aimee Cheek reference at least nine Ohio conventions before the additional nine that Foner and Walker list between 1849 and 1865. As Jewon Woo points out in her essay in this volume, in 1849 Douglass's *North Star* announced that "annual conventions [in Ohio,] we dare say, have been more faithfully and regularly held than those of the colored freemen of any other state in the Union." "Colored Citizens of Ohio," *North Star* (Rochester, NY), June 29, 1849; William Cheek and Aimee Lee Cheek, *John Mercer Langston and the Fight for Black Freedom, 1829–65* (Urbana: University of Illinois Press, 1989), 133.

17. Another Black representative from Virginia, the long-serving Robert "Bobby" Scott, wouldn't be elected until more than a century later. He was elected in 1993 and was still serving at the time of this writing.

18. Convention for the Improvement of the Free People of Color, Third Annual (1833: Philadelphia, PA), *Minutes and Proceedings of the Third Annual Convention, for the Improvement of the Free People of Colour in these United States, Held by Adjournments in the City of Philadelphia, from the 3d to the 13th of June Inclusive, 1833*, Colored Conventions Project, http://coloredconventions.org/items/show/275. For more on how the conventions were counted and why the meeting that initiated the movement wasn't considered the first annual convention, see Brown, *The Meeting That Launched a Movement*.

19. Here I refer not to the first (gradualist) movements for abolition, those epitomized by Benjamin Lundy's *Genius of Universal Emancipation*, which a young Garrison joined and also edited. Instead, my claim is that antebellum antislavery in its more radical form tended to dance with or follow, not lead, Black-organized efforts in the antebellum era.

20. Elsa Barkley Brown, "To Catch the Vision of Freedom: Reconstructing Southern Black Women's Political History, 1865–1880," in *African American Women and the Vote, 1837–1965*, ed. Ann Gordon, Bettye Collier-Thomas, John H. Bracey, Arlene Avakian, and Joyce Berkman (Amherst: University of Massachusetts Press, 1997), 77, 80.

21. Barkley Brown, 77, 80. Martha Jones also notes that "through community-wide gatherings, African Americans created their own political culture. While only a select few men attended such meetings with a delegate's formal credentials, many more men, women, and children filled meeting halls and public assembly grounds. The right to 'vote' was fully exercised within these gatherings, as activists took up the issues of the day." While Jones does not mention conventions explicitly here, and it turns out that the "select few men" numbered in the thousands, her spot-on analysis resonates nowhere as soundly as with the conventions she features on her front cover.

Martha S. Jones, *All Bound Up Together: The Woman Question in African American Public Culture, 1830–1900* (Chapel Hill: University of North Carolina Press, 2007), 14.

22. Steven Hahn, *A Nation under Our Feet: Black Politic Struggles in the Rural South from Slavery to the Great Migration* (Cambridge, MA: Harvard University Press, 2003; Audible, 2018), audiobook, 01:47:12–29. By 2018, the Senate had only had nine Black senators from its founding through Kamala Harris's appointment, and a third of those (Hiram Revels, Roland Burris, and William Maurice "Mo" Cowan) were short-term appointments to fill vacancies. At the time of this essay's composition, since the nineteenth century, two Black governors have been elected to office: Douglas Wilder and Deval Patrick.

23. For examples, see Cheek and Cheek, *John Mercer Langston*; John Ernest, *Liberation Historiography: African American Writers and the Challenge of History, 1794–1861* (Chapel Hill: University of North Carolina Press, 2004); Glaude, *Exodus!*; Jones, *All Bound Up Together*; Patrick Rael, *Black Identity and Black Protest in the Antebellum North* (Chapel Hill: University of North Carolina Press, 2002); and Derrick Spires, *Black Theories of Citizenship in the Early United States, 1787–1861* (Philadelphia: University of Pennsylvania Press, 2019). These scholars are among the very few who substantially integrate nineteenth-century Black conventions into their full-length works. Jones is the only of these authors to examine conventions in the postbellum period. Ernest, Glaude, and Spires are among the rare scholars who differentiate Black conventions as discrete subjects within chapters of their books.

24. Colored Citizens of Norfolk (1865: Norfolk, VA), *Equal Suffrage: Address from the Colored Citizens of Norfolk, Va., to the People of the United States; Also, an Account of the Agitation among the Colored People of Virginia for Equal Rights; With an Appendix Concerning the Rights of Colored Witnesses before the State Courts, June 5, 1865*, 11, Colored Conventions Project, http://coloredconventions.org/items/show/563.

25. George Michael Hahn was the state's (first) Republican governor at the time; he was elected in February 1864, which could have made such a meeting less dangerous than in other parts of the South. See Philip S. Foner and George E. Walker, *Proceedings of the Black National and State Conventions, 1865–1900* (Philadelphia: Temple University Press, 1986), 38n82.

26. State Convention of the Colored People of Louisiana (1865: New Orleans, LA), *State Convention of the Colored People of Louisiana, January 9th, 10th, 11th, 12th, 13th, and 14th, 1865*, Colored Conventions Project, http://coloredconventions.org/items/show/271. The *New Orleans Tribune* was the subject of resolutions of support and adopted as an official organ.

27. This was the first convention held in the South, with the exception of the one antebellum Maryland convention, which was marked with such violence that many delegates fled the city earlier. The editorial cited here is included in the minutes in State Convention of the Colored People of Louisiana (1865), *State Convention*.

28. State Convention of the Colored People of North Carolina (1865: Raleigh, NC), *State Convention of the Colored People of North Carolina, Raleigh, September 29, 1865*, Colored Conventions Project, http://coloredconventions.org/items/show/561.

29. State Convention of the Colored People of North Carolina (1865).

30. Convention of Colored Citizens of the State of Arkansas (1866: Little Rock, AK [*sic*]), *Proceedings of the Convention of Colored Citizens of the State of Arkansas: Held in Little Rock, Thursday, Friday and Saturday, Nov. 30, Dec. 1 & 2*, 189, Colored Conventions Project, http://coloredconventions.org/items/show/559.

31. Convention of Colored Citizens of the State of Arkansas (1866), 191.

32. Also see the accompanying exhibit by Carolyne King based on the essay included in this volume by Erica L. Ball, *The "Conventions" of the Conventions: The Practices of Black Political Citizenship*, digital exhibit, Colored Conventions Project, https://coloredconventions.org/black-political-practices.

33. "BRETHREN AND FELLOW CITIZENS:—YOUR BRETHREN OF THE North, East,

and West have been accustomed to meet together in National Conventions, to sympa-thize with each Other, and to weep over your unhappy condition. In these meetings, we have addressed all classes of the free, but we have never until this time, sent a word of consolation and advice to you." This is from the published account of what was presented in debate at the 1843 national convention and then again at the 1847 con-vention. National Convention of Colored Citizens (1843: Buffalo, NY), *Minutes of the National Convention of Colored Citizens; Held at Buffalo; On the 15th, 16th, 17th, 18th, and 19th of August, 1843; For the Purpose of Considering Their Moral and Political Con-dition as American Citizens*, Colored Conventions Project, http://coloredconventions .org/items/show/278.

34. Andre Johnson, ed., *An African American Pastor before and during the American Civil War*, vol. 3, *The Literary Archive of Henry McNeal Turner: American Reconstruc-tion, 1866–1880* (Lewiston, NY: Edwin Mellen, 2013), 166.

35. Johnson, 166.

36. Johnson, 166.

37. See Denise Burgher's digital exhibit, *Before Garvey! Henry McNeal Turner and the Fight for Reparations, Emigration and Black Rights*, based in part on Andre John-son's essay in this volume, at Colored Conventions Project, https://coloredconven tions.org/before-garvey-mcneal-turner; emphasis mine. The map displaying newspa-per coverage of the convention was created by Samantha de Vera.

38. This is widely cited; see *Freedom's Journal*'s inaugural issue itself or, e.g., Jona-than Birnbaum and Clarence Taylor, eds., *Civil Rights since 1787: A Reader on the Black Struggle* (New York: New York University Press, 2000), 41.

39. Henry McNeal Turner, "Colored National Convention Called," *Voice of Missions* (Atlanta), October 1, 1893.

40. Two of Jonathan Gibbs's children (Thomas Van Renssalaer Gibbs [https:// en.wikipedia.org/wiki/Thomas_Van_Renssalaer_Gibbs] and Julia Pennington Gibbs) are named after famous Black convention goers. Frederick Douglass named a son after Black reformer and fellow antislavery speaker Charles Remond, and one of Mar-tin Delany's famously named children was also named for Remond. James McCune Smith named a child who didn't live long Frederick Douglass. William Still's daugh-ter Frances Ellen Still was the namesake of the family's close friend Frances Ellen Watkins Harper. William Catto named one of his first children to be born in the North (the brother of the murdered activist Octavius Catto) Beman Garnet Catto, after convention goers and activists Amos Beman and Henry Highland Garnet. Still more Black reformers followed Delany and John Mercer Langston in naming their children after revolutionary leaders of the Black diaspora. While reformers such as the Crafts, Cattos, Stills, Remonds, and Purvises also named children after white abolitionists including Charles Torrey, William Wilberforce, Wendell Phillips, and multiple Garrisons, scholars have yet to deeply consider the close circuits that these intragroup naming practices signal within Black reform communities. For the Cat-tos and Bemans on this subject, see Daniel R. Biddle and Murray Dubin, *Tasting Freedom: Octavius Catto and the Battle for Equality in Civil War America* (Philadelphia: Temple University Press, 2010), 95. Thanks to Jonathan Schroeder, Shirley Moody Turner, Syl Woolford, Susanna Ashton, Eric Gardner, Paul Erickson, and Anna Mae Duane for a lively online discussion about this topic, January 9–12, 2018.

41. Jonathan C. Gibbs attended conventions in Troy, New York, in 1855 and 1858 and then in Syracuse in 1864. The language quoted comes from the Colored Conventions Project, https://omeka.coloredconventions.org/items/show/570.

42. Like the Langston brothers, who often attended Ohio conventions together, Jonathan Gibbs's brother Mifflin, who became the first Black elected judge in the United States, also was active in the convention movement. While Jonathan was at the New York state convention, Mifflin, after moving west to build a business during

the gold rush, attended the 1855 California State Convention—out of which the Black paper *Mirror of the Times* was launched—and the 1856 California convention. After leading a Black exodus from California to Canada when facing entrenched segregation and violence, Mifflin attended national conventions in postwar South Carolina and Nashville, where he served as president in 1876, as well as Cincinnati in 1875 and Nashville in 1879. Mifflin Wistar Gibbs, *Shadow and Light: An Autobiography with Reminiscences of the Last and Present Century* (M. W. Gibbs, 1902).

43. The convention held November 20–24, 1865, was covered in the *Mobile Register and Advertiser* (November 24, 1865, p. 3) and in the Black paper the *Nationalist*. Sources from uncatalogued pamphlet, Special Collections Document, Talladega College, Talladega, AL. The proceedings have yet to be recovered at the time of this printing. See also Talladega College promotional materials in "Talladega College History," Talladega College, accessed February 4, 2020, http://www.talladega.edu/history.asp.

44. The American Moral Reform Society met between 1836 and 1841. In addition to Joan Bryant's article in this volume, see Howard Holman Bell, "The American Moral Reform Society, 1836–1841," *Journal of Negro Education* 27, no. 1 (Winter 1958): 34–40. See also *The Minutes and Proceedings of the First Annual Meeting of the American Moral Reform Society: Held at Philadelphia, in the Presbyterian Church in Seventh Street, below Shippen, from the 14th to the 19th of August, 1837*, 64, Daniel Murray Collection, Library of Congress, https://www.loc.gov/resource/lcrbmrp.t2117.

45. Alexander, *Army of Lions*, xiii. *An Army of Lions* suggests that journalists T. Thomas Fortune and John Bruce called the league together because they agreed that "organization was needed—and in a form in which the community had no prior experience" (7). The Afro-American League structure had state meetings that directly mirrored state Colored Convention meetings with a shared focus on school segregation (26) and the courts (27) that mirrored the work that conventions had been doing all over the country for decades. Again following Black conventions, the league chose Nashville as a place for a national meeting to convene; at least four state and two national Colored Convention meetings had been held from 1865 to 1879. Likewise, the league recruited John Mercer Langston into its leadership. Yet *An Army of Lions* names the abolitionist movement and the Irish struggle as the league's inspirations and antecedents. When Alexander first mentions the convention movement, he notes that the league hoped to do "what the earlier Convention movement did not: provide an apparatus for sustained activity" (29). *An Army of Lions* situates the league as a first and a model rather than as an outgrowth and extension of long-established and continuing civil rights activism firmly grounded in the convention movement.

46. Jones, *All Bound Up Together*, 4–6. Public culture, she asserts, is an "expansive rubric that encompasses the deliberations of African Americans within their own institutions and their engagements with overlapping publics" (6).

47. National Convention of Colored Men (1864: Syracuse, NY), *Proceedings of the National Convention of Colored Men; Held in the City of Syracuse, NY, October 4, 5, 6, and 7, 1864; With the Bill of Wrongs and Rights; And the Address to the American People*, Colored Conventions Project, coloredconventions.org/items/show/282. See also John Ernest, *A Nation within a Nation: Organizing African-American Communities before the Civil War* (Chicago: Ivan R. Dee, 2011), 119, for his attention to this convention.

48. See Psyche Williams-Forson's essay in this volume.

49. Jenn Briggs and Anna E. Lacy, *What Did They Eat? Where Did They Stay? Black Boardinghouses and the Colored Conventions Movement*, digital exhibit, Colored Conventions Project, https://coloredconventions.org/boardinghouses; Samantha de Vera, *Black Women's Economic Power: Visualizing Domestic Spaces in the 1830s*, digital exhibit, Colored Conventions Project, https://coloredconventions.org/women-economic-power.

50. National Conference of Colored Men of the United States (1879: Nashville, TN),

Proceedings of the National Conference of Colored Men of the United States, Held in the State Capitol at Nashville Tennessee, May 6, 7, 8 and 9, 1879, Colored Conventions Project, http://coloredconventions.org/items/show/323.

51. Jones, *All Bound Up Together*, 5.

52. Elizabeth Stordeur Pryor, *Colored Travelers: Mobility and the Fight for Citizenship before the Civil War* (Chapel Hill: University of North Carolina Press, 2016), 45.

53. Pryor, 45.

54. Pryor, 48–49.

55. Pryor, 76.

56. National Convention of Colored Citizens (1843), *Minutes*. See list of delegates.

57. Colored National Convention (1848: Cleveland, OH), *Report of the Proceedings of the Colored National Convention Held at Cleveland, Ohio, on Wednesday, September 6, 1848*, Colored Conventions Project, coloredconventions.org/items/show/280. For more on Sydna Edmonia Robella Francis, see Heather Sinkinson, "Sydna E. R. Francis," in *Prosperity and Politics: Taking Stock of Black Wealth and the 1843 Convention*, by Sarah Patterson, digital exhibit, Colored Conventions Project, https://coloredconventions
.org/black-wealth/biographies/sydna-e-r-francis.

58. Convention of Colored Newspaper Men (1875: Cincinnati, OH), *Convention of Colored Newspaper Men Cincinnati, August 4th, 1875, Wednesday A.M.*, Colored Conventions Project, http://coloredconventions.org/items/show/455.

59. ColoredConventions.org launched in 2012. It didn't begin its efforts to include calls, coverage memorials, and petitions in earnest until 2017–18, when it created a "seeking records" curriculum and shifted platforms in response to the technical complexities of housing multiple items associated with one convention event, in the terminology of digital archives, in Omeka Classic.

60. Howard Holman Bell, *A Survey of the Negro Convention Movement, 1830–1861* (New York: Arno, 1969).

61. Bell's *A Survey of the Negro Convention Movement, 1830–1861* was published in 1969 from his dissertation by the important Arno Press, which is responsible for much of the Black scholarship that emerged in the 1960s. During this time Arno Press partnered with the NAACP to publish back issues of the *Crisis*, signing a contract to reissue the first fifty years of the magazine's publications.

62. A copy of Howard Holman Bell, *Minutes of the Proceedings of the National Negro Conventions, 1830–1864* (New York: Arno, 1969), was selling for $435.47 on Amazon on September 26, 2017. On February 1, 2018, it was selling on Amazon for $3,476.80. See Colored Conventions (@CCP_org), "Edition of national conventions to 1861, $435.47 on Amazon," Twitter, September 26, 2017, https://twitter.com/CCP_org/status/912772128327524352; and Colored Conventions (@CCP_org), "$3476.80 is today's price for the print collection of 12 national antebellum Convention proceedings on Amazon. $3476.80," Twitter, February 1, 2018, https://twitter.com/CCP_org/status/959085552338456577.

63. Ernest's *Liberation Historiography* and *A Nation within a Nation* both end at the Civil War. His thorough research and analysis might have analyzed and uncovered more postbellum conventions had that period been his focus. Following the collected primary sources, he notes that Douglass was "an influential presence in the latter phase of the black national Convention movement that extended from 1830–1864." Ernest, *Liberation Historiography*, 250. See his entire section on the antebellum national convention movement (250–76). Eddie Glaude's fine chapter "The Initial Years of the Black Convention Movement" in *Exodus!*, takes as its focus respectability and emigration in the national conventions of the 1830s. Glaude notes that the public and "democratic debate and exchange the conventions formalized . . . became the principal agency for black activism from 1830 up to the Civil War," again emphasizing the antebellum period without mention of the postbellum conventions (Glaude, *Exodus!*, 114). See Jones, *All Bound Up Together*, 3, for more on how Black women asserted

their rights and leadership not in separate spheres but in the public culture they shared with men. The cover of her book is an illustration of the 1869 national Colored Convention held in Washington, DC. Her work extends beyond the antebellum meetings, but her chapter "Right Is of No Sex: Reframing the Debate through the Rights of Women" takes the 1848 national meeting in Cleveland as its organizing focus.

64. Foner and Walker, *Proceedings of the Black State Conventions.*

65. While Bell ends at the start of the war, Foner and Walker's two volumes of convention proceedings end in 1865, just as conventions exploded.

66. In their meticulously researched biography, William Cheek and Aimee Lee Cheek have documented these twenty-one Ohio conventions and their leaders in detail. Cheek and Cheek, *John Mercer Langston,* 133–63, esp. 163n12.

67. Convention of the Colored Inhabitants of the State of New York (1840: Albany, NY), *Minutes of the State Convention of Colored Citizens, Held at Albany, on the 18th, 19th, and 20th of August, 1840, for the Purpose of Considering Their Political Condition,* Colored Conventions Project, coloredconventions.org/items/show/620. One example of the focus on national conventions is Ernest, *Liberation Historiography,* 250–76, esp. 260.

68. Garnet was twenty-five at his first state convention, held in New York in 1840. Reason, who would become the first Black professor at a white university, was twenty-two. Crummell was born in 1819 and was likely twenty-one. All were alumni of the African Free Schools in New York City, and all would go on to have distinguished careers as leading Black intellectuals who shaped not only their own generations but also those that followed on their heels. A year before his death in 1898, for example, Crummell cofounded the Black-led American Negro Academy in Washington, DC, in which a new generation of Black activist intellectuals such as W. E. B. Du Bois figured prominently. Many of the older founding members had participated in the convention movement. "Seeking Records Curriculum," Colored Conventions Project, accessed July 21, 2020, https://coloredconventions.org/about-conventions/submit -records/.

69. National meetings include those held in Washington, DC, St. Louis, New Orleans, Nashville, Louisville, and Cincinnati. Philip Foner and George Walker note in the introduction to their postbellum volume (to 1870) that it was one of three projected editions, though the others were never published. In the summer of 2015, the Colored Conventions Project (CCP) sent team member Nathan Nikolic to the Tamiment Institute Library and Robert F. Wagner Labor Archives, where Foner's papers are housed. Making his way through twenty linear feet in nineteen record cartons and two drawers in the newly released records, Nikolic found what CCP leadership hoped he would: the table of contents for the volumes that hadn't been published. In 2016, the Foner estate also graciously granted permission for the CCP to include the rich editorial notes found in all of Foner and Walker's published editions. The CCP is extending their work, and that of Bell, in this collective effort.

70. Bell, *Survey,* iii. Convention petitions to state legislatures and to Congress tell an important story. New York state conventions gathered approximately 2,000 Black signatures and 600 from white allies in favor of a non-racially-restricted franchise, reports Carla Peterson in her essay in this volume. Placing these petitions alongside the calls, proceedings, and subsequent coverage allows scholars to trace the circuits of exchange and activism that reach well beyond the convention delegates named in proceedings. The CCP will soon begin that process in earnest.

71. Samuel Ringgold Ward, *Autobiography of a Fugitive Negro: His Anti-slavery Labours in the United States, Canada, and England* (London: John Snow, 1855; Documenting the American South, 1999), 269–70, http://docsouth.unc.edu/neh/wards/ward .html.

72. Johnson, *African American Pastor,* 199–200, 224.

73. The *Liberator* and *Provincial Freeman* narrated the contentious emigration

arguments. See "Post-convention News Coverage," in *The Fight for Black Mobility: Traveling to Mid-century Conventions*, by Jessica Conrad and Samantha de Vera, digital exhibit, Colored Conventions Project, https://coloredconventions.org/black-mobility /post-convention-news-coverage.

74. For example, Richard Allen, Samuel Cornish, Abraham Shadd and his children, Mary Ann Shadd Cary and Isaac Shadd.

75. The Convention of Colored People (1873: Dover, DE), *Proceedings of the Convention of Colored People Held in Dover, Del., January 9, 1873*, Colored Conventions Project, http://coloredconventions.org/items/show/297.

76. *Delaware State Journal* (Wilmington), January 11, 1873, third column from the right, bottom; and January 25, 1873, both in *Chronicling America* database, accessed February 1, 2018.

77. *Delaware State Journal*, January 11, 1873, third column from the right, bottom, *Chronicling America* database, accessed February 1, 2018.

78. *Delaware State Journal*, January 11, 1873, third column from the right, bottom, *Chronicling America* database, accessed February 1, 2018.

79. Denise Burgher's early research on the Delaware convention can be found in "Recovering Black Women in the Colored Conventions Movement," *Legacy* 36, no. 2 (2019): 259.

80. Ernest, *Liberation Historiography*, 265; Ernest, *Nation within a Nation*, 125.

81. See Christine Anderson and Nancy Yerian, *Colored Convention Heartland: Black Organizers, Women and the Ohio Movement*, digital exhibit, Colored Conventions Project, https://coloredconventions.org/ohio-organizing. See esp. the sections "Women Activists: 'A Great Many Females Being Present,'" https://coloredconventions.org/ohio -organizing/women-activists; and "Frances Ellen Watkins Harper," https://colored conventions.org/ohio-organizing/biographies/frances-ellen-watkins-harper. See also "Excerpt from 1858 Cincinnati Convention Proceedings," Colored Conventions Project, accessed February 10, 2018, http://coloredconventions.org/items/show/1539.

82. Ernest, *Liberation Historiography*, 265.

83. Rochester would host a national convention in 1853, shortly after the reading room shuttered.

84. These groups debated emigration when this was the issue conventions took up. Their membership in different cities included delegates, their family members, and their circles. New York's Phoenix Society executed its plans to "establish circulating libraries in each ward for the use of people of colour on very moderate pay, to establish mental feasts, and also lyceums for speaking and for lectures on sciences." Elizabeth McHenry, *Forgotten Readers: Recovering the Lost History of African American Literary Societies* (Durham, NC: Duke University Press, 2002), 53. There's much to be done on Black papers and conventions in the postbellum period. Other convergences include Louis Roudanez's *New Orleans Tribune* and Henry McNeil Turner's *Voice of Missions* (1893–1900) and *Voice of the People* (1901–4).

85. McHenry, *Forgotten Readers*, 53.

86. Convention for the Improvement of the Free People of Color, Third Annual (1833), *Minutes and Proceedings*.

87. Ernest, *Nation within a Nation*, 116. See also Convention for the Improvement of the Free People of Color, Third Annual (1833), *Minutes and Proceedings*.

88. Boston's William Cooper Nell, who also attended conventions, was a founding member of the Adelphic Union Literary Society, which was founded in 1836. Other groups that organized around mutual aid, such as the New York African Dorcas Society, which provided clothing to Black youth so they could attend school—another critical issue that was a focus of conventions—had overlapping leadership structures. Henrietta Ray, convention leader Charles Ray's first wife, served on the Dorcas Society's governing board. For more on the overlapping spheres of nineteenth-century

Black public culture, and on the multiple resonances of the term itself, see Jones, *All Bound Up Together*, esp. 5–6.

89. Iowa State Colored Convention (1868: Des Moines, IA), *Proceedings of the Iowa State Colored Convention: Held in the City of Des Moines; Wednesday and Thursday, February 12th and 13th, 1868*, Colored Conventions Project, http://coloredconventions .org/items/show/567.

90. See, for example, the ColoredConventions.org visualization of the Reported Societies in the Northeast and the "West," 1843. See visualization by Caleb Trotter from Sarah Patterson's exhibit, *Prosperity and Politics: Taking Stock of Black Wealth and the 1843 Convention*, https://coloredconventions.org/black-wealth/tables-and-maps/, from *Report of the Committee upon the Condition of the Colored People Presented at the 1843 National Convention of Colored Citizens at Buffalo, NY*. See also Ernest, *Nation within a Nation*, 116; Ernest asserts that one great purpose of the conventions was "to promote the organization of conventions of numerous societies, and thus to promote community through voluntary associations." National Convention of Colored Citizens (1843), *Minutes*.

91. McHenry, *Forgotten Readers*, 61.

92. McHenry, 57. Whipper attended conventions in 1831–35, a state convention in 1848, and national conventions in Rochester, Philadelphia, and Washington, DC, in 1853, 1855, and 1869, or over thirty-eight years. He died in 1876. Thanks to Jim Casey for his leadership in starting the name index that formed the foundation of the ColoredConventions.org data set from which this information was pulled.

93. McHenry, 57.

94. McHenry, 57.

95. Cornish edited *Freedom's Journal*, the *Rights of All*, and the *Weekly Advocate*. Ray is best known for his leadership of the *Colored American*. Bell was a leader in Black papers all over the country, from New York to California. Delany's *Mystery* eventually became the *Christian Recorder*; he joined Douglass's first venture, the *North Star*. Douglass's paper became, some argue, the unofficial national organ for the convention movement. When Shadd Cary launched the *Provincial Freeman*, she became the first Black woman editor in North America. Day edited the weekly *Aliened American*, and Townsend, William Newby, and others published California's Black paper, the *Mirror of the Times*. This is just a small sampling of antebellum newspaper involvement. There's much more work to be done on the role of editors and papers and the conventions.

96. McHenry, *Forgotten Readers*, 113.

97. The 1855 California convention is one such example. The Publishing Committee of five included William Newby and served to "procure the printing of the proceedings of this Convention and that each delegate should receive five copies to distribute." First State Convention of the Colored Citizens of the State of California (1855: Sacramento, CA), *Proceedings of the First State Convention of the Colored Citizens of the State of California: Held at Sacramento Nov. 20th 21st, and 22d, in the Colored Methodist Chuch [sic]*, Colored Conventions Project, http://coloredconventions.org/items /show/265. See also Iowa State Colored Convention (1868), *Proceedings*.

98. National Convention of Colored People and Their Friends (1847), *Proceedings*.

99. The meeting was held there and at Liberty Street Presbyterian Church, where Garnet presided as pastor. For more on Liberty Street Church (which also hosted the 1841 New York State convention), see the recent site-specific media art project *Spectres of Liberty: The Ghost of the Liberty Street Church*, accessed December 16, 2017, http://www.aspectmag.com/works/ghost-liberty-street-church.

100. Nathan Johnson and his wife, Mary (or Polly, as she was known), owned a block of buildings and businesses in New Bedford, Massachusetts, where Polly was famous as a confectioner. There they hid those on the run from slavery. Nathan attended the 1832, 1833, 1834, and 1835 national conventions. Also at the 1847 convention, among

many others, was James Pennington, who, readers of Douglass's 1845 *Narrative* will remember, married Anna and Frederick Douglass. James McCune Smith, also at this meeting, went on to write the introduction to Douglass's second narrative, *My Bondage and My Freedom*, published in 1855. The famous passage about Nathan Johnson and Douglass choosing a new name to take Douglass into freedom appears in chapter 11. I quote here from Frederick Douglass, *Narrative of the Life of Frederick Douglass, an American Slave* (Boston: Anti-Slavery Office, 1845; Documenting the American South, 1999), http://docsouth.unc.edu/neh/douglass/douglass.html. Conventions make available Black networks of collaboration and influence that have been so well mined when it comes to interracial activism and abolition.

101. National Convention of Colored People and Their Friends (1847), *Proceedings*.

102. National Convention of Colored People and Their Friends (1847).

103. National Convention of Colored People and Their Friends (1847).

104. National Convention of Colored People and Their Friends (1847).

105. "Report of the Committee on a National Press," in the National Convention of Colored People and Their Friends (1847).

106. "Report of the Committee on a National Press." With the exception of the *Ram's Horn* and Martin Delany's *Mystery*, the papers noted in the report are barely known. According to Derrick Spires, "The *Disfranchised American* was a paper coming out of Cincinnati in 1847. A *Black Abolitionist Papers'* footnote places it in Cincinnati, running concurrently with Delany's *Mystery* (*BAP*, 4:128n5), and the *National Era* lists it as a 'new paper' in a May 27, 1847, notice. The paper started coming out of Philadelphia sometime in 1849. A November 23, 1849, editorial from *North Star* denigrates the paper and complains that it was unnecessarily competing with *Ram's Horn* and others. Apparently, Douglass didn't write the editorial, because he printed an apology and disavowal of it a few issues later. Spires adds, "The apology was addressed to a 'Mr. Sumner.' This is perhaps A. M. (Alphonso?) Sumner, who represented Cincinnati at the 1843 meeting."

According to James McCune Smith, the paper had "'disappeared' by 1851 (27 November 1851)." Derrick Spires, email to author, December 18, 2017. Jim Casey adds that the "title may have applied to three different/related publications in the 1840s. My hunch is that Alphonso M. Sumner kept starting a newspaper and using the same name to draw on whatever recognition he had been able to get in the last go-round. At least, I have commentary in '43, '47, and '49 by other editors on the launch of a 'new' paper called the *Disfranchised American*." Jim Casey, email to author, December 18, 2017. The *Northern Star and Freeman's Advocate* should not be confused with Douglass's *North Star*, which was in its planning stages at the 1847 convention. As Jim Casey notes, in 1842, Stephen Myers launched the paper in Albany, which he coedited with Charles Morton, John G. Stewart, and his wife, Harriet Myers, "before merging the paper with James W. C. Pennington's Hartford, CT paper called *The Clarksonian*. By 1849, the latest iteration of the paper merges with Samuel Ringgold Ward's paper to become the *Northern Star and Colored Farmer*. In 1849, Douglass complains that people are mistaking the *Northern Star* for the *North Star* (even though the Myers/Ward paper predates his by five years). So Ward decides to re-name his paper to the *Impartial Citizen*, starting in Syracuse and then Boston before it fails in 1851 and he goes to Canada," Casey states. "Ward's *Citizen* survives in a sizable run." Jim Casey, Derrick Spires, and Benjamin Fagan, emails to author, December 18, 2017. Spires notes that Irvine G. Penn places the *National Watchman* in Troy beginning in 1842, edited by William G. Allen (the second Black professor [1850] at a white university, New-York Central College, in what was then McGrawville, with Charles Reason, and author of *The American Prejudice against Color: An Authentic Narrative, Showing How Easily the Nation Got into an Uproar* [1853] and *A Personal Narrative* [1860]). Allen was "assisted by Henry Highland Garnet," who, like Allen, attended the Oneida Institute. See I. Garland Penn, *The Afro-American Press and Its Editors* (Springfield, MA: Wiley,

1891), 52. As of this moment, notes Casey, no extant copies have been found; Casey, email to author, December 18, 2017. Here it is possible to trace concrete and overlapping circuits of Black newspapers, Black convention goers, and convention planning and debates that have gone largely unexamined. Thanks to Casey, Fagan, and Spires, three of the best-informed scholars on the early Black press, for this rich discussion.

107. "Report of the Committee on a National Press."

108. Convention of Colored Newspaper Men (1875), *Convention*.

109. Convention of Colored Newspaper Men (1875).

110. Jim Casey, "Connected by Ourselves: Networks of Antebellum African American Editors, 1827–1863," (PhD diss. draft, University of Delaware, November 2016), 2.

111. Casey, 2.

112. See Ashley Durrance, Hannah Harkins, Nicholas Palombo, Leslie Rewis, Melanie Berry, Christy Hutcheson, Eli Jones, and Morgan Shaffer, *The Early Case for a National Black Press*, digital exhibit, Colored Convention Project, http://coloredconventions.org/exhibits/show/national-press-1847. Also see Benjamin Fagan, *The Black Newspaper and the Chosen Nation* (University of Georgia Press, 2016).

113. See Benjamin Fagan's essay in this volume.

114. I borrow the term "inspired borrowings" from the 2016 American Literature Association conference and panel sponsored by the Pauline Hopkins Society; "Conferences," Pauline Elizabeth Hopkins Society, January 1, 2017, http://www.paulinehopkinssociety.org/conferences.

115. John Ernest, "Life beyond Biography: Black Lives and Biographical Research," *Common-Place* 17, no. 1 (2016), http://commonplace.online/article/life-beyond-biography. See also Ernest, *Liberation Historiography*.

116. Stephen G. Hall's forthcoming book is titled *History as a Communal Act: African American Historians and Historical Writing Past and Present*. I quote Stephen G. Hall, "History as a Communal Act: The History of Black History Month," *Black Perspectives* (blog), AAIHS, February 1, 2017, www.aaihs.org/history-as-a-communal-act-the-history-of-black-history-month.

117. "Resolved, That a Committee of three be appointed to draw up an address to our people, setting forth our duties in relation to the foregoing resolution, and to the cause of human rights in general. Resolved, That the Committee consist of Henry H. Garnet, C. B. Ray, and Theodore S. Wright." See Convention of the Colored Inhabitants of the State of New York (1840), *Minutes*. This was Garnet's first convention, three years before the famous 1843 national convention. The 1841 state convention is preserved through its address to the state's electors printed in the *National Anti-Slavery Standard*. Its address is also plural rather than singular: "May we not, then, in behalf of that class among us who feel the evil inflicted upon them, and who labor under all the consequent disadvantages, address you upon this long-continued grievance, to them more than to all others? Nay, more, ought we not to do so?" The address, as the report says, was "prepared and adopted" by the New-York State Convention of Colored Citizens, held in Troy. New York State Convention of Colored Citizens (1841: Troy, NY), *New-York State Convention of Colored Citizens, Troy, August 25–27, 1841*, Colored Conventions Project, http://coloredconventions.org/items/show/231.

118. This convention offers another glimpse of the internal workings of collective writing: the Committee on the Address reported that it had met, each member had proposed a written abstract of what such an address should be, and the committee had appointed one of its number from the various abstracts to put together an address. "F. Douglass here read the substance of the different abstracts, that the Convention might know the substance of the address. The action of the Committee was approved." The addresses were often revised after being discussed by the delegates to account for feedback and objections. This was the case with the 1843 address (often called Garnet's "Address to the Slaves"), which was ultimately voted down. Colored National Convention (1848), *Report of the Proceedings*.

119. Iowa State Colored Convention (1868), *Proceedings*. Emphasis mine.

120. See Derrick R. Spires's essay in this volume. See also Harrison Graves and Jake Alspaugh, *Henry Highland Garnet's "Address to the Slaves" and Its Colored Conventions Origins*, digital exhibit, http://coloredconventions.org/exhibits/show/henry-highland-garnet-address.

121. The full text available at Archive.org is one such example presenting the full document but identifying the author as Robert Purvis; see Robert Purvis, *Appeal of Forty Thousand Citizens, Threatened with Disfranchisement, to the People of Pennsylvania* (Philadelphia: Merrihew and Gunn, 1838), https://archive.org/details/ASPC0001845400. As Derrick Spires argues, "Groups organized specifically to address constitutional franchise restrictions date back to at least 1837, when Robert Purvis and a group of black activists meeting [in] Pittsburgh, PA, formally protested the soon-to-be-successful attempt to disenfranchise black men in Pennsylvania. Their 'Appeal of Forty Thousand Citizens, Threatened with Disfranchisement, to the People of Pennsylvania' outlines the legal and historical basis for black citizenship in Pennsylvania, with a blistering critique of justifications for black disenfranchisement." See Spires, *Black Theories of Citizenship*, introduction and chap. 3. I thank Derrick Spires for the rich discussions that inform this section.

122. For the full text, see Purvis, *Appeal*. Emphasis mine.

123. See Spires's essay in this volume.

124. Garnet served on both the Business and the Correspondence Committees—again, with Ray, with whom he'd served on previous New York state convention committees that also penned collective addresses.

125. State Convention of the Colored Citizens of Ohio (1849: Columbus, OH), *Minutes and Address of the State Convention of the Colored Citizens of Ohio, Convened at Columbus, January 10th, 11th, 12th, & 13th, 1849*, Colored Conventions Project, https://omeka.coloredconventions.org/items/show/247. Emphasis mine.

126. See Manisha Sinha, *The Slave's Cause: A History of Abolition* (New Haven, CT: Yale University Press, 2017), 2; and William L. Andrews, *Slavery and Class in the American South: A Generation of Slave Narrative Testimony, 1840–1865* (New York: Oxford University Press, 2019).

127. Sinha, *Slave's Cause*, 2.

128. Hahn, *Nation under Our Feet*, audiobook, 12:11–13:31.

129. Hahn, 12:11–13:31.

130. Some sources report Lewis H. Douglass to be Lewis Henry, but several books, records, and contemporaneous newspapers call him Lewis Hayden Douglass, after the once enslaved Boston businessman, Underground Railroad conductor, Boston Vigilance Committee leader, and state congressman. See, for example, the March 1, 1871, edition of New York's *Newspaper Press* reporting that Douglass's paper, the *New National Era*, would be under the supervision of Lewis Hayden Douglass while Frederick Douglass and Lewis's brother Charles were in Santo Domingo. Several contemporary books and museums refer to him by this name, including the *Black Studies Reader*, edited by Jacqueline Bobo, Cynthia Hudley, and Claudine Michel. Thanks especially to Reginald Pitts for our rich discussion about naming practices.

131. Ward, *Autobiography*, 269–70. For more on the CCP's agreement with Gale Cengage, see "Historic Agreement: Library Announces Historic Agreement with Gale Cengage Learning, Colored Conventions Project," *UDaily*, September 3, 2015, www1.udel.edu/udaily/2016/sep/library-agreement-090315.html.

132. For the agreement with Accessible Archives, see "Accessible Archives: New Agreement Will Enhance Research for Colored Conventions Project," *UDaily*, May 11, 2016, www1.udel.edu/udaily/2016/may/colored-conventions-accessible-archives-051116.html.

133. The first twentieth-century Douglass Day involved nine host institutions, which came together to transcribe and celebrate. On the 200th anniversary of Douglass's

birth, the CCP coordinated and partnered with the Smithsonian Transcription Center and the National Museum of African American History and Culture to transcribe Freedmen's Bureau papers. More than eighty hosts from all over the United States, Canada, and Europe took part in this collective work. "Douglass Day: February 14, 2020," Colored Conventions Project, accessed January 1, 2020, http://colored conventions.org/hbd. Since then, the CCP and Douglass Day have collaborated with Black museums and repositories such as the African American Museum of Philadelphia and the Moorland Spingarn Research Center to make February 14 and Douglass Day a day of "collective love for Black History." See Kylie Hubbard, "UT Community Members Gather to Celebrate Frederick Douglass," *Daily Beacon* (Knoxville, TN), February 14, 2018, http://www.utdailybeacon.com/news/ut-community-members-gather -to-celebrate-frederick-douglass/article_fbca4c04-11e3-11e8-a5a2-0f57b73be485.html.

134. See "History of Douglass Day," *Douglass Day*, http://douglassday.org/history-of -douglass-day; and "A Short History of Douglass Day," *Douglass Day*, YouTube video, 2:47, https://youtu.be/cjqfeO2F90c. For more on previous CCP Douglass Days, see "Douglass Day: February 14, 2020." See also DouglassDay.org.

135. Years later Coppin would become an important AME bishop and activist throughout the Black diaspora. At this moment, as a young man, he was grieving the loss of his first wife and child. His second wife was educator Fanny Coppin, after whom Coppin State University is named.

136. See David A. Joens, "Illinois Colored Conventions in the 1880s," *Journal of the Illinois State Historical Society* 110, no. 3–4 (Fall/Winter 2017). See also Victoria L. Harrison, "We Are Here Assembled: Illinois Colored Conventions, 1853–1873," *Journal of the Illinois State Historical Society* 108, no. 3–4 (Fall/Winter 2015).

137. Sebastian Page wrote saying he was working at the "British National Archives and have found a pamphlet covering the above convention at more length than do Foner and Walker. I think it may be a unique copy." It was, he reported later, a report filed by a labor recruiter from Trinidad: "*The Minutes of the State Convention of the People of Color of the State of Indiana*, CO 295/174, stamped page nos. 394–398, all both recto and verso [10 images]." Sebastian Page, emails to author, January 15, 25, 2016.

138. Following the CCP model, the Iowa CCP team included graduate and undergraduate researchers, librarians, IT leaders, and community members. Emily Nelson, "UI Class Uncovering Little-Known Aspect of Black History in Iowa," *Iowa Now*, May 1, 2019, https://now.uiowa.edu/2019/05/ui-class-uncovering-little-known-aspect -black-history-iowa.

139. For an earlier call for such protocols, see P. Gabrielle Foreman, "A Riff, a Call, and a Response: Reframing the Problem That Led to Our Being Tokens in Ethnic and Gender Studies; or, Where Are We Going Anyway and with Whom Will We Travel?," *Legacy* 30, no. 2 (2013).

140. CFP: "Colored Conventions in the Nineteenth Century and the Digital Age," April 24–26, 2015, University of Delaware and the Delaware Historical Society, Colored Conventions Project, https://coloredconventions.org/events/symposium/.

141. See Haley Di Pressi, Stephanie Gorman, Miriam Posner, Raphael Sasayama, and Tori Schmitt, "A Student Collaborators' Bill of Rights," with contributions from Roderic Crooks, Megan Driscoll, Amy Earhart, Spencer Keralis, Tiffany Naiman, and Todd Presner, *HumTech Blog*, Humanities Technology, UCLA, June 8, 2015, http://cdh .ucla.edu/news/a-student-collaborators-bill-of-rights.

142. Michel-Rolph Trouillot, *Silencing the Past*: *Power and the Production of History* (Boston: Beacon, 1995), 27.

A WORD FITLY SPOKEN

Edmonia Highgate, Frances Ellen Watkins Harper,
and the 1864 Syracuse Convention

Eric Gardner

The list of delegates to the National Convention of Colored Men held in Syracuse in October 1864 would leave any student of African American culture star struck. Frederick Douglass was elected to preside. Activist Peter Clark and author-activist William Wells Brown joined him on the Credentialing Committee. Poet, teacher, and intellectual leader George Boyer Vashon, after a journey immortalized in the recently rediscovered poem "In the Cars," served on key committees; there, he tried without luck to make peace between firebrand minister Henry Highland Garnet and entrepreneur George T. Downing.[1] *Christian Recorder* editor Elisha Weaver was present, as were Robert Hamilton (whose family produced the *Anglo-African Magazine* and the *Weekly Anglo-African*) and minister and slave narrative author James Pennington. Massachusetts abolitionist and attorney John Rock likely rubbed shoulders with Ohio attorney and future congressman John Mercer Langston. Singer Thomas J. Bowers, nationally known as the "Colored Mario," attended, joining a Pennsylvania delegation that included longtime activists such as Joseph Bustill as well as young lions such as Octavius Catto and future African Methodist Episcopal bishop Benjamin Arnett.

Think for a moment about the intellectual and moral power gathered there.

That power is even more striking given the very real risks that Black attendees took when they went (sometimes far from their homes) to a convention. The *Liberator*, copying from various Syracuse papers, reported in its October 14, 1864, issue that, on the Wednesday of the convention, "one or two rowdies attacked the Rev. Highland Garnet in front of the St. Charles hotel, where he is stopping. He was struck and knocked down, and lost a valuable gold cane."[2] The October 21 *Liberator* raised the number of attackers to "three or four" and reported that one "struck him a violent blow on the side of his face, and knocked him down; not a word having been spoken or the slightest provocation given for the assault."[3] This story also noted that "a night or two after this, another colored man who came to attend the

Convention was violently assaulted by another copperhead rowdy."[4] The October 14 report suggested that, after the attack on Garnet, "the Mayor sent for the gentlemen composing the committee of arrangements, and offered the support of his whole constabulary force," but the October 21 issue submitted that this didn't stop "an occasional satanic scowl as colored men passed about the streets."[5]

That tension shouldn't surprise students of the period. By October 1864, the United States had retaken Atlanta, and Ulysses S. Grant's "total war" approach, embodied in the aggressive advances of generals such as William T. Sherman and Philip Sheridan, suggested that the Union might at long last crush the rebellion. Some, both north and south, understood that Black troops —including units such as the Massachusetts Fifty-Fourth—represented an important piece of the Union's changing fortune. The long battles to gain African Americans basic rights saw progress beyond the entry of Black men into the military: the compensated emancipation in Washington, DC, in 1862 turned into the more radical Emancipation Proclamation, and the June 1864 repeal of key fugitive slave laws further increased hope. But the North was far from united on the mission of the war. The rabid racism embodied in the July 1863 draft riots in New York City—not all that far from Syracuse—and especially in the December 8, 1863, Proclamation of Amnesty and Reconstruction suggested that many white northerners, Abraham Lincoln included, were, in the language of the Syracuse meeting's "Address of the Colored National Convention to the People of the United States," "not only ready to make peace with the Rebels, but to make peace with slavery also."[6] Neither of the major parties' platforms for the 1864 election promised anything like the kinds of changes Black activists hoped for, and the Syracuse convention's "Address" recognized "powerful re-actionary forces arrayed against us."[7] What the "Address" called the "immeasurable horror" of the massacre of Black troops at Fort Pillow served as a compelling reminder that "reintegrating" Rebels might lead to a business-as-usual approach to slavery and racism generally.[8]

The convention thus pushed hard for civil rights—demanding, per the initial sentence of the "Address," "complete emancipation, enfranchisement, and elevation of our race."[9] The convention argued especially strongly for voting rights and tied those arguments directly to Black military service, asking, "Are we good enough to use bullets, and not good enough to use ballots?"[10] No wonder, then, that white fear of change led a group of Syracuse men to attack Garnet—who used a cane because he had lost part of a leg decades earlier—in a direct reminder to convention attendees about the state of the nation right outside the convention hall. Reading the attendees' names and thinking about their action and their heroism is thus also a reminder of how marginalized the convention was—and remains— by American history and of the continuing threats to Black bodies and souls by white fear and violence.

Still, these names also serve as a reminder of the margins *within* that marginalized group, embodied in part by the specification "Colored *Men*" in the very name of the convention. In the spirit of the calls of the Colored Convention Project (CCP) "to commit to confronting the underrepresentation of women in the convention minutes and articulate their substantial contributions to reform and organizational movements of the nineteenth century," this essay addresses the forgetting and erasure of women's work tied to the convention movement—work that happened amid dangers as, and sometimes more, frightening than the assault on Garnet and work that must be remembered as essential to any real sense of nineteenth-century Black activism.[11] In this, the essay recognizes, as does Psyche Williams-Forson's contribution to this volume, that crucial tasks surrounding the convention fell to women—preparing and serving food, aiding the massive number of out-of-town attendees, and offering a host of other labor without which *no* convention could take place—and that, as Williams-Forson so cogently argues, such "domestic" efforts gave women direct access to delegates, opened extra-convention conversations at the table and the parlor to women, and placed women firmly in the broader moments of the conventions. It recognizes, as well, that women were occasionally able to jockey for entry and participation at early state-level conventions—as Jewon Woo's essay demonstrates through studying a selection of Ohio conventions—arguably expanding their level of engagement significantly and setting the stage for later women's efforts.

But this essay also emphasizes that we do not always need to go "beyond the podium" to locate women's work in the Colored Conventions movement—especially if we move beyond standard methods and sources. The 1864 Syracuse convention especially presaged the larger—though still often circumscribed—inclusion of Black women in national conventions later in the nineteenth century. Specifically, while women *were* excluded in myriad ways from convention activities there, two women, Edmonia Goodelle Highgate and Frances Ellen Watkins Harper, not only worked beyond the podium but actually *took* the podium. This essay reflects on what brought these women to the podium, how their work was represented, and what their work and its recovery mean to our scholarship. In so doing, it reconsiders the boundaries of inclusion at and around the Syracuse meeting and the limits, demands, and potential for broader work reconsidering the Colored Conventions. The essay opens by recognizing that convention proceedings are not only exciting records but also inherently impoverished tools for fully understanding the riches of the Colored Conventions movement and so serve as beginnings of our study rather than ends. Such an approach demands that we gather, share, and carefully consider as much of the "ephemeral," "nonauthorized," and "noncanonical" material on the conventions as we can—ranging from newspaper reports of individual speeches and events to trace descriptions of convention work in sources such as diaries and letters. Studying these additional sources and rediscovering just how important women were to the Colored Conventions movement can provide an even fuller sense of the intellectual and moral power, the national importance, and the real courage central to that movement.

———————

What the official 1864 Syracuse convention proceedings say about Highgate and Harper is exceedingly brief. On the convention's second night, after a speech by J. Sella Martin, Douglass quipped that "as the audience were now in such good humor," they would "be visited by the Finance Committee, after which they would be addressed by a young colored lady. He said 'you have your Anna Dickinsons; and we have ours. We wish to meet you at every point.'"[12] The program ordering shifted, though, and "after a song was called for and sung by Mr. Robert Hamilton"—the New York delegate was not only a print activist but also a sought-after musician—"the President introduced Miss Edmonia Highgate, an accomplished young lady of Syracuse. Miss Highgate urged the Convention to trust in God and press on, and not abate one jot or tittle until the glorious day of jubilee shall come."[13] She was followed by John Mercer Langston, whose speech the proceedings report in much more depth. The body adjourned for the night soon after, as Revs. J. C. Gibbs and Henry Highland Garnet declined to speak due to the "late hour," with Garnet named to speak first the next day.[14] No additional details of Highgate's address are included in the published proceedings.

On the convention's third night, after another speech by Martin that the proceedings called "able and eloquent," "Mrs. Frances Ellen Watkins Harper was then introduced, and spoke feelingly and eloquently of our hopes and prospects in this country."[15] This single sentence is all the published proceedings offer on Harper's speech. They note that the chair moved on to the business of creating a nominating committee for the National League, the organization that would come out of the convention to try to help coordinate battles for suffrage and civil rights writ large, and the meeting adjourned soon after for the evening.

Because the presences and absences surrounding Highgate and Harper in the published proceedings are so critical to initial study of their convention work, that document itself and surrounding texts are worth some discussion. The production of the published proceedings as a material and political object and their dissemination into a hostile American print culture were set up by not only past published proceedings but also coverage in the white abolitionist and Black presses. The *Liberator*, for example, ran a long story drawn from the "telegraphic reports of the Boston Journal" in its October 14, 1864, issue that noted several of the attendees, discussed key resolutions, and shared powerful documents such as the "Address" noted above and a text that would be included in the proceedings as the "Declaration of Wrongs and Rights," which articulated both the wrongs done to African Americans by the nation and the rights that they claimed "as natives of American soil" and "citizens of the Republic."[16] In a similar vein, the *Christian Recorder* featured a long article written by Weaver himself on its second page. From this base, delegate Robert Hamilton advertised "a full report of this important gathering" in the November 12, 1864, *Christian Recorder*, which he offered for fourteen cents.[17] That said, it is clear that Hamilton's report—which has not yet been found—was not the convention's sanctioned document. By its December 23, 1864, issue, the *Liberator* was reporting, under the heading "An Interesting Pamphlet," that the editors had "received, in handsome pamphlet form, the Proceedings of the National Convention of Colored Men, held in Syracuse, N.Y., on the 4th, 5th, 6th, and 7th October; with the Bill of Wrongs and Rights, and the Address to the American People."[18] The *Liberator* called the pamphlet "deeply interesting" and asserted that the proceedings "evince talent of a superior order on the part of those who participated."[19]

This was the document that quickly became the central public memory of the convention, in part because it was far less ephemeral than the press coverage and in part because it was convention sanctioned. The convention had agreed to the pamphlet's publication during the convention, with no less than John Mercer Langston successfully moving that "all money in the hands of the Finance Committee be placed in the hands of the Treasurer of the [National] League, William Rich, to pay for the printing of the Minutes, and the other expenses connected therewith."[20] Charged (along with William Howard Day) with preparing the pamphlet, John Rock and George Ruffin, both of Boston, went to George C. Rand's printing house, which many students of African American literature will recognize as, among other things, the printer of Harriet Wilson's *Our Nig*.[21] It was this sixty-four-page pamphlet that Rock and Ruffin advertised. One such ad—in the April 15, 1865, *Recorder*—said that the pamphlet could be mailed for thirty-five cents for a single copy, a dollar for three copies, three dollars for ten copies, or, "to State or Local Leagues, $25.00 per hundred."[22] And it is this pamphlet—printed in quantity in a geographic and philosophic center of organized abolition and shepherded into hands across the nation by the Black press, the white abolitionist press, and promoters such as Rock and Ruffin—that is reproduced in various sources, including the CCP website.[23]

Thinking through the ways this material object was constructed and distributed highlights the distinctions between official proceedings and surrounding documents—and, in essence, demonstrates the ways in which convention leadership often created specifically authorized texts (the "canon" of the Colored Conventions movement, if you will) and used a range of resources (financial, human, social) to ensure the widest possible dissemination of those authorized texts, even as the broader white-dominated American print culture sought to ignore or dismiss them. The expectation of the supposed ephemerality of texts such as press reports, on one level, made such dissemination essential—and the potential variations of such reports (to say nothing of separate documents such as Hamilton's) made a case for telling a single story to the broader publics, hostile or not.

Studying the *Proceedings* is as rich and vexed an act as reading the list of convention attendees, for it also emphasizes centers and margins. What's both exciting and disappointing about the pamphlet is that Highgate and Harper are mentioned—but essentially only mentioned. Some of this comes from the fact that the Syracuse proceedings function in dialogue with the form and content of earlier convention proceedings, which document procedures, votes, and actions rather than most individual speeches and share communal addresses such as the "Address" and the "Bill of Rights and Wrongs." Nonetheless, the Syracuse proceedings *do* offer some summative and evaluative comments on *some* speeches—just not (much) on Harper's and Highgate's remarks. In short, the Syracuse pamphlet, like many other documents from various conventions, was not designed to think about "women's work" inclusively.

Outside of the remarks on Highgate and Harper, the pamphlet barely mentions women—and does not even include the kind of resolution thanking the city's women for their support of the convention that appeared, for example, in some California convention proceedings.[24] In a speech, Paschal Beverly Randolph pauses after saying "of manhood" to add "of womanhood," and the "Declaration of Rights and Wrongs" speaks of "wives" and "daughters."[25] Nonetheless, the "Declaration" firmly places the convention's voice as male and fatherly: "We have been denied the ownership of our bodies, our wives, homes, children, and the products of our own labor," and "we" have seen "our daughters ravished, our wives violated."[26] Indeed, between Douglass's almost tokening comparison between Highgate and white lecturer Anna Dickinson and the marking of Highgate as a "young" woman talking about "jots" and "tittles," the failure to report much of her speech (or Harper's) looks like a move to cordon off women from the "work" of the convention. At the very least, it places them among the less important delegates—those who participated but did not have their words (if they spoke) recorded.[27]

The first lesson is that Colored Convention proceedings need to be studied as multivocal texts loaded with gaps and silences—and that close analysis can help think through the stories they tell and don't tell. The larger lesson is that, as documents produced by specific entities to write specific cultural memories, the proceedings of Black conventions are a starting point for understanding those conventions rather than an end point. To build beyond the official *Proceedings*, we thus need to explore the biographies of participants and press coverage of the conventions themselves in much more depth, as such moves into the context and paratexts offer a fuller sense of these stories and, ultimately, of the amazing cultural moments afforded by the Colored Conventions.[28]

In Highgate's case, biographical investigation highlights a figure who deserves much more study.[29] Born in 1844 into an activist family who regularly interacted with both Black leaders (ranging from Garnet to Jermain Loguen) and white abolitionists (such as Samuel J. May), Edmonia Highgate was educated in Syracuse and graduated from the almost completely white Syracuse High School in 1861 only to be denied a teaching job in the city because of her race. After teaching in Montrose, Pennsylvania, and Binghamton, New York, Highgate, like a number of African American women teachers, applied to the American Missionary Association to help educate the newly freed people of the South. Teaching in and around Norfolk, Virginia, with a corps of Black women teachers that included Sallie Daffin, Highgate found her efforts both exhilarating and exhausting. She wrote to the American Missionary Association's George Whipple in a June 1, 1864, letter that working with "so many of my people who have spent most of manhood's and womanhood's freshness in slavery" produced "peculiar crushing emotions which, at first, check even my utterance."[30] Paired with immensely difficult physical conditions at Norfolk, those "crushing emotions" and the stresses of aiding underresourced and exhausted Black soldiers eventually took a toll on Highgate. In an undated letter (likely written in mid-to-late September) and published in the October 8, 1864, *Recorder*, Daffin reported that Highgate was suffering from "aberration of the mind" and had to be taken back to Syracuse to recover.[31]

But by the time that letter appeared, Highgate had already taken the podium at the Syracuse convention, continuing her calling to speak out for Black rights. Soon after, she would return to teaching newly freed people, first in Maryland and then in Louisiana, where she would live through both the 1866 New Orleans Massacre and continued harassment from "unreconstructed" white terrorists in rural Louisiana. During these years, she wrote more than a dozen lively pieces for the *Recorder*; that work may have sprung, in part, from her interactions with editor Elisha Weaver at the Syracuse convention. Her *Recorder* work talked back to Henry David Thoreau and Margaret Fuller, challenged lackluster Reconstruction efforts, and began to articulate a protofeminist, transcendentalist liberation theology of practice. When she died in 1870 at only thirty-six, a bright light was snuffed.

While Harper's biography has been better documented and she has entered courses and scholarship in both African American and wider American literature and culture in significant ways, looking at her life through the lens of the 1864 convention reminds us that she is a figure we like to *think* we know. Scholars such as Carla Peterson and Frances Smith Foster have done massive work gathering documents and offering germinal analysis of Harper, but we don't, at the moment, have anything on Harper like, say, Lois Brown's biography of Pauline Hopkins. Indeed, Harper is often pushed into a single sentence or two—as she was in the 1864 Syracuse *Proceedings*—without context or full recognition of her power.[32]

The years 1864 and 1865 are comparatively absent in most studies of Harper, which often simply note that, following the May 1864 death of her husband of almost four years, Fenton Harper, she returned to lecturing. But Harper was actually already lecturing again before her husband died, suggesting that she was already thinking about how to use her talents to provide for her family and/or that she was drawn to public speech because of the press coverage of national events.[33] Soon after the Syracuse convention, she began speaking throughout the Northeast, mainly in New England but with a trip to her birth state of Maryland, building from her earlier emphasis on abolition to the kind of civil rights focus embodied by the Syracuse meeting. Such work can especially be seen in her efforts in her soon-to-be-permanent home in Philadelphia, where she offered several lectures, including one for the Social, Civil, and Statistical Association of the Colored People of Pennsylvania for "the benefit of freedmen, sick and wounded soldiers, &c" on February 27, 1865, that was set up by her old friend William Still and featured both "Black Swan" Elizabeth Greenfield and the Black post band from Camp William Penn.[34] While the later 1860s and 1870s would see her become a national institution in African America—publishing poetry collections and serialized novels and lecturing on tours that crisscrossed the South, Northeast, and Midwest—we still need a much fuller sense of her activism, artistry, savvy networking, skilled self-promotion, and intersections with later conventions, in part because the Syracuse meeting may well have helped propel her full return to lecturing.

The fragments we have on Highgate and Harper remind us of how much African American history has been neglected, lost, or stolen—and of the fact that efforts such as the CCP, which provides free high-quality resources to a broad audience, are far too rare. In many cases, digitization, for example, has *not* meant wide access; several key resources remain locked behind high paywalls or in locations where there isn't even support *for* digitization.[35]

To be sure, weighing these fragments in context similarly reminds us that many extant and available documents that tell us more about the conventions may *still* not tell us about women's involvement. The *Liberator's* October 14, 1864, account of the Syracuse convention, for example, ignored Highgate and Harper completely. Harper was named but not discussed in—and Highgate was absent from—an October 15, 1864, account in the *National Anti-Slavery Standard* that had been copied from the October 7, 1864, *Syracuse Journal*.[36] The rough handwritten notes about the convention made by Ruffin and shared in the *Black Abolitionist Papers* make no mention of Highgate or Harper either.[37] Elisha Weaver's October 15, 1864, *Recorder* report lists several "persons of note" and then says that "among the lady portion, we met Mrs. Ellen Watkins Harper, who is celebrated for her wonderful eloquence and powers of diction, and Miss Edmonia G. Highgate, who has just returned from Norfolk, Virginia, where she had been acting in the capacity of teacher among the freedmen."[38] But even this piece, which offers us a bit more information and asserts the presences of a "lady portion" of the convention, separates women from the business of the convention; such reporting only repeats with variation the gendered gaps in the proceedings.

Nonetheless, careful digging can get us closer to a sense of Harper and Highgate's "women's work" at the 1864 Syracuse convention. The content of Harper's speech can be guessed at from a set of corollary material. First, the

Syracuse convention placed great emphasis on the ongoing war. One of the most emotionally charged moments at the meeting, for example, was when the battle flag of the First Louisiana Colored Troops was loaned to the convention: "The beautiful flag was then presented by Rev. Mr. Garnet," who led the committee that had requested use of the flag.[39] Garnet introduced "Capt. Ingraham, who led the attack at Port Hudson when the brave Cailloux fell. Capt. Ingraham then gave a feeling narrative of the events connected with the flag. His remarks were greeted with great applause. The whole audience rose, and united in giving three hearty cheers for Capt. Ingraham, the brave men who were with him, and the battle-flag which they bore."[40] Whatever Harper said in Syracuse, we know that it was in this spirit. We also know that many lecturers often prepared a single adaptable text for a tour. Thus, consider the titles of lectures Harper gave in the months surrounding the convention: on two nights in May 1864 in Indianapolis, "The Mission of the War"; on November 12 in New Haven, "The Mission of the War"; on December 28 in Philadelphia, "The Mission of the War"; and on February 27, 1865, again in Philadelphia, "The Cause and Effects of the War."[41] And while Jermain Loguen offers no specifics on what Harper said, for example, his letter published in the November 5, 1864, *Weekly Anglo-African* tells us that Harper, "our long tried friend," was, "as usual, GRAND."[42]

While I haven't yet been able to recover Harper's specific language at Syracuse, her lectures in Indianapolis, according to a May 21, 1864, *Recorder* report, not only walked her audience through the war's progress but also outlined "the faithless performances of the Government toward the colored man . . . and what the Government must perform in good faith . . . before she can ultimately triumph."[43] Part of those lectures also "depicted slavery in all its horrors, at times causing the audience"—which was racially mixed—"to weep."[44] The *Recorder* quoted the Indianapolis *Daily Journal*'s assessment of Harper's lecture that

> the character and influence of slavery and the slave-power, its desperation and suicidal policy, the pro-slavery war policy and measures of the National Government, its slow awakening to a conviction of its error, [and] its final comprehension of the question and magnitude of the work and just measures were all clearly discussed. The future of the nation, conditions of reconstruction, [and] the relation of the blacks to that future were canvassed with clear and cogent logic and appeal, and through all was traced the progress of the idea of liberation to the slave. She closed with an earnest appeal for a national recognition of the colored man as a freeman and citizen.[45]

Similarly, in a November 15 speech (whose title and location are not given in "an extract" from the speech shared in the December 31, 1864, *Recorder*), Harper spoke of the dream of "full, broad, and unconditional freedom" and asserted that "the Union of the past, thank God, is gone. Darkened by the shadow of a million crimes, it has sunk beneath the weight of its guilt, and now we stand upon the threshold of a new era—an era whose horizon is gilded with promise and flushed with hope."[46] In answer to "the Democrats" who "tell us that this war has been a failure," she said, "Go ask a hundred thousand freedmen in Maryland if the war be a failure, and let them point you to the homes which no soul-driver invades by law, where the crack of the whip, and the shrieks of tortured women, and groans of outraged men, no longer rise as swift witnesses to God against the terrible wrongs of slavery."[47] She argued that "national defeats have been national gains" and specifically that "in the early part of the war, we needed the defeats of McClellan, and others, more than the victories of Sherman, Sheridan, and Grant" because those defeats taught the North what the war was about and how it would need to be pursued.[48] These were the ideas that likely brought Weaver to note Harper's reputation for "wonderful eloquence," and they charted a course deeply in line with those of the Syracuse convention and the *Recorder*'s sense of the final year of the war.

We can get closer to Highgate's convention remarks—both in terms of their character and their language—through two documents. The first has essentially been missed in all scholarship on the Syracuse convention and on Highgate. Loguen's *Weekly Anglo-African* letter follows his comments on Harper by mentioning "our own colored Anna E. Dickinson," another naming of the famous lecturer who was often compared to Harper.[49] But his language doesn't fit as applied to Harper and reminds us, per the convention proceedings, that when Frederick Douglass introduced *Highgate* to the convention, he specifically compared her to Dickinson. Loguen writes: "Our old friend Mrs. Frances Watkins Harper, was, as usual, GRAND. But our own colored Anna E. Dickinson was more than grand. Fresh from the South, where she had been teaching the children of the freedmen and soothing the hearts of the sick and wounded colored soldiers, in and about Norfolk, by gathering from her Northern friends the comforts necessary for them, her words were 'like apples of gold in pitchers [sic] of silver,' sparkling and brilliant, touching every true heart as with coals of fire."[50] Though Loguen did not name Highgate, this description—from the pivot "but" to the mention of a recent return from Norfolk and the description of work with newly freed children (and adults) and Black soldiers—leaves no doubt that it was Highgate who was "more than grand."

The October 26, 1864, *New Orleans Tribune* gives the fullest account of Highgate's speech yet found—one that, placed in context, pushes her speech far beyond what a reader of the *Proceedings* might think and into the realm of Loguen's high praise. Notably, it begins by recognizing that "Miss Highgate was unwell, and labored under a little difficulty in speaking."[51] Undoubtedly, just back from Norfolk under the care of friend and fellow teacher C. C. Duncan, she was still suffering from exhaustion. Some of the convention attendees may well have known something of this: Syracuse was, of course, Highgate's hometown, and area residents in the audience may have known her or her family; in addition to her work on the front lines of the freedom struggle, she had probably been invited to speak in part because family friends from Jermain Loguen to Frederick Douglass were major forces at the convention; and, beyond the formerly enslaved people in the audience (and there were several), many of the convention attendees had firsthand experience working with newly freed people and feeling something like the "peculiar crushing emotions" Highgate described. Recovering this sense of the occasion, I submit, enriches our sense of the multiple layers of Colored Conventions' "women's work" even more; that is, even when we recover the words of individual speakers, we still have much to do to understand convention moments as *events*—performative, layered, interactive.

No wonder, given these circumstances, that, again per the *Tribune*, "her remarks were most attentively listened to by all, except when they were interrupted by applause."[52] The *Tribune* also suggests much more play with the gendering of her speech: "Miss Highgate said she would not be quite in her place, perhaps, if a girl as she is"—early on, she had noted that she was twenty—"she should tell the Convention what they ought to do; *but* she had, with others, *thought* about what [had] been proposed, and those thoughts she would tell them."[53] The reporter seems to have caught on to some of this play, as the next section of the story says that "Miss Highgate was evidently a strong *Lincoln* MAN," with "man" in all caps.[54] Regardless, she did indeed tell the audience that they should, as she did, support Lincoln and should work both to repair the fissures over the 1864 Republican Party nomination and to push the party's occasional and partial antislavery leanings into consistent antiracist policy and practice. In reporting her final words, the *Tribune* says nothing of "jots" or "tittles" but instead says that "Highgate urged the Convention to press on, to not abate hope until the glorious time spoken of tonight shall come."[55] She "urged them to trust in God, who never fails, and concluded by thanking the President, the Convention, and audience for their attention and kindness in hearing her."[56]

These differences from the published proceedings are crucial—to both a sense of women's work at this convention and a number of larger questions. Highgate's use of gendered expectations to create room for her own political speech, for example, surely has resonance with the work of other women, both Black and white, in the period. "Matching" Anna Dickinson one for one, to use Frederick Douglass's introductory words, might well be an understatement for the ways Black women such as Highgate and Harper found voice in and surrounding the Colored Conventions as they worked toward a hoped-for "glorious time."

Loguen's "apples of gold" language deserves special discussion in this frame, as it gives Highgate a rich variation of Elisha Weaver's sense of Harper's "wonderful eloquence." It is drawn from Proverbs 25, a chapter that early on (in its second verse) submits that "the honour of kings is to search out a matter." This specific verse in the King James Version reads, "A word fitly spoken is like apples of gold in pictures of silver" (25:11); it is rendered as "A word fitly spoken is like apples of gold in a setting of silver" by the *New*

Oxford Annotated Bible.[57] In short, Loguen marked Highgate's participation at the 1864 National Convention of Colored Men as powerful in its delivery and keen in its Solomon-like wisdom—a burst of gold amid already beautiful silver, words "fitly spoken."

These are the kinds of voices we begin to hear more fully when we consider the presence of women in the Colored Conventions movement—but only if we simultaneously recognize that the authorized proceedings of the various conventions are beginnings, sketches of the multifaceted and multivocal sets of events, doors that open onto a complex and messy history. To do that work, we need to think of the proceedings as material texts, consciously constructed and disseminated by convention leaders for specific purposes and audience—and we need to then use that study to locate and carefully consider other, perhaps more "ephemeral" and less "canonical" or "authorized" accounts of the conventions in dialogue, with the end goal of recovering as full a sense as we can of these amazing moments in African American culture.

NOTES

1. On "In the Cars," see Eric Gardner, Aldon Nielsen, Keith Leonard, Evie Shockley, and Tara Bynum, "George Boyer Vashon's 'In the Cars': A Poem and Four Responses," *American Periodicals* 25, no. 2 (2015): 177–87; and Eric Gardner, *Black Print Unbound: The* Christian Recorder, *African American Literature, and Periodical Culture* (New York: Oxford University Press, 2015), 196–204.

2. Untitled item, *Liberator* (Boston), October 14, 1864.

3. "A Copperhead Victory," *Liberator*, October 21, 1864.

4. "Copperhead Victory."

5. "Copperhead Victory."

6. "Address of the Colored National Convention to the People of the United States," in *Proceedings of the National Convention of Colored Men, Held in the City of Syracuse, N.Y.; October 4, 5, 6, and 7, 1864; With the Bill of Wrongs and Rights; And the Address to the American People,* by National Convention of Colored Men (1864: Syracuse, NY), 52, Colored Conventions Project, http://coloredconventions.org/items/show/282.

7. "Address of the Colored National Convention," 48.

8. "Address of the Colored National Convention," 48.

9. "Address of the Colored National Convention," 44.

10. "Address of the Colored National Convention," 58.

11. "Instructor Memo of Understanding," Colored Conventions Project, accessed September 12, 2015, http://coloredconventions.org/memo-of-understanding.

12. "Address of the Colored National Convention," 14. Dickinson was a noted white woman lecturer active in, among other causes, abolitionist work.

13. "Address of the Colored National Convention," 15.

14. "Address of the Colored National Convention," 15.

15. "Address of the Colored National Convention," 25.

16. "The National Convention of Colored Men," *Liberator*, October 14, 1864; "Address of the Colored National Convention," 42.

17. "For Sale," *Christian Recorder* (Philadelphia), November 12, 1864.

18. "An Interesting Pamphlet," *Liberator*, December 23, 1864.

19. "Interesting Pamphlet."

20. "Address of the Colored National Convention," 30.

84 ERIC GARDNER

21. See "Address of the Colored National Convention," 17, 19, 35, for more on the convention's publishing committee.

22. "Minutes of the Great National Convention," *Christian Recorder*, April 15, 1865.

23. See National Convention of Colored Men (1864), *Proceedings of the National Convention of Colored Men*.

24. See, for example, *Proceedings of the Second Annual Convention of the Colored Citizens of the State of California Held in the City of Sacramento, Dec. 9th, 10th, 11th, and 12th, 1856*, in *Proceedings of the Black State Conventions, 1840–1865*, ed. Philip S. Foner and George E. Walker (Philadelphia: Temple University Press, 1980), 2:150.

25. National Convention of Colored Men (1864), *Proceedings of the National Convention of Colored Men*, 22, 41.

26. National Convention of Colored Men (1864), 41.

27. That said, even the Publication Committee itself carefully marked the *Proceedings* as incomplete in its letter of submission reproduced on the pamphlet's second page: the committee members "respectively submit[ted] the result of their labors in collecting, and, so far as they could, arranging the papers containing the proceedings of the Convention," noting that they "found the Secretary's report incomplete, and some important papers . . . missing" (National Convention of Colored Men [1864], *Proceedings of the National Convention of Colored Men*, 2). They "supplied several omissions from a private report of one of the members, and have endeavored to give them to you as correct as we could make them" (2).

28. This work has been nobly begun by a number of the exhibits developed by the CCP, some of which are cited in this volume.

29. See Eric Gardner, "'Each Atomic Part': Edmonia Goodelle Highgate's African American Transcendentalism," in *Toward a Female Genealogy of Transcendentalism*, ed. Jana L. Argersinger and Phyllis Cole (Athens: University of Georgia Press, 2014), 277–99; and Gardner, *Black Print Unbound*, esp. chap. 6.

30. Quoted in Gardner, *Black Print Unbound*, 187. On Daffin, see Eric Gardner, *Unexpected Places: Relocating Nineteenth-Century African American Literature* (Jackson: University Press of Mississippi, 2009), 139–52.

31. Sallie [Daffin], "Our Norfolk Correspondence: The Wounded Soldiers," *Christian Recorder*, October 8, 1864.

32. Key early texts on Harper include the sections on her life and work in William Still, *The Underground Railroad* (Philadelphia: Porter and Coates, 1872); Frances Smith Foster, ed., *A Brighter Coming Day: A Frances Ellen Watkins Harper Reader* (New York: Feminist Press of CUNY, 1990); Frances Smith Foster, ed., *Minnie's Sacrifice, Sowing and Reaping, Trial and Triumph: Three Rediscovered Novels by Frances E. W. Harper* (Boston: Beacon, 1994); Melba Boyd, *Discarded Legacy: Politics and Poetics in the Life of Frances E. W. Harper 1825–1911* (Detroit: Wayne State University Press, 1994); Maryemma Graham, *Complete Poems of Frances E. W. Harper* (New York: Oxford University Press, 1988); Carla Peterson, "Literary Transnationalism and Diasporic History: Frances Watkins Harper's 'Fancy Sketches,' 1859–1860," in *Women's Rights and Transatlantic Antislavery in the Era of Emancipation*, ed. Kathryn Kish Sklar and James Brewer Stewart (New Haven, CT: Yale University Press, 2007), 189–208; Carla Peterson, *"Doers of the Word": African American Women Speakers and Writers in the North, 1830–1880* (New York: Oxford University Press, 1995); and Margaret Washington, "Frances Ellen Watkins: Family Legacy and Antebellum Activism," *Journal of African American History* 100, no. 1 (Winter 2015): 59–86.

More recent work that demonstrates how much we have left to learn about and from Harper includes Johanna Ortner, "Lost No More: Recovering Frances Ellen Watkins Harper's Forest Leaves," *Common-Place* 15, no. 4 (Summer 2015); Eric Gardner, "Sowing and Reaping: A 'New' Chapter from Frances Ellen Watkins Harper's Second Novel," *Common-Place* 13, no. 1 (October 2012); Meredith McGill, "Frances Ellen Watkins Harper and the Circuits of Abolitionist Poetry," in *Early African American Print*

Culture, ed. Lara Langer Cohen and Jordan Alexander Stein (Philadelphia: University of Pennsylvania Press, 2012), 53–74; Eric Gardner, "Frances Ellen Watkins Harper's 'National Salvation': A Rediscovered Lecture on Reconstruction," *Common-Place* 17, no. 4 (Summer 2017); and Eric Gardner, "African American Literary Reconstructions and the 'Propaganda of History,'" *American Literary History* 30, no. 3 (Fall 2018): 429–49. On Harper's marriage and experiences surrounding the Civil War, see esp. Eric Gardner, "Frances Ellen Watkins Harper's Civil War and Militant Intersectionality," *Mississippi Quarterly* 70/71, no. 4 (Fall 2017/2018): 505–18.

33. See G, "From Indianapolis, Ind.," *Christian Recorder*, May 21, 1864.

34. Untitled advertisement, *Christian Recorder*, February 11, 1865; William Still, "Mrs. F. E. Watkins Harper," *Christian Recorder*, February 25, 1865.

35. For more on these issues, see Ryan Cordell, Elizabeth Hopwood, Benjamin Fagan, Kim Gallon, Jeffrey Drouin, and Amanda Gailey, "Forum: Digital Approaches to Periodical Studies," *American Periodicals* 26, no. 1 (2016): 1–24; and Joycelyn Moody, Rian E. Bowie, Barbara McCaskill, Benjamin Fagan, John Ernest, and Eric Gardner, "Forum: Where are the Women in Black Print Culture Studies?" *Legacy* 33, no. 1 (2016): 1–30.

36. "National Convention of Colored Citizens," *National Anti-Slavery Standard* (New York), October 15, 1864.

37. George Lewis Ruffin, "Draft Minutes [of the National Convention of Colored Men at Syracuse] by George Ruffin," October 4–7, 1864, Ruffin Papers, Moorland-Spingarn Research Center, Howard University Library, Washington, DC, accessed via *Black Abolitionist Papers* database, September 15, 2015, http://bap.chadwyck.com.

38. "National Convention of Colored Men in America," *Christian Recorder*, October 15, 1864.

39. National Convention of Colored Men (1864), *Proceedings of the National Convention of Colored Men*, 13.

40. National Convention of Colored Men (1864), 13.

41. For these titles, see G, "From Indianapolis, Ind."; William W. Grimes, "New Haven Correspondence," *Christian Recorder*, December 31, 1864; "Lecture," *Christian Recorder*, January 7, 1865; "An Extract from the Speech of Mrs. F. E. W. Harper, Delivered Nov. 15th, 1864," *Christian Recorder*, December 31, 1864; and Still, "Mrs. F. E. Watkins Harper." Notably, Frederick Douglass also gave lectures titled "The Mission of the War" during this period.

42. J[ermain] Loguen, "The Late National Colored Convention," *Weekly Anglo-African* (New York), November 5, 1864.

43. G, "From Indianapolis, Ind."

44. G.

45. G.

46. "Extract from the Speech of Mrs. F. E. W. Harper."

47. "Extract from the Speech of Mrs. F. E. W. Harper."

48. "Extract from the Speech of Mrs. F. E. W. Harper."

49. Loguen, "Late National Colored Convention."

50. Loguen. The slight error in the quoted passage—"pitchers" should be "pictures"—may have been in Loguen's original or may have simply been a mistake at the *Anglo-African*.

51. "National Convention of Colored Men," *New Orleans Tribune*, October 26, 1864.

52. "National Convention of Colored Men," *New Orleans Tribune*.

53. "National Convention of Colored Men," *New Orleans Tribune*. First emphasis mine; second emphasis in the original.

54. "National Convention of Colored Men," *New Orleans Tribune*.

55. "National Convention of Colored Men," *New Orleans Tribune*.

56. "National Convention of Colored Men," *New Orleans Tribune*.

57. Herbert G. May and Bruce M. Metzger, eds., *New Oxford Annotated Bible with the Apocrypha* (New York: Oxford University Press, 1977).

WHERE DID THEY EAT? WHERE DID THEY STAY?

Interpreting the Material Culture of Black Women's Domesticity in the Context of the Colored Conventions

Psyche Williams-Forson

[It is what I call] "the humility of things." . . . The surprising conclusion is that objects are important, not because they are evident and physically constrain or enable, but often precisely because we do not "see" them. The less we are aware of them the more powerfully they can determine our expectations by setting the scene and ensuring normative behaviour, without being open to challenge. They determine what takes place to the extent that we are unconscious of their capacity to do so.

—Daniel Miller, "Materiality: An Introduction"

The low status of [Black female] work and unexamined assumptions about the absence of "working-class consciousness" made women, particularly poorer women and women of color, appear largely "unworthy" of sustained examination in the minds of far too many historians and others scholars. Consequently, the realities of their waged and unwaged work remained lost.

—Sharon Harley, "Speaking Up: The Politics
of Black Women's Labor History"

At the New York meetings held in Troy in 1858 to discuss the question of Black suffrage in the state the women did not participate in the debate. They did, however, arrange a table loaded with the most palatable refreshments, which were eaten during the recess, with a relish.

—James Horton, "Freedom's Yoke:
Gender Conventions among Antebellum Free Blacks"

Early in the minutes of the September 14, 1858, Suffrage Convention of the Colored Citizens of Troy, New York, the recorder documents that delegates "took a recess until 2½ o'clock." Immediately following this detail, the notetaker writes, "The ladies, in the meantime, arranged, in an adjoining hall, a table loaded with the most palatable refreshments, which were eaten during the recess, with a relish."[1] The remainder of the minutes goes on to detail other political events covered during the convention. It is curious that the chronicler of the events includes this detail. One might wonder why this feature was mentioned, especially since most readers note, as James Horton does, that "at the New York meetings held in Troy in 1858 to discuss the question of Black suffrage in the state the women did not participate in the debate." Most often, such minutiae are not recorded—especially when they involve women or domestic labors. Historian Martha Jones observes, "The records of the first 'colored' conventions do not make even passing mention of female attendees, even as providers of meals or entertainment, roles women most assuredly filled during men's extended deliberations." So the inclusion of the reference to "the most palatable refreshments" at the Troy convention is both curious and noteworthy for the material culturalist. Mention of the quotidian act of arranging a table of refreshments enables us to consider the myriad ways that, using food, women—even when not allowed to participate directly in the debates—nonetheless exerted some influence over the politics of the day.

Anthropologist Daniel Miller describes this kind of assertion as the "humility of things." Daily, we engage the world and the things therein so that there is a continuous, invisible exchange taking place between us, our objects, and our environments. As Miller explains, objects and things often escape our intellectual attention because "[they tend] towards presentational form, which cannot be broken up as thought into grammatical sub-units, and as such they appear to have a particularly close relation to emotions, feelings and basic orientations to the world."[2] We expect food provisioning and lodging to fall within the realm of women's work, so we tend to see it less as part and parcel of political activity. Rather, it is "simply" an aspect of domesticity. Explaining Ernst Gombrich's perspective, Miller maintains, "When a frame is appropriate we simply don't see it, because it seamlessly conveys to us the appropriate mode by which we should encounter that which it frames."[3]

How does one study an ephemeral product such as food? And how does one study the politics of food? David Davis notes, "Food is so intricately braided with other elements of culture that cross-disciplinary analysis is essential to understanding the topic."[4] Taking an interdisciplinary methodological approach informed by American cultural studies, this essay brings together multiple sources to analyze how and why food activities and events where food is served are a useful lens through which to analyze some of the political activities of African American women historically. By documenting where convention delegates lodged and quite possibly ate, this chapter suggests that the material world provides important insights into the nexus between political activism and Black female domestic labor and entrepreneurship.

The varying roles played by nineteenth-century Black women in liberation politics have been well established.[5] Indeed, any discussion of the Colored Conventions must include the contributions of Mary Ann Shadd Cary and would be remiss to ignore the rampant neglect and discrimination she experienced in seeking to be heard. Alongside Maria Stewart, Sojourner Truth, Sarah Remond, and others, Cary was tireless in her efforts and adamant in her beliefs in women's equality, refusing to be silenced or relegated to the role of a "helpmate" providing refreshments and entertainments for male repasts. Yet some women did perform these roles, enabling them to combine domestic labor with social activism. What, then, do we do with their domesticity? Do we dismiss it as quotidian women's work undeserving of attention and merit? Or might we reconsider preexisting theoretical frameworks and read these instances for what they can suggest about African American women's contributions to the struggle of emancipation and liberation, all while participating in American materialism and consumption?[6] Taking this query as a starting point, this essay asks: Where did convention attendees lodge, and where and what did they eat while attending conventions? This examination argues for a reconsideration of women's domestic participation as furthering the cause of freedom.

The essay has two parts. First, there is an examination of how Black women's domestic labor and acts of commensality served as a form of activism. With this, I urge a retheorizing of Black women's pursuits of freedom and citizenship by considering how they used African American domestic spaces to engage the market economy and enact social change. Next, I turn to an analysis of African American boarding and lodging advertisements found in such newspapers as the *Liberator*, the *Freedom's Journal*, and the *Delaware County (PA) American* to consider what these ads can reveal about definitions of home, domesticity, and respectability for Black women. In doing so, I argue for the ways in which Black women participated in the sociopolitical activities of the day using food and commensality. Using food as a lens enables us to consider not only how domestic labor was radicalized as a source of female empowerment but also how we can glean new insights about Black women's participation in political life.

Commensality and Social Activism

In 1849, Frederick Douglass issued an apology to the citizens of East Bloomfield, New York, in his paper the *North Star*. His regret was that he had not acknowledged sooner his gratitude "to the many kind friends in that place who contributed so generously and bountifully for the refreshment table." His sentiments were most sincere, given that the ladies of East Bloomfield "were not informed of the intention to hold a fair until the evening previous; yet in the short space of time intervening, [the ladies] brought together a most liberal supply of delicious cakes, tarts, jellies, and pies of all descriptions. One gentleman donated a roast pig."[7] It was a common occurrence for women— white and African American—working for the cause of antislavery or Black political efforts to hold fundraising fairs and bazaars, a tradition begun in Baltimore in 1827. Beverly Gordon argues that the practice of holding fundraising fairs and bazaars, though considered trivial and inconsequential, was significant largely because they were women-centered spaces that "functioned as an arena for fellowship and community, aesthetic expression, and aesthetic experience . . . [and they were] a reflection of American consumer culture." Because they were "pliant and adaptable," fundraising fairs and bazaars were meaningful occasions for women engaged in various causes. These affairs enabled African American women, who have long since been engaged in the market economy, to raise money for their churches and other social action causes.[8] By the time the First Colored Female Society was organized and the Colored Female Anti-Slavery Society (later the Salem Female Anti-Slavery Society) was established at midcentury, the practice of providing and selling refreshments from lemonade to ice cream was well under way.[9]

Foods and meals tell stories. Food carries cultural and spiritual meaning; thus it signifies social relationships and creates and reflects a sense of identity. Moreover, it has the ability to mediate human relationships.[10] Food is part of the social organization to which people subscribe, so arguably, food and food practices (or foodways) play a constitutive role in shaping cultural, social, and ethnic traditions. Food is a demarcation of group identity, so what is consumed and the choices made surrounding that consumption speak volumes about individual and community identity. Using their cookery and homemaking skills not only to provide refreshments but also to decorate and create an atmosphere of welcome in public and private spaces, some Black women throughout the antebellum era exerted influence "over men's public virtue" through acts of commensality.[11]

Commensality, generally, refers to when people gather "to accomplish in a collective way some material tasks and symbolic obligations linked to the satisfaction of a biological individual need.[12] Claude Grignon stresses the importance of commensality as a means to understanding social morphology. He also maintains that consuming food and drinks together "activate[s] and tighten[s] internal solidarity; but it happens because commensality first allows the limits of the group to be redrawn, its internal hierarchies to be restored and if necessary to be redefined."[13] Within these interstices of restoration and redefinition, African American women used commensality as a political tool. Choices of refreshment became very politicized, because while the refreshments served to nurture interracial ties, they were also provided at events set up to restore the group by "closing it, [as] a way to assert or to strengthen a 'We' by pointing out and rejecting, as symbols of otherness, the 'not We,' strangers, rivals, enemies, superiors or inferiors."[14] This kind of "segregative," or "exceptional," commensality, both in the public sphere and in boarding and lodging houses, allowed for "in-group conviviality," where "a means of scrutinising itself, of pointing out its divisions, its hierarchies, on occasion its antagonisms, of activating and reactivating its functioning, its internal life, i.e. the relationships of solidarity, competition, and even conflict between its members," could be displayed.[15]

In these surroundings, food brought together those who could and would tell distinctly Black stories in places where alliances and allegiances could be forged and renewed and particular in-group intimacies could be shared. The fundraising fair, the convention, and the space of daily meal setting allowed for various kinds of influence to be exercised by Black women even as they served the function of providing sustenance—points elaborated on later in this essay. For now, it is important to stress that some women were able to use food preparation, commensality, and other domestic skills to influence decision-making and help foster social change. Martha Jones explains:

> Female influence was the primary rubric through which African American activists considered women's standing in early antebellum public culture. . . . Female influence had emerged in the post-Revolutionary era to capture a new set of assumptions about how middle-class, white, Republican wives might exert moral force over men's public virtue. In exchanges between antebellum African Americans, female influence was recrafted to reflect the particular challenges facing Black public culture. Some invoked female influence as a prescriptive, attempting to police women's extradomestic endeavors. For others, female influence was a malleable and capacious rubric. Cloaked in it, Black women might foray into public culture, particularly politics. . . . The home was explained as the most powerful realm of female influence.[16]

Using domestic labor, Black women led the charge in social uplift—feeding, clothing, educating, and training generations of young men and women—in their communities. Convention halls and fundraising fairs, along with boarding and lodging houses, were some of the sites where Black women could apply their skills and work toward the causes of freedom and liberty.

Boarding and Lodging during the Colored Conventions

In her turn-of-the-century novel, *Contending Forces* (1900), Pauline Hopkins provides a window into the commensal goings-on in a late nineteenth-century lodging or boarding house. Mrs. Smith, a widow, owns a house in the West End of Boston. Her son, Will, and daughter, Dora, live with her. Her house is a center for the social and political meetings of her children's friends. On any given Sunday, for example, Ma Smith's boardinghouse is filled with guests and boarders enjoying "good things to eat"—from sandwiches to sherbet and cake with hot chocolate. Between the eating and socializing, "the young people in the room had gathered in a little knot, and were discussing many questions of the day and the effect on the colored people."[17] When Ma Smith uses her home to host events such as a sewing circle and other women's clubs activities, including a fundraising fair to pay off her church's mortgage, the women take the opportunity to discuss "the events of interest to the negro which had transpired during the week throughout the country." These are not impromptu conversations, as "[the] facts had been previously tabulated upon a Blackboard, which was placed upon an easel, and occupied a conspicuous position in the room."[18] My purposes here are to draw attention to Hopkins's deep engagement with historical sites, spaces, and geographies and to focus on how the private house, and especially the Black parlor, was the center not only for social gatherings but also specifically for important public affairs and women's political engagement.

Hopkins's rendition gives life to the abbreviated records of women's political activities in Black domestic spheres cited in convention minutes and newspaper advertisements. The boarding or lodging house was a real hive of activity in its eighteenth- and nineteenth-century heyday. It was a common practice, in rural and urban areas, to take in strangers and nonrelatives, who received room and board in exchange for labor, currency, or other services. In addition to providing shelter, boarding and lodging houses, most of which were run by women, offered live-in support, and they were a ready means of supplementing meager family incomes, given that opportunities for work were scarce.[19] Wendy Gamber notes that social historians have estimated that somewhere "between a third and a half of nineteenth-century urban residents either took in boarders or were boarders themselves." Despite the ubiquitous nature of the practice, though, Gamber notes it is hard to pinpoint the existence of boarding and roominghouses on the landscape, because landladies often "adopted vague and confusing terminology" in their advertisements, having been previously "stung by accusations that allied them with a heartless marketplace."[20] For Black women in particular, such accusations were even more acute. Always having had their femininity and respectability questioned, Black women embraced some practices of mainstream society but also moved beyond them, advertising by word of mouth through various church affiliations, associations, and lyceums but also in Black newspapers.[21]

Newspaper advertisements offer opportunities to investigate the kinds of political activities engaged in by African American women who used their domestic skills in the home and in the space of public culture.[22] A diligent search for boarding and lodging announcements, as well as for those announcing refreshments and oysters, reveals several in the *North Star*, the *Liberator*, *Freedom's Journal*, the San Francisco *Elevator*, and many others. The frequency with which these notices appeared makes them too important to go unanalyzed.[23] As a result, these ephemera are ripe for shedding light on the social and political milieu. For example, in 1828, Mrs. Eliza Johnson posted an advertisement in *Freedom's Journal* indicating that "Boarding and Lodging" was available "for the accommodation of Genteel persons of Colour" at her home at 28 Elizabeth Street in Philadelphia. Along with her husband, David, Eliza Johnson repeatedly advertised in the paper on a weekly basis. Perhaps this was because she was in competition with others such as Grace Jones, who also lived in Philadelphia at that time and was particularly keen to indicate the availability of "refreshments, oysters, & c. served up at the shortest notice." And then there was Mrs. Serena Gardiner and her

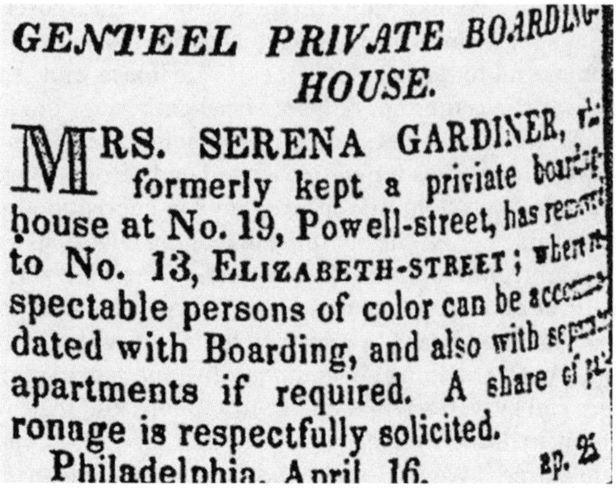

GENTEEL PRIVATE BOARDIN
HOUSE.
MRS. SERENA GARDINER,
formerly kept a priviate board
house at No. 19, Powell-street, has re
to No. 13, ELIZABETH-STREET; where
spectable persons of color can be acc
dated with Boarding, and also with sep
apartments if required. A share of pa
ronage is respectfully solicited.
Philadelphia, April 16. ap. 25

FIGURE 4.1. Advertisement for Mrs. Gardiner's "Genteel Private Boardinghouse." *Liberator*, May 30, 1835.

husband, who, ten years after Johnson's announcement ran in the paper, indicated that she and her husband were also moving to Elizabeth Street and would be continuing their own practice of offering lodging and boarding.[24]

An advertisement by Mrs. Gardiner in the May 30, 1835, issue of the *Liberator* (fig. 4.1) coincided with the fifth annual Colored Convention. It would prove to be profitable for the Gardiners because they played host to several of the political delegates. There were, in fact, over twenty visitors to the Gardiner house during the convention; they published a thank-you to, and concomitantly offered an endorsement of, the "select" boardinghouse of Mrs. Serena Gardiner (fig. 4.2).[25]

Amelia Shad is more specific in her solicitation of convention attendees and is keen to inform them that "no care or expense will be spared to render her house agreeable to all who may favor her with their company" (fig. 4.3). Not only is the house of the widowed Ms. Shad "situated in Pine Street, No. 178, with an open lot running back to little Pine-street," and thus in close proximity to the convention location, but also the location "renders it one of the most healthy and pleasant situations of the kind in the city."

In emphasizing the location, Ms. Shad engages in a shrewd marketing strategy even while extending a welcome invitation to those men who will undoubtedly be weary from the day's convention events.[26] Though published a decade apart in one instance and in different newspapers in the other, the nature of each of these advertisements invites unpacking in order to better understand the complex interplay between these boardinghouse proprietors—Mrs. Johnson, Mrs. Gardiner, and Ms. Shad—who may or may not have been well acquainted. Often, these proprietors were keen to include the

A CARD.

We, the undersigned, having availed ourselves during the session of the colored Convention, held in Philadelphia, June, 1835, of Mrs. Serena Gardiner's select boarding house, No. 13, Elizabeth street, are happy to say, that with its pleasant situation, the cleanliness of its apartments, the good order therein preserved, and its good table, we were highly pleased; and to persons of color visiting this city, who are prepared to appreciate the above advantages, we freely recommend her house, as possessing superior inducements to their patronage and support.

FIGURE 4.2. Thank-you card and an endorsement of Mrs. Serena Gardiner's boardinghouse. *Liberator*, July 11, 1835.

BOARDING & LODGING FOR GENTEEL PERSONS OF COLOR.

THE Subscriber would beg leave to call the attention of those who may visit Philadelphia, during the Convention of people of color, to her house, now open for the accommodation of Boarders and Visitors. Her house being situated in Pine Street, No. 178, with an open lot running back to little Pine-street, renders it one of the most healthy and pleasant situations of the kind in the city.

No care or expense will be spared to render her house agreeable to all who may favor her with their company.

AMELIA SHAD.

Philadelphia, April 14, 1835.   4t

FIGURE 4.3. Advertisement for Ms. Shad's "Boarding and Lodging for Genteel Persons of Color." *Liberator*, May 30, 1835.

adjectives "respectable," "genteel," or "pleasant," because, as Wendy Gamber notes, "respectability carried distinctive importance in combatting the
notion that African Americans and 'negro boarding-houses' were 'hot beds
of filth and of the vilest degradation.'"[27] So, embodied in these descriptors
is the promotion of an ethic of care that demarcates good home manage-
ment, excellent taste, and "proper" domesticity—neat, clean, and without
vice. Furthermore, the politics of respectability almost demanded this practice. African Americans, especially women, were frequently maligned and
accused of being outside the realm of "proper" domesticity because of their
race and gender. Regardless of their status as free, African American women
were always associated with being loose and immoral and thus not afforded
the courtesies or protections given to their white middle-class counterparts.
The wording of the advertisements also suggests a sense of the decorum
that is expected by the hostess and that awaits the guest. But even more
than this, these adjectives signal to the reader that these Black women govern homes filled with virtue, purity, and goodness—critical attributes that
debunk the stereotypes that constantly surrounded them. To this end, it
is worthy to note that most of the women proprietors were keen to publish
their names with the appropriate title "Mrs." Affixing an honorific signals
the virtue of the home, because its proprietor is married or, in the case of
Shad, widowed.[28] Moreover, it signals that the keeper of the house expected
a level of respect to be bestowed. These homes were alternatives spaces of
empowerment for Black women because of the mercantile benefits, and they
aided in uplifting the race by enabling women to host political gatherings,
shelter runaways, and feed those in need. They also served as "proof of respectability, achievement, and progress, all of which are virtues that needed
to be defined and defended rather than taken for granted."[29]

The use of the term "genteel" also denotes the invitation to an older, more
distinguished, and stable clientele. So then, it is not necessarily surprising
that a number of the fifth annual convention attendees would opt to partake
of Mrs. Gardiner's cordiality and warmth. The wording in her announcement about the move to Elizabeth Street suggests that she has a reputation
that will continue to be upheld in the new (perhaps larger) location. The
response of the visitors who took the time to write and publish a thank-you
card to Mrs. Gardiner suggests that the house did not disappoint. Indeed,
her home, with its "cleanliness of apartments," "good order," and "good
table," made for an overall "pleasant situation," which left the men "highly
pleased." Despite the fact that boarders, in general, and convention boarders, specifically, might have found themselves sleeping on a sofa or the floor
or even sharing a bedroom with others for a small fee, Mrs. Gardiner seems
to have provided her guests with all the accoutrements and rituals of home.
This includes family meals and quite possibility lively or quiet moments in
the parlor to continue the discussions of the day. Given this atmosphere, it
is difficult to believe that an air of conviviality did not continue to exist after
the convention meeting was adjourned, because by all accounts, in the home

of Mrs. Gardiner, communities came together. As Carla Peterson explains, "In the domestic sphere . . . living arrangements reflected an adaptation of African family patterns; households were based not primarily on nuclear family structures but rather on larger domestic networks that often included non-kin members, for example, boarders who were gradually incorporated into the household and contributed to its maintenance."[30]

These in-kind contributions—in conversation and in labor—when and where possible, were much appreciated, because being the keeper of a boarding and lodging house was nothing short of laborious. Menus required planning, shopping, and cooking, and cleaning had to be done. One can imagine that with numerous people in and out, such as during convention times, there were always dishes to be washed and maybe also laundry to be completed before the next day's events. If none of these women employed any kind of help, then this, too, meant additional work. Wendy Gamber explains, "An old lodger's departure or a new one's imminent arrival produced the flurry of activity that surrounded the 'fitting up' of a vacant chamber— thoroughly sweeping, putting down new carpet or oilcloth (sometimes varnishing the latter), and arranging furniture as the new occupant wished."[31] This level of detail is not lost on the African American proprietors discussed above. In fact, these aspects of well-kept surrounders were used as a marketing strategy to promote the atmosphere of home away from home.

We move here beyond simply an ethic of care. To be sure, it certainly was *an* aspect of the boarding/lodging enterprise. However, other, more likely facets such as earning a living and racial uplift were central to the advertisements we find in the Black press. Writing specifically about Boston, Lois Horton explains that survival was, at best, "precarious" for Blacks in the antebellum era. To assist in overcoming such odds, "community based social activism" was all but the norm for survival.[32] Many of the boarding and lodging house owners—male and female—worked in some kind of domestic or unskilled laborer capacity. This group, defined by Carla Peterson as the "Black subaltern class," consisted of members such as Sojourner Truth and Jarena Lee. The "men were employed as sailors, waiters, or mechanics, the women as domestics and laundresses. Though less literate, this group was rooted in oral and folk culture and formed the bedrock of Methodist and Baptist churches." Though somewhat separated from the likes of their elite sisters and brothers—Episcopalians and Presbyterians, "freeborn, Northern-rooted, and light-skinned populations," who were literate and steadily employed as ministers, teachers, doctors, and lawyers—these groups nonetheless came together for social activism and reform.[33]

Among the best-preserved physical locales available for understanding the history of African Americans in Boston are the Smith Court Residences, along with the African Meeting House and the Abiel Smith School. The Smith Court Residences are considered "typical homes of Black families built between 1799 and 1853," which served at times as boardinghouses, rented to numerous African American men and their families. The tenants ranged from mariners and laborers to barbers, waiters, activists, and abolitionists. Starting in 1830, 3 Smith Court was rented to numerous African American men and their families and by all accounts was a major site for the causes of abolition and antislavery, which is why it is now known as the James Scott and William C. Nell House. James Scott, a clothier, is said to have lived at this residence for nearly fifty years, during which time he participated in many emancipation efforts. In 1851, Scott was arrested in his shop and charged with spearheading the rescue of fugitive slave Shadrach Minkins. Though he was ultimately acquitted for lack of evidence, Scott was known for assisting other fugitives and self-emancipated slaves. William Cooper Nell, one of Boston's most ardent advocates for school integration, a community activist, and an abolitionist, apparently sheltered or aided numerous self-emancipated slaves at 3 Smith Court.[34] Who fed these people when they boarded at Scott's home? Who carried out this work? And how did the work of feeding, clothing, and sheltering tie into the political and social reform activities of the day?

In the context of these questions, these boardinghouses, along with Black churches and mutual aid societies, served as central institutional structures. Women such as Johnson, Gardiner, and Shad, along with the women of the Scott/Nell house at 3 Smith Court, may very well have been considered community brokers. We know that Serena Gardiner's husband, Peter, was well acquainted with lumberyard entrepreneur and abolitionist William Whipper and fellow boarding and lodging host/hotelier/tavern keeper Charles Short. Peter was also himself involved in political meetings, though not the Colored Conventions. It is quite possible that Serena Gardiner and Charles Short's wife, Rebecca, were friends or at the very least consorted in discussions of domestic affairs. These women may well have been conduits between their husbands, their husbands' friends, and their own sewing circles or other female companions in communicating the changes they wanted to see happen. Lois Horton's insight furthers this observation:

> For the large transient proportion of the population the system of boarding was especially important, since hotels and other transient facilities were not open to Blacks. Finding places in private homes undoubtedly eased the adjustment of newcomers to the community. Contacts with the host family provided immediate access to the social life of the community, to information about employment opportunities, and to the special types of information and knowledge, which enabled Blacks to function and survive in an alien environment. For fugitive slaves, such information about where Blacks could move freely or where they could expect trouble with authorities was of crucial importance. Their continued freedom could depend on their ability to merge unobtrusively into the community—a process facilitated by the contacts which boarding provided.[35]

Food Provisions and Black Liberation Politics

The February 23, 1895, issue of the *Cleveland Gazette* announced that Mr. J. H. Cisco was elected a Twenty-First District delegate to the National Republican League Convention. The announcement went on to say that the convention would meet in June. One column over from the convention publication, and not for the first time, was a notice that "Mrs. John J. Buckner has opened a first-class boarding and lodging house at No. 482 Central Avenue. *Table de hote* [*sic*] from 2 to 4 p.m. Sunday. Roomers have the privilege of the bath."[36] Similar to contemporary society where African American women play the culinary dozens to see who can outdo the other in preparing the best meals or dishes, nineteenth-century boardinghouse proprietors did the same. Historian Juliet E. K. Walker indicates that about five percent of free Black women operated boardinghouses, and through advertising in the antebellum Black press they heavily competed, charging lower rates and offering more amenities.[37] Mrs. John Buckner not only indicated that her home offered "the privilege of the bath" but also introduced the *table d'hôte* menu. In modern parlance this is a *prix fixe* menu—a fixed-price meal where the courses are set and the choices limited. Other homes offered oysters and other choice refreshments. What has gone unnoticed, however, is how women like the fictional Ma Smith as well as the historical Mrs. Buckner and other female entrepreneurs often used their homes for building avenues of political power.

Feeding and sheltering were productive political forms of work. While provisioning, women were also forming networks and exchanging information. While cooking, they may have discussed political issues with those within earshot. They lobbied husbands, sons, male relatives, and guests and helped one another formulate plans for encouraging and nudging the men in their lives to make important decisions in political affairs. If women could not debate issues on the convention floor, they could certainly do so in their parlors and kitchens or other rooms of their house, during sewing circles, and while selling tickets to reading room events. In this and other ways, women were political actors in their own right and active participants in providing sites of Black intellectual production.[38]

Both during and at the close of convention meetings, food and refreshments were most likely present, even though more often than not this was not documented. Sometimes details are provided in the form of committee reports and receipt accounts. Or, as with Frederick Douglass's editorial, the details are included in a newspaper column. Most of the time we learn that there were a range of confections and ice creams along with lemonade and other dainties. The newspapers also tell us that some boardinghouse keepers offered their lodgers raw or baked oysters, and in some instances chilled champagne. Qualitative questions about food consumption tend to generate those about preparation, delineating who has access to what foods, when, and where. Food is never simply about the object itself, nor is a food event merely about a gathering of friends or strangers. Boardinghouse owners who extended lodging to conventioneers were very cognizant of the relationship between commensality and politics—another reason they clearly advertised the choicest foods such as oysters and other delicacies. It is entirely possible that these hostesses provided regional foods for their guests once the boarders were confirmed precisely so that the foods did the work of communicating affinity and shared political stances. Sending south for an opossum, for example, or serving fried chicken and even champagne and homemade cake sends messages of community building. So, it is instructive when the *Delaware County American* advertises: "Mrs. Amie Long has fitted up refreshment rooms in South Avenue, near the Court House, which will prove a great public convenience, especially during the session of Court. She dispenses hot cakes and coffee, ham, soups, eggs, and variety of admirably prepared edibles, and those suggestors of Christmas times, mince pies, which were so hugely appreciated by hands, are to be considered as specimens of her culinary abilities, commend us say we, to her proficiency to this especial department." Mrs. Long's "proficiency to this especial department" is not simply in her culinary abilities but in her knowing how to influence convention attendees, given that she, like Ms. Shad, resides adjacent to one of the convention halls. Mrs. Long has the express ability to chat with her customers and to learn more about the topics of the day. In so doing, she may gently influence her boarders' thinking on a subject. This kind of engagement goes far when efforts toward freedom were constant and information was essential currency.

Given this means of exercising influence and power, it would be unfortunate to render invisible the culinary labor of women during the Colored Conventions, because it was multilayered—deliberate as much as it was political. As illustrated by Mrs. Amie Long's advertisement and the details of the menu she offered, "cooking and feeding others is almost never a completely spontaneous act, reliant as it is on knowledge, supplies, and other existing resources. Even people who described a practice of feeding friends who 'just drop by at dinner time,' [are] working from a storehouse of prior knowledge."[39] It was not necessarily easy work to learn how to be hospitable to different groups of people at the same time. Moreover, providing different social arrangements through shared meals was a learned skill. The levels of work involved, the kinds of foods offered—hot and cold, sandwiches and full meals, sweet and savory—necessitated careful planning. This, coupled with boundary setting within a household—such as determining who had access to which spaces and when, how guests were served, or how and when they served themselves—was critical to the smoothest transitions in the home space. According to the 1830 census, for example, Eliza and David Johnson had a young child residing in their home along with other boarders, a washer named K. Jackson and a woman named Catherine Wright.[40] How much did the people living at the Johnsons' house interact with the delegates, if at all? Moreover, did the number of people in the household contribute to the fact that their home disappeared from advertisements for lodgers years later? Serena and Peter Gardiner, by contrast, were able to entertain many delegates from the fifth annual convention, perhaps because their home was seemingly otherwise unencumbered or occupied.[41] Amelia Shad was a widow who rented her home to sixty-year-old Charles Perret, a dyer, which might have contributed to why her home was open during the convention to both "Boarders and Visitors."[42]

Attention to this level of detail requires thinking through proper and necessary provisions and preferences, cleaning, preparing, and cooking. It thus belies Marjorie DeVault's assertion in *Feeding the Family* that women are often unaware of the level of work they extend daily to produce meals for their family because the work is often disguised as "caring" work, rendering it invisible.[43] While this is certainly possibly true for Black women in the antebellum era, more likely than not they were very clear about the ways in which food production and provision in the private sphere coincided with public affairs and about the critical importance of this work for conveying their skills, talents, and abilities. Alice Julier maintains, "For women of color, participation in food production crossed public and private divides and exists in a complicated nexus of both empowerment and oppression."[44] Thus, when Black women (and men) accepted visitors into their homes, fed and sheltered them during these conventions, they invited with them public discourses. Consequently, embedded in the values of home were the atrocities and indignities faced by Black women and men who moved about outside this domain. For Black people, Julier further suggests, "[an] understanding of hospitality is shaped by the history of the African American experience in the United States, notably the ways in which sociability and community sharing were integral to group survival.[45] If we believe this then it is not difficult to believe that the home was intimately tied to the public affairs, and vice versa. When women prepared refreshments and brought them to the convention hall and when the conventioneers came into their homes, group survival in all of its parts, politics included, was being played out.

So then, when the *Proceedings of the Black State Conventions, 1840–1865* reveal that, at the New York meetings held in Troy in 1858, women did not participate in the debates on Black suffrage but did arrange "a table loaded with the most palatable refreshments, which were eaten during the recess, with a relish," we should not look askance at such participation. Rather, we might read this participation as occupying alternative spaces of power or as being part of the liminal space that functions, "however temporarily, as [Black women's] 'center,' offering them greater possibilities of self-expression as well as the potential to effect social change . . . [so that] these women were not purely 'outside of' but remained 'a part of.'"[46] This participation included creating the necessary order and control at the dinner table or during the processional flow to the refreshment table. We can only speculate how this may have happened, as very little evidence exists to provide any direct indication. What seems quite likely, based on the fact that graphic artists and illustrators included women in their renderings of political meetings, conventions, and parades, is that women believed it was their *right* to participate in political affairs, whether in the private or public sphere. Moreover, they understood the ability of commensality, enjoyed in boarding or lodging situations or in convention halls, to ensure their involvement.

Given this discussion, this essay takes umbrage with the notion that lack of direct participation suggests that African American women did not shape the votes and the political decisions of Black men. Elsa Barkley Brown says as much in her essay "Negotiating and Transforming the Public Sphere" when she takes to task Mary Ryan, who argues, "Black women's participation [was] buried beneath the public sphere."[47] I contend the opposite: Their participation was evident in myriad ways, including the refreshment table where social and material meanings of objects can be interpreted because goods are imbued with complex economic, social, political, and cultural meanings. Objects like food reveal interactions between societies of people and therefore studying the quotidian illuminates major structures of daily life and charts their changes. A study of these boarding and lodging announcements is critical because food consumption is among the most representative and important investments in people's everyday lives. And in this context, food and lodging provide opportunities for commensality. In this way, they act as conduits for Black women's convention participation and social activism.

We approach the conventions with a keen desire to uncover the past, and we should move beyond the obvious—the political content of the minutes—to venture into analysis and explanation of that which seems to be irrelevant: songs that were sung, locations and spaces of the meetings, moments when refreshments tables were provided. Doing so blends these material and expressive forms into the wider currents of political historical scholarship. Choosing to employ material evidence can bring insights that are both absent from and present in many of these written records. Along with the written content of the minutes—details of the debates, decisions, and actions—food and lodging are important personal relics of the past, shaped by the complexities of their time of creation and their history of use. Thus, their mention and their presence are central to the larger conversations taking place, begging us to approach this set of objects with questions and seeking forthcoming answers. As a result of this process, our historical accounts will be more richly conceived and perhaps even better understood as the conflation of gender, race, class, material culture, citizenship, and belonging for African Americans unfolds.

NOTES

I would like to thank Mary Corbin Sies, P. Gabrielle Foreman, and the anonymous reviewers for their comments on earlier versions of this essay. Thanks also to the Colored Conventions Project team for expanding and challenging my thinking on this subject.

1. Suffrage Convention of the Colored Citizens of New York (1858: Troy, NY), *Suffrage Convention of the Colored Citizens of New York, Troy, September 14, 1858*, Colored Conventions Project, https://omeka.coloredconventions.org/items/show/239.

2. Daniel Miller, *Material Culture and Mass Consumption* (Hoboken, NJ: Wiley Blackwell, 1997), 107.

3. Daniel Miller, "Materiality: An Introduction," in *Materiality*, ed. Daniel Miller (Durham, NC: Duke University Press, 2005), 5.

4. David Davis, "A Recipe for Food Studies," *American Quarterly* 62, no. 2 (June 2010): 365–74.

5. The literature on African American female activism in the antebellum era is robust. Many of those resources can be found cited throughout this essay. In addition, see Jacqueline Jones, *Labor of Love, Labor of Sorrow: Black Women, Work and the Family, from Slavery to the Present* (New York: Random House, 1985); Darlene Clark Hine, ed., *Black Women in America: An Historical Encyclopedia*, vol. 1 (Brooklyn: Carlson, 1990); Shirley Logan, *With Pen and Voice: A Critical Anthology of Nineteenth-Century African-American Women* (Carbondale: Southern Illinois University Press, 1995); Evelyn Brooks Higginbotham, *Righteous Discontent: The Women's Movement in the Black Baptist Church, 1880–1920* (Cambridge, MA: Harvard University Press, 1993); Deborah Gray White, *Too Heavy a Load: Black Women in Defense of Themselves, 1894–1994* (New York: W. W. Norton, 1999); and Martha S. Jones, *All Bound Up Together: The Woman Question in African American Public Culture, 1830–1900* (Chapel Hill: University of North Carolina Press, 2007).

6. Alice Taylor, "Selling Abolitionism: The Commercial, Material, and Social World of the Boston Antislavery Fair, 1834–1858" (PhD diss., University of Western Ontario, 2008).

7. Frederick Douglass, "Letter from the Editor," *North Star* (Rochester, NY), September 28, 1849.

8. For more on the market activities of slave women, see Ira Berlin and Phillip Morgan, *Slaves' Economy: Independent Production by Slaves in the Americas* (London: Frank Cass, 1991); Roderick A. McDonald, *The Economy and Material Culture of Slaves: Goods and Chattels on the Sugar Plantations of Jamaica and Louisiana* (Baton Rouge: Louisiana State University Press, 1993); and Psyche Williams-Forson, *Building Houses out of Chicken Legs: Black Women, Food, and Power* (Chapel Hill: University of North Carolina Press, 2006), 38–79. See also Beverly Gordon, *Bazaars and Fair Ladies: The History of the American Fundraising Fair* (Knoxville: University of Tennessee Press, 1998).

9. Gordon, *Bazaars and Fair Ladies*, 37; Hine, *Black Women in America*, 39; Dorothy Sterling, ed., *We Are Your Sisters: Black Women in the Nineteenth Century* (New York: W. W. Norton, 1984), 113.

10. See Sydney Mintz and Christine DuBois, "The Anthropology of Food and Eating," *Annual Review of Anthropology* 31 (October 2002): 99–119; and Carole Counihan, *The Anthropology of Food and Body: Gender, Meaning, and Power* (New York: Routledge, 1999).

11. Carole Counihan argues for recognizing two forms of power: coercion and influence. On the latter, she says that women's influence comes through the act of giving, of feeding, and of satisfying hunger. Because most often it is women who provide the means to fulfill this raw, basic need, food takes on social and symbolic significance. See Carole Counihan, "Female Identity, Food, and Power in Contemporary Florence," *Anthropological Quarterly* 61, no. 2 (April 1988): 51–62; and Williams-Forson, *Building Houses*, esp. chaps. 4–6.

12. Claude Grignon, "Commensality and Social Morphology: An Essay of Typology," in *Food, Drink and Identity: Cooking, Eating, and Drinking in Europe since the Middle Ages*, ed. Peter Scholliers (Oxford: Berg, 2001), 24. See also Claude Fischler, "Commensality, Society, and Culture," *Social Science Information* 50, no. 3–4 (2011):

528–48; and Joan Burton, "Women's Commensality in the Ancient Greek World," *Greece and Rome* 45, no. 2 (October 1998): 143–65.

13. Grignon, "Commensality and Social Morphology," 28.

14. Grignon, 28–29.

15. Grignon, 29.

16. Martha Jones, *All Bound Up Together*, 28.

17. Throughout her work—novels, short stories, and editorial contributions—Pauline Hopkins deeply engages history and, as an editor for the *Colored American Magazine*, print culture. See Pauline Hopkins, *Contending Forces: A Romance Illustrative of Negro Life North and South*, Schomburg ed., with introduction by Richard Yarborough (New York: Oxford University Press, 1991), 110 and introduction. For more on Hopkins's use of contemporaneous historical debates, historical figures, and locations, see also Claudia Tate, *Domestic Allegories of Political Desire: The Black Heroine's Text at the Turn of the Century* (New York: Oxford University Press, 1992); and P. Gabrielle Foreman, *Activist Sentiments: Reading Black Women in the Nineteenth Century* (Urbana: University of Illinois Press, 2009).

18. Hopkins, *Contending Forces*, 143.

19. The practice of African Americans taking in boarders to supplement income in the antebellum era is discussed in Sterling, *We Are Your Sisters*, 97–98, 216–17, 361–62; James Horton, "Freedom's Yoke: Gender Conventions among Antebellum Free Blacks," *Feminist Studies* 12, no. 1 (Spring 1986): 51–76; James Horton and Lois Horton, *In Hope of Liberty: Culture, Community and Protest among Northern Free Blacks, 1700–1860* (New York: Oxford University Press, 1998), 98, 114; and Gayle Tate, *Unknown Tongues: Black Women's Political Activism in the Antebellum Era, 1830–1860* (East Lansing: Michigan State University, 2003), 120–21.

20. Wendy Gamber, *The Boardinghouse in Nineteenth-Century America* (Baltimore: Johns Hopkins University Press, 2007), 3. See also Wendy Gamber, "Tarnished Labor: The Home, the Market, and the Boardinghouse in Antebellum America," *Journal of the Early Republic* 22, no. 2 (Summer 2002): 177–204.

21. Gamber explains that most people who took in boarders never advertised or listed themselves in city directories. By not doing so, "genteel" proprietors shielded themselves and their customers from the ills of crime and vice associated with boardinghouses of the time. African Americans, on the other hand, often did advertise, if the notices in newspapers of the time are taken as evidence (Gamber, *Boardinghouse*, 35–36). For more on Black respectability politics, see Higginbotham, *Righteous Discontent*; and E. Frances White, *Dark Continent of Our Bodies: Black Feminism and Politics of Respectability* (Philadelphia: Temple University Press, 2001). See also Anne Boylan, "Benevolence and Antislavery Activity among African-American Women in New York and Boston, 1820–1840," in *The Abolitionist Sisterhood: Women's Political Culture in Antebellum America*, ed. Jean Fagan Yellin and John Van Horne (Ithaca, NY: Cornell University Press, 1994), 119–38.

22. I am referring to Martha Jones's interpretation of public culture. In Jones's *All Bound Up Together*, public culture speaks to the "interrelatedness of various sites of African American life," where Black women activists "engaged a broad array of intellectual currents" (4–5). For more on some African American women who offered lodging during the Colored Conventions, see Samantha de Vera, *Black Women's Economic Power: Visualizing Domestic Spaces in the 1830s*, digital exhibit, Colored Conventions Project, http://coloredconventions.org/exhibits/show/womens-economic-power.

23. A search for "boarding" and "lodging" in the African American newspaper database for the period 1827–98 reveals over 4,000 references. Many of these advertisements are the same and appear weekly or biweekly. This kind of inundation was not uncommon for the time. James Gordon Bennett, journalist and founder of the *New York Herald*, is credited with having limited ads to a two-week run and later to a

single day, believing that doing so forced readers to scrutinize ads more carefully. For more on Bennett, see William M. O'Barr, "A Brief History of Advertising in America," *Advertising and Society Review* 11, no. 1 (2010).

24. In the online exhibit pertaining to the Johnsons and other women who opened their homes to lodgers and boarders, de Vera maps the community in which these proprietors lived. See "David and Eliza Johnson," in de Vera, *Black Women's Economic Power*, https://coloredconventions.org/women-economic-power/boarding-houses/david-eliza -johnson.

25. Accordingly, the men traveled to Philadelphia from as far away as New Orleans, Louisiana, and Providence, Rhode Island, and as close as Carlisle, Pennsylvania, to the 1830s convention, where temperance and moral reform were on the agenda. Two lodgers, Augustus Price and John F. Cook of Washington, DC, were appointed vice president and corresponding secretary, respectively, as agents for the Annual Convention of the Free People of Color. Special thanks to Kabria Baumgartner, who graciously shared this and other advertisements from the *Liberator*. See William Goodell, *Liberator* (Boston), July 11, 1835; and "Serena and Peter Gardiner," in de Vera, *Black Women's Economic Power*, https://coloredconventions.org/women-economic-power/boarding -houses/serena-peter-gardiner.

26. "Amelia Shad," in de Vera, *Black Women's Economic Power*, https://coloredconven tions.org/women-economic-power/boarding-houses/amelia-shad.

27. See Gamber, *Boardinghouse*, 58, for more on African American boardinghouse keepers.

28. Even though she is widowed, Ms. Shad does not attach an honorific to her name in the advertisement, opting simply for "Amelia Shad." On the other hand, Pauline Hopkins chose to add "Mrs." to her protagonist.

29. Hanna Wallinger is referring here to Hopkins's *Contending Forces* and thus is referencing a time later in the century. But the ideals to which she refers are applicable as early as the 1830s, if not earlier. Hanna Wallinger, *Pauline E. Hopkins: A Literary Biography* (Athens: University of Georgia Press, 2005), 158.

30. Carla Peterson, *"Doers of the Word": African American Women Speakers and Writers in the North, 1839–1880* (New York: Oxford University Press, 1995), 10. See also de Vera's digital discussion of Gardiner's boardinghouse in "Serena and Peter Gardiner."

31. Gamber, *Boardinghouse*, 61.

32. Lois Horton, "Community Organization and Social Activism: Black Boston and the Antislavery Movement," *Sociological Inquiry* 55, no. 2 (April 1985): 182–99.

33. Peterson, *"Doers of the Word,"* 8–9. According to the 1830 census, Peter Gardiner was a botanical doctor and boot cleaner. "Serena and Peter Gardiner."

34. "Smith Court Residences," National Park Service, accessed March 12, 2015, http://www.nps.gov/boaf/learn/historyculture/smith-court-residences.htm.

35. Lois Horton, "Community Organization," 186.

36. *Cleveland (OH) Gazette*, February 23, 1895.

37. Juliet Walker explains that many boardinghouses, especially those in the South owned and operated by quadroons, were obtained through the plaçage system, a highly complex negotiated and consensual sexual relationship between Black women and white men. See Juliet Walker, "Boardinghouse Enterprises and Property Ownership," in *The History of Black Businesses in America*, ed. Juliet Walker, 2nd ed. (Chapel Hill: University of North Carolina Press, 2009), 143–46.

38. As I have referenced repeatedly, the Colored Conventions Project's interactive online discussion of this essay and several others is unparalleled for expanding on the details of the meetings and roles that women played in the process. "Boarding Houses: Sites of Black Intellectual Production," in de Vera, *Black Women's Economic Power*, https://coloredconventions.org/women-economic-power/boarding-houses, provides an excellent overview of the topic, because it expounds on some of the details

that time and space do not permit me to expand on here. See de Vera, *Black Women's Economic Power*; and Jenn Briggs and Anna E. Lacy, *What Did They Eat? Where Did They Stay? Black Boardinghouses and the Colored Conventions Movement*, digital exhibit, Colored Conventions Project, https://coloredconventions.org/boardinghouses.

39. Alice Julier, *Eating Together: Food, Friendship, and Inequality* (Urbana: University of Illinois Press, 2013), 9.

40. "David and Eliza Johnson."

41. "Serena and Peter Gardiner."

42. "Amelia Shad."

43. Marjorie DeVault, *Feeding the Family: The Social Organization of Caring as Gendered Work* (Chicago: University of Chicago Press, 1991), 13.

44. Julier, *Eating Together*, 9.

45. Julier, 25. Briggs and Lacy provide an interactive menu of Mrs. Long's provisions in *What Did They Eat?*, https://coloredconventions.org/boardinghouses/what-did-they-eat-mrs-amie-longs-menu.

46. Peterson, *"Doers of the Word,"* 17–18.

47. See Elsa Barkley Brown, "Negotiating and Transforming the Public Sphere: African American Political Life in the Transition from Slavery to Freedom," *Public Culture* 7, no. 1 (Fall 1994): 120n26. See also Willie Coleman, "Architects of a Vision: Black Women and Their Antebellum Quest for Political and Social Equality," in *African American Women and the Vote, 1837–1965*, ed. Ann D. Gordon, Bettye Collier-Thomas, John H. Bracey, Arlene Avakian, and Joyce Berkman (Amherst: University of Massachusetts Press, 1997), 24–41.

RECONSTRUCTING JAMES McCUNE SMITH'S ALEXANDRINE LIBRARY

The New York State/County and National Colored Conventions (1840–1855)

Carla L. Peterson

"**T**he New York City riots of 1863, among other disasters, has caused the destruction of nearly all the printed minutes of these conventions— our Alexandrine Library—from which some of the noblest pages in the history of our people could have been selected."[1] So wrote James McCune Smith in his 1865 "Sketch of the Life and Labors of Henry Highland Garnet" only a few short months before his own death in November of that year. Smith was referring to the famed Library of Alexandria established at the beginning of the third century BC during the reigns of Kings Ptolemy I and II. Under the guidance of its first major collector, Demetrius of Phaleron, a former member of Aristotle's Peripatetic school, it became a repository of the most important works of scholarship in Greek philosophy, literature, law, and science. Just as Demetrius had sought to preserve the writings of the man who theorized concepts of constitution and citizenship, so Smith hoped to do the same for the records of his community; indeed, despite his fears, many of the conventions' printed minutes have survived the ravages of man and time.

What, then, were "these conventions" to which Smith was referring? What material other than the printed minutes should today's scholars place in "our Alexandrine Library"? How can we conceptualize, and then compose, "the noblest pages in the history of our people"? Members of the Colored Conventions Project are spearheading this effort, mining the archives to bring "lost" items to the surface and infuse them with new life.

Contrary to current scholarly assumptions, Smith's statement was a reference not to the national conventions movement initiated in 1830 to bring together Black leaders from across northern and midwestern states but to the several conventions held in various "provincial cities" throughout New York State. Smith's concern here demands that *we* shift *our* critical focus. Until recently, we have tended to privilege national over state and local (city and county) conventions, perhaps because on a practical level they have been relatively easier to locate in the archives or perhaps because on a substantive level we have been convinced that that is where the most significant speeches were delivered; witness the attention awarded to Henry Highland Garnet's controversial call to arms at the 1843 Buffalo national convention.

Digging through the archives tells us that New York State's Black leaders held their first state convention in 1840, three years after Ohio's 1837 Convention of Colored People.[2] Following Smith's lead, I suggest that we expand our field of inquiry to include non-national meetings in order to gain a fuller picture of Black Americans' intellectual work and political activism during this period and of the leaders who stood at the vanguard. Smith himself underscored the equal significance of the early state conventions to the later national ones. Noting that the printed minutes of the 1844 Schenectady state convention were the only records available to him, Smith proceeded to compare them to those of the recently held 1864 Syracuse national convention, concluding that, with few exceptions, "there is a singular sameness in the Resolutions, and the recommendations, and general proceedings."[3] Such comparative study of national and non-national meetings further demonstrates how issues discussed at the local level were subsequently introduced at national conventions where they became central topics of debate. Finally, it illuminates how different states approached similar issues in divergent ways, reflecting the varied, if not conflictual, nature of antebellum African American sociopolitical thought.

Smith's statement underscores his preoccupation with the fate of the conventions' printed minutes. But here we should perhaps consider shifting *Smith's* focus and widening *his* lens to reconsider what constitutes a convention's proceedings. The published printed pamphlet, as Derrick Spires has suggested, does not always give us the full narrative.[4] We must consider pre- and postconvention material as well. Preconvention material consists of the "call" that laid the groundwork for the convention and at times resulted in contentious debate over procedure or content. Postconvention material addressed the gathering's outcome, considering whether the proposed actions did in fact occur and, if so, determining how successful they were. As with the call, postconvention commentary sometimes revealed deep ideological fissures or personal disagreements that the official minutes had taken pains to obscure. When a contentious debate erupted at the Schenectady convention, for example, it was merely summarized in the official printed pamphlet that Smith referred to in his sketch.

To track down this framing material we need to expand our research to include newspapers of the day, which, I suggest, deserve an equal place in our Alexandrine Library. The *Colored American* assiduously reported on the preparation and aftermath of the 1840 New York State convention. The *North Star* did the same for later national conventions, as did its successor, *Frederick Douglass' Paper*. When the *Colored American* ceased operation in 1841, white abolitionist newspapers took over this function; it was the *National*

Anti-Slavery Standard that detailed the rancorous debate at the Schenectady convention.

Writing the noblest pages of our history necessitates finally that we read convention proceedings seriatim. A single convention may merely be one chapter of a longer narrative; we must then locate subsequent chapters in order to obtain a better sense of the larger story. In reading about each convention, at least three factors emerge as separate, but ultimately interrelated, focal points; arising within each convention, they thread their way serially from one to the next. The first factor is ideological principle, the stand taken by the convention concerning Black civil rights (education, voting, trade, agriculture, etc.); the second is strategy, the most efficacious way of thinking about and then determining what course of action to take; the third is the action itself. In each instance, principle informs strategy and vice versa, and action results from the two.

I seek to fill in some of the gaps in Smith's history by adding some pages of my own based on both printed minutes and newspaper accounts, employing the methodology proposed above. My essay examines the proceedings of New York State and County conventions held in the 1840s and 1850s, as well as the national conventions held in Troy in 1847, Rochester in 1853, and Philadelphia in 1855. I begin by addressing the single-minded concern of Black leaders in New York State over the issue of Black male suffrage, and then trace how this concern evolved into a more expansive analysis of the U.S. Constitution and the meaning of citizenship in the national conventions. The debates in New York State and County conventions, I argue, served as a proving ground for the development of later national conventions.

Even as I widen my conceptual lens, I narrow my focus to spotlight two men—James McCune Smith, joined later by Frederick Douglass—whose voices resonate throughout these conventions and beyond. Although less well known to us today than Douglass, by the late 1830s Smith had already emerged as a dominant force in the Black community. Born in New York City in 1813, Smith attended the Mulberry Street African Free School, where he stood out even then for his intellectual prowess. After graduation, he attended the University of Glasgow medical school, graduated at the top of his class, and then returned to New York to set up practice as a doctor and pharmacist. A genuine Renaissance man, Smith was a scientist, essayist, and political activist who commanded the greatest respect. From the late 1830s on, he was intellectually and organizationally engaged in the fight for Black civil rights, laying the foundation on which Douglass, who was just then escaping from slavery, would later build. Attending to the crucial roles Smith and others played at these early state conventions brings these Black leaders out of the obscurity into which Douglass's historiographical preeminence has cast them until recently. Indeed, it was Smith, not Douglass, who envisioned the Colored Conventions to be, in his words, "conventions of ideas."[5]

New York State and County Colored Conventions, 1840–1855

Throughout the 1840s and 1850s New York State's Black leaders organized approximately ten state and county conventions of which the most important were Albany (1840), Troy (1841), New York County (1841), Schenectady (1844), Cazenovia (1850), Albany (1851), and Troy (1855 and 1858). Black leaders were motivated by one dominant issue, grounded in the local—restitution of Black male suffrage throughout the state—but holding much broader implications—the right to citizenship. As New York State politicians prepared for emancipation in the early decades of the nineteenth century, they worried about the potentially increasing numbers of free Blacks in the state. Arguing that Blacks were intellectually inferior, and thus could easily be swayed to give away or sell their votes to one particular party, in 1821 the legislature passed an amendment declaring that Black men would need to prove their intelligence by acquiring property and then, as propertied men, meet a voting qualification of $250. On the surface, the issue appeared to be a state rather than a national one; it did not apply, for example, to Massachusetts, where all Black men retained the right to vote throughout the antebellum period.

It is difficult to tell who among New York State's Black male population could vote. A few statistics do exist for New York City; in 1835, approximately 15,000 Blacks lived in the city, eighty-four of whom were taxed and sixty-eight of whom met the voting requirements of the 1821 amendment. In 1845, the number of Black New Yorkers dropped by about 2,000; although the number of taxed had risen to 255, only a mere ninety-one were entitled to vote. State-wide numbers are harder to determine. At the 1844 Schenectady convention, Henry Highland Garnet asserted that the towns of Geneva and Syracuse contained small Black populations of approximately 800 inhabitants each but had the same number of Black voters (ninety-one) as New York City; he attributed their ability to vote to landownership as well as a more tolerant racial environment.[6]

The *Colored American* provides the back story to the organization of state and county conventions in the early 1840s. Throughout the 1830s, New York City's Black leaders agitated for the repeal of the 1821 amendment. In 1838, they established the New York Association for the Political Elevation and Improvement of the People of Color; its purpose was to circulate petitions for signatures to be submitted to the state legislature. Seeking to move beyond the confines of the city, organizers called for the statewide creation of similar associations and requested that their representatives meet at a state convention "to devise measures whereby we could all act in concert."[7]

The convention took place in Albany in August 1840. It was preceded by a published call followed by several preparatory meetings—all covered extensively by the *Colored American*—that were almost as important as the convention itself. During the meetings, a contentious debate erupted over what appeared to be strategy—whether racially separate conventions were a good idea or not—but in fact hinted at underlying tensions that would eventually rise to the surface concerning the meaning and use of racial categories. Prominent men such as restaurateur Thomas Downing and *Colored American* editor Charles Ray stated their case in favor of separate conventions as proof of Black autonomy and self-reliance. Others were opposed, but their reasons varied. Educator John Peterson based his argument on expediency: since the majority of New York State's population was white and hostile to Black political rights, Blacks as a minority had no hope of "influencing the said white majority, neither by interest, fear, nor by superior intellectual power." Hence, an all-Black convention would be counterproductive.[8]

Adopting a different perspective, James McCune Smith shifted the terms of the debate to demonstrate how strategy and principle were in fact inextricably intertwined. In the preconvention meetings, Smith, with the support of his former classmate Peter Guignon, insisted that "separate action distinguished by the complexion of the skin [is] a virtual acknowledgment that there are *rights peculiar to the color of a man's skin*," and thus promotes racial difference. According to Smith, "a movement based on the complexion of the skin will end in riveting still more firmly the chains which bind us"; in contrast, "*a movement based on principle* will effect our enfranchisement."[9] Rights, he insisted, are based on principles broader than racial identity.

Smith's distinction here is crucial, as it anticipates the thrust of his later arguments. Convention delegates readily agreed on goals—the restitution of Black male suffrage in New York State—but shaded their arguments differently. Whereas most placed emphasis on racial wrongs, Smith grounded his points in the principle of citizenship rights. The former is a restrictive principle based on (racial) difference that leads to special pleading ("rights peculiar to the color of a man's skin"); in contrast, Smith invoked an expansive principle that puts aside difference to embrace inclusiveness and universality.

Smith lost the battle, and the Albany meeting took place without him as a separate convention. In addition to Charles Ray, other Black men who would later rise to eminence were in attendance, among them school teacher Charles Reason and his brother Patrick, an engraver; Presbyterian minister and radical activist Henry Highland Garnet; and Episcopal theologian Alexander Crummell. The only complaint about racial separation was voiced by the editors of the *National Anti-Slavery Standard* who raised yet a third objection, arguing that separation would confirm white ideas of Black inferiority. Some whites were present in the audience, however; many were leading Whig politicians whom convention delegates hoped to convert to their cause. The 140 delegates present saw themselves as representatives of their Black brethren denied the franchise. They argued not so much for the right to suffrage as for its extension, and they based their points on a set of twin and interrelated principles: common humanity and Republican values. The franchise should be extended to Black men because it was their birthright privilege: they were freemen, native not foreign born, and had proved their loyalty to the nation through military service in the wars of Independence and 1812. To deny them the right to vote was to grant them nominal freedom only, reducing Black men to political slavery and extracting the "life blood" of the Black community, inhibiting its religious, literary, and educational aspirations.[10]

The Albany convention made a series of decisions that the *Colored American* reported in great detail. Mostly organizational in nature, they served as models for later local and, indeed, national conventions: compile statistics about the condition of Blacks in the state; create county committees to supervise petition drives; and collect signatures for petitions to be submitted to the state legislature. By February 1841, organizers had gathered approximately 2,200 signatures from the Black population and about 600 from sympathetic whites.[11]

A year after the Albany convention, Black leaders met in Troy, where Smith was again absent. While delegates repeated the principle of the right to vote based on birthright privilege, they amplified their earlier arguments that in turn resulted in a subtle shift in strategy. They now asserted that denial of suffrage inflicted damage not only on the Black community but on the entire state: "The State, by this policy, inflicts a wound upon herself, and detracts from her real strength." To deprive the state of the energy of Black men is to cripple it. To encourage this energy is to empower the entire body politic. As proof, they pointed to the example of Massachusetts, where Black men were deemed responsible voters who benefited the state. In making this argument delegates sought to appeal beyond their Black constituents and the few elite whites in attendance and reach the broader white community.[12] Such a shift at least tacitly acknowledged John Peterson's point concerning the inefficacy of separate conventions.

The Troy convention concluded by encouraging delegates to take action by calling county conventions, and indeed a month later Black leaders came together at a New York County convention. This time Smith was present and his voice dominated the proceedings. Still determined to move beyond a focus on racial discrimination, he based his appeal on constitutional rights arising from taxation. Prior conventions had briefly contended that the 1821 amendment violated the principle of "no taxation without representation," but as chair of the business meeting, Smith made it the cornerstone of his argument. The amendment, he declared, contravened republicanism because it 1) "is contrary to the spirit, tendency, and letter" of the state constitution; 2) "enforces the feudal doctrine that the rights of men are to be graduated according to their possessions in land"; 3) "fixes the current value of every citizen's vote, and demeans the State into a seller of the right to vote"; 4) imposes on Colored citizens excluded from voting both direct (real estate) and indirect (articles of import) taxes "without granting them a voice in the representation which imposes those taxes"; and 5) infringes of the right of Colored citizens denied the franchise "by depreciating the value of their (unrepresented) labor."[13] Even while white abolitionist William Lloyd Garrison, whose influence on Black political thought was still considerable, was insisting that the U.S. Constitution was a proslavery document, Smith was more interested in understanding the constitutional principles that undergirded republicanism (as distinguished from feudalism) that apply to all citizens, including those who were Colored.

Later state conventions—in particular those held in Schenectady (1844), Geneva (1845), Albany (1851), and Troy (1855)—continued to focus on the issue of Black male suffrage. Smith attended only the Troy convention, but his intellectual influence was pervasive even in his absence. At the Albany convention, for example, the Committee on Elective Franchise wrote a report arguing that since the U.S. Constitution had declared that "the citizens of each State shall be entitled to all the privileges and immunities in the citizens of several States," the New York State Constitution had violated that clause by denying Black men the right to vote.[14]

Perhaps Smith felt discouraged and chose not to attend most of the state conventions of the early 1850s because a bold proposal he had put forth at the 1844 Schenectady convention had been ignored: to hold a "general convention" in conjunction with delegates from other states—namely Pennsylvania and Connecticut—whose Black population labored under similar forms of disfranchisement, with the theory that greater numbers would create more effective strategies and actions.[15] The resolution was never adopted because the convention was derailed by intraracial conflict that pitted Black men not against state power but against one another. It was the *National Anti-Slavery Standard* that published the full report of this conflict, only summarized in the official printed minutes. Fascinatingly, Smith never alluded to it in his 1865 "Sketch" and even excised the summary when inserting the official minutes into his narrative. Perhaps the omission reflected his state of mind in 1865: nearing death, he might have wanted to emphasize harmony over conflict in order to honor his friend Henry Highland Garnet. Yet his omissions serve to remind us of the subjective and fragmented nature of the archives and of our need for critical vigilance.

Here is what happened. At the poorly attended Rochester state convention held the year before in 1843, Garnet and others had passed a resolution stating that, if granted the franchise, Black men would not "vote with either of the pro-slavery parties of the land, since that would be, in our judgment, giving our suffrages against ourselves." This resolution violated the Troy convention's promise to separate franchise rights from support of political party. Smith and his supporters attempted to lodge a protest but were opposed by Garnet. A heated debate ensued, arguments flew in all directions—on substance (the resolution itself) and on procedure (the legitimacy of the Rochester convention)—until Smith rose to make a request: he was merely asking, he said, for the right of constituents to be heard by submitting his protest and having it accepted. A vote was taken and the protest rejected. Smith and other delegates resigned, claiming that "a primary and inalienable right of their constituents had been violated."[16]

The conflict at the Schenectady convention was intraracial, not interracial, arising out of tension between race-based collective activism on the one hand and the inalienable rights of constituents on the other. Smith's efforts to serve as the voice of reason anticipate his later role at the national conventions. Abiding by the principles of republican constitutional law, he was making a simple plea based on the expansive right of dissenting citizens to lodge a protest and for the protest to be heard. Unfortunately, he was not heard.

The general convention that would have brought together delegates from New York State, Connecticut, and Pennsylvania never took place. Connecticut did not hold a state convention until an 1849 meeting in New Haven. Pennsylvania began organizing state conventions a year after New York; yet, although Black Pennsylvanians faced similar forms of disfranchisement, their response differed from that of their neighbor. The 1790 Pennsylvania State Constitution had stipulated that all "freemen" over the age of twenty-one were entitled to vote provided they were residents of the state for a minimum of two years and had been assessed a county tax. The question boiled down to who was a "freeman." White advocates for Black Pennsylvanians contended that any Black who was not a slave was perforce a freeman; opponents maintained that simply by virtue of their race, Blacks could never be considered freemen. Unlike New York's Black leaders, who envisioned themselves as representatives of their disfranchised brethren, their Pennsylvania counterparts viewed the franchise as an elite issue around which the broader Black community would not rally, and hence were reluctant to interfere.

Their attitudes changed, however, after Pennsylvania's 1837 state reform convention, which repealed Black men's right to vote for several interrelated reasons: raw racial prejudice, fears of the rise of abolitionism, and a desire to preserve the Union by accommodating the South.[17] Black leaders reacted immediately, outlining their position in three main documents: Robert Purvis's 1838 "Appeal of Forty Thousand Citizens, Threatened with Disfranchisement, to the People of Pennsylvania"; the proceedings of the 1841 Pittsburgh state convention; and the proceedings of the 1848 Harrisburg state convention. These documents' line of argument went as follows: blame the American Colonization Society for its attempts to repeal what had been a right of Black Americans in order to induce them to leave the country; assert that the reason for their disfranchisement was racial—"founded upon complexion" and "on account of color," as they put it; and claim that Blacks deserved the franchise given their proof of racial elevation (entrepreneurship, military service, volunteer work during the yellow fever epidemic of 1793). Yet by 1848 the Harrisburg convention bitterly rejected the elevation argument, lamenting that whatever Blacks might achieve, "the vulgar voice of the populace would still cry out they are a degraded people, because they are black."[18] By not directly addressing constitutional issues, Black Pennsylvanians might well be charged, in Smith's words, with launching arguments "based on the complexion of the skin [that] will end in still more riveting the chains which bind us" rather than on "a movement based on principle [that] will effect our enfranchisement."

National Colored Conventions, 1847, 1850, and 1853

Frederick Douglass made his presence known at the New York state conventions when he attended an 1850 meeting referred to as the Cazenovia Fugitive Slave Law Convention. Yet this was not Douglass's first convention appearance. He had already attended several national meetings—Buffalo in 1843, Troy in 1847, and Cleveland in 1848—and had emerged at the forefront of northern Black leadership. Smith was absent at both the Buffalo and Cleveland conventions, in which the constitutional issues of citizenship, suffrage, and taxation were barely raised. Instead, the Buffalo meeting was dominated by Garnet's address to southern slaves to arm themselves and rebel against their oppressive masters and by Douglass's vehement opposition to this call for violence. Although much less acrimonious, the Cleveland convention raised another contentious issue, that of women's rights, where Douglass prevailed in passing a motion in support of the decision that, when referring to delegates, the word "persons" would include women.

Absent in Buffalo and Cleveland, Smith was at the 1847 Troy convention, where both he and Douglass made their voices heard. They readily agreed on two major issues: the creation of an industrial college for Black youth and the worthiness of white abolitionist Gerrit Smith's gift of land to settle Black families in Upstate New York. But they crossed swords on the question of establishing a national press, Smith arguing for and Douglass against (out of concern that it would hurt his newly founded *North Star*). Smith won the battle and authored the convention report favoring a national newspaper.[19] Douglass, however, won the war: his several newspapers would serve as national organs over the next decade and a half.

Yet Smith and Douglass quickly became close friends and collaborators. Smith was a frequent contributor to *Frederick Douglass' Paper* and in 1855 replaced white abolitionist William Lloyd Garrison to write the preface to Douglass's second autobiography, *My Bondage and My Freedom*. In turn, Douglass used the pages of his newspaper to praise Smith and acknowledge his preeminence among Black leaders.

The 1853 Rochester and 1855 Philadelphia conventions refocused attention on constitutional issues. It was here that both Smith and Douglass affirmed their commitment to the principles embedded in the U.S. Constitution. The nation's founding document was key to the arguments they sought to advance. Grounded in Enlightenment principles, its ideals are universal in application and not limited by caste or class. Hence, the document grants Black Americans full permission to participate in national political debate and to define the meaning of citizenship—nowhere specified in the Constitution—on their own terms.

Yet a careful reading of the conventions' proceedings underscores the different shadings each man gave to his argument. Having recently broken ties with Garrison, Douglass was intent on reaffirming his abandonment of Garrisonian interpretations of the Constitution as a proslavery document. Many of his other pronouncements echo the debates—in particular Smith's positions—of the earlier New York state conventions. By contrast, Smith was moving forward in his thinking. Long convinced that the Constitution was an antislavery document, he worked to refine his arguments of the decade before, asserting fundamental principles of citizen rights; beyond that, however, he began to question the very term "citizen" in order to invoke that of universal "person."

We need to be grateful for the fact that *Frederick Douglass' Paper* did become a national organ, given the assiduousness with which the newspaper reported on the conventions' proceedings—the call, the meetings, and the outcome.

The calls made clear the significance of both conventions in the minds of Black leaders. The Rochester announcement noted that it had been four long years since the last national convention, while the Philadelphia call was republished at least fifteen times during the summer and fall of 1855. Most readers offered excited support, although some expressed worry. One person lamented that conventions cost too much money, that too few attended, and that nothing came of them. "In a word," he opined in highly metaphoric language, "*conventions* among us may be aptly compared to a beautiful sky-rocket that ascends, and, for a moment, illumines the surrounding space, but soon comes down, leaving all around wrapped in darkness."[20]

The figure of James McCune Smith dominated the calls. Witness an editorial published a month before the Rochester convention that praised him in elaborate terms:

Among the colored men of note in this country, distinguished for their talents and learning, and for their known devotion to the cause of their oppressed people, there is not one who has risen to his position so noiselessly and steadily, and so entirely without rivals, as Dr. James McCune Smith. . . . Nor has he . . . lost sight of his "vocation" as a scholar. It was as a scholar that we needed a James McCune Smith, and he has seemed thoroughly to understand this need, and nobly devoted his time, talents and learning, without fee or reward to supply it. . . .

Industriously pursuing his professional labors in New York, he is seldom tempted beyond the limits of that city. . . . The emergency must be pressing, and the call must not be merely for someone, but for him, in order to bring him out. He is too wise to be forward; yet too brave to shrink from duty, at whatever peril, or against whatever odds. When there comes an assault of a peculiarly injurious character, threatening great damage to our people, and requiring strength and skill to repel it, the arm of James McCune Smith is seen uplifted.[21]

Both Smith's scholarly vocation and uplifted arm were on full display in the calls for the 1855 Philadelphia convention. Surveying the ever-deteriorating condition of his people, Smith accused white abolitionists of betrayal, pointing out with particular venom that "the blame falls with cursing effect on Mr. Garrison and his party." Not only had Garrison sowed disunion between white and Black abolitionists, Smith lamented, but the Black leadership itself had been torn apart by "divided-ners." Of leaders, "we have none." To rectify this situation, Smith concluded, delegates needed to follow the example of "old Thomas Aquinas" and join forces in a "CONVENTION OF IDEAS."[22] In thus invoking the venerable theologian, Smith was urging Black leaders to adopt the rigorous model of the medieval disputatio. In such a public debate, an authoritative leader poses a question to a group; an answer is then proposed, followed by one or more objections; the debate is concluded once the leader determines the correct position.[23] Smith wanted two main ideas disputed. The first, centering on principle, was the true meaning of the Constitution; the second, a strategy, concerned the establishment of a national council that would facilitate greater activism.[24]

The 1853 Rochester convention initiated these ideas. Douglass opened the meeting, delivering an address on the very first morning that underscored both his own intellectual development and his determination to institutionalize his political beliefs within the Colored Conventions movement. As Gregg Crane has noted, the early 1850s marked a turning point in Douglass's thinking. The former slave had recently returned from England where for the first time he had experienced something akin to true freedom. Chafing under Garrison's continued tutelage, he announced his break with the white abolitionist at the 1851 meeting of the American Anti-Slavery Society by declaring the U.S. Constitution to be an antislavery document and by siding with those whom Crane calls "radical antislavery constitutionalists." By focusing on its abstract language, Crane argues, Douglass was able to separate the Constitution from its extrinsic historical context and insist that it was in fact affirmatively antislavery. It constituted, Douglass declared in his 1852 speech "The Meaning of July Fourth for the Negro," "a glorious liberty document," universal and egalitarian in character, promoting the unity of humanity, and committed to justice for all, including Black Americans.[25]

Douglass began his address by reaffirming these ideals, rendered in capital letters in the printed proceedings pamphlet: "THE CONSTITUTION OF THE UNITED STATES WAS FORMED TO ESTABLISH JUSTICE, PROMOTE THE GENERAL WELFARE, AND SECURE THE BLESSING OF LIBERTY TO ALL THE PEOPLE OF THE COUNTRY." He went on to argue that these obligations extended to Blacks because "we are . . . American citizens asserting their rights on their own native soil," and he based his arguments on the following claims: 1) Black men are citizens of New York State, since nowhere does the word "white" appear in its constitution and since they had all been voters before 1821; 2) according to the U.S. Constitution, "the citizens of each State shall be entitled to all the privileges and immunities of citizens in the

United States"; 3) therefore, as citizens of New York State, Black men were perforce citizens of the United States.[26] It is impossible not to hear echoes of the earlier New York state and county suffrage debates, spearheaded by James McCune Smith, in this address.[27] How can we not conclude that the single-minded historiographical focus on national conventions and the singular figure of Douglass has obscured the role of local conventions and Black leaders such as Smith?

Two years later, it was Smith's turn to deliver the major address at the 1855 Philadelphia convention. Much like Douglass, Smith drew his argument from the very abstractness of the Constitution. But, in contrast to Douglass and to his own pronouncements of the 1840s, Smith now eschewed the term "citizen," which the Constitution seldom invoked and never defined, to adopt the document's more frequently used word "person." He provided ample footnotes to several of its articles and amendments as well as to a number of related legal speeches to buttress his case. All human beings, Smith argued, are persons, not things or property. Since Blacks are human beings, they must perforce be persons; hence, according to the Constitution, they cannot be deprived of liberty and must fall within the purview of the national "general welfare." Given that the Constitution guarantees that each state in the union must have a republican form of government, these provisions apply nationwide. Echoing Douglass, Smith called on his fellow delegates to vindicate "our glorious Constitution," concluding that "there can be no higher praise of the Constitution, than that its workings are absolute—if rightly interpreted, for Freedom—if wrongly, for Slavery—to all."[28]

Although he specifically limited his citations to legal documents, Smith was silently invoking philosophical traditions concerning personhood embedded in the thinking of "old Thomas Aquinas," who, centuries earlier, had "held such a meeting when he discovered that 'all men are created equal.'"[29] In his disputations, Aquinas had argued that human beings are persons created in the image of God; born of a divine source, they are defined by their essence—universal in nature—that is the soul. The soul is immaterial and spiritual (and hence raceless). It is unique to each person, dynamic, and capable of evolving and of striving for self-actualization. It is what endows human beings with dignity, reason, and free will and makes them masters of their own selves.[30] At once scholar and activist, Smith conjoined theology and secular law in his Philadelphia speech to articulate a powerful concept of universal personhood.

Smith concluded his address by calling on delegates to unite in concerted action. Yet postconvention accounts in *Frederick Douglass' Paper* acknowledged that, like the local meetings, national conventions often resulted in disharmony. William J. Wilson, aka Ethiop, principal of Brooklyn's Colored School No. 1 and Smith's close friend, assiduously adopted the role of the conventions' unofficial reporter. According to Wilson, Smith made every effort to be the voice of reason much as he had at the earlier Schenectady convention. With his "peculiar and inimitable tact and . . . promptness of action almost intuitive with him," Smith, he claimed, was a formidable leader who managed the opposition without its ever realizing it. But tact failed Smith after the Philadelphia convention. His speech created, in Ethiop's word, a "house divided," pitting Smith and Douglass against men from Boston and Philadelphia such as Robert Purvis, William Nell, Charles Remond, Junius Morell, and John Rock who still held to the Garrisonian view that the Constitution was a proslavery document. It fell to Douglass to win over their opponents: "As a lion, fairly roused from his den . . . he crushed out, first their vitality, and then pulverized their meager skeletons ere he buried them."[31]

The National Council of the Colored People, 1853–1855

Nowhere was Smith's tact more necessary than in his strategy to transform his second idea—the creation of a National Council of the Colored People—into action. From the start, the council was identified as Smith's brainchild. An apologetic editorial in *Frederick Douglass' Paper* acknowledged, "It was not, we beg to state, Frederick Douglass, as our printers have proclaimed, that reported to the colored National Convention, the plan for a National organization, styled the National Council, but Dr. J. McCune Smith. . . . We are sure that our friend, the Dr., must have smiled at the seeming coolness with which we lugged off his 'thunder.'"[32]

Smith proposed his plan in his calls for the Rochester and Philadelphia conventions. Delivered immediately after Douglass's address at the Rochester meeting, Smith's speech explaining the National Council of the Colored People was received with great excitement, as was the printed document, published and distributed at year's end. In structuring the council, Smith followed the same trajectory that he had in formulating his constitutional arguments by turning once again to the nation's founding document.

Smith conceived of the council as a permanent legislative body designed to organize "a Union of colored people of the free States."[33] Meeting every six months, it would provide greater regularity and consistency than the conventions, and thus be more efficacious. A strategy for action, it was nevertheless firmly embedded in a principle: that of representative democracy.

The national conventions were to elect two members from each state to the national council. Returning to their respective states, these representatives were to hold a poll every two years open to all voters who paid a tax of ten cents. The vote would result in the election of twenty delegates, who would make up the state councils; they, in turn, would elect additional members of the national council, one for every 2,000 Black inhabitants, who would also hold office for two years. The officers of the national council included a president, vice president, secretary, and treasurer; various committees would attend to specific issues of the day. Smith's plan thus brought together several salient features of Articles I and II of the Constitution. It combined both fixed and proportional representation (calculated according to the number of inhabitants in a given state), as well as direct and indirect elections (conducted through the intermediary of delegate-electors).

The goals of the national council were lofty. "The hour has come," members intoned, "for us to take a direct and forward movement. . . . The time is come when our people must assume the rank of a first-rate power in the battle against caste and Slavery. . . . We must maintain our citizenship and manhood in every relation civil, religious and social throughout the land."[34] The council's activism focused on three principal issues: antislavery efforts, the franchise, and the establishment of an industrial college for Black youth.

Sadly, very little came of the council's activities. As anti-Black sentiment hardened in the decade before the Civil War, its failure is hardly surprising. Moreover, like the conventions, this legislative body was riven by dissension. Part of the problem might have been due to Smith's plan itself. Despite his attempts to balance the interest of all states and voters much as the Constitution had, states with smaller Black populations might well have thought themselves overshadowed by those with larger ones, and the power of electors might well have led to charges of favoritism. In a heartfelt letter to *Frederick Douglass' Paper*, one member took the Ohio delegates to task over their dogged opposition to unspecified decisions made earlier in New York:

> This Council would be sustained by the people, and act in unity among themselves. In this I have been disappointed yea, sadly, disappointed. . . . While much has been done . . . it appears to me that there never was a time when our people seemed so much divided in cliques and parties as the present. We have, it is true, good men in the National Council; but even among the small number of eleven that met in Cleveland, I found that the spirit of discord had entered, to distract, to divide and to destroy. Indeed, it was clearly manifest that there was a determination that nothing should be done by the Council, unless, in the first place, the Council would pass a vote of censure on the doing of the meeting at New York in November last, and then follow that by a vote rejecting all that was done by the Convention at Rochester, and thence begin anew on a plan that might perhaps meet the views of the *Ohio Councilmen*.[35]

It is not clear how long the national council remained in existence, but after 1855 there appears to be no reference to it in Douglass's paper.

James McCune Smith vs. Roger B. Taney

The 1857 *Dred Scott* decision delivered a death sentence to the rights of Black Americans and to constitutional arguments in favor of Black citizenship. The national Colored Conventions movement disbanded and did not hold another meeting until 1863. Smith, however, refused to be silenced and, as in earlier years, turned to print media to voice his protest. In May 1859 he published an essay titled "Citizenship" in the recently founded *Anglo-African Magazine*. Ever the tactician, Smith realized that he now needed to discard the category of "person" and revert to that of "citizen." Roger B. Taney, chief justice of the United States, according to Smith, had based his infamous opinion on the denial of personhood to Black Americans. Negroes were not persons but things, "bought and sold, and treated as an ordinary article of merchandise and traffic whenever a profit could be made by it."[36] In a statement that captivated the public imagination, Taney felt free, Smith wrote, to conclude that "negroes had no rights which white men were bound to respect." But personhood, Smith insisted, had not been the basis of the Court's decision. Rather, the Court had reasoned that Dred Scott "was a slave in the state of Missouri, according to the laws thereof, and *therefore* not a citizen of the United States within the meaning of the Constitution." Determined to challenge the Court on its own terms, Smith knew that his already difficult task was compounded by the American public's reluctance to engage with the "broad principles which underlie the discussion, [namely] the relation which individuals bear to the state, and the limits of the power of the judiciary to alter such relations."[37]

Smith continued by pointing out that since the Constitution nowhere defined the word "citizen," he himself would need to seek its exact meaning by independent means. Marshaling all of his scholarly resources yet again, he turned to the historical record and came to rest at the Roman Republic: "The word citizenship," he wrote, is "of latin derivation [and] gathers its purport and exact meaning from the Roman republic; it originated and *grew* under the Romans." Smith then proceeded to interpret its purport and meaning. Enumerating the rights of Roman citizens—both private and public—Smith maintained that "possession of all or any of them constituted citizenship on the part of the individual holding them."[38] Turning to the United States, he argued that free Blacks–at all times or only at certain times–and even some slaves, enjoyed all or some of these same rights. Tapping into Aristotelian and medieval rhetorical traditions, Smith created a syllogism. If the rights he enumerated were those of Roman citizenship, and if any Americans— including free Blacks—enjoyed any one of these rights in the United States, they were perforce citizens of the United States. Or, in his words:

> Such are the rights which were attached to citizenship among the Romans. Such are the rights which constitute citizenship as expressed in the Constitution of the United States, because, in the absence of any definition of the word in that Constitution, the word must bear the meaning which language itself attaches to it under like circumstances, to wit, when it expresses the relation of the individual to the general government. As in Roman polity, the possession of any one of these rights constituted the possessor a citizen of the Republic, so it might be safely argued, that in these United States, the possession of any one of these rights confer citizenship on the possessor.

Those in power did not read Smith's essay, and even if they had, they would not have agreed with his argument. Indeed, Smith was less interested in the letter of the law than in its spirit, hoping against hope that the United States could rival the ideals of "lofty Rome."[39] History proved otherwise. Two years later, the civil war broke out. Smith lived long enough to celebrate the abolition of slavery and the preservation of the Union. But he would not survive to witness passage of the Fourteenth and Fifteenth Amendments granting citizenship to "all persons born or naturalized in the United States," and the right to vote to these new citizens.

Reconstructing Our Alexandrine Library

The ancient Library of Alexandria declined slowly over the centuries, victim of both internal dissension and foreign invasion, and by the end of the fourth century disappeared entirely. But efforts to revive it, begun in the 1970s, led to its 2002 revival as the Bibliotheca Alexandrina. Much the same can be said of James McCune Smith's Alexandrine Library that African American studies scholars are painstakingly reconstructing by mining the archives for Black writing in all fields and genres and recomposing "the noblest pages in the history of our people." As we rebuild our library, we have sought to reinvigorate our own reading practices, resurrecting voices obscured by history, reassessing the import of seemingly insignificant texts, and tracing the threads that lead from one text to another to uncover larger histories. One of these histories—which Smith feared would be lost—is the determined quest for citizenship by antebellum northern Blacks that ultimately culminated in the reconstruction of the nation with the passage of the Thirteenth, Fourteenth, and Fifteenth Amendments.

NOTES

1. James McCune Smith, "Sketch of the Life of and Labors of Henry Highland Garnet," introduction to *A Memorial Discourse by Henry Highland Garnet, Delivered in the Hall of the House of Representatives, Washington D.C., on Sabbath, February 12, 1865*, by Henry Highland Garnet (Philadelphia: J. M. Wilson, 1865), 34.

2. *Philanthropist* (New Richmond, OH), September 8, 1837; and October 17, 1837. I thank Professor Kate Masur for her recent discovery of this early Ohio State Convention of Colored People.

3. Smith, "Sketch," 41.

4. Derrick Spires, "Imagining a State of Fellow Citizens: Early African American Politics of Publicity in the Black State Conventions," in *Early African American Print Culture*, ed. Lara Langer Cohen and Jordan Alexander Stein (Philadelphia: University of Pennsylvania Press, 2012), 276.

5. *Frederick Douglass' Paper* (Rochester, NY), October 3, 1855.

6. Rhoda Golden Freeman, *The Free Negro in New York City in the Era before the Civil War* (New York: Garland, 1994), 93; Smith, "Sketch," 37–38.

7. *Colored American* (New York), November 17, 1838; and July 27, 1839.

8. *Colored American*, August 8, 1840. See also Carla L. Peterson, *Black Gotham: A Family History of African Americans in Nineteenth-Century New York City* (New Haven, CT: Yale University Press, 2011), 124–26.

9. *Colored American*, August 15, 1840. Emphasis mine.

10. *Convention of the Colored Inhabitants of the State of New York, August 18–20, 1840,* in *Proceedings of the Black State Conventions, 1840–1865,* ed. Philip S. Foner and George E. Walker (Philadelphia: Temple University Press), 1:7, 16.

11. *Colored American,* February 13, 1841.

12. "Proceedings of the New York State Convention Held in the City of Troy, August 25th, 26th, and 27th, 1841," *Colored American,* September 11, 1841.

13. "Proceedings of the New York County Convention, Held in the City of New York," *Colored American,* October 30, 1841.

14. *Proceedings of the State Convention of Colored People Held at Albany, New York on the 22nd, 23rd, and 24th of July, 1851,* in Foner and Walker, *Proceedings,* 1:70; also available at Colored Conventions Project, https://omeka.coloredconventions.org/items/show/235.

15. Convention of the Colored Citizens of the State of New York, Fifth Annual (1844: Schenectady, NY), *Minutes of the Fifth Annual Convention of the Colored People of the State of New York, Held in the City of Schenectady, on the 18th, 19th, and 20th of September, 1844,* 6, Colored Conventions Project, https://omeka.coloredconventions.org/items/show/602.

16. *National Anti-Slavery Standard* (New York), October 24, 1844, reprinted in *The Protest, State Convention of the Colored Citizens of New York, Held at Schenectady, September 18–20, 1844,* in Foner and Walker, *Proceedings,* 1:32, 35.

17. Julie Winch, *Philadelphia's Black Elite: Activism, Accommodation, and the Struggle for Autonomy, 1787–1848* (Philadelphia: Temple University Press, 1988), 134–42.

18. Robert Purvis, "Appeal of Forty Thousand Citizens, Threatened with Disfranchisement, to the People of Pennsylvania," in *Pamphlets of Protest: An Anthology of Early African American Protest Literature, 1790–1860,* ed. Richard Newman, Patrick Rael, and Philip Lapsansky (New York: Routledge, 2001); *Proceedings of the State Convention of the Colored Freemen of Pennsylvania, Held in Pittsburgh, on the 23rd, 24th, and 25th of August, 1841, for the Purpose of Considering their Condition, and the Means of Improvement,* in Foner and Walker, *Proceedings,* 1:106–16 (also available at Colored Conventions Project, https://omeka.coloredconventions.org/items/show/240); *Minutes of the State Convention of the Coloured Citizens of Pennsylvania, Convened at Harrisburg, December 13th and 14th, 1848,* in Foner and Walker, *Proceedings,* 1:132 (also available at Colored Conventions Project, https://omeka.coloredconventions.org/items/show/241).

19. National Convention of Colored People and Their Friends (1847: Troy, NY), *Proceedings of the National Convention of Colored People, and their Friends Held in Troy, N.Y., on the 6th, 7th, 8th, and 9th October, 1847,* 18–21, Colored Conventions Project, https://omeka.coloredconventions.org/items/show/279.

20. *Frederick Douglass' Paper,* June 17, 1853; May 13, 1853.

21. *Frederick Douglass' Paper,* June 3, 1853.

22. *Frederick Douglass' Paper,* October 5, 1855.

23. James J. Murphy, *Rhetoric in the Middle Ages: A History of Rhetorical Theory from St. Augustine to the Middle Ages* (Berkeley: University of California Press, 1974), 102–4.

24. *Frederick Douglass' Paper,* September 21, 1855; October 3, 1855; May 20, 1853; June 3, 1853.

25. Gregg D. Crane, *Race, Citizenship, and Law in American Literature* (Cambridge: Cambridge University Press, 2002), 108–11, 115–21.

26. Colored National Convention (1853: Rochester, NY), *Proceedings of the Colored National Convention, Held in Rochester, July 6th, 7th and 8th, 1853,* 8, 11–12, Colored Conventions Project, https://omeka.coloredconventions.org/items/show/458.

27. See also John Stauffer, *The Black Hearts of Men: Radical Abolition and the Transformation of Race* (Cambridge, MA: Harvard University Press, 2001), 160–61.

28. Colored National Convention (1855: Philadelphia, PA), *Proceedings of the Colored*

National Convention, Held in Franklin Hall, Sixth Street, below Arch, Philadelphia October 16th, 17th and 18th, 1855, 32, Colored Conventions Project, https://omeka.colored conventions.org/items/show/281.

29. *Frederick Douglass' Paper*, October 5, 1855.

30. Jove Jim S. Aguas, "The Notions of the Human Person and Human Dignity in Aquinas and Wojtyla," *Kritike* 3, no. 1 (June 2009): 44–45, 55.

31. *Frederick Douglass' Paper*, August 19, 1853; November 23, 1855.

32. *Frederick Douglass' Paper*, July 22, 1853.

33. *Frederick Douglass' Paper*, July 23, 1853; May 20, 1853; June 3, 1853; October 26, 1855; December 16, 1853; May 18, 1855.

34. *Frederick Douglass' Paper*, May 18, 1855.

35. *Frederick Douglass' Paper*, September 1, 1854.

36. "The Dred Scott Decision," *American Memory: Slaves and the Courts, 1740–1860*, https://www.loc.gov/item/17001543, 11.

37. James McCune Smith, "Citizenship," *Anglo-African Magazine*, May 1859, 144, 145. Smith's quotations do not reproduce the exact wording of Taney's decision.

38. Smith, "Citizenship," 146–47. According to Smith, the private rights of Roman citizens were the right of liberty, of family, of marriage, of a father, of legal property, of making a will and succeeding to an inheritance, and of tutelage or wardship. Public rights were the right of census, of serving in the army, of being taxed, of voting, of holding office, and of ministering to sacred things.

39. Smith, 149.

PART 2

ANTEBELLUM DEBATES

*Citizenship Practices, Print Culture,
and Women's Activism*

FLIGHTS OF FANCY

Black Print, Collaboration, and Performance in
"An Address to the Slaves of the United States of America
(Rejected by the National Convention, 1843)"

Derrick R. Spires

Scholars have long pointed to the 1843 National Convention of Colored Citizens in Buffalo and the debate around "An Address to the Slaves of the United States of America" delivered by Henry Highland Garnet as a flashpoint in the history of Black activism. Garnet directed the "Address" to his enslaved "brethren and fellow citizens," calling on them to stage a general strike and to fight if their enslavers refused to comply with their just claims as citizens: "You had far better all die—*die immediately*, than live slaves, and entail your wretchedness upon your posterity."[1] This tone and forthrightness led Herbert Aptheker to anthologize the "Address" in *A Documentary History of the Negro People in the United States* (1951) as "Garnet's Call to Rebellion, 1843"; Sterling Stuckey has framed it as part of the "ideological origins of black nationalism"; and most recently Stanley Harrold and Manisha Sinha have analyzed it as part of the "rise of radical abolitionism," a touchstone for a "distinct black abolitionist tradition of protest."[2] At the same time, the 1843 convention itself, the first known national Colored Convention since 1835, was rife with the tensions plaguing abolitionism and Black activism more broadly: political affiliations (Liberty Party versus nonalignment), abolitionist tactics ("color-blind" moral suasion versus Black political activism), and regional differences, to name a few.[3] The "Address" became a point around which many of these tensions erupted and remains a centerpiece in scholarship probing the complexities of antebellum Black activism. Yet, this essay argues, the way the convention minutes and subsequent press coverage report these fault lines around the "Address," the convention's eventual decision not to print it, and the document's ultimate path to publication provide an ideal case study, not just for limning these political and personal differences but also for thinking about Colored Conventions as choreographed public performances of collective Black politics, for examining Colored Conventions' dynamism as collaborative enterprises that included oft-uncited women's labor, and for thinking about the importance Black activists placed on making collective authorship and print practices visible.

Delegates at the 1843 convention twice rejected printing the "Address," both by close margins. In the months after the 1843 convention, multiple accounts of the "Address" appeared in newspapers such as the *Liberator* and the *Emancipator and Free American* and later in the official convention minutes. But these accounts primarily described the ensuing debate about printing the address, not the address's contents. Garnet delivered a version of the "Address" again during the 1847 National Convention of Colored People in Troy, New York; however, the convention's official "Report of the Committee on Abolition" tacitly rejected the address's sentiments as "absurd, unavailing, dangerous and mischievous ravings."[4] Another year would elapse before Garnet finally published "An Address to the Slaves of the United States of America (Rejected by the National Convention, 1843)" as an addendum to his printing of the second edition of David Walker's *Appeal to the Colored Citizens of the World* in 1848. By then, many of Garnet's detractors would hold up Walker's *Appeal* and the "Address" as expressing a consensus that a more aggressive abolitionism was needed. Finally, in 1865 James McCune Smith would include yet another version of the "Address" in his biographical introduction to Garnet's *A Memorial Discourse by Henry Highland Garnet, Delivered in the Hall of the House of Representatives.*

These twists in the performance, reception, and print history of the "Address" suggest that analyzing it involves working on a constellation of at least three distinct yet mutually constituting print events: 1) the 1843 convention's minutes, 2) newspaper accounts describing Garnet's performance and ensuing debate, and 3) the divergent editions of the "Address" published in 1848 and 1865. None of these iterations gives direct access to what Garnet read or to his performance in 1843. They instead point to an absence, a black hole; we know it happened, and we have a sense of its shape because of how the surrounding discourse responded to its gravity, but we cannot *see* it. In that sense, we need to read each moment—minutes, newspaper accounts, and editions—as a distinct interpretation of a performative text that simultaneously offers a reception history of Garnet's delivery and reenacts his performance in the rendering.[5]

In attending to the trajectory of the "Address" from composition to convention and print, this essay foregrounds the 1843 convention as a deliberative space meant to encourage rather than foreclose critical debate. The 1843 convention's rejection of the "Address" has often been used to demonstrate the personal battles between Frederick Douglass and Garnet and as a sign of divisions within the convention movement, yet the debate around Garnet's "Address" shows the delegates' insistence on the power of collective action and collective authorship. Even as the printed minutes show the fissures within the convention, their style and form emphasize a collaborative process, perhaps most visibly around the convention's most contentious moments. Rereading the "Address" through its print and reception histories—even in its rejections—highlights Colored Conventions as having a democratic process of textual production that in its very nature resisted reduction to individual authorship or a cult of personality. That Garnet delayed publication and cited the 1843 convention in the title reinforces the importance of Colored conventions' imprimatur to the meaning of the "Address." More, among Garnet's collaborators was Julia Williams Garnet, his wife. Acknowledging her role further destabilizes interpretations of the "Address" as "Henry Highland Garnet's 'Address to the Slaves,'" of conventions and the "Address" as products of exclusively male spaces, and of Black radicalism as a male project. The Colored Conventions' insistence on creating spaces—physically and in print—where Black people could discuss issues germane to Black life also reveals the gaps between white perceptions of the conventions, Black activism as primarily abolitionist in nature, and participants' focus on a much broader notion of Black citizenship with emancipation as just the beginning.

Conventional Document, Unconventional Address

The "Address to the Slaves" was never meant to be "Henry Highland Garnet's 'Address to the Slaves.'" The "ritual" in which the convention would adopt the address and print it as its own statement, however, did not go as planned.[6] Garnet prepared the "Address" in his capacity as chair of the 1843 convention's Business Committee, and if all had gone according to plan, the "Address" would have been titled something like "An Address to the Slaves of the United States from the National Convention of Colored Citizens" or "from Their Colored Fellow Citizens." Like the "Conventional Addresses" and declarations of sentiments from Colored Conventions of the 1830s and the addresses to voters and Black citizens from the state conventions of the 1840s, the address was composed to be a corporate public assertion of the convention's intentions—part manifesto, part historical assessment of abolitionism, and part vehicle for creating and sustaining a national Black movement that linked explicitly northern racism and enslavement.[7] And the 1843 convention would not have been the first convention to address enslaved people. Two white abolitionists, Gerrit Smith and William Lloyd Garrison, had delivered addresses to enslaved people within the past year that were adopted and printed on behalf of the New York Antislavery Society (1842) and the New England Anti-Slavery Society (1843), respectively.[8] If these organizations were advising enslaved people, why not their northern brethren, many of whom had been enslaved themselves and had family and loved ones still enslaved? And in back of all this work was Garnet's engagement with David Walker's *Appeal* (1829), still invoked in print in the early 1840s.[9]

Garnet, then, was not breaking new ground; rather, he was putting his own stamp on an evolving tradition. Though the "Address" represented a radical departure from typical antislavery tropes of the enslaved as powerless victims, it was in keeping with a tradition of Black political theory outlined in Walker's *Appeal*, rhetoric coming out of white-led organizations, and the way free Black citizens had begun addressing each other. Indeed, this history, and the somewhat expected nature of Garnet's remarks, becomes clearer if we situate Garnet's "Address" less in the debates among competing abolitionist organizations and more in the political philosophies Garnet, Theodore S. Wright, Charles B. Ray, Samuel H. Davis, and others developed during suffrage campaigns through New York state Colored Conventions in the 1840s.

The synergy between the 1840 New York Colored Convention's addresses, the 1843 convention's "call," and Davis's address as convention president suggests that Garnet grounded the "Address to the Slaves" in a political discourse that would have been familiar to his (New York) audience and those who had been following New York events through the *Colored American*.[10] As the 1840 New York convention's Address Committee chair, Garnet helped craft that convention's addresses to "Their Colored Fellow Citizens" and to "the People of the State." Both articulate an aggressive politics of agitation grounded in claims to birthright citizenship and the language of republicanism.[11] "In a community," they argue, "man sustains various relations, and possesses powers adapted to them—which, if not permitted a natural and legitimate exercise, are turned upon himself and follows with augmented and fearful capacity for evil, from the fact of having been diverted from a natural channel."[12] Bereft of legally sanctioned channels for exercising natural political energies, people (disenfranchised Black New Yorkers in this case) would find other, potentially destructive outlets. Any state claiming to be republican would recognize this fact and work to incorporate, rather than exclude, any and all men (specifically gendered and rendered as able-bodied) into the body politic. The state refusing to do so, the convention implies, was inviting unrest—potentially violent. The convention then urges Black citizens to "put forth our own exertions," because history has demonstrated that only the oppressed can force change.[13] Such agitation was morally and politically justified, divinely sanctioned, and basic human nature.

Both the 1843 national convention's "call," most likely drafted by Garnet as chair of the Correspondence Committee, and Davis's opening remarks follow from this state-level emphasis on agential citizenship and direct political engagement.[14] "Come in strength of the Lord," the call proclaims, "and prepared to take a *bold stand* for truth and suffering humanity" (3). Davis's opening remarks amplify the emphasis on the power of independent self-assertion: "We, ourselves, must be willing to contend for the rich boon of freedom and equal rights, or we shall never enjoy that boon" (7). Addressing free Black citizens, Davis scales New York's strategy up to the national level. Black citizens needed to shape their own institutional spaces and they needed to claim full citizenship on their own terms. By the time Garnet stepped to the podium, the convention would have been primed for a politically engaged statement.

Yet Garnet innovates on earlier models by merging Walker's *Appeal* and previous addresses with a definition of citizenship that extended the New York convention's precepts to include enslaved people as rights-bearing citizens. "Forget not that you are native-born American citizens," Garnet tells enslaved men in an echo of the New York convention, "and as such, you are justly entitled to all the rights that are granted to the freest."[15] Garnet combines this birthright citizenship discourse with the narrative of Christian duty that Walker outlined in *Appeal*: "Have we any other master but Jesus Christ alone? Is he not their master as well as ours?" asks Walker. "What right then, have we to obey and call any other master, but Himself?"[16] Garnet transposes Walker's invocation of the first commandment ("Thou shalt have no other gods before me") to argue that enslavement—like disenfranchisement—runs counter to human nature and divine law: "He who brings his fellow down so low, as to make him contented with a condition of slavery," Garnet posits, "commits the highest crime against God and man."[17] Even as Garnet condemns enslavers, he turns a critical eye on enslaved men in particular, mirroring masculinist constructions of citizenship in state and national Colored Conventions and in public discourse at large: "TO SUCH DEGRADATION IT IS SINFUL IN THE EXTREME FOR YOU TO MAKE VOLUNTARY SUBMISSION."[18] Men have a Christian duty to protect their wives and children and to refuse to support, even passively, a system built on rape and theft. It's one thing to remain enslaved when the conditions of enslavement impose submission through brutality and forced ignorance, Garnet argues in echo of Walker. It's quite another for enslaved men to willingly support the institution, even if that support comes through inaction.

In a final callback to the New York state conventions, Garnet then delivers the crux of the "Address" as an algorithmic application of agential citizenship and natural political energies. Enslaved men should 1) announce to their enslavers "that YOU ARE DETERMINED TO BE FREE" and support this assertion with an appeal to "their sense of justice"; 2) offer "renewed diligence in the cultivation of the soil" in exchange for fair wages, using the success of British emancipation in the West Indies as evidence; and 3) warn "of the righteous retributions of an indignant God."[19] If reason, economic incentives, and the threat of damnation fail and their enslavers "then commence the work of death," Garnet assures his audience that "they, and not you, will be responsible for the consequences. You had far better all die—*die immediately*, than live slaves, and entail your wretchedness upon your posterity."[20] Presenting Denmark Vesey, Nathaniel Turner, Joseph Cinque, and Madison Washington as a transatlantic and transhistorical hall of faith with "Moses, Hampden, Tell, Bruce, and Wallace, Touissaint L'Overteur [sic], Lafayette and [George] Washington," Garnet calls on enslaved men to follow historical precedent and "act for yourselves."[21] "It is an old and true saying," Garnet continues, "that 'if hereditary bondmen would be free, they must themselves strike the blow.'"[22] Garnet used this same Byron quote as the epigraph for the 1840 "Address of the New York State Convention to Their Colored Fellow Citizens" to emphasize the need for increased political activism.[23] Yet, in this context, "strike the blow" has more ominous implications, and (Garnet's audience feared) when addressed to his imagined enslaved audience, it suggested a plan leading inexorably toward violent insurrection.

Delivery and Debate: Convention Minutes as Curated Space

Both the ensuing debate around the "Address" and the silences about its content in the official record invite us to attend to the convention experience and printed matter as forming a dialectical relationship, one that convention delegates noted and tried to manage actively. Delegates accepted the "Address" as a live oration; making it the convention's official printed statement was a different matter. One was an approval of general sentiments expressed live, the details of which would be inaccessible to those reading the minutes; the other would be a printed text open to closer scrutiny and interpretation and willful misinterpretation. Ray, former editor of the *Colored American* and chair of the convention's Committee upon the Press, drew attention to the difference early on, moving that the "Address" be referred "to a select committee of five" with Garnet as chair so "it might pass through a close and critical examination, and perceiving some points in it that might in print appear objectionable, to have it somewhat modified" (12). The words themselves (or the ideas behind them) were not objectionable, but, Ray implies, print could not be trusted to simply convey meaning; it could not carry Garnet's inflections, tones, and embodied gestures nor could it communicate accurately his performance's unique vibe before that audience at that moment in that space. Ray's caution also reiterates a general concern about the convention as an act of collective self-fashioning and the minutes' role as an overly burdened presentation of the delegates' actions and words to hostile and racist readers.[24]

Ostensibly, there was nothing unusual about the committee route; conventions usually attributed their adopted addresses to a committee. The addresses from the 1840 New York convention, for instance, went through a committee with Garnet as the chair.[25] Yet Garnet seems to have taken the motion for referral in 1843 and the fact that he was singled out as the author as a personal rebuke or as an attempt to derail, rather than promote, the "Address." Adamant that "the address should be adopted by the convention, and sent out with its sanction" and that the minutes record it as such, Garnet defended his work:

> He reviewed the abominable system of slavery, showed its mighty workings, its deeds of darkness and of death—how it robbed parents of children, and children of parents, husbands of wives; how it prostituted the daughters of the slave; how it murdered the colored man. He referred to the fate of Denmark Vesey and his accomplices—of Nat Turner; to the burning of McIntosh, to the case of Madison Washington, as well as to many other cases—to what had been done to move the slaveholders to

let go their grasp, and asked what more could be done—if we have not
waited long enough—if it were not time to speak louder and longer—to
take higher ground and other steps. (13)

This record in the minutes strategically draws attention to the occasion: the
"abominable system of slavery" and an urgent need for new tactics. It provides an interpretive reconstruction, not a transcription, of Garnet's defense
that structurally and thematically reports his central premises through the
kind of argument many readers would have found appealing: slavery was
a crime against humanity and against heteronormative gender paradigms
in particular; it calls on the history of insurrections (successful and not) as
rallying cry and revolutionary pantheon; and it ends with an exhortation to
increase agitation that resonates with both Walker's and William Lloyd Garrison's admonitions to "be as harsh as truth, and as uncompromising as justice."[26] That the minutes provide this much detail suggests sentiments that,
even if the delegates did not adopt them formally, spoke to a growing consensus. If, as Garnet biographer Earl Ofari observes, "the fact that [the "Address"] was presented and seriously discussed legitimized it," then the fact
that this debate took up so much printed space meant that Garnet's claims,
if not his document, were guaranteed an audience beyond the convention.[27]

Yet Garnet would have neither the only nor the final word, and if the
minutes legitimized his claims, they similarly legitimized the counterargu-
ments from the convention's other young rising star, Frederick Douglass,
who was in the midst of the Hundred Conventions tour and was, along with
Charles L. Remond, determined to hold the moral suasion line. The record
of their back-and-forth emphasizes the overall spirit of critical debate as
both archive and model for readers to follow. "There was too much physical
force" in Garnet's rhetoric, Douglass argued, and "could it reach the slaves,
and the advice, either of the address or the gentleman, be followed, while
it might not lead the slaves to rise in insurrection for liberty, would, nevertheless, and necessarily be the occasion of an insurrection" (13). Garnet,
however, reasserted his stance: "If the master refused" slaves' just request
for liberty, enslaved people should "tell them, then we shall take it, let the
consequence be what it may" (13). If violence occurred, enslavers, not the enslaved, would be to blame. The minutes bookend the detailed portion of the
debate with Douglass's rejoinder: "He wanted emancipation in a better way,
as he expected to have it" (13). Would delegates side with Garnet's principled
stand or with Douglass's practical concerns? Would they embrace a potentially apocalyptic, but justified, confrontation as the last resort, or would
they be patient just a while longer?

The minutes frame this moment in a way that stages the convention as a
dialogic space and promotes, even demands, ongoing reenactment in other
meetings, reading rooms, and parlors and among a broader Black public. As
Douglas Jones notes, the minutes "functioned as (intended) continuations
of something of the happening itself . . . a script perhaps, that impelled its

reading publics to *do* something."[28] They provide a template and talking points for reviewing antislavery activities and the horrors of enslavement up to the present. Readers might be justified—even compelled—to choose a side but in the choosing would also be compelled to defend and act on that choice. If the time had come for "other steps," as Garnet argued, take them. If one preferred instead "trying the moral means a little longer," as Douglass argued, do so and prove Garnet wrong (13).

The "Address" wasn't finished at the convention just yet. The debate over whether to refer it to committee lasted into Wednesday evening, and the next morning the convention voted to do so "by a large majority" (14), with Garnet chairing a group of five that included Douglass, Alphonso M. Sumner, S. N. Davis, and R. Banks. Upon their return Thursday afternoon, the committee presented a second version "with some very slight alterations" (17) that perhaps included—as does the 1848 edition—a passage resonating with Douglass's caution: "We do not advise you to attempt a revolution with the sword, because it would be INEXPEDIENT. Your numbers are too small, and moreover the rising spirit of the age, and the spirit of the gospel, are opposed to war and bloodshed" (96). We may never know if this passage was part of the original address or if the phrasing was more Douglass's or Garnet's, but the 1847 convention's "Report on the Committee of Abolition," which Douglass had a central hand in crafting, used similar language: "The slave is in the minority, a small minority," and all the powers of government, "press and pulpit" support their continued enslavement, making any turn to violence "suicidal."[29] What we do know is that even in 1843, we are confronted with at least two versions of the "Address," and even in 1843 we are confronted with an image of Douglass and Garnet not just as antagonists but also as collaborators, albeit reluctant ones. The committee closed its report with a resolution that supporters "come forward and sign it in the name of the ever living God, and that measures be taken to print 1000 copies for circulation" (17).

Delegates at the 1843 convention subsequently debated and voted 18–19 against printing this revision. But the "Address" was not dead. After a day of discussing reports from committees on the press, agriculture, and "the condition of the colored people," R. Frances (Rochester, New York) called for a revote because "he had changed his mind in respect to the merit of the address" (23). Frances's reasons remain unclear—maybe the committee reports reinforced Garnet's sense of urgency—but the motion reopened the debate for the rest of that evening and resulted in a revote Friday morning, which Garnet again lost 9–14. This time, given the chance to vote, Ray and three others voted against adopting the address and R. Frances yet again voted "nay."

The voting patterns cannot be boiled down to moral objections or neatly mapped along radical versus conservative, political versus moral suasionist, or pro- versus anti–Liberty Party lines. I can only speculate, but Ray and others may well have ceded the point on the "Address," given the apparently insufficient alterations, in favor of maintaining a united front in the convention as a whole. Beyond that, the Ohio delegation's objections did not follow these fault lines nor did they seem to involve a battle over leadership, at least not on the individual level. This group was second largest after New York's (though New York was not a unified front), and their fear of violence—white violence against them in their home state—ultimately decided both rounds for them. Sumner (Cincinnati), who participated in the revision process with Garnet and Douglass, articulated the Ohio consensus: printing the "Address" "would be fatal to the safety of the free people of color of the slave States, but especially so to those who lived on the borders of the free States" (18). Sumner was concerned more about northern white reactions to reading an "Address to the Slaves" from a convention of colored citizens than about the possibility of enslaved people acting on it. He alluded to recent anti-Black violence in Cincinnati during celebrations on August 1, 1841, when an armed white mob attacked Cincinnati's Black business district in what historians have described as "the most severe urban outbreak against Blacks in pre–Civil War America."[30] Though armed and organized Black defenders beat back the attack, white rioters destroyed businesses, the dead (Black and white) were uncounted, and the city capitulated to enforcing Ohio's Black Codes more rigorously.[31] As their defense of Black Cincinnati demonstrated, Sumner and his fellow Ohioans were "prepared" to resist "unprovoked" incursions with violence if necessary, but they did not wish "injudiciously to provoke difficulty" (18), a sentiment echoed in the 1848 printing of the "Address." At the same time, their comments likely served as a reminder to other delegates of their own precarious positions, no matter how distant from the South.

Perhaps with this tenuous position in mind, the minutes as a whole suggest a stance that balances Garnet's call for agential citizenship, Douglass's caution about violent language, and a broad consensus around Sumner's determination to defend Black communities: the antislavery movement is at a crossroads, but the issues facing free and enslaved Black people remain constant; Black citizens would do well to review and take inspiration from the history of world revolutions and slave insurrections; they should proceed prudently, but deliberately; and Black activists need to develop independent national and local institutions to facilitate communication and collective action. The tensions don't disappear. Instead, the minutes make them do productive work. They shape the convention's sometimes acrimonious debate into proceedings adhering to a republican style of politics that uses the way Black activists disagree as part of the argument.

The collaboration involved in the production process—from taking notes to producing the final document—highlights this care and collective authorship. Ray, Jas. W. Duffin, and Abner H. Francis were official secretaries for the convention, but the minutes do not identify who recorded events at a given moment (8). At some point between the meeting and publication, one of them likely compiled notes, perhaps standardized the text's language, and decided principles for exclusion and inclusion. The convention also named a "committee to publish the proceedings" that included Ray, Garnet, Wright, and W. P. McIntosh (25). This committee likely had a hand in shaping the narrative as well and probably made more direct decisions about how much to include based on cost of publication. What I want to emphasize here is that both points in the process were at least nominally collaborative, with representatives from an array of positions. The number of people involved and the care with which the minutes lay out the account I've just outlined suggest that as much as conveners wanted to present a historical record, they also carefully considered how the proceedings would be perceived and read, a concern subsequent reviews of the event would prove justified.

Reception and Dissemination: A Tale of Two Addresses

The way the minutes represent Garnet's delivery and the absence of the address's content demonstrates the degree to which reading Colored Conventions can be a practice of following threads and assessing gaps that go well beyond printed minutes or the immediate weeks leading up to or following the meeting. Circulating narratives describing the convention and ensuing debates, not the "Address" itself, shaped public impressions of the document between 1843 and 1848. Minding these gaps places in sharper relief the performative elements of Colored Conventions—both event and minutes—and delegates' attempts to manage representations of Black performance in a racist print culture eager to manipulate Black presences toward its own ends.

The 1843 minutes are generally silent on how listeners responded throughout the convention, adopting instead a parliamentarian style foregrounding statements from official delegates and the convention's deliberative character. This style characterized many antebellum convention proceedings, which did not record extended descriptions of audience participation beyond delegate responses, often leaving that kind of work to newspaper correspondents and others. For instance, where outside accounts agree that Garnet "fairly enchained the audience, over whose passions, affections and actions" he had "perfect control," the minutes only note, "The business committee reported, by their chairman, H. H. Garnit [sic], an address to the slaves of this land, prepared for the occasion, which was read and accepted" (12).[32] That is the official record of Garnet's performance or the original content of the "Address." Practically, including more details might have been financially prohibitive.[33] Beyond stylistic and financial concerns, the Publication Committee may have been concerned about avoiding any representations that would play into racist tropes of Black public gatherings as dangerously emotional, lacking in substance, or disorderly.

This formal tendency makes deviations, as in the case of Garnet's extemporaneous defense of the "Address," all the more significant. The minutes describe it as "a masterly effort" leaving "the whole convention, full as it was . . . literally infused with tears. Mr. Garnit [sic] concluded amidst great applause" (13). The only other moment in the minutes that comes close to this level of affective detail occurs during Amos Beman's objection to the revised version later in the convention: "The remarks of Mr. Beman were of great force, and produced [an] effect upon the audience" (23). The break in the pattern around Garnet and Beman punctuates just how singular the moment was, how strongly attendees supported Garnet, and just how careful delegates were about what they put in *print*. Including the audience's unequivocal approbation gave Garnet's sentiments, as represented in the minutes, as close to an endorsement as he could receive without official approval. The fact that Ray, Garnet, Wright, and Francis were involved in the recording and publication process also suggests that the stylistic break might have been as carefully orchestrated as the rest of the document. Though Ray, Wright, and Francis spoke against printing the "Address" when given an opportunity, Ray at least was in favor of printing a softer version and was explicitly concerned with print reception.

How *did* wider audiences attending and writing about the 1843 convention respond to Garnet? As with many Colored Conventions, newspaper accounts provide crucial material on a range of issues, including audience demographics and response and performative elements that convention minutes tended not to reveal. Like the minutes, most accounts of the 1843 convention are silent on the content of the "Address"; instead, they flesh out the event as a participatory theatrical *experience*. An account first published in the *Buffalo Commercial Advertiser* and reprinted in the *Emancipator and Free American*, for instance, excludes debate particulars in favor of commentary on black statecraft and on the "abilities displayed by the delegates, as business men and men of talent."[34] In this account, Theodore S. Wright appears as the elder statesman, "a peace-maker during the whole sitting" and a stalwart of "high-toned feelings of morality and religion," while Garnet represents the convention's energy as he "evinced that he may, equally with the whites, lay claim to the highest order of eloquence." Together, they formed "the back-bone of the convention," which itself was a masterful display of statecraft and stagecraft.[35]

The *Advertiser* leans into this theatricality, beginning its account of the debate with a description of Garnet's body: Garnet "drew up his fine figure to its full height" and controlled his posture and movement to produce a "thrilling portraiture of his own feelings."[36] This description would have been all the more potent for readers who knew of Garnet's prosthetic leg (his leg was amputated at the knee in 1841). The movement suggesting a stance beyond the simple straightening of one's back. The correspondent describes Garnet using his body and voice to guide his audience's thoughts and emotions as a master conductor: "his ridicule" of potential opposition had "the audience . . . in an almost continual roar of laughter," while his account of enslavement and "the wrongs of his race" through his own narrative of enslavement and escape gave "utterance to sentiments, and enforced them by a graceful action" so that "the whole assembly, were moved in tears."[37] Even stoic (white) lawyers "found they could not restrain their feelings" and would have been embarrassed, the review reports, had not everyone else been "too much occupied with his own case, and the speaker, to notice them."[38] Garnet's final tonal move wrenches listeners from pity to righteous anger with such force that "the tear was instantly dried, the fist involuntarily clenched, and a very prevalent disposition to jump from the seats" spread through the hall. "I may verily believe," the reviewer notes, "that at the close, it would have been dangerous to a slave-holder to have been in sight."[39] The delegates responsible for voting for or against publishing the "Address" might have debated its tactical effectiveness and potential for misreading as a printed manifesto; the general audience, however, seemed primed to act then and there. The lawyers' response in particular demonstrates Garnet's rhetorical prowess, mitigates assumptions about his audience's susceptibility to sentiment, and reinforces the sense from the minutes that there was something irresistible about Garnet's presence, for good or ill. If people experienced his words, they would act, but the words also depended on Garnet himself to have proper effect.

Writers for the *Liberator*, by contrast and in confirmation of Ray's caution, had a dourer interpretation that played on racist tropes more familiar to Thomas Jefferson and minstrelsy than to the statehouse. E. A. Marsh's and Maria Weston Chapman's accounts play up dissension, isolate Garnet, and, perhaps most troubling for convention organizers, trade in the discourse of white paternalism that the Colored Conventions were meant to counter. Where the minutes and other reviews describe a democratic process, Marsh dramatizes a battle between the forces of good and evil. Douglass, Remond, and William Wells Brown emerge as "contend[ing] nobly for freedom" and "the interests of the slaves" against Garnet, Ray, and convention organizers' antidemocratic, misguided "sophistry" and their "evil, hatred, force, revenge, and littleness," as Chapman put it.[40] Marsh provides the most detailed contemporaneous articulation of the central premise of the "Address": "that the slave was to go to his master, tell of the injury of slavery, the duty of immediate emancipation—to refuse to work another hour, unless paid." He quotes Garnet as calling on slaves to "strike for liberty" if their masters "remained inexorable."[41] (This phrasing, while not in the minutes, does appear in the version of the "Address" printed in 1865.)[42] The other details Marsh includes (and excludes), however, heighten the interpretation that Garnet was inciting violence and that he increasingly began losing control of his emotions and rhetoric. The subtle manipulation of pathos and reason described in the *Advertiser* gets flattened into quixotic noise: "The Rev. gentleman grew eloquent [in his defense of the address]; axioms of Patrick Henry and others were pressed into service on the occasion—'Give me liberty, or give me death.' 'Resistance to tyrants is obedience to God.' The time has come. He was ready for 'war to the knife, and knife to the hilt.'"[43] Marsh's reporting of *these* references without mention of more recent slave insurrections or Garnet's own enslavement paints Garnet as having taken "flights of fancy."[44] Rather than addressing potential Madison Washingtons and Joseph Cinques, or even his own family history, Marsh figures Garnet as addressing "a gang of crushed and imbruted slaves, despoiled of all rights, and without the means of successful resistance" as if they were or could ever become revolutionaries. Instead of an address to "brethren" from a collective with shared intellectual, familial, and political stakes, Marsh reconstructs an address coming from a delusional demagogue who "did not forget, however, that Mason and Dixon's line was some hundreds of miles south of him and his family."[45]

Focusing on Garnet individually rather than on the convention as a whole allowed Marsh to turn the event into a battle of wills and character and reduced the convention's political stakes to a narrowly defined abolitionism. Marsh does not note the strong consensus around starting a Black press, convening national conventions annually and supporting state conventions, establishing a corps of traveling lecturers, or acknowledging that "the disabilities of the nominally free people in this country flow from slavery" (22). That these resolutions were "read and adopted without debate" (21) underscores how widely delegates shared the sense that abolition was just one aspect of Black activism. It also reminds us that our own scholarly tendency to refer to Black activists as abolitionists effaces Black activism and flattens a multivalent range of activities. Such was the case in Marsh's report, and it reinforced the sense that white activists had much to say about enslaved Black people but very little to free Black citizens and that Black activism was best understood as a subset of and answerable to white organizations, not Black communities.

Marsh's dismissive tone and trade in anti-Black tropes cannot be underestimated, as his account's publication in the *Liberator* gave it wide circulation and authority that could confirm foregone conclusions drawn by those not in attendance and could authorize others to inflict even more damage.[46] His narrative enabled Chapman, who did not attend the convention, to treat it as a failure of the organizers to resist the "bad counsels" of white men, particularly the Liberty Party.[47] "Little must the man of color have reflected," Chapman benevolently warns in a September 22, 1843, editorial, "who does not see that the white man who now stimulates his feelings of revenge" would abandon "him, should he be weak and rash enough to yield to such promptings."[48] Far from a master orator carrying an audience, Chapman castigates Garnet as an emotionally "enchained" mouthpiece for the Liberty Party. Chapman's language—"weak and rash," overstimulated, lacking the capacity for reflection, susceptible to emotional manipulation—combines misogynist and racist coding that placed Black men in the position of the "weaker sex" in need of direction (and perhaps unprepared for public scrutiny); echoes Thomas Jefferson, who in *Notes on the State of Virginia* famously claimed that slaves' "existence appears to participate more of sensation than reflection"; and, as I discuss in the next section, erases Black women altogether while elevating white voices.[49] Chapman positions herself, the

Liberator (in her capacity as acting editor), and the American Anti-Slavery Society (AASS) as the only institutions authorized to sanction and manage Black voices and bodies.

Chapman's attacks, and even the *Advertiser*'s attention to presentation over substance, also underscore the absence of a prominent Black newspaper, such as the *Colored American*, an institution that simultaneously chronicled Black citizenship practices, invited critical debate among Black folk, and provided necessary counters to white high-handedness.[50] As the 1843 convention's Committee upon the Press argued, a healthy press allowed members of a national Black community to speak to and for themselves "and correct the false views and sentiments entertained of us" (28). When the *National Anti-Slavery Standard* launched similar ripostes against the New York state conventions in 1840 and 1841, the *Colored American* dedicated space to rebuttals and printed Black opinions for and against the gatherings from "Sidney," James McCune Smith, and William Whipper.[51] At the same time, the paper published editorials and letters directly challenging the *National Anti-Slavery Standard*'s characterizations and the AASS's apparent unwillingness to place Black activists in leadership positions.[52] Conventioneers did not have to argue for the reflection that went into shaping a convention, because the *Colored American* showed them engaging in that process from the start. A Black paper with similar institutional heft did not exist in 1843, leaving the convention organizers—former editors of the *Colored American* among them—without a print venue comparable to the *Liberator* through which to consolidate and mount a consistent defense. Subsequent Colored Conventions would benefit from the presence of the *North Star*, *Frederick Douglass' Paper*, the *Aliened American*, the *Provincial Freeman*, and other papers that were not official organs of Colored Conventions but that nevertheless had cultural capital and wider circulation.[53]

Chapman's condescension and her refusal to recognize Black political agency outside of abolitionism forced Garnet to defend the very nature of Black public discourse, while the convention's rejection and vacuum left by the *Colored American*'s closure forced him to do so as an individual. Had the convention adopted the "Address" or had a Black newspaper championed his autonomy, if not his message, Garnet might have been less susceptible to ad hominem attacks, or at the very least, Chapman and others would have had to take on more than one Black opponent. As it was, Garnet was simultaneously isolated and made into a symbol for the follies of Black activism. Garnet recognized these stakes, and his response to Chapman in the *Emancipator and Republican* (reprinted in the *Liberator* on December 8, 1843) excoriates her for attempting "to sink me again to the condition of a *slave*": "If it has come to this, that I must think and act as you do, because you are an abolitionist, or be exterminated by your thunder, then I do not hesitate to say that your abolitionism is abject slavery."[54] What good was abolitionism if its white practitioners expected Black people to become their institutional and intellectual dependents? At the heart of his response, Garnet declares his intellectual independence "either from the men of the West, or the women of the East" and defends his right to choose his own path. Douglass would express similar sentiments over a decade later, when he noted in *My Bondage and My Freedom* (1855) white leaders' admonition to "give us the facts . . . we will take care of the philosophy."[55] While these moments rightly draw the eye, however, one of Garnet's most critical moments is subtler, but no less sharp. It depends on readers' attention to his revealing that he did in fact consult with others while composing the "Address to the Slaves," including his wife, Julia Williams.

Julia Williams Garnet: Critic and Collaborator

When Garnet responded to Chapman, he revealed that he consulted two people: "One was a colored brother, who did not give me a single word of counsel, and the other was my wife; and if she did counsel me, it is no matter, for 'we twain are one flesh.'"[56] In so doing, Garnet gives hints at Julia Williams's potential contributions to the "Address to the Slaves" as among the first to critique it and makes her presence part of his counter to Chapman. Garnet's note that her contribution was of "no matter" illustrates the ease with which women's voices might have been heard and incorporated into a convention's proceedings and simultaneously taken for granted as not requiring official citation. While dismissive on the face, however, it also suggests that her contribution might indeed have been substantive. Why mention her, if not to signal an intellectual debt? What if Williams's name was itself an authenticating document, both a rhetorical barb thrown in Chapman's face and a signal to Boston's Black activist community, female antislavery community, and the AASS more broadly, one that depends on Williams's presence and very visible activism to underscore that Garnet was not alone in his refusal to be an intellectual "slave"? To begin to answer some of these questions, I offer an extended discussion of Williams's public life leading up to the 1843 convention. Williams's experience with organizing and crafting addresses for antislavery conventions would have made her an ideal consultant as Garnet drafted the "Address," and her history would have made her the perfect cosigner in a response to Chapman and others.

By the time Amos Beman performed the Garnets' marriage ceremony on August 19, 1841, in Troy, New York, Williams had already developed an activist career and network as wide ranging—if not as visible in print archives—as Garnet's. Williams was born in 1811 in Charleston, South Carolina, and her family moved to Boston, Massachusetts, at some point during her childhood.[57] During these early Boston years, Williams might have read Walker's *Liberator* articles and the *Appeal*, and she may have heard or read Maria Stewart's lectures. Stewart in particular was active in Boston when Williams would have been in her early twenties, and I can only speculate about whether Williams, an ardent student and scholar, would have been a member of Boston's Afric-American Female Intelligence Society. If she was, she might have heard Stewart proclaim, "I am willing to die for the cause that I have espoused," during her address to that society in 1832, a tantalizing connection that could situate Stewart's influence on the "Address" more concretely alongside Walker's.[58] Williams's subsequent activities certainly suggest her sympathies with Stewart, for she seemed always at the vanguard of fights around Black uplift. She was a student at Prudence Crandall's School for Negro Girls from 1833 to 1834, when the combination of white violence and litigation forced the school's closure. Williams then continued her education at the short-lived Noyes Academy in 1835, where she met Garnet along with others who would become prominent leaders within the Colored Conventions: Alexander Crummell, Thomas Sidney, and Thomas Paul Jr. She was there and active with a crutch-bearing, shotgun-wielding Garnet in protecting Noyes students as a white mob destroyed the academy's buildings.[59] A year later, Williams and Garnet would meet again in New York City, where they were delegates at the American Female Anti-Slavery Society and the AASS conventions, respectively. Henry would describe Julia in an 1837 letter to Crummell: "Modest and chaste. She seems to have everything which beautifys [sic] a female. A good christian [sic], and a scholar."[60] The letter leaves the impression that Henry viewed Julia, a year his senior, as his intellectual superior. These connections demonstrate not only Williams's determination but also the many institutional networks linking Black activist cohorts and generations, from academies and literary societies to newspapers and conventions.

Williams was as experienced in Boston as Garnet was in New York, and like Garnet, she was likely experiencing how white organizations could leverage Black visibility but also mute or ignore Black voices. As Garnet was making a name for himself organizing and speaking for Black activists and the Liberty Party in New York State, Williams was similarly engaged in local and national organizing through the Boston Female Anti-Slavery Society (BFASS). The BFASS was an interracial organization founded in 1833 that engaged in multiple activities, including organizing antislavery fairs, funding a Samaritan Asylum and a school for Black children, and issuing addresses that combined calls for immediate abolitionism with feminist critique.[61] Williams taught at Martha and Lucy Ball's school for "young ladies of color" and represented the BFASS as one of its two Black delegates at the 1837 and 1839 antislavery conventions.[62]

Williams was not only a prominently visible figure in the BFASS but also a rising figure in Black Boston. As Anne Warren Weston (Maria Weston Chapman's sister) put it, "the coloured people regard[ed] [Julia Williams] as one of themselves," making her an ideal choice as a delegate and an important member of the BFASS (even if tokenized in print).[63] Williams was named to the 1837 convention's committee charged with revising an "Address to Free Colored Americans" along with several other attendees including Rebecca Downing and Sarah M. Grimké (though their addition to the committee may have been more a symbolic gesture, since the address had already been read and accepted).[64] Williams, then, was well known within Black activist circles and to Boston abolitionists, including Chapman (a chief organizer of the BFASS) and William Lloyd Garrison, with whom she traveled to the 1837 convention in New York.[65]

While Garnet was based in a Black New York activist community with mentors such as Theodore S. Wright and Gerrit Smith who supported his commitment to the clergy and to political activism, Chapman and Weston essentially isolated Williams in Boston when the antislavery establishment split in part over women's participation and the role of the clergy in antislavery activism. The two flagged her as one of the few Black women to vote against them, as the BFASS fractured into pro- and anti-Garrison factions in the late 1830s. Williams was apparently so outspoken in her support of Black clergymen and the role of churches in Black activism more generally that white Garrisonians pressured Boston's Black leaders into disavowing her and projects associated with her. In a December 15, 1839, letter, Weston notes with satisfaction, "Some of the colored men would not contribute to Julia Williams' school because she" supported an anti-Garrison organization, leading to the school's closure.[66] Weston's lack of concern for the collateral damage is clear in her reaction: "I thought that this was well."[67] One could imagine that from Williams's perspective, divisions within a largely white antislavery establishment affected Black men's willingness to contribute to an institution dedicated to serving Black children and Black girls in particular. Her experiences during the height of the BFASS might have shown her the power of interracial organizing in securing funds for community work and carving out space for women's (or white women's) rights, but it would also have given her insights, similar to those Garnet expressed, into how easily Black interests as articulated by Black people could become pieces maneuvered within and for white abolitionist politics.

Garnet, Chapman, and at least some of the *Liberator*'s readers knew Williams's Boston history. Mentioning Williams in his response to Chapman signaled (in a not so subtle way for those in the know) that Garnet was not alone in his refusal to submit to white guidance and that previous attempts by Chapman and others to control Black activists had contributed to the dissolution of organizations such as the BFASS and the Balls' school. Neither Chapman nor the *Liberator* spoke for all abolitionists. Neither Garnet nor Williams would temper their activities to please a white abolitionist establishment.

At the same time, this history and Williams's prominence suggest that Garnet's allusion to her in this context (to a Boston antislavery audience and in response to Chapman in particular) was more than a simple aside. Williams was a highly visible figure in these circles, both because of her brilliance and because of how white activists would have rendered her hypervisible. She was also a fixture in Boston's free Black community and quickly becoming one in New York. In that sense, invoking Williams acts as both rebuke and, perhaps more interesting, authorization. Absent the convention's imprimatur or a prominent Black newspaper to support Garnet, Julia Williams stands in as a cosigner in a way that prefigures Garnet's use of David Walker's *Appeal* to authorize his publication of the 1848 edition of the "Address." And, maybe, that's all Garnet needed. Where Garnet's "brother" offered little in the way of assistance (and maybe name impact), Williams provided both intellectual and institutional support that, while rendered nearly invisible in Garnet's language, would have been clear to those familiar with her.

If, as Stanley Harrold notes, "Garnet's letter reveals the angst that led to the outraged masculinity of his Address to the Slaves," Williams's presence in the letter offers a trace of her own "angst" and anger at constantly having to respond not just to enslavement, northern racism, and colonization but also to racism within white abolitionist ranks, feminist and otherwise.[68] As Manisha Sinha aptly notes in her recent history of abolitionism, the moment at the very least suggests that "the notion of appeals to slave resistance as a masculinist discourse must be rethought. Black women, it seems, were no less militant."[69] While Garnet's stated audience might have been his Black "brethren," Williams's own history and their collaboration suggests the document had roots in a vision of Black activism that Henry and Julia shared. Williams, for instance, had a sister, Diana, who was still enslaved in South Carolina and whom she and Garnet would help gain freedom in the late 1850s.[70]

More broadly, Williams's collaborations with Garnet once they were married point to women's participation in the Colored Conventions (organizing local meetings and fairs, editing and drafting documents, overseeing activities while their husbands traveled as lecturers and delegates, building a literate political base, etc.) even when they were not in the conventions or the minutes. And this practice was not rare. Harriet Johnson Myers, for instance, "provided a skilled editorial hand" for Stephen A. Myers's writing (or writing attributed to him) in the *Northern Star and Freeman's Advocate* and managed their household in Albany, a major station on the Underground Railroad.[71] In a similar vein, the fact that Garnet singled Williams out as one of two who had read the "Address" and the only one who may have offered substantive critique suggests she may also have had a hand in vetting and crafting other addresses and documents for conventions and other venues from the early 1840s on. Garnet biographer Martin B. Pasternak describes these years as an activist and intellectual partnership: "Julia shared most church activities with her husband. Generally, she taught the adult reading program while Garnet instructed the children. Henry ran a Young Man's Literary Association, while Julia headed the ladies auxiliary. They shared the teaching responsibilities in the Sabbath School. On the numerous occasions when Garnet was out of town, Julia ran the programs herself."[72] In 1849 Williams directed a fair in aid of the *Impartial Citizen*, a paper edited by Samuel Ringgold Ward. The fair, held September 11–13 in Syracuse, New York, included singing and speaking and was organized by people familiar to the Colored Conventions, including Martha M. Wright, J. W. Loguen, and Mary A. Jeffrey.[73] These activities in Troy, Syracuse, and elsewhere also suggest that she played a key role in creating infrastructure for the 1847 National Convention of Colored People, held in Troy. This history compels us to acknowledge and find ways of documenting how other women participated in crafting Colored Conventions' statements and ideological positions and contributed to their infrastructure, not just as influencers but rather as uncredited collaborators: writers, critics, listeners, and intellectual pillars.[74]

1848 and 1865: Working through Multiple Editions

I have built the above analysis based on passages common to the 1848 and 1865 editions of "An Address to the Slaves," because the overlap points to sentiments most likely derived from an 1843 source. Yet the two printed editions of the "Address" differ significantly in key moments. The 1848 edition includes the proviso that enslaved people should not "attempt a revolution with the sword, because it would be INEXPEDIENT." [75] This passage might be original to the 1843 delivery, the committee might have suggested it in 1843, or Garnet might have added it sometime between the convention and the 1848 publication, perhaps in response to the 1847 Troy convention's "Report on the Committee of Abolition."[76] The version of the address James McCune Smith included in his introduction to Garnet's 1865 *Memorial Discourse*, however, does not include this proviso. It offers instead one of the most direct and most quoted passages of the "Address": "Brethren, arise, arise! Strike for your lives and liberties. Now is the day and the hour" (see table 6.1).[77]

How should we parse these changes, and what do they mean for how we read the "Address" and the Colored Conventions? Harrold has argued that either Smith or Garnet revised portions of the 1865 edition to reflect the post–Civil War, pre–Thirteenth Amendment climate. That Smith or Garnet would update the number of enslaved referenced in the text from 3 million (1848) to 4 million (1865) and call on freed people to "strike for your lives and liberties" rather than wait for federal action makes sense. Similarities between Marsh's 1843 account and the 1865 edition, however, complicate this timeline. Marsh quotes Garnet as having called on slaves to "strike for liberty" during the 1843 delivery, a phrase that's absent from the 1848 printing and one of the few relatively direct quotations from someone who witnessed the first reading. This phrasing appears in the 1865 edition, exactly where the inexpedient proviso appears in the 1848 printing. Whether the passage was in the 1843 delivery depends on how willing one is to rely on Marsh's phrasing. Even so, the correspondence suggests that the 1865 edition may more accurately reflect the "Address" as delivered. There is, then, at least one other possibility: Garnet may have provided Smith with an earlier manuscript, which

TABLE 6.1. Content and typographical comparison between the 1848 and 1865 editions of Garnet's "Address to the Slaves"

1848	1865
We do not advise you to attempt a revolution with the sword, because it would be INEXPEDIENT. Your numbers are too small, and moreover the rising spirit of the age, and the spirit of the gospel, are opposed to war and bloodshed. But from this moment cease to labor for tyrants who will not remunerate you. Let every slave throughout the land do this, and the days of slavery are numbered. You cannot be more oppressed than you have been—you cannot suffer greater cruelties than you have already. RATHER DIE FREE-MEN. THAN LIVE TO BE SLAVES. Remember that you are THREE MILLIONS.	Brethren, arise, arise! Strike for your lives and liberties. Now is the day and the hour. Let every slave throughout the land do this, and the days of slavery are numbered. You cannot be more oppressed than you have been—you cannot suffer greater cruelties than you have already. *Rather die freemen than live to be slaves.* Remember that you are FOUR MILLIONS!

he, Smith, or both may have updated for *A Memorial Discourse*. In that case, the passage would reflect both an update to spur newly freed people and the reintroduction of Garnet's 1843 militancy in a more receptive post–Civil War world. It would suggest consistency in Garnet's logic but also support the idea that the "slightly modified" 1848 edition more directly reflected collective sentiments, the 1843 convention's collaborative effort, and their effects on Garnet's print practices at the time.[78]

The distinction might seem insignificant or esoteric, given other passages in both editions calling on enslaved people to defend themselves against recalcitrant enslavers. Both, for instance, include the admonition, "There is not much hope of Redemption without the shedding of blood. If you must bleed, let it all come at once—rather, *die freemen, than live to be slaves*."[79] Methodologically, however, these are two *editions*, and we need to read them as such, accounting for reception and context. At the same time, we need to develop diachronic analyses of how and with what other texts the "Address" circulated and was received over time in a way that sets the editions in conversation. And we need to develop synchronic narratives based on the texts' overall intellectual grounding in a longer Colored Conventions movement that continued through the 1890s yet drew on many of the themes articulated in the 1830s: citizenship, economic empowerment, overcoming white supremacy, and education.

Individuals and groups endorsing the "Address" between 1848 and 1865 were endorsing the 1848 edition, with the proviso and presented as an addendum to David Walker's *Appeal*, not the more direct "call to rebellion" found in the 1865 edition. They would have read it in the wake of the U.S.-Mexico War, new anti-Black legislation in states across the country, and the prospect that enslavement was spreading despite decades of antislavery agitation. Readers of the 1865 edition of the "Address" would have encountered it in the middle section of a biographical narrative hailing Garnet's oratorical successes in the (failed) struggle for unqualified suffrage in New York State that framed the "Address," as I do in this essay, as continuous with the New York Colored Conventions. In contrast to Garnet's 1840s listeners and readers, Smith *emphasizes* the violent undertones of the "Address," suggesting that John Brown financed its 1848 publication. Smith packaged the text for newly emancipated and newly literate readers (and listeners) as evidentiary in nature, an object "most elegant [in] style" and an "heir-loom of their past condition" "to be published and handed down to future generations" as a bridge between ante- and postbellum activism, as much memorial as call.[80] In so doing, Smith connected implicitly suffrage activism in New York conventions to calls for full citizenship and enfranchisement in 1865 and the explosion of Colored Conventions being organized around the country. In that sense, the "Address" constitutes part of a syllabus for understanding antebellum Black activism and for shaping an ongoing agenda.

This context and the shifts in content suggest that we should be more vigilant in identifying which text we're citing and for what purposes. Treating either document as if it were a direct transcription of the speech delivered in 1843, as if the "Address" were solely Garnet's creation, or as if the editions are interchangeable ignores a protracted and collaborative composition and publication process and anachronistically reads Garnet's most forthright printed call for insurrection in the 1865 edition as if readers had access to it in the 1840s and 1850s. Some collections already do this work. The *Black Abolitionist Papers* reprints the 1848 edition, and Philip Foner and Robert Branham cite their reprint of the "Address" in *Lift Every Voice: African American Oratory, 1787–1900* (1987) as the 1865 version from *A Memorial Discourse*, with an explanatory note referring readers to "an alternate version" in the *Black Abolitionist Papers*. That seems to be the ideal way to deal with the "Address" bibliographically. Yet other foundational anthologies—Herbert Aptheker's *A Documentary History*; Sterling Stuckey's *The Ideological Origins of Black Nationalism* (1972); and Richard Newman, Patrick Rael, and Phillip Lapsansky's *Pamphlets of Protest* (2001), to name a few—reprint the 1865 edition either as the 1843 address (Aptheker) or with 1848 as the publication date (Newman, Rael, and Lapsansky). More recently, the latest edition of the *Norton Anthology of African American Literature* (third edition, 2014) also prints the 1865 edition with 1848 as the publication date. And though it is difficult to canvass all the digital instances, it appears that pages featuring transcriptions without an accompanying facsimile of the source material are susceptible to the same error.

Scholarship on Garnet's "Address" citing these versions may not note the differences, though whether a work quotes the 1848 figure of "three million" slaves or the 1865 figure of "four million" provides an easy identifier. The discrepancy does not invalidate these studies or anthologies; they remain fundamental to our understanding of antebellum Black writing, and we should continue consulting and citing them. We might still read "An Address to the Slaves" as a call to rebellion, and it certainly remains a key text of early Black Nationalism. But we should also attend to which edition a source cites and to which edition or moment we are referring in making our own arguments about the "Address," the conventions, and the audiences that either embraced or rejected it. Not doing so unintentionally recapitulates the tactics detractors used to discredit the 1843 convention: flattening the history Garnet himself encodes into the title of the "Address" and forcing Garnet (again) to represent ideas developed in collaboration with and in response to specific historical moments.

My point here is not that one edition is more accurate than the other but rather that attending to their distinctive differences opens new avenues for analysis, particularly when coupled with print and material culture methodologies. The changes, for instance, extend to typography (a key factor in distinguishing new editions from new printings). As Marcy Dinius's work on Walker's *Appeal* demonstrates, such changes can be significant and intentional.[81] Garnet's famous concluding lines about resistance show marked typographical differences that should lead us to think about Garnet's use of Walker's *Appeal* as a thematic and formal resource (see table 6.2). The 1865 edition adheres more to Walker's escalating typography, suggesting a text calibrated for public reading, as Garnet's 1843 original was meant to be circulated among enslaved people or, just as likely, was meant for public reading among newly freed people in 1865. Paragraph breaks in this edition punctuate Vesey's, Turner's, Cinque's, and Madison Washington's places in the "constellation of true heroism."[82] While the 1848 edition does not use escalating typography, it does use changes in type—particularly small caps— more frequently to give emphasis. Overall typographic differences in passages that the editions share might also suggest shifting points of emphasis (as they do in Walker's *Appeal*). The 1848 edition, for instance, seems to use small caps to accentuate biblical principles, while the 1865 edition does not (see table 6.3). We may never know who was responsible for the changes from one edition to the next, or the balance between Garnet's meaning, expense, and available typeface, but this print history does underscore that the "Address" was collaborative from the start and each printing was deeply engaged with the events of the moment.

Ironically, only after Garnet printed the "Address" with Walker's *Appeal* in 1848 as a stand-alone book did conventions—state conventions—endorse

TABLE 6.2. Consistent bolded small caps vs. intensifying type in the 1848 and 1865 editions of Garnet's "Address to the Slaves"

1848	1865
Let your motto be **RESISTANCE!** **RESISTANCE!**	Let your motto be resistance! *resistance!*
RESISTANCE!—No oppressed people have ever secured their liberty without resistance.	RESISTANCE! No oppressed people have ever secured their liberty without resistance.

TABLE 6.3. Small caps to emphasize religious references in the 1848 edition of Garnet's "Address to the Slaves"

1848	1865
It is impossible, like the children of Israel, to make a grand Exodus from the land of bondage. THE PHARAOHS ARE ON BOTH SIDES OF THE BLOOD-RED WATERS!	It is impossible, like the children of Israel, tomake a grand exodus from the land of bondage. The Pharaohs are on both sides of the blood-red waters!

it.[83] While the 1848 Pennsylvania state convention does not mention Garnet or Walker directly, the convention's "Appeals" to white voters and Colored citizens invoke the two rhetorically. The next year, the 1849 Ohio state convention resolved, "We still adhere to the doctrine of urging the slave to leave immediately with his hoe on his shoulder, for a land of liberty, and would accordingly recommend that five hundred copies of Walker's *Appeal*, and Henry H. Garnet's Address to the slaves, be obtained in the name of the convention, and gratuitously circulated."[84] This resounding endorsement signals two shifts: generational (David Jenkins appears to be the only holdover from the 1843 convention) and political (Ohio's new Black Laws along with the annexation of Texas and the U.S.-Mexico War suggested that no amount of Black meekness would stave off white supremacist legal and physical aggression). And Douglass, once Garnet's most vocal opposition, also endorsed the *Appeal* and the "Address" and reprinted Garnet's biography of Walker in the *North Star*.[85] By 1851, Charles H. Langston figured the link between northern Black politics and emancipation in explicitly violent terms: "I would vote under the United States Constitution on the same principle . . . that I would call on every slave, from Maryland to Texas, to arise and assert their *liberties*,

148   DERRICK R. SPIRES

and cut their masters' throats if they attempt again to reduce them to slavery."[86] By 1865, Smith would praise the "Address" in his biographical preface to Garnet's *Memorial Discourse*, noting that Black people should "adopt it as their watchword of conduct should any" person or institution "attempt to fasten another gyve upon their now fetterless limbs."[87]

"An Address to the Slaves," then, is a living document, and each appearance—even in its modern anthologizing—speaks to a particular historical moment even as it documents the past. The September 1964 issue of *Ebony* magazine, for instance, featured an account of the 1843 Buffalo convention by Lerone Bennett Jr. describing Garnet as "the Thomas Paine of America's second revolution." That same issue also featured the article "The Mystery of Malcolm X," a profile outlining Malcolm X's activism after his break with the Nation of Islam.[88] We might rightly say that Garnet's "Address"—and the Colored Conventions movement—was indeed a "[flight] of fancy," a counterfactual performative speech act intended to conjure the "victorious army" Garnet was and continues to address *through* the act of addressing it.[89] And, as the ongoing circulation of the "Address" indicates, that army keeps marching on.

NOTES

1. Henry Highland Garnet, "Address to the Slaves of the United States of America. (Rejected by the National Convention, 1843)," in *Walker's Appeal, with a Brief Sketch of His Life: And Also Garnet's Address to the Slaves of the United States of America*, by Henry Highland Garnet and David Walker (New York: J. H. Tobitt, 1848), 90, 94, *Slavery and Anti-Slavery: A Transnational Archive*, Gale (DS4103107272); Henry Highland Garnet, "An Address to the Slaves of the United States of America. (Rejected by the National Convention, 1843)," in *A Memorial Discourse Delivered in the Hall of the House of Representatives, Washington City, D.C., on Sabbath, February 12, 1865 with an Introduction by James McCune Smith, M.D.* (Philadelphia: J. M. Wilson, 1865), 49. Subsequent citations give corresponding pages for the 1848 and 1865 editions where they align.

2. Herbert Aptheker, *A Documentary History of the Negro People in the United States*, vol. 1, *From Colonial Times through the Civil War*, 7th ed. (New York: Citadel, 1969), 226; Sterling Stuckey, ed., *The Ideological Origins of Black Nationalism* (Boston: Beacon, 1972), 17; Stanley Harrold, *The Rise of Aggressive Abolitionism: Addresses to the Slaves* (Lexington: University Press of Kentucky, 2004); Manisha Sinha, *The Slave's Cause: A History of Abolition* (New Haven, CT: Yale University Press, 2016), 418–19. The scholarship on Garnet's "Address to the Slaves" is extensive and varied. This essay draws mainly on Aptheker, *Documentary History*; Leslie Alexander, *African or American? Black Identity and Political Activism in New York City, 1784–1861* (Urbana: University of Illinois Press, 2008); Howard Holman Bell, *A Survey of the Negro Convention Movement, 1830–1861* (New York: Arno, 1969); John Ernest, *Liberation Historiography: African American Writers and the Challenge of History, 1794–1861* (Chapel Hill: University of North Carolina Press, 2004); Phyllis Field, *The Politics of Race in New York: The Struggle for Black Suffrage in the Civil War Era* (Ithaca, NY: Cornell University Press, 1982); Eddie S. Glaude Jr., *Exodus! Religion, Race, and Nation in Early Nineteenth-Century Black America* (Chicago: University of Chicago Press, 2000); Harrold, *Rise of Aggressive Abolitionism*; Douglas A. Jones, *The Captive Stage: Performance and the*

Proslavery Imagination of the Antebellum North (Ann Arbor: University of Michigan Press, 2014); Leslie Harris, *In the Shadow of Slavery: African Americans in New York City, 1626-1863* (Chicago: University of Chicago Press, 2003); Leon F. Litwack, *North of Slavery: The Negro in the Free States 1790–1860* (Chicago: University of Chicago Press, 1961); Earl Ofari, *Let Your Motto Be Resistance: The Life and Thought of Henry Highland Garnet* (Boston: Beacon, 1972); Martin B. Pasternak, *Rise Now and Fly to Arms: The Life of Henry Highland Garnet* (New York: Garland, 1995); Joel Schor, *Henry Highland Garnet: A Voice of Black Radicalism in the Nineteenth Century* (Westport, CT: Greenwood, 1977); and David E. Swift, *Black Prophets of Justice: Activist Clergy before the Civil War* (Baton Rouge: Louisiana State University Press, 1989).

3. For foundational overviews of the tensions within the Colored Conventions, see Bell, *Survey*, 27–82; and Jane H. Pease and William H. Pease, "Negro Conventions and the Problem of Black Leadership," *Journal of Black Studies* 2, no. 1 (September 1971): 29–44. See also Alexander, *African or American?*, 63; and Glaude, *Exodus!*, 116.

4. *Proceedings of the National Convention of Colored People and Their Friends, Held in Troy, N.Y. on the 6th, 7th, 8th and 9th October, 1847*, 10, 31, in *Minutes of the Proceedings of the National Negro Conventions, 1830–1864*, ed. Howard Holman Bell (New York: Arno Press and the *New York Times*, 1869); also available at Colored Conventions Project, http://coloredconventions.org/items/show/279.

5. For a slightly different reading of Garnet's "Address" and performance, see Douglas A. Jones, *Captive Stage*, 114–24.

6. See Erica Ball's essay in this volume; and Carolyne King and Erica L. Ball, *The "Conventions" of the Conventions: Political Rituals and Traditions*, digital exhibit, Colored Conventions Project, http://coloredconventions.org/exhibits/show/the-performance-of-convention.

7. See, e.g., the "Conventional Address, to the Free Colored Inhabitants of the United States," from the 1833 Convention for the Improvement of the Free People of Colour, in Bell, *Minutes*, 31–36 (also available at Colored Conventions Project, http://coloredconventions.org/items/show/275); and the 1840 *Convention of the Colored Inhabitants of the State of New York, August 18–20, 1840*, in Foner and Walker, *Proceedings*, 1:5–26 (also available at Colored Conventions Project, http://coloredconventions.org/items/show/620).

8. For a book-length analysis of the relation between the three addresses from Smith, Garrison, and Garnet, see Harrold, *Rise of Aggressive Abolitionism*.

9. See Ernest, *Liberation Historiography*, 247–50; and Glaude, *Exodus!*, 152–60.

10. See "Address of the New York State Convention to Their Colored Fellow Citizens," reprinted in *Colored American* (New York), November 21, 1840.

11. See also Carla Peterson's essay in this volume; Derrick R. Spires, *The Practice of Citizenship: Black Politics and Print Culture in the Early United States* (Philadelphia: University of Pennsylvania Press, 2019), chap. 2.

12. *Convention of the Colored Inhabitants of the State of New York, August 18–20, 1840*, in Foner and Walker, *Proceedings*, 1:19–20; also available at http://coloredconventions.org/items/show/620. On the New York state conventions, see Carla L. Peterson's essay in this volume; Alexander, *African or American?*, 97–120; and Derrick R. Spires, "Imagining a State of Fellow Citizens: Early African American Politics of Publicity in the Black State Conventions," in *Early African American Print Culture in Theory and in Practice*, ed. Jordan Alexander Stein and Lara Cohen (University of Pennsylvania Press, 2012), 274–89.

13. *Convention of the Colored Inhabitants of the State of New York*, 1:16.

14. *Minutes of the National Convention of Colored Citizens: Held at Buffalo on the 15th, 16th, 17th, and 19th of August, 1843*, in Bell, *Minutes*, 4; also available at Colored Conventions Project, http://coloredconventions.org/items/show/278. All subsequent citations of this work in this essay are included parenthetically in the text.

15. Henry Highland Garnet, "Address" (1848), 94; Henry Highland Garnet, "Address" (1865), 48. For an insightful analysis of Garnet's reprint of the *Appeal*, see Lori Leavell, "Recirculating Black Milantancy in Word and Image: Henry Highland Garnet's 'Volume of Fire," *Book History* 20 (2017): 150–87.

16. David Walker, "Appeal to the Colored Citizens of the World" in Garnet and Walker, *Walker's Appeal*, 27.

17. Henry Highland Garnet, "Address" (1848), 92; Henry Highland Garnet, "Address" (1865), 47.

18. Henry Highland Garnet, "Address" (1848), 94; Henry Highland Garnet, "Address" (1865), 47.

19. Henry Highland Garnet, "Address" (1848), 94; Henry Highland Garnet, "Address" (1865), 48–49.

20. Henry Highland Garnet, "Address" (1848), 94; Henry Highland Garnet, "Address" (1865), 48–49.

21. Henry Highland Garnet, "Address" (1848), 95; Henry Highland Garnet, "Address" (1865), 50.

22. Henry Highland Garnet, "Address" (1848), 93; Henry Highland Garnet, "Address" (1865), 48.

23. *Convention of the Colored Inhabitants of the State of New York*, 1:15.

24. Delegates demonstrate this concern elsewhere when they vote to have a failed resolution affirming birthright citizenship "expunged from the minutes," because, as several delegates argued, even debating the point potentially legitimated counterclaims (17, 24).

25. *Convention of the Colored Inhabitants of the State of New York*, 1:16.

26. William Lloyd Garrison, "To the Public," *Liberator* (Boston), January 1, 1831, 1, ProQuest American Periodicals, Document ID 91273238.

27. Ofari, *Let Your Motto*, 43.

28. Douglas A. Jones, *Captive Stage*, 35.

29. *Proceedings of the National Convention of Colored People and Their Friends*, 31.

30. William Cheek and Aimee Lee Cheek, "John Mercer Langston and the Cincinnati Riot of 1841," in *Race and the City: Work, Community, and Protest in Cincinnati, 1820–1970*, ed. Henry Louis Taylor Jr. (Urbana: University of Illinois Press, 1993), 46–49; Nikki M. Taylor, *Frontiers of Freedom: Cincinnati's Black Community, 1802–1860* (Athens: Ohio University Press, 2007), 121–26.

31. Cheek and Cheek, "John Mercer Langston," 49.

32. "Convention of Colored Men," *New York Evangelist*, August 31, 1843. This account quotes from an article on Garnet originally appearing in the *Daily Gazette*.

33. Ray closes the convention minutes with a complaint that delegates' failure to provide the needed funding forced the Publication Committee members to partially fund the printing themselves (39).

34. "Convention of Colored Persons," *Buffalo (NY) Commercial Advertiser*, reprinted in *Emancipator and Free American* (New York), October 12, 1843.

35. "Convention of Colored Persons."

36. "Convention of Colored Persons." Douglas Jones has noted that the 1843 convention illuminates "the power of . . . affect, presence, and theatricality" in the Colored Conventions and Black activism more broadly. See Douglas A. Jones, *Captive Stage*, 118. While the *Emancipator* was a Liberty Party–supporting abolitionist paper based in Boston, the *Advertiser* was a general political weekly. The *Advertiser*'s account also appears in the *Newburyport (MA) Herald* (October 23, 1843). It would seem that the convention and Garnet were of as much interest to a general readership as they were to abolitionist and Black activist circles.

37. "Convention of Colored Persons."

38. "Convention of Colored Persons."

39. "Convention of Colored Persons."

40. E. A. Marsh, "The Colored Convention," *Liberator*, September 8, 1843; Maria Weston Chapman, "The Buffalo Convention of Men of Color," *Liberator*, September 22, 1843. See also Douglas A. Jones, *Captive Stage*, 119–20.

41. Marsh, "Colored Convention."

42. Henry Highland Garnet, "Address" (1865), 51.

43. Marsh, "Colored Convention."

44. Marsh.

45. Marsh.

46. The *Northern Star and Freeman's Advocate* (Albany, NY), edited by Black activist Stephen A. Myers, based its assessment of the convention and Garnet in part on the *Liberator*'s accounts. "The National Convention," *Northern Star and Freeman's Advocate* reprinted in *Liberator*, September 29, 1843.

47. Chapman, "Buffalo Convention"; Henry Highland Garnet, "A Letter to Mrs. Maria W. Chapman," *Emancipator and Free American* (New York), November 30, 1843.

48. Chapman, "Buffalo Convention."

49. Thomas Jefferson, *Writings* (New York: Library Classics of America, 1984), 270.

50. It's not that no Black papers were in circulation at this time. Myers's *Northern Star and Freeman's Advocate*, for instance, was being published out of Albany. Rather, these papers lacked the *Colored American*'s reach and institutional heft.

51. See Carla L. Peterson's essay in this volume.

52. See Spires, "Imagining," 277–80. For a sampling of this coverage for the 1840 and 1841 New York state conventions, see "Colored Convention," *National Anti-Slavery Standard* (New York), June 18, 1840; "The National Anti-Slavery Standard vs. the Convention," *Colored American*, July 11, 1840; "Samuel Ringgold Ward to Nathaniel Press. Rogers," in *The Black Abolitionist Papers*, ed. C. Peter Ripley (Chapel Hill: University of North Carolina Press, 1985–92), 3:341; "Four Letters by Sidney," in Stuckey, *Ideological Origins*, 149–64; and "Three Letters by William Whipper," in Stuckey, *Ideological Origins*, 252–60.

53. For a discussion of the ways Black papers and Colored Conventions sometimes functioned synergistically, see Eric Gardner, "Early African American Print Culture and the American West," in *Early African American Print Culture*, ed. Lara Langer Cohen and Jordan Alexander Stein (Philadelphia: University of Pennsylvania Press, 2012), 75–89. For a more general discussion on the centrality of Black and antislavery institutions to circulating Black texts, see Joanna Brooks, "The Unfortunates: What the Life Spans of Early Black Books Tell Us about Book History," in Cohen and Stein, *Early African American*, 40–42.

54. Henry Highland Garnet, "Letter." See also Howard Holman Bell, "National Negro Conventions of the Middle 1840's: Moral Suasion vs. Political Action," *Journal of Negro History* 42, no. 4 (October 1957): 247–60; and Harrold, *Rise of Aggressive Abolitionism*, 93–96.

55. Frederick Douglass, *My Bondage and My Freedom* (New York: Miller, Orton, and Mulligan, 1855; Documenting the American South, 2000), 361, https://docsouth.unc.edu/neh/douglass55/douglass55.html.

56. Henry Highland Garnet, "Letter." As far as I can determine, this is Garnet's only reference to Julia Williams in relation to the "Address."

57. Though records on Julia Williams are scarce, the Colored Conventions Project has a developing biography of her life as a part of its mission to recover Black women's activities in the Colored Conventions movement. What I reconstruct here relies on work by Debra Gold Hansen and Ross Pasternack and the smattering of articles and letters mentioning Williams in the 1830s and 1840s. Details on Williams's activities leading up to the 1843 convention can most often be found in scholarship on the Boston Female Anti-Slavery Society and the tensions within what Hansen aptly

calls the "strained sisterhood" between white and Black women abolitionists. See Debra Gold Hansen, "The Boston Female Anti-Slavery Society and the Limits of Gender Politic," in *The Abolitionist Sisterhood: Women's Political Culture in Antebellum America*, ed. Jean Fagan Yellin and John C. Van Horne (Ithaca, NY: Cornell University Press, 1994), 45–66; Debra Gold Hansen, *Strained Sisterhood: Gender and Class in the Boston Female Anti-Slavery Society* (Amherst: University of Massachusetts Press, 1993); Steve Sebzda, "Julia Williams Garnet," in *Prosperity and Politics: Taking Stock of Black Wealth and the 1843 Convention*, by Sarah Patterson, digital exhibit, Colored Conventions Project, https://coloredconventions.org/black-wealth/biographies/julia-williams-garnet; Sinha, *Slave's Cause*, 418; James McCune Smith, "Sketch of the Life of and Labors of Henry Highland Garnet," introduction to Henry Highland Garnet, *Memorial Discourse*; and Pasternak, *Rise Now*, 36.

58. Elizabeth McHenry notes that the society's reception of Stewart was lukewarm at best. Elizabeth McHenry, *Forgotten Readers: Recovering the Lost History of African American Literary Societies* (Durham, NC: Duke University Press, 2002), 68–74. Anne Warren Weston's description of Williams suggests that she was not necessarily a member of Boston's Black elite.

59. Smith, "Sketch," 30; Schor, *Henry Highland Garnet*, 15.

60. Garnet to Crummell, May 13, 1837, Alexander Crummell Papers, Schomburg Collection, New York Public Library, quoted in Swift, *Black Prophets*, 120.

61. Hansen, "Boston Female Anti-Slavery Society," 46–49.

62. Hansen, 46–49.

63. Hansen, *Strained Sisterhood*, 14, 58; Anne Warren Weston to Deborah Weston, April 18, 1837, Rare Books Department, Boston Public Library, http://ark.digital commonwealth.org/ark:/50959/wm117v69p.

64. *Proceedings of the Anti-Slavery Convention of American Women* (New York: W. S. Dorr, 1837), 11.

65. See William Lloyd Garrison to Helen E. Garrison, May 6, 1837, in *A House Dividing against Itself, 1836–1840: The Letters of William Lloyd Garrison*, ed. Louis Ruchames (Cambridge, MA: Belknap Press of Harvard University Press, 1971), 260–61.

66. Hansen, "Boston Female Anti-Slavery Society," 56; Anne Warren Weston to Deborah Weston, April 18, 1837.

67. Anne Warren Weston to Deborah Weston, April 18, 1837.

68. Harrold, *Rise of Aggressive Abolitionism*, 94.

69. Sinha, *Slave's Cause*, 418.

70. The best account of these events I've been able to locate appears in William Gould, *Diary of a Contraband: The Civil War Passage of a Black Sailor* (Stanford, CA: Stanford University Press, 2002), 34–38.

71. See "Harriet Myers," *Anglo-African* (New York), August 26, 1865; and Ripley, *Black Abolitionist Papers*, 3:378n3.

72. Pasternak, *Rise Now*, 36.

73. Julia W. Garnet, "Circular by the Provisional Committee of the Impartial Citizen August 1849," *Impartial Citizen* (Syracuse, NY), September 5, 1849, reprinted in Ripley, *Black Abolitionist Papers*, 4:38–41. See also Martha S. Jones, *All Bound Up Together: The Woman Question in African American Print Culture, 1840–1900* (Chapel Hill: University of North Carolina Press, 2007), 84.

74. Here, I draw on Martha S. Jones's description of a shift from "female influence to the rights of women" over the 1840s; Martha S. Jones, *All Bound Up Together*, 61.

75. Henry Highland Garnet, "Address" (1848), 96.

76. Pease and Pease suggest that Garnet added the passage after the initial delivery to tone the address down in response to criticism, but Bell speculates that "it is probable that not too much revision was made" at the 1843 convention (78). Harrold, however, argues that the passage was likely in the original, based on his reading of

the internal logic of the "Address." See Harrold, *Rise of Aggressive Abolitionism*, 33–35; and Jane H. Pease and William H. Pease, *They Who Would Be Free: Blacks' Search for Freedom, 1830–1861* (New York: Athenaeum, 1974), 239.

77. Henry Highland Garnet, "Address" (1865), 51.

78. Henry Highland Garnet, "Address" (1848), preface on p. 89.

79. Garnet, 94; Henry Highland Garnet, "Address" (1865), 49. But even here punctuation and capitalization differences shift the resonance of words such as "Redemption" (not capitalized in 1865).

80. "Rev. H. H. Garnet's *Memorial Discourse*," *Christian Recorder* (Philadelphia), July 1, 1865; Smith, "Sketch," 52.

81. Marcy J. Dinius, "'Look!! Look!! At This!!!!': The Radical Typography of David Walker's Appeal," *PMLA* 126, no. 1 (2011): 55–72.

82. Henry Highland Garnet, "Address" (1865), 51. The 1848 edition places them in the "constellation of freedom"; Henry Highland Garnet, "Address" (1848), 96.

83. Smith's introduction to *A Memorial Discourse* provides the principal evidence for this association. See Smith, "Sketch," 52.

84. *Minutes and Address of the State Convention of the Colored Citizens of Ohio, Convened at Columbus, January 10th, 11th, 12th, and 13th, 1849*, in Foner and Walker, *Proceedings*, 1:229.

85. "Sketch of the Life and Character of David Walker," *North Star* (Rochester, NY), July 14, 1848, 4.

86. *Minutes and Address of the State Convention of the Colored Citizens of Ohio*, 1:263.

87. Smith, "Sketch," 52.

88. Lerone Bennett Jr., "Pioneers in Protest: Nay-sayer of the Negro Revolt," *Ebony*, September 1964, 67. See also "Garnet beyond the 19th Century," in *Henry Highland Garnet's "Address to the Slaves," and Its Colored Conventions Origins*, by Harrison Graves, Jake Alspaugh, and Derrick Spires, digital exhibit, Colored Conventions Project, https://coloredconventions.org/garnet-address-1843/garnet-beyond-the-19th-century.

89. As Douglas Jones notes, "The performative strives for some sort of change by way of its very enactment or utterance, and in Garnet's case that was the transformation of his listening audience into the insurrectionary body that would begin the work of eradicating slavery with physical might." Douglas A. Jones, *Captive Stage*, 121. See also Spires, "Imagining," 274.

PERFORMING POLITICS, CREATING COMMUNITY

Antebellum Black Conventions
as Political Rituals

Erica L. Ball

Introduction

Specialists in African American history have long recognized the state and national Colored Convention proceedings of the antebellum era to be documents of extraordinary political importance. As early as 1969, in the introduction to his collection *Minutes of the Proceedings of the National Negro Conventions, 1830–1864*, historian Howard Holman Bell declared that antebellum Black conventions must be understood as "the first 'national association for the advancement of colored people.'"[1] Roughly one decade later, in the introduction to their collection of the *Proceedings of the Black State Conventions, 1840–1865*, Philip S. Foner and George E. Walker wrote that "for keen analyses of the issues outlined and for breadth of research and argument," the proceedings offer examples of the most "outstanding political documents of the period."[2] And in recent decades, scholars have irrefutably demonstrated that the antebellum state and national Black conventions were essential for the development of African American political consciousness.

It is no surprise, then, that for the last half century, the minutes of these conventions have served as an invaluable resource for historians investigating the antislavery and civil rights activism of free Blacks living in the antebellum North. Much of this work has focused on analyzing the recurring themes and shifting political stances that defined Black protest thought in the period: debates over whether to prioritize emigration outside the United States or to remain in the country, or whether to pursue interracial coalitions or promote racial separatism, for example. More recently, scholars have turned to antebellum state and national convention proceedings to gain insight into the factors shaping the emergence of a free Black leadership class, the expansion of African American print culture, and the growth of Black women's public activism.[3]

This essay seeks to contribute to this conversation by exploring the ways that the very *conventions* of antebellum Colored Conventions generated meaning for elite and aspiring women and men of African descent living in the nominally free North. Rather than analyzing the competing political arguments and debates printed in the convention proceedings, this chapter considers the possibilities that emerge when we contemplate the significance of the convention as an event itself. Focusing on representative state conventions from Ohio, New York, and Pennsylvania and drawing upon the work of scholars who examine the rites and routines that defined the political culture of the early American republic, this chapter examines the ways that civic traditions and rituals generated political meaning for participants in the state Colored Conventions of the 1840s and 1850s.[4] I argue that antebellum state Colored Conventions must be understood as collective experiences where free Blacks reaffirmed for each other their commitment to antislavery living by embodying the gender-specific republican virtues and personal traits increasingly understood as essential for demonstrations of political capacity. Organized around a set of familiar procedures, customs, and rhetorical strategies, and relying on the active participation and public performances of spectators and delegates alike, conventions served as civic rituals for the northern free Black population, events that simultaneously situated people of African descent within the political culture of the United States and at the vanguard of a diasporic Black nation. In the process, antebellum state Colored Conventions functioned as collective, public demonstrations of a uniquely northern free, Black, middle-class political consciousness.[5]

Race, Gender, and Political Capacity

By the 1840s, when northern free Blacks began meeting in state and national conventions with frequency, political conventions had become an established feature of the American political landscape, popular expressions of the "meeting place democracy" of the era.[6] Indeed, David Gellman and David Quigley note that "one of the most striking features of nineteenth-century American politics was the regularity with which states came together to revise their constitutions," offering an opportunity for those affiliated with the Whig and Democratic Parties to remake the laws of their states.[7] In addition to this proliferation of state constitutional conventions, rank-and-file white men and third-party representatives frequently organized alternative political conventions for their communities. Recognized as "legitimate unofficial bodies" deriving their authority "from the constitutional precedent of the right of the people to assemble and petition the government," these public meetings ranged from less polished spontaneous conventions to more formal gatherings.[8] They offered a space for those with alternative points of view to sidestep the official party system, craft political opinion on their own terms, and represent the wishes of their constituents to elected officials. And their popularity in white communities reflected the extent to which participation in the political process was coming to be understood as an expansive, democratic, white male prerogative rather than a privilege for a small group of aristocratic white male elites.[9]

Men of African descent living in northern states in these years found that even though recent emancipation laws had outlawed slavery in the region, free Black men remained excluded from these and other popular early nineteenth-century rituals of American civic inclusion. In fact, even as elected officials took steps to expand the white male electorate, northern lawmakers simultaneously moved to disenfranchise men of African descent. For example, in 1821, when New York lawmakers removed all property qualifications for the state's white male voters, they limited Black voter eligibility to those few African American men who had lived in the state for three years and owned at least $250 in property. As a result, the size of the Black electorate declined immediately, leaving only 16 of New York City's 12,499 Blacks and 298 of New York State's African Americans eligible to vote in 1826, the year before New York became the last northern state to outlaw slavery. In 1822, Rhode Island's legislature moved to bar African American men from the ballot box, while in 1838, Pennsylvania voters approved new constitutional provisions barring African American men from the polls. And by 1840, with the exception of the New England states of Maine, New Hampshire, Vermont, and Massachusetts, all northern state constitutions severely restricted or prohibited free Black men from voting. Additionally, African American organizations and individuals were generally excluded from participating in the public rituals, processions, and celebrations of public holidays so important to the political culture of the era. And by the 1840s, attacks on free Blacks became an integral part of the way some whites claimed their status as citizens and celebrated national holidays such as Independence Day.[10]

It was this early nineteenth-century political ethos that ensured that Colored Conventions would be understood by northern free Blacks as affairs with a precise set of political meanings. Arguing that by holding conventions, men of African descent could create spaces to represent the wishes of their constituents, hone their political abilities, and articulate a distinct political agenda for the race, supporters of Colored Conventions insisted that northern free Blacks could claim the American convention as a political institution of their own and remake it for the benefit of Black people, both free and enslaved. In keeping with an older eighteenth-century republican vision of civic virtue that based the health and future prospects of the nation on the existence of a class of virtuous, independent men capable of representing the best interests of their family and community, supporters of state Colored Conventions hoped to provide a space for the rising generation of young Black men to hone their political talents, embody ideal Black manliness, and represent the best interests of the race. As an early advocate for Colored Conventions, "Long Island Scribe" wrote in the *Colored American* that conventions were necessary for training "our Statesmen and Lawyers," as well as for "proving that we have political talents."[11] "From the petty town meeting" on up to Congress, the writer pointed out, "our rights are not defended in any of those councils"; thus, Colored Conventions provided an opportunity for free Black men to enact citizenship.[12]

Antebellum conventions, then, served as spaces for delegates to demonstrate Black male political capacity and engage in a complex process of political representation. And for these reasons, state conventions were often publicized and styled as explicitly male and thoroughly political affairs. For example, after declaring that "the object of this Convention is our elevation, moral, intellectual and political," the call for the Ohio state convention of 1849 charged the county committee with the task of "bringing together, to form this Convention, a body of independent, fearless and talented men—men in whose hearts burns unquenchably the love of liberty; and who will permit no surmountable obstacle to work any intermission in their efforts to come at once into the most complete enjoyment of that liberty which they love."[13] Declaring their intention to transact their business "in a manner creditable to ourselves, our immediate constituents," as well as the states in which they lived, delegates to the 1841 Pennsylvania state convention understood the gathering to be an explicitly political one, an event that allowed male representatives to discuss politics and represent the wishes of their people in a public forum.[14] And when the delegates to the 1848 state convention of Pennsylvania composed an "Appeal to the Voters of the Commonwealth of Pennsylvania," they presented themselves as "the representatives of the Colored Citizens" of the state.[15]

At times, delegates were even able to secure state buildings and courthouses for their meetings, buildings that heightened the political grandeur for the spectators in attendance and reinforced the gendered political actions of the male delegates on the floor. The formality of the space, recognizable as a public arena for male deliberation on political issues, made it an ideal forum for free Black men to enact citizenship and, in the process, demonstrate their political capacity to all observers. The use of official state buildings further reinforced the fact that the male delegates were engaging in a complex process of representation, serving as legislators for their people, exemplars of the very identities they hoped the state would soon recognize. For these reasons, northern free Blacks understood their conventions to be political in "viable, visible," and "direct" ways that, as Derrick Spires has noted, distinguished the conventions from the antislavery fairs and August 1 celebrations so popular among antebellum Black activists and their white abolitionist allies.[16]

Conventions as Civic Rituals

As uniquely political gatherings, state Colored Conventions required careful attention to structure, presentation, and form, elements that elevated the gatherings from simple meetings to recognizable political rituals. Indeed, the initial call for convention itself was "modeled on a long American tradition of calls for public meetings," which explicitly invoked "a set of established conventions" that would have been familiar to northern residents both Black and white alike.[17] In every Colored Convention—both state and national—participants were expected to follow a precise order of events from the dissemination of the call to convention and the seating of the delegates to the closing address and the subsequent publication of the proceedings. After arriving at the hall, delegates presented their credentials to the Credentials Committee for approval. And after the opening remarks, the delegates elected officers for the proceedings. Carefully adhering to the rules of parliamentary procedure throughout the day's sessions, the delegates debated contentious points, passed resolutions addressing a variety of social, economic, and political concerns, deliberated in small committees, and then returned at regular intervals to present reports to the entire body. Before adjourning, delegates presented all the finalized committee reports, speeches, and petitions prepared over the course of the multiday gathering, closing the event with a prayer and a song.[18]

As legal studies scholar Mark Weiner explains, ritual events such as these are best understood as "performances" that "achieve symbolic power because they proceed according to a pre-determined set of rules." In other words, one of the reasons that they "'work' [is] because they follow a conventional structure."[19] It was adherence to these practices that marked state Colored Conventions as a precise form of political engagement (as a political *convention*, rather than some other form of community or antislavery gathering) in keeping with early nineteenth-century political culture. Moreover, it was the repetition of these familiar elements—the call to convention, the election of delegates, the presentation of credentials, the election of the president and officers, the opening remarks, the speeches, the songs—in state after state, convention after convention, that gave these particular gatherings a unique cultural and political significance that extended beyond the sum of the individual acts themselves. In fact, the combination of repetition, expectation, and familiarity transformed these acts from mere practices into powerful civic rituals for those in attendance.

At the same time that these rituals affirmed the precise political nature of the event, these formal *conventions* of the conventions also served as barriers that restricted access to the convention floor to "respectable" elite and aspiring male members of free Black communities, making them performances rife with class and gender symbolism. Scholars have long noted the overwhelmingly male nature of antebellum Black conventions—"the conspicuous dearth of women among their ranks"—and, with the notable exception of emigration conventions, which welcomed women as delegates and leaders, their tendency to exclude women from the convention floor.[20] Indeed, since Howard Holman Bell first published his study of the convention movement in the 1950s, historians have identified and highlighted only a few instances when women appear in the published proceedings. As historian Martha Jones has argued, moments where women such as Barbara Ann Steward arrived at conventions claiming the right to represent their districts and deliberate alongside male delegates are best understood as disruptive events, moments when women inserted themselves into the "male" public sphere, forcing African American activists to contend with the "woman question" in what was otherwise understood to be a space for male political figures.[21]

The convention rituals also served as public affirmations and collective celebrations of a specific Black, middle-class political ethos. As I have argued elsewhere, elite and aspiring free Black men and women created their own distinct political worldview and cultural ethos in the decades preceding the Civil War. Simultaneously respectable and subversive, they embraced the gendered values and cultural practices of the region's emerging middle class, redefining them in some cases and imbuing them with political significance. Arguing that their community's increasing education, morality, virtue, and independence demonstrated the "falsity" of the claims of proslavery theorists and politicians, who consistently characterized people of African descent as inherently servile, degraded, and unfit for freedom and incorporation into the body politic, free Black activists and writers urged elite and aspiring free Black men and women to embody their antislavery principles and serve as living, breathing refutations of the nation's increasingly popular proslavery discourse, to live what the Reverend Samuel Ringgold Ward called "an antislavery life." Simultaneously distinct from yet complementary to the public, organized abolitionist *activism* in which so many northern free Blacks engaged, much of antislavery living was done in private—at home with family and friends, in prayer at the fireside hearth, or in less overtly political forums such as in church, in reading rooms, and in schools, where free Blacks might model exemplary behavior for each other. But awareness of the politics of the white gaze and the practice of what historian Patrick Rael calls racial synecdoche (the white tendency to use examples of "degraded" free Black behavior as evidence to support arguments in favor of the colonization movement or the expansion of slavery) ensured that elite and aspiring northern free Blacks understood their personal embodiment of the period's gender and class ideals in unquestionably political terms.[22]

Conventions provided the space for northern free Blacks to embody their conception of respectability in a public, political forum. Declaring their intention to transact their business "in a manner creditable to ourselves, our immediate constituents," and the states in which they lived, participants behaved in ways that concretely and symbolically constructed Black male political "capacity."[23] Delegates to antebellum state Colored Conventions believed their own elevated status, or "mental and moral improvement," was demonstrated by their very ability "to elect and send representatives to a council in which they know their rights are sacredly regarded."[24] And when all was said and done, participants in antebellum Colored Conventions hoped they could look back on their conventions and see that "we are a more talented, a better educated, more improved and elevated people than we had any anticipation we were."[25] Blurring the lines between late eighteenth-century notions of virtue and independence and emerging early nineteenth-century middle-class ideals of respectability, supporters of antebellum Colored Conventions viewed these events as key vehicles for a larger race-building enterprise, a movement toward Black self-sufficiency, an ideal community, and ultimately, independence.

Spectators and Delegates, Call and Response

Constructed and understood by northern free Blacks as quintessentially political affairs, these civic rituals demanded the presence of an audience. This in and of itself was not unusual, for as the historian Mary Ryan has explained, publicity remained an essential feature of early nineteenth-century American political culture. "Antebellum citizenship," she writes, "was most always exercised in association with one's fellows: To the pioneers of antebellum democracy, the sacred civic act was not a private exercise of conscience of the individual practice of intellect but, in the words of the Loco-Focos, 'speechifying and resolutions at political meetings.'"[26] Moreover, as Nancy Isenberg reminds us, "to a significant extent publicity remained a joint fabrication, constructed by the viewer or spectator as much as by the actual participants."[27] Thus, the presence of an interested and engaged audience, one upon which the legitimacy of the gathering ultimately depended, was as crucial a part of antebellum Colored Conventions as the subsequent publication of the proceedings in print form.[28]

Although it is tempting to think of this aspect of publicity as one involving an audience of passive spectators who merely observed the delegates' activity on the convention floor, this does not appear to be the case in antebellum Colored Conventions. This is especially apparent when we consider the ways that convention audiences responded to the words, speeches, and declarations made by delegates on the convention floor. Rather than simply detailing the content of a speech, the minutes often contain descriptions of an audience's spirited reaction to a delegate's rhetorical abilities. At times, recording secretaries took pains to record the response of the audience as well as an assessment of the speech. For example, not only did the minutes of the 1858 New York state convention remark that "Mr. Garnet's speech on Tuesday evening exhibited rare points of analysis, logic, wit and eloquence," but they additionally noted that it "was listened to with the greatest pleasure and applause."[29] After describing the audience at the Ohio state convention of 1856 as "large and enthusiastic," the minutes recorded that "every evening, the large and commodious City Hall was filled to its utmost capacity with anxious listeners, both white and colored." They further noted that "the speeches made by Langston, Clark, Gaines, and others, were logical, pointed and eloquent, and were delivered with earnestness and great power."[30] And the minutes of the Ohio state convention of 1849 lauded the presidential address, making sure to recount that the speech "was received with deafening shouts of applause."[31] A white reporter for a local newspaper covering the event agreed with the recording secretary's assessment, saying, "The address was a strong and a good one, and was enlivened by sparks of genuine wit, which elicited frequent and tumultuous applause." He then reminded his readers of the connection between fine oratory, citizenship, and manliness, declaring that "the speaker himself was an evidence of what a soul can do, even under the pressure of extraordinary difficulties. In this case it has made a man."[32]

These references to anxious listeners, enthusiastic spectators, and deafening shouts of applause reflect the extent to which northern free Blacks shared prevailing beliefs about the significance of male oratory. Oratory, considered "a political as well as literary art" in the period, was so important in early nineteenth-century American political culture that "would-be orators" would often "seek advice and even instruction" to improve their technique.[33] Those attending Colored state conventions shared this assessment of the power of oratory and praised those Black men who distinguished themselves on the speaker's platform. In addition to serving as examples of the success of the convention ritual, these responses to male oratory were understood as key indicators of the manliness of the speaker. For African American delegates—men who had long been admonished to live antislavery lives, that is, lives that were antitheses of proslavery discourse—their ability to move audiences in this way was rife with powerful cultural and political implications.

Additionally, the vocal responses of those in attendance also suggest that antebellum Black state and national conventions relied on an especially active reciprocal relationship between delegates and the audience. And because their very presence was necessary to confer legitimacy on the proceedings— both in terms of the delegates' claims to leadership and the very political nature of the convention itself, we must consider these nondelegates in attendance to be essential for the success of the convention ritual and cocreators of the convention experience. In other words, Colored Conventions must be understood as spaces where both spectators and delegates participated in the rituals required to affirm both the political capacity of the male delegates and the respectable nature of the Black community being represented. As Weiner explains, "The involvement of community members in ritual events, as either participants or spectators, enables them not only to acknowledge but also actively to affirm and define the character of the community."[34] Antebellum Black conventions, it seems, served as key spaces to do just that.

This, in turn, requires us to reconsider the role of women in antebellum state conventions, for these active and engaged audiences included free Black women as well as men. Indeed, evidence suggests that even though they were rarely seated as delegates, African American women attended the Black national and state conventions of the 1840s and 1850s in considerable numbers. Newspaper coverage of the 1840 New York state convention described "numerous" spectators, "both of male and female," who remained "in attendance morning, afternoon and evening" and "manifested no less interest than the delegates themselves."[35] When speakers rose to present a formal address to the assembly, they sometimes addressed their remarks to the "*Ladies and Gentlemen*" present at the public sessions.[36] In 1841, the Pennsylvania state convention delegates passed a resolution thanking "the ladies" for their presence throughout the convention.[37] Similarly, the publishing committee prefaced its publication of the minutes of an Ohio state convention, noting that "the weather was very cold, and the hall where the session was held was cold, but the ladies, God bless them! cheered us with their smiles, and wishes and approbation, and for which I thank them, not for myself alone, but for the millions with whom I am identified in suffering and wrong."[38]

There are also moments where the proceedings record examples of African American women performing some kind of collective gesture during the meeting and the delegates responding with a resolution formally acknowledging them and registering their "thanks." So when "the Ladies attending" the Ohio state convention of 1850 "proposed to defray the expenses of the house for the sitting of the Convention," the delegates then moved and resolved "that the Convention tender their sincere thanks to [the ladies] for their genuine patriotism."[39] And "at the close of the last evening's exercises" of the 1856 state convention of Ohio, "Rev. Mr. Turban came forward and presented the Convention five dollars in behalf of the ladies of Bethel Church." In response, the delegates unanimously resolved "that the thanks of the Convention are due, and are hereby tendered to the ladies of Bethel Church, for their liberal donation."[40] These sorts of gestures and responses served as ceremonial acts solidifying the community's commitment to political organization and collective activism. And it was for this reason that the New York state delegates of 1840 would proclaim: "We call for the exertion of the entire people. We call upon age . . . upon youth . . . upon that portion of the people whose influence is tender, gentle, and benign—we call upon the women."[41]

Perhaps the most extensively recorded example of one of these dramatic moments of reciprocity took place at the Ohio state convention of 1856, where the delegates received the gift of a written statement from the Ladies' Anti-Slavery Society of Delaware. Penned by a twenty-year-old Oberlin student of African descent named Sara Stanley, and read to the convention by a male delegate, the address saluted the gentlemen of the convention for their efforts "to concoct measures for obtaining those rights and immunities of which unjust legislation has deprived you."[42] She urged them to "press on!" insisting that "manhood's prerogatives are yours by Almighty fiat." "To you, gentlemen, as representatives of the oppressed thousands of Ohio, we look hopefully," she declared, praising their work and expressing her organization's "earnest hope that such determination and invincible courage may be evinced by you in assembly as are requisite to meet the exigencies of the times."[43] Then in a rhetorical move increasingly popular with free Black writers of the period, Stanley harkened back to a classical martial tradition, positioned the women of her Ladies' Anti-Slavery Society as supportive mothers, sisters, and daughters, and urged the male delegates onward, proclaiming, "It was a Spartan mother's farewell to her son, 'Bring home your shield or be brought upon it.' To you we would say, be true, be courageous, be steadfast in the discharge of your duty. The citadel of Error must yield to the unshrinking phalanx of truth. In our fireside circles, in the seclusion of our closets, we kneel in tearful supplication in your behalf. As Christian wives, mothers and daughters, we invoke the blessing of the King, Eternal and Immortal . . . to rest upon you." She then concluded, "Again we say, be courageous; be steadfast; unfurl your banner to the breeze—let its folds float proudly over you, bearing the glorious inscription, broad and brilliant as the material universe: '*God and Liberty!*'"[44]

Free Black women such as Sara Stanley understood their role as audience members—restricted though it was—to be one that was neither passive nor inconsequential. Rather, it was their presence as spectators that imbued conventions with the class and gender ethos required for political legitimacy in the period. As Nancy Isenberg has argued in her analysis of the Whig conventions of the era, "Having women in the audience . . . upheld the masculine code of chivalry, in which male virtue required the displays of social decorum and verbal prowess before the female gaze." Moreover, as David Waldstreicher notes in his analysis of white American political practices in the early republic, "The inclusion of these women even at the margins of celebration was a significant aspect of the republican public sphere, but one that broadcast its own limits: respectability."[45] What I would like to suggest here is that African American conventioneers pushed this construct even further. It was not simply that the presence of elite and aspiring middle-class Black women gave virtue and legitimacy to the actions of the Black men on the floor. Rather, given the spirited call-and-response nature of audience participation, women such as Sara Stanley were in deliberate dialogue with the delegates on the convention floor and, consequently, coparticipants in the ritual and cocreators of the drama of the event as a whole. In the process, they claimed a kind of gendered political power rarely afforded to women of African descent in the era—whether free or enslaved.

It was this interplay, this reciprocal relationship between convention delegate and spectator, that made antebellum Black conventions profound and empowering collective experiences for those who attended. We can see this illustrated most clearly in the closing moments of the 1841 Pennsylvania state convention. As the gathering drew to a conclusion after three days of committee work, spirited rhetoric, and lively debate, President John Peck rose to congratulate the body on the "appropriate manner [of its] various doings . . . [and] the pleasing fact that so large a Delegation had been together for three days, [and] had transacted such deeply interesting business." After Peck finished with his remarks, "the whole assembly" joined together in song, singing two hymns: "Before Jehovah's Awful Throne" and "Old Hundred." As the proceedings described it, the attendees sang the hymns "with indescribable fervor and pathos; the voices of the ladies, who crowded the gallery, uniting with those of the men from below, producing an effect, which to be appreciated must have been heard." Then, after a "solemn and appropriate prayer" by the Reverend Lewis Woodson, "on motion, the Convention adjourned, *sine die.*"[46]

Conclusion

Careful attention to moments such as these—discursive snapshots that allow us not just to analyze the arguments of the delegates but to consider the drama of the event, the interactions with the audience, and the responses of the spectators—reminds us that conventions functioned as powerful po-litical rituals for antebellum free Black communities. As public affirmations, collective celebrations, and opportunities for antebellum free Blacks to, as John Ernest has argued, embody an ideal "imagined African American com-munity," conventions were carefully choreographed civic rituals requiring the active participation of delegate and spectator alike.[47] Finally, antebel-lum Colored state conventions also allowed free African Americans to enact citizenship—even without the formal recognition of the state. During conventions, delegates could perform the very political privileges they de-manded in the proceedings, embody ideal middle-class manliness before an audience of virtuous male and female observers, transform themselves from dependents into political agents, and in the process, challenge the very boundaries of antebellum political culture itself.

NOTES

1. Howard Holman Bell, ed., *Minutes of the Proceedings of the National Negro Con-ventions, 1830–1864* (New York: Arno, 1969), i.

2. Philip S. Foner and George E. Walker, eds., *Proceedings of the Black State Conven-tions, 1840–1865* (Philadelphia: Temple University Press, 1979–80), 1:xvi.

3. For analysis of the ways these debates played out in conventions, see Bella Gross, *Clarion Call: The History and Development of the Negro People's Convention Move-ment in the United States from 1817–1840* (New York: printed by the author, 1947); How-ard Holman Bell, *A Survey of the National Negro Convention Movement* (New York: Arno, 1969); Julie Winch, *Philadelphia's Black Elite: Activism, Accommodation and the Struggle for Equality, 1787–1848* (Philadelphia: Temple University Press, 1988); C. Peter Ripley, ed., *The Black Abolitionist Papers*, vol. 3, *The United States, 1830–1846* (Chapel Hill: University of North Carolina Press, 1991), introduction; Stanley Harrold, *The Rise of Aggressive Abolitionism: Addresses to the Slaves* (Lexington: University Press of Kentucky, 2004); Patrick Rael, *Black Identity and Black Protest in the Antebellum North* (Chapel Hill: University of North Carolina Press, 2002); Leslie M. Harris, *In the Shadow of Slavery: African Americans in New York City, 1626–1863* (University of Chi-cago Press, 2002), chaps. 6, 7; John Ernest, *Liberation Historiography: African Ameri-can Writers and the Challenge of History* (Chapel Hill: University of North Carolina Press, 2004); Harry Reed, *Platform for Change: The Foundations of the Northern Free Black Community, 1775–1865* (East Lansing: Michigan State University Press, 1994); Stephen Kantrowitz, *More Than Freedom: Fighting for Black Citizenship in a White Republic, 1829-1889* (New York: Penguin, 2012); and Derrick R. Spires, *The Practice of*

Citizenship: Black Politics and Print Culture in the Early United States (Philadelphia: University of Pennsylvania Press, 2019).

4. Elizabeth R. Varon, *We Mean to Be Counted: White Women and Politics in Antebellum Virginia* (Chapel Hill: University of North Carolina Press, 1998); David Waldstreicher, *In the Midst of Perpetual Fetes: The Making of American Nationalism, 1776–1820* (Chapel Hill: University of North Carolina Press, 1997); Mary Ryan, *Civic Wars: Democracy and Public Life in the American City during the Nineteenth Century* (Berkeley: University of California Press, 1997); Nancy Isenberg, *Sex and Citizenship in Antebellum America* (Chapel Hill: University of North Carolina Press, 1998); Glenn C. Altschuler and Stuart M. Blumin, *Rude Republic: Americans and their Politics in the Nineteenth Century* (Princeton, NJ: Princeton University Press, 2001). These sources all explore aspects of political theater in the political culture of the early nineteenth century.

5. For analyses of the politics of antebellum Black respectability and middle-class consciousness, see Erica L. Ball, *To Live an Antislavery Life: Personal Politics and the Antebellum Black Middle Class* (Athens: University of Georgia Press, 2012), chaps. 1, 2; Kantrowitz, *More Than Freedom*, chap. 4; Rael, *Black Identity*, esp. chaps. 4, 5; Elizabeth Rauh Bethel, *The Roots of African-American Identity: Memory and History in Free Antebellum Communities* (New York: St. Martin's, 1997), chap. 5; and Frederick Cooper, "Elevating the Race: The Social Thought of Black Leaders, 1827–50," *American Quarterly* 24 (December 1972): 604–25. See also "Political Rituals and Routines," in *The "Conventions" of the Conventions: The Practices of Black Political Citizenship*, by Carolyne King and Erica L. Ball, digital exhibit, Colored Conventions Project, https://coloredconventions.org/black-political-practices/rituals-and-routines.

6. Ryan, *Civic Wars*, 96.

7. David N. Gellman and David Quigley, eds., *Jim Crow New York: A Documentary History of Race and Citizenship, 1777–1877* (New York: New York University Press, 2003), 249.

8. Isenberg, *Sex and Citizenship*, 16.

9. Gellman and Quigley, *Jim Crow New York*, 249.

10. Leon F. Litwack, *North of Slavery: The Negro in the Free States, 1790–1860* (Chicago: University of Chicago Press, 1965), 93; Rhoda Golden Freeman, *The Free Negro in New York City in the Era before the Civil War* (New York: Garland, 1994), 92; Ryan, *Civic Wars*, 87–91.

11. *Colored American* (New York), June 16, 1838.

12. *Colored American*, June 16, 1838. For work that explores the ways Black Americans insisted on more expansive interpretations of freedom and citizenship, see Spires, *The Practice of Citizenship*; Kantrowitz, *More Than Freedom*; Martha S. Jones, *Birthright Citizens: A History of Race and Rights in Antebellum America* (Cambridge: Cambridge University Press, 2018); and Manisha Sinha, *The Slave's Cause: A History of Abolition* (New Haven: Yale University Press, 2016).

13. *North Star* (Rochester, NY), December 15, 1848.

14. *Proceedings of the State Convention of the Colored Freemen of Pennsylvania, Held in Pittsburgh, on the 23d, 24th and 25th of August, 1841, for the Purpose of Considering Their Condition, and the Means of its Improvement*, in Foner and Walker, *Proceedings*, 1:107.

15. *Minutes of the State Convention of the Coloured Citizens of Pennsylvania Convened at Harrisburg, December 13th and 14th 1848*, in Foner and Walker, *Proceedings*, 1:123.

16. Derrick R. Spires, "Imagining a State of Fellow Citizens: Early African American Politics of Publicity in the Black State Conventions," in *Early African American Print Culture*, ed. Lara Langer Cohen and Jordan Alexander Stein (Philadelphia: University of Pennsylvania Press, 2012), 275.

17. Rael, *Black Identity*, 30.

18. Foner and Walker, *Proceedings*, 1:xvi.

19. Mark S. Weiner, *Black Trials: Citizenship from the Beginnings of Slavery to the End of Caste* (New York: Alfred A. Knopf, 2004), 14–15.

20. Rael, *Black Identity*, 29.

21. Martha S. Jones, *All Bound Up Together: The Woman Question in African American Public Culture, 1830–1900* (Chapel Hill: University of North Carolina Press, 2007), 102–6; Shirley Yee, *Black Women Abolitionists: A Study in Activism, 1828–1860* (Knoxville: University of Tennessee Press, 1992), 144.

22. Ball, *To Live an Antislavery Life.*

23. *Proceedings of the State Convention of the Colored Freemen of Pennsylvania*, 107.

24. *Colored American*, June 16, 1838.

25. *Colored American*, August 29, 1840; also reprinted in Foner and Walker, *Proceedings*, 1:6.

26. Ryan, *Civic Wars*, 96.

27. Isenberg, *Sex and Citizenship*, 70.

28. Rael, *Black Identity*, 30.

29. *Suffrage Convention of the Colored Citizens of New York, Troy, September 14, 1858*, in Foner and Walker, *Proceedings*, 1:101; also published in *Liberator* (Boston), October 1, 1858.

30. *From the Proceedings of the State Convention of Colored Men, Held in the City of Columbus, Ohio, Jan. 16th, 17th, & 18th, 1856*, in Foner and Walker, *Proceedings*, 1:307.

31. Minutes and Address of the State Convention of the Colored Citizens of Ohio (1849: Oberlin, OH), *Minutes and Address of the State Convention of the Colored Citizens of Ohio, Convened at Columbus, January 10th, 11th, 12th, & 13th, 1849*, Colored Conventions Project, https://omeka.coloredconventions.org/items/show/247, 3.

32. *Minutes and Address of the State Convention*, 23.

33. Waldstreicher, *In the Midst*, 221.

34. Weiner, *Black Trials*, 14–15.

35. *Colored American*, August 29, 1840; reprinted in Foner and Walker, *Proceedings*, 1:6.

36. *From the Proceedings of the State Convention of Colored Men*, 321.

37. *Proceedings of the State Convention of the Colored Freemen of Pennsylvania*, 111.

38. *State Convention of Colored Men of the State of Ohio, Held in the City of Columbus, January 21st, 22d, and 23d, 1857*, in Foner and Walker, *Proceedings*, 1:318.

39. *Convention of the Colored Citizens of Ohio, Convened at Columbus, January 9th, 10th, 11th, and 12th, 1850*, in Foner and Walker, *Proceedings*, 1:250.

40. *From the Proceedings of the State Convention of Colored Men*, 307.

41. *Convention of the Colored Inhabitants of the State of New York August 18-20, 1840*, in Foner and Walker, *Proceedings*, 1:16–17.

42. Ellen NicKenzie Lawson, *The Three Sarahs: Documents of Black Antebellum College Women* (Lewiston, NY: Edwin Mellen, 1985), 49, 50.

43. *From the Proceedings of the State Convention of Colored Men*, 313.

44. *From the Proceedings of the State Convention of Colored Men*, 314.

45. Isenberg, *Sex and Citizenship*, 19; Waldstreicher, *In the Midst*, 84.

46. *Proceedings of the State Convention of the Colored Freemen of Pennsylvania*, 111–12.

47. Ernest, *Liberation Historiography*, 252.

COLORED CONVENTIONS, MORAL REFORM, AND THE AMERICAN RACE PROBLEM

Joan L. Bryant

At its 1836 inaugural meeting, the American Moral Reform Society (AMRS) launched one of its first reform campaigns with open letters to northern Black and white Protestant churches. The aim was to persuade the institutions to end their reliance on racial constructions. Reformers were convinced that organizations that accepted race as a valid category of human difference could not do the work required of Christians.[1]

The letter to white congregations—"PROFESSED FOLLOWERS OF JESUS CHRIST"—decried their exclusion and marginalization of Black Christians. By deploying "invidious distinctions," it argued, churches propagated perverted notions of human difference that contracted the spheres of sympathy. They invoked specious "physical peculiarities" to suggest that it was "*morally impossible*" to include Colored people within their networks of love and obligation. This notion was at odds with reformers' understanding of the biblical declaration that God made all nations "of one blood." They believed that scripture upheld "the identity of the human race—our common origin, and natural equality."[2] Congregations that refused to affirm the unity of the human species thus flaunted their sins and ignorance.

In Colored churches, assumptions about racial categories threatened to limit members' capacity to instigate a comprehensive economic attack on slavery. Reformers urged the congregations to boycott items produced with slave labor. They reasoned that slavery's sinfulness made the use of such products evil. It was tantamount to stealing a person's God-given right to freedom. To highlight Colored people's culpability, the group estimated that their consumption of cotton, tobacco, rice, sugar, and molasses generated an annual net yield of $150,000 to slaveholding planters. Incredulously, they asked, "Is this doing nothing for the support of slavery? Can the colored churches wink at this?"[3] The letter condemned the excuse that the Colored population was powerless against the slave system. Noting that God made "no distinction in complexion," reformers insisted that there was no valid basis for correlating moral obligations with skin color. They warned that on Judgment Day, no one would be able to justify the failure to perform Christian duties by pleading, "We are *Colored*."[4]

In attacking the assumption that racial distinctions were logical and legitimate bases of religious obligations, moral reformers insisted that they were
fulfilling a mandate of the 1835 national Colored Convention address, which
pledged delegates to help churches "rid themselves of the sin of slavery and
immorality."[5] This connection, along with the absence of any other forum
convening as a national convention in 1836, lends plausibility to the idea that
the AMRS continued the work of the national Colored Conventions. However, other factors suggest a different scenario. By their own account, moral
reformers sought to push beyond the long-standing convention objective of
improving Colored people. They were anxious for the public to appreciate
the "newness and greatness" of their endeavor to spark a "moral revolution"
that would reform the nation.[6] Scholars also distinguish the AMRS from the
conventions. For example, historians Jane and William Pease argue that the
group's rejection of racial designations contradicted the conventions' "main
purpose" of promoting "race pride and cohesion."[7]

Navigating tensions between continuity and disruption entails exploring
the basis of the Reform Society's repudiation of race and the debates it inspired. These issues elucidate the group's significance in the history of Colored Conventions. AMRS ideas and the conflicts they occasioned illuminate
how the conventions evolved as a discrete form of collective action framed
by distinctive rituals and documentation. They highlight the importance
of looking beyond official proceedings to understand the ideas and politics
that shaped convention discourse and records. The initiatives of reformers
working in the gap between the first set of national conventions and the
state gatherings that revived annual proceedings help to explain how conceptions of race configured early African American reform.

How did the AMRS come to temporarily disrupt the course of early national
conventions? Exploring the development of the organization means contending with the ideas of its central architect, William Whipper of Philadelphia and Columbia, Pennsylvania. His views and controversies shed light
on reformers' misgivings about the logic and ethics of racial classifications.
Whipper was one of the few constants in the first series of national conventions that began in 1830. The forums were in flux from their inception, as
competing conceptions of reform defined their agendas. The disparate concerns of a fluctuating slate of participants shifted convention priorities from
year to year. A twenty-six-year-old delegate to the inaugural meeting, Whipper became the only person to continue in this capacity at the five annual
meetings that followed. He is a relatively insignificant character in prevailing accounts of Black American activism, known as a chief advocate of moral
reform and pacifism and as something of an outlier for repudiating race.
Sterling Stuckey concludes that Whipper simply heeded the directives of
white benefactors.[8] The principle of moral suasion that William Lloyd Garrison championed clearly informed Whipper's thinking, just as it influenced

such prominent abolitionists as Frederick Douglass, William Cooper Nell, Charles Remond, and Robert Purvis. However, while their reform careers evolved in alliances with Garrison and other white abolitionists, Whipper's perspectives developed squarely within Black reform arenas. They reflect the evolution of the conventions as Black-controlled spaces and illustrate how doubts about the idea of essential human difference fueled challenges to race constructions. His participation situates challenges to race as critical aspects of the unwieldy process of enacting freedom in reform organization.

By the time he delineated the conceptual basis of the AMRS, Whipper was not merely a seasoned delegate; he was a pivotal figure in the national conventions. He had helped direct their focus after the founding meeting, where Richard Allen oversaw the creation of the American Society of Free Persons of Colour for Improving their Condition in the United States; for Purchasing Lands; and for the Establishment of a Settlement in Upper Canada. In the wake of Allen's death, Whipper and his Philadelphia colleague, Belfast Burton, issued a call for a second gathering of individuals who had no interest in emigration. They hoped to ensure that the 1831 convention devoted its attention to advancement in America. To disempower delegates who insisted on addressing emigration, they maneuvered a structural change, designating their meeting as the First Annual Convention of the People of Colour. In theory, the mutual aid society created under Allen's leadership continued to exist as an auxiliary of the convention. However, reorganization meant that support for emigration would not be the central basis of the conventions. Instead, they were to serve as representative bodies to reform Colored people in the United States.[9]

The Reform Society was the outgrowth of a new vision of reform that Whipper formulated at the 1834 national convention. He prepared for the proceedings by laboriously drafting a Declaration of Sentiment, which delegates voted to adopt as the convention's platform. The reform press praised the document for its nobility, Christian ideals, and "manly style."[10] There is no record of concerns about individuals typically identified as needing reform carrying out the moral duties of citizens and Christians. This platform fundamentally altered the logic of the conventions by shifting their focus away from improving Colored people.

The conviction that Colored people could and should practice freedom and citizenship through reform endeavors led Whipper and his allies to propose the creation of a new society at the 1835 convention. They envisioned it as a venue through which to reform the nation, rallying Americans "without distinction of caste or complexion."[11] The rationale for the project lay in the Declaration of Sentiment. It is unclear whether they intended to displace the conventions. Nevertheless, by design or disorganization, the AMRS helped disable national conventions until 1843.

For Whipper, James Forten Sr., Robert Purvis, and other AMRS stalwarts, repudiating the validity of race designations and distinctions was a premise of the organization they sought to build. Their stance prompted a diverse set of reformers to grapple with the meanings of race for much of the society's six-year career. Conflict emerged slowly. On the eve of the second AMRS meeting, in 1837, there were no signs of the debates that accompanied its inception in the 1835 convention or of the dissension that was to come. The group's commitment to "moral principle" won praise in the columns of the *Colored American*. Participation indicates early interest in the project. Moral reformers counted 100 people among its initial members and delegates. Forty individuals from this group—a number comparable to the size of the 1830 national convention—officially participated in the proceedings.[12]

The implications of excluding race categories from AMRS initiatives became clear after the 1837 meeting. Early supporters who endorsed the society's denunciations of race practices in churches opposed a drive to exclude color designations from its endeavors. They viewed the refusal to name Colored people as the specific beneficiaries of reform as an unconscionable attempt to shirk obligations. Vehement reactions sparked arguments among former convention participants who had initially supported the Reform Society, believing it would generate positive outcomes. Two days of debate failed to settle conflicts over the appropriateness of using color labels to define moral reform objectives. Squabbles ended when James Forten Sr. exercised his prerogative as AMRS president and ordered members to drop racial references.[13]

Although official accounts suggest Forten's directive resolved the issue, editorials and letters in the reform press chart ongoing controversy. Samuel Cornish, Presbyterian editor of the *Colored American*, was unable or unwilling to publish all the correspondence he received concerning the society. Many of the submissions were, reportedly, "not at all suited" to the paper. Most of the letters he printed were critical of Whipper and the AMRS. Cornish confessed to excluding one letter merely because it mentioned the Reform Society; he warned the writer to confine future commentary to the national conventions.[14]

Protracted debate over the AMRS shows that moral reformers were not alone in harboring doubts about racial distinctions. It reveals how difficult it was to speak coherently about the meanings and import of color designations. With no solid discursive tradition on which to draw, reformers struggled to factor clear conceptions of race into their understanding of reform obligations. The notion that color labels were benign, useful, or malleable signifiers could not trump misgivings about their validity as markers of essential human difference and rank.

Debates surrounding the AMRS were not simply conflicts between separatists and integrationists. Individuals who disparaged segregated associations and welcomed the participation of white people in their forums were among the group's harshest critics. They were not attacking an integrationist agenda. Frederick Hinton, a former convention delegate who supported the formation of a National Moral Reform Society, assailed the idea that Colored reformers had any obligation to assist white people. Such a notion was "absurd and preposterous," he argued, because white people possessed all the advantages that Colored people were trying to secure. Hinton was no separatist. He had recommended that the Reform Society invite all presidents of antislavery societies and "other friends of our cause" to participate in its meetings. Even AMRS critics who advocated a return to the national conventions were not necessarily advocating segregated forums. A former convention delegate from New York, distressed that the national conventions had lapsed, appealed to leading AMRS members to redirect their energies to reviving them. The pseudonymous "Hamilton" acknowledged that the conventions had not been perfect. Inexperience had compromised delegates' ability to manage authority, convince Colored people of "the necessity of union," and wring coherence out of the Colored population's "discordant elements." Despite these limitations, he extolled the arenas as fruitful sites of integration because they had fostered friendships with "the white brethren."[15]

Many early critics of the AMRS focused attention on how to name the objects of reform. They felt the society's principal purpose was to improve free people of color. Thus, it was logical and necessary to identify them as such. The matter appeared to be so straightforward that the refusal of Whipper, James Forten, Robert Purvis, and their allies to identify free people of color "by name" seemed inexplicable and morally indefensible. Nevertheless, there was a broad spectrum of ideas about the term "colored" among the society's detractors. It was variously a phenotypic description, a designation of social circumstances, and a caste label. The indefinite character of the term meant that people attached multiple and conflicting meanings to it simultaneously.

Frederick Hinton had proposed that the AMRS promote education specifically for free Colored people. Upon defecting over the group's rejection of color designations, he explained that he had referred to free people of color simply to distinguish them from slaves. He interpreted opposition to the term as tantamount to a refusal to identify with "the peculiarities of their people." The label "Colored" referred to skin and the name God created. Individuals who scorned it as a *"badge of . . . degradation"* were slighting Colored people for the way God made them and rejecting natural facts.[16] Such people could not be trusted with the cause of reform.

Critics who cast Whipper as a misguided crusader against race harbored their own misgivings about the concept even as they defended racial designations. Samuel Cornish was among the most vocal challengers of the AMRS. He had no tolerance for its stand on color categories because it concerned mere "trifles" that ignored the unique circumstances facing the Colored population. He confessed to being "as much opposed to complexional distinctions as brother Whipper or any other man." Nevertheless, "SPECIAL" needs required reformers to specify for whom the society was promoting reform.[17] Yet Cornish's ridicule of moral reformers masked his own struggles to clarify his ideas about race and the status of Colored people. As editor of the short-lived *Rights of All*, he had decried the "ridiculous doctrine" that they comprised a "*separate people,* [with] *separate interests.*"[18] When establishing the *Colored American*, he insisted that the term "colored" denoted the population's distinctive contours and needs. Names mattered. Moral reformers should welcome being called "colored," he reasoned, because it was superior to the alternative of being "nothing else but NEGROES, NEGROES." The designations "*Negroes, Africans,* and *blacks*" were all "names of reproach" that compromised claims to American identity.[19] He acknowledged that some might dismiss the name of his paper as just another signifier of subjugation. "Why draw this cord of caste?" he asked. The "peculiarity" of Colored people's circumstances and needs supplied the answer.[20] Although he perceived color designations as markers of stratification, he was convinced that they could function as a useful way to distinguish among Americans.

Concerns about accuracy and pragmatism compelled Baltimore preacher and teacher William Watkins to criticize moral reformers' ideas even as he remained part of the AMRS. He construed its purpose as indistinguishable from that of the national conventions, namely to improve the moral and mental condition of Colored people. Accordingly, it was appropriate to use the term "colored" in reform endeavors. Despite objecting to its "prodigal" use, he found the "endearing" designation superior to the label "African." To bring conceptual and ethical clarity to the issue, he explained that the term "colored" was "philosophically correct" because there was a customary link between it—"the sign"—and "the thing signified."[21] The arbitrary moniker was no different from other forms of speech that derived their logic and efficacy from usage.

Watkins appreciated his colleagues' attempts to distinguish moral discourse from race categories. He explained that the fact of "being *colored*" was not a reason for targeted reforms. However, it was a reliable proxy for identifying individuals who lacked moral resources. Naming Colored people as the exclusive targets of reform efforts would make the society more practical and provide a corrective to the "sweeping" designation "American." The title betrayed a lack of propriety among individuals "just emerging from darkness," purporting to reform a nation comprised of people "thoroughly indoctrinated" in the ideal of universal liberty.[22]

———————

Strife transformed the Reform Society's antirace premise into its focus. Notwithstanding its array of measures, including recurring convention themes of morality, slavery, education, and public decorum, the group gained a reputation for one thing: the repudiation of color designations.[23] Concerns about identifying Colored people as beneficiaries of reform obscured the conceptual basis and the stakes of objections to race designations. The AMRS position did not arise from questions about how to accurately identify objects of reform. Nor was it a pragmatic gesture about how to effectively implement reforms. It flowed from the same convictions about the unity of the human species that shaped the society's critique of churches. In short, a common origin determined human relations and thus fixed the boundaries of obligation. Racial and color designations were incompatible with reform endeavors because they were flawed configurations of human difference that distorted conceptions of duty for American reformers. This logic of human equality paved the foundations of moral reform.

Overcoming false notions of difference was both a premise and a goal for moral reformers. Their call for Colored people to eschew racial constructs was noteworthy; yet it relied on familiar claims about the illogical and fallacious character of race that reformers used to condemn colonization efforts and discrimination. It was an attempt to hold them to standards of truth that they applied to others. Two examples illustrate the early reform practice of challenging race. In 1813, James Forten invoked the principle of species unity to challenge the legitimacy of differential treatment between white and Black Philadelphians. Writing as a "Man of Colour," he issued a series of letters protesting a proposal to prohibit Colored people from migrating to Pennsylvania and to require existing Colored residents to register their presence. The injustice of the plan lay in its assumption that Black people were fundamentally different from white people. He condemned it, asking the question, "Has the God who made the white man and the black, left any record declaring us a different species?"[24]

In 1832, Forten collaborated with Robert Purvis and Whipper to oppose race categories in Pennsylvania's plan to repeal protections for fugitive slaves and again attempt to bar free Colored people from migrating to the state. Their protest to the state legislature argued that the action against fugitives compromised Pennsylvania's status as a free state. The proposed ban on migrants was worse. Its reliance on the arbitrary and dubious criteria of color differences violated the very principle of liberty. The attempt to regulate autonomy using "wavering and uncertain shades of white" placed freedom on unstable and illusory foundations.[25]

The AMRS tried to alter the terms of reform by calibrating initiatives to the nature of humanity. Skin complexion and color designations were of no moral consequence; they neither created nor defined obligations. The only valid categories for understanding human difference were "virtues and vices."[26] Whether viewed in terms of ethics or nature, a "color" was not something a person could be.

The rationale for challenging race extended beyond the obligations reformers associated with citizenship and a common humanity. Everyday experiences provided compelling warrants for repudiating race distinctions. They demonstrated that the categories were not merely benign or self-evident descriptors. Whipper cited a host of wrongs that proved otherwise. Schools, churches, employment, transportation services, courts, the legislative arena, and social settings were among the many sites of discrimination and exclusion that prevented Colored people from standing on "equal footing with 'white people.'" The root of the problem was the "odious distinction in language, principle, and practice that confers . . . favor on those that are known by the distinctive appellation of 'white people.'"[27] Race categories did not merely justify inequality, but they embodied and structured it. They were linguistic, ideological, and behavioral tools that regulated access to social, political, economic, legal, and religious opportunities by inventing and maintaining whiteness. The caprice of individual prejudice was inadequate to explain the injustices Colored people faced. Hierarchies were intrinsic to the discourse of "color." Deploying race designations gave credence to invalid notions of difference and rank. Moral reformers thus had a duty to reject them.

Whipper pleaded guilty to accusations that he and his allies had lost sight of their oppressed status as Colored people. With an air of moral superiority, he confessed that they had indeed forgotten that they were "degraded." This was hardly a cause for lament because they had buried the perception in the nobility of their undertaking as Christian citizens. He stopped short of concluding that Colored people could make race categories disappear by abandoning them. Nevertheless, standards of rectitude compelled reformers to act on "correct principles." Embracing race categories made them "equally guilty" of facilitating oppression. As long as the terms persisted as part of common speech, there could be no hope of abolishing the color-coded injustice they structured. They would endure until "all the different SHADES mingle into ONE."[28]

The desire for change that fueled the Reform Society's origins shaped its demise as northern states disenfranchised Colored men. The threat that legislative action posed was far more formidable than criticism from other reformers. The Philadelphians who dominated the leadership of the AMRS felt the impact most acutely in 1838, when Pennsylvania joined Connecticut and New York in adopting constitutional provisions restricting the franchise to white men.[29] Disenfranchisement undermined a fundamental premise of the AMRS. Although its designation as "American" expressed a nationalist sentiment rather than a claim about its geographic reach, the group's reform vision was expansive. Claims to American citizenship created the imperative and license for Whipper's activism. They grounded his insistence that "moral power" transcended complexional and state boundaries. Pennsylvania's action forced him to contend with the fact that states regulated the terms of citizenship; it was not a national phenomenon. The situation left him outraged and dismayed. He decried the fact that there was no "American government" for Colored people—"no federal union" that transcended their varied experiences in individual states. A diminished sphere of citizenship mutated the long-standing problem of finding a common basis for reform and made it appear more intractable.[30]

Ultimately, political exclusion hardened Whipper's position on the immorality of color distinctions. It disabused him of any lingering attachment to the idea that moral improvement was a key to rights. He assailed the popular claim that citizenship rights were a function of moral rectitude, insisting that it veiled the structure of injustice and gave credence to discrimination. He assured *National Reformer* readers of the power of religion, humanity, and even legislation to overcome social evils because morality was a virtue in its own right. However, he urged them to jettison the false view that moral elevation was a strategy for winning rights. That notion, he argued, should have been "annihilated at its birth."[31] If any impediment to rights required a remedy, it was white people's hearts, not Colored people's morals. The imposition of a moral test for rights would illustrate this need by disenfranchising "half the white population."[32] Birth was the sole legitimate qualification for citizenship rights. To suggest that religion, morality, or mental ability were conditions for political privileges was to commit a "fatal error." Immorality, wickedness, ignorance, and "impiety" had nothing to do with disenfranchisement. It stemmed from the "wicked principle" of color distinctions.[33]

Political barriers and the decline of the Reform Society brought Whipper and AMRS opponents to a turning point. He insisted on the need for "new terms" for reformers to confront injustice. He made conciliatory gestures toward his critics, conceding that the society had failed to transpose its principles into a viable reform association. As a result, free Colored people were bereft of the broad base of representation they had in national conventions. Yet his closing words to *National Reformer* readers suggest just how little he was willing to compromise. The AMRS paper expired with his renunciation of "all COMPLEXIONAL ALLEGIANCE with every class of mankind."[34]

———————

Challenges to race constructions survived the demise of the AMRS. Questions about the validity of race kept pace with the evolution of conventions and other reform organizations led by Colored people. Delegates to the 1840 Albany convention decried New York's restrictions on Colored voters as a "toleration of complexional difference" that sullied republican principles, making rights a function of "arbitrary" and "unnatural" distinctions.[35] Participants in the 1841 New York county convention deadlocked over whether it was more appropriate to base suffrage claims on the "common humanity" and natural equality they shared with other citizens or on the notion of collectively inherited rights from Colored men.[36]

Although scholars perceive heightened militancy in national conventions of the 1840s and 1850s, these forums were not immune to concerns about race constructions and citizenship claims. Titles offer a small glimpse of their orientation. The 1843 forum signaled a familiar commitment to morality and rights with its unwieldy description as a convention of "Colored Citizens" who met to consider "their Moral and Political Condition as American Citizens." More to the point was the 1847 gathering of "Colored People and their Friends." Both meetings engaged traditional reform issues affecting the status of Colored people; the second forum made a point of spreading temperance principles "without a thought of color."[37] Other delegations issued apologetic assurances that autonomous endeavors did not mean that they viewed themselves as different from other human beings. The 1848 convention asserted that "general complexion," shared subjugation, and public perception brought disparate elements of the Colored population together as "one people." This fusion was a provisional basis of collective action with which delegates were uncomfortable. They confessed that organizing along color lines contradicted their belief in "human brotherhood." However, they felt they had no choice and regretted that circumstances would compel them to meet in this manner for some time. They urged others to take up the cause of reform "without exclusiveness" and to act "without distinction of color." The group that convened five years later repudiated color distinctions altogether. Declaring themselves "members of the human family," participants assailed racial designations to pinpoint the wrongs of disenfranchisement and establish their citizenship claims. They condemned the term "white" as antithetical to American identity. This "modern word"—used to deprive Colored citizens of their rights—was the creation of "modern legislators."[38] They perceived it as a violation of the spirit of the American Revolution and foreign to the founders of the republic.

The significance of William Whipper and the American Moral Reform Society extends beyond the gap they created between conventions. AMRS adherents eventually returned to state and national conventions and societies. Whipper remained prominent in the cause of antislavery and citizenship rights. Although he and his allies never spearheaded another reform organization, the misgivings about race that distinguished moral reformers permeated other venues. Their ideas, which circulated through convention proceedings, minutes, editorials, speeches, and letters, are critical to mapping the narrative arc of antebellum reform. Their endeavors help explain how Black-controlled reform arenas and print media provided venues and resources for questioning race, debating its logic, and trying to reinterpret it.

NOTES

1. This essay is based on portions of the author's book manuscript, "Reluctant Race Men: Black Opposition to the Practice of Race in Nineteenth-Century America," contracted with Oxford University Press.

2. *National Enquirer and Constitutional Advocate of Universal Liberty* (Philadelphia), December 3, 1836. The biblical reference to "one blood" is in Acts 17:26.

3. *National Enquirer*, November 12, 1836.

4. *National Enquirer*, November 12, 1836.

5. *Minutes of the Fifth Annual Convention for the Improvement of the Free People of Colour in the United States, Held by Adjournments, in the Wesley Church, Philadelphia, from the First to the Fifth of June, Inclusive, 1835*, 26, 29, in *Minutes of the Proceedings of the National Negro Conventions, 1830–1864*, ed. Howard Holman Bell (New York: Arno, 1969).

6. *Minutes and Proceedings of the First Annual Meeting of the American Moral Reform Society* (Philadelphia: Merrihew and Gunn, 1837), in *Early Negro Writing, 1760–1837*, ed. Dorothy Porter (Boston: Beacon, 1971), 211, 225–41.

7. Jane H. Pease and William Pease, *They Who Would Be Free: Blacks' Search for Freedom, 1830–1861* (Urbana: University of Illinois, 1990), 121–22.

8. Sterling Stuckey, *Slave Culture: Nationalist Theory and the Foundations of Black America* (New York: Oxford University Press, 1987), 203.

9. *Minutes and Proceedings of the First Annual Convention of the People of Colour, Held by Adjournments in the City of Philadelphia, from the Sixth to the Eleventh of June, Inclusive, 1831*, 14, 4, 5, 10, 12, 15, in Bell, *Minutes; Liberator* (Boston), July 2, 1831.

10. *Minutes of the Fourth Annual Convention for the Improvement of the Free People of Colour, in the United States, Held by Adjournments in the Asbury Church, New York (New York, 1834)*, 31, 35, in Bell, *Minutes; Colored American* (New York), September 23, 1837.

11. Proponents of an "American" society ignored the vote to launch a *"National Moral Reform Society."* Whipper's opponents clearly envisioned future convention gatherings. His position is ambiguous. He and Robert Purvis recommended that a committee name the "Conventional board" for the next year, and Whipper was chosen to serve on this selection committee. Evidence of the machinations surrounding the formation of the AMRS appear in the preamble of its constitution drafted by Whipper, Stephen Smith, Augustus Price, Edward Crosby of New York, and William Powell of New Bedford. The document, which became part of the convention minutes, maintains that the society came into being at the 1834 convention. Although Whipper and John Jackson of Newtown, New York, had proposed such an action, there is no evidence that the convention considered it. *Minutes of the Fifth Annual Convention*, 4, 5, 8–9, 11, 15, 31.

12. The proceedings identified thirty-one delegates and seventy other members. *Minutes and Proceedings of the First Annual Meeting*, 224, 225; *Colored American*, March 4, 1837; and September 16, 1837.

13. *Minutes and Proceedings of the First Annual Meeting*, 217–19, 221, 223, 231, and passim; *Colored American*, September 2, 1837.

14. *Colored American,* September 9, 1837.

15. Sterling Stuckey interprets conflicts over the Reform Society's position as a fight between separatists and integrationists. Stuckey, *Slave Culture*, 208; *Colored American*, September 2, 1937; and September 23, 1937; *Minutes and Proceedings of the First Annual Meeting*, 216.

16. *Colored American*, September 2, 1837. Emphasis in the original.

17. *Colored American*, May 20, 1837; July 29, 1837; August 19, 1837; August 26, 1837; September 9, 1837; March 15, 1838; March 29, 1838.

18. *Rights of All* (New York), August 14, 1829, as quoted in Floyd Miller, *The Search for a Black Nationality: Black Emigration and Colonization, 1787–1863* (Urbana: University of Illinois Press, 1975), 89.

19. *Colored American*, August 19, 1837.

20. *Colored American*, March 4, 1837.

21. *National Reformer*, October 1838.

22. *National Reformer*, October 1838.

23. For descriptions of the issues that the AMRS considered each year, see Julie Winch, *Philadelphia's Black Elite: Activism, Accommodation, and the Struggle for Autonomy, 1787–1848* (Philadelphia: Temple University Press, 1988), 109–28; and Howard Holman Bell, "The American Moral Reform Society, 1836–1841," *Journal of Negro Education* 27, no. 1 (Winter 1958): 34–39.

24. *Freedom's Journal* (New York), February 29, 1828.

25. *Liberator*, April 14, 1832.

26. *Colored American*, September 9, 1837.

27. *Colored American*, September 16, 1837.

28. *Colored American*, February 10, 1838; March 29, 1838; September 16, 1837; *National Reformer*, November 1838.

29. Paul Finkelman, "Prelude to the Fifteenth Amendment: Black Legal Rights in the Antebellum North," *Rutgers Law Journal* 17 (Spring and Summer 1986): 415–82; Rhoda Golden Freeman, *The Free Negro in New York City in the Era before the Civil War* (New York: Garland, 1994), 92–93.

30. *National Reformer*, November 1838; September 1838; January 1839.

31. *National Reformer*, December 1839.

32. *National Reformer*, December 1839.

33. *National Reformer*, December 1839.

34. *National Reformer*, December 1839.

35. *Convention of the Colored Inhabitants of the State of New York, August 18–20, 1840*, in *Proceedings of the Black State Conventions, 1840–1865*, ed. Philip S. Foner and George E. Walker (Philadelphia: Temple University Press, 1980), 2:8.

36. *Colored American*, October 30, 1841; December 4, 1841; *Convention of the Colored Inhabitants*, 2:13. The New York state convention had requested voting petitions from each county in the state.

37. *Minutes of the National Convention of Colored Citizens: Held at Buffalo, on the 15th, 16th, 17, 18, and 19th of August, 1843 for the Purpose of Considering their Moral and Political Condition as American Citizens*, in Bell, *Minutes*; *Proceedings of the National Convention of the Colored People and their Friends, Held in Troy on the 8th and 9th of October, 1847*, 7, 19, 17, in Bell, *Minutes*.

38. *Report of the Proceedings of the Colored National Convention, Held at Cleveland, Ohio, on Wednesday, September 6, 1848*, 18–20, in Bell, *Minutes*; *Proceedings of the Colored National Convention, Held in Rochester, July 6th, 7th, and 8th, 1853*, 12–15, in Bell, *Minutes*.

DELETED NAME BUT INDELIBLE BODY

Black Women at the Colored Conventions
in Antebellum Ohio

Jewon Woo

The "other side" has not been represented by one who "lives there." And not many can more sensibly realize and more accurately tell the weight and the fret of the "long dull pain" than the open-eyed but hitherto voiceless Black Woman of America.

—Anna Julia Cooper, *A Voice from the South*
by a Black Woman of the South (1892)

During the evening session on Friday, January 17, 1849, at the Columbus Convention of Colored Citizens of Ohio, a group of Black women threatened to boycott the convention unless they were permitted to participate on an equal basis with men. Led by Jane P. Merritt, the women submitted a resolution to the chairman of the Business Committee: "Whereas we the ladies have been invited to attend the Convention, and have been deprived of voice, which we the ladies deem wrong and shameful. Therefore, *Resolved*, That we will attend no more after tonight, unless the privilege is granted."[1] Even though two men, W. Hurst Burnham of Muskingum County and George J. Reynolds of Erie County opposed, the committee adopted the resolution and granted women an equal voice in the proceeding by "inviting the ladies to share in the doings of the Convention."[2] Among those who favored the resolution from the outset were John L. Watson, John Mercer Langston, and T. J. Merritt. In particular, T. J. Merritt, as a member of the Business Committee and Jane's husband, helped Jane by initially bringing the women's resolution to the floor.[3] The Central Committee of the 1849 convention started with a call for participants by appealing to Black manhood: "You, *gentlemen*, are expected to co-operate with the Central Committee in bringing together, to form this Convention, a body of independent, fearless and talented *men—men* in whose hearts burns unquenchably the love of liberty."[4] Notably, after Jane P. Merritt and the women's protest of 1849, the minutes of the next year's convention begin with the resolutions that mention "persons" instead of "men" or "gentlemen" when they declare, "*Persons* present from their respective counties, who have credentials, and those who have been regularly elected, constitute this Convention."[5] This essay argues that Merritt and the other women's interruption in the masculine narrative of the convention destabilizes Black male political subjectivity, as they revised the meaning of Black citizenship that had been exclusively applied to men.

Colored Conventions in Ohio not only confirmed that western abolition was not an eastern import; they also united various African Americans to envision Black citizenry beyond the boundary of abolitionism.[6] The state had at least twenty-one conventions led by Black people, including three national and eleven state Colored Conventions between 1837, when Ohio had its first state Colored convention, and the end of the Civil War.[7] Convention delegate Frederick Douglass's *North Star* praises the Ohio conventions: "These annual conventions[,] we dare say, have been more faithfully and regularly held than those of the colored freemen of any other state in the Union."[8] Indeed, the record of frequency and longevity of the conventions in Ohio is unmatched in any other state. It is not coincidental that Black women such as Jane P. Merritt spoke out against the male-dominant culture at the convention in Ohio, where African Americans had frequent meetings to actualize democracy by claiming the race's civil rights.

However, even though the proceedings are crucial to our examination of Colored Conventions, they often do not allow us to have a full view of Black women activists. The convention proceedings are "a narrative of Black citizenship authentically 'written by itself'" because it "seek[s] to manufacture the very citizenship practices from which the delegates had been excluded."[9] Yet, as John Ernest observes, this narrative centers male voices while the conventions functioned as a stage for Black male leadership.[10] The proceedings of Colored Conventions gloss over Black women participants when compared to the attentive records of male leaders' speeches, debates, and occasionally nonverbal actions. In fact, not only has women's activism rarely been detailed in the few remaining documents in addition to the proceedings, but even these documents often survived only in the form of untraceable fragments. Instead of confirming the lack of their audible voice in the proceedings, this essay illuminates the performative aspect of Black women activists' participation in conventions and proceedings despite their (in)voluntary silence and namelessness, in order to delineate the indelible mark of their influence on the history of Colored Conventions.

This essay revolves around Jane P. Merritt because her name, as it once appears in the record, becomes a thread that leads us to others, the majority of whom are barely named in written history but who, we know from the traces in proceedings and newspaper coverage, actively attended conventions. In attempting to historicize Merritt, we can hardly render her as observable as other Black reformers who produced their own writings, from narratives to newspaper articles. Her very absence from "History" to some extent disrupts seemingly homogeneous narratives generated from the conventions.

As Hortense Spillers suggests with terms such as "pentimento" and "palimp-sest," these absences still carry "traces of preceding moments that alter the contemporaneous rendition, making the latter both an 'originality' and an 'affiliated,' or the initiation of a new chain of signifying as well as an instance of significations already in intervened motion."[11] However, when this blank-ness is replaced with a radical resignification, the forces that Jane P. Merritt and other Black women resisted may remain unmarked, as if those women's independent recognition of agency always existed regardless of these forces. Moreover, the women in the blankness could easily be projected by our pre-sentism and historical expectation, which unintentionally undermines their struggle to speak for themselves. Saidiya Hartman would call this practice "trespass[ing] the boundaries of the archive" through "further violence in [a scholar's] own act of narration."[12] According to Hartman, scholarly work on the archive of slavery inevitably fails to give voice to nameless and silent en-slaved people, while justifying the pattern of what cannot be recovered. This critic equates an effort to reconstruct the past with "an attempt to describe obliquely the forms of violence licensed in the present, that is, the forms of death unleashed in the name of freedom, security, civilization, and God/ the good."[13] In other words, regarding their absence as a sign of disruptive power against "History" oversimplifies the margins where these silenced women were situated. For this reason, it is important to resist the tempta-tion to mythologize Jane P. Merritt as a representative figure of all free Black women in antebellum Ohio or at Colored Conventions.

   Without radically re-signifying her reticence as if our discovery of her si-multaneously would empower her to speak up out of the archival lacuna, this essay considers Jane P. Merritt firmly present with strategic absence of her audible voice to create space for Black women in the history that had failed to notice their significance. What Eve Allegra Raimon describes as "a very present absence," or aporia, can help us explain Merritt's subversively silent presence in history.[14] If we believe that being voiceless or silenced in history is a sign of powerlessness, we reinforce the oppressor's historiogra-phy to glorify the dehumanization of the oppressed as achievement. Rather, we can assume that this absence of Black women's voices or refusal to keep them audible in print indicates Black women's performative strategy to keep their presence intact from unjust authorities' attempts to delete them as meaningless instead of being singled out as unconventional, and therefore socially "less desirable," women with "loud" voices in public. This strategy appears obvious when we engage in their performance with our effort to explore their "present absence" in the archive. Carla Peterson defends specu-lations that emerge in the penumbra of this kind of lacuna, arguing that they can serve as a liberating tool for both scholars and African American women subjects: "Speculative activity may place the feminist researcher in liminal spaces on the margins of established institutions where she may come to test and challenge institutional conventions and constraints."[15] For this reason, Merritt in this essay remains where both the forces, which try to unremember her presence in history, and other voices, which may be different from hers but equally forgotten, coexist. In that place, she makes her way among those forces and voices by maintaining the "very present absence" for liberation out of the racially and sexually discriminatory practices in historiography.

Colored Conventions excluded women from their leadership. However, Black women's textual absence from the proceedings does not simultaneously indicate their actual withdrawal from these public meetings. The proceedings of the first two Colored Conventions—1830 and 1831, both held in Philadelphia—completely omit female attendees, even as providers of meals and entertainment, roles that women mostly filled during men's extended deliberations. When Mary Ann Shadd Cary delivered her speech at the 1855 National Convention of Colored Men, in Philadelphia, one reporter for the *British Banner* denounced the participation of women in conventions even though he noticed her oratorical skill: "Such Conferences are not the place for woman, whose province is ample enough for all her energies of mind and heart—energies alike powerful and precious in their appropriate field; but that field is not the arena of discussion and debate."[16] In the same year, Barbary Anna Stewart was "stricken out" from a discussion on political organization during the 1855 New York state convention in Troy, when "several gentlemen [were] objecting to it on the ground that it is not a Woman's Rights Convention."[17] Nevertheless, numerous Black women undauntedly appeared to be vigorous at conventions. Many "nameless" women were present at the conventions as singers and facilitators. The 1849 Ohio state convention minutes say, "A song was here sung by the Ladies; which elicited much applause." The next year's state convention minutes record that Black women actively secured their seats: "The Ladies attending the Convention proposed to defray the house for the sitting of the Convention."[18] The proceedings of the 1851 Ohio state convention at last began to include several women correspondents, "ladies of Columbus," such as Lucie Ann Stanton, M. J. Hopkins, L. M. Jenkins, C. Hacley, S. Mason, S. P. Scurry, and L. Harper. Therefore, it must be a foregone conclusion that the conventions solely served to confirm Black masculinity as the evidence of African American historical self-consciousness and the representation of their civic qualification.

Both printed and digitized sources provide scant biographical information about Jane P. Merritt. In her study of Black women abolitionists, Shirley Jo-ann Yee laments that census records published before the twentieth century offer little help in searching for the details of Black women's lives. Until 1850, not all free Blacks were included in the federal census. Even when the census included them, it usually listed only Black men as heads of households.[19] The 1840 United States Federal Census records one "Thomas Merritt" under the category of "Free Colored Persons" living in Pickaway County with three men and two women under age twenty-three. The census does not explain their relationship to one another. They were only marked for taxation depending on their age and sex. "Jane Merritt" is found in the 1870,

1880, and 1900 censuses. The widowed "Jane Merritt," who was born in Virginia and a "Black" or "mulatto" female, lived with her grown-up children in Greene County, about sixty miles away from Pickaway County. The 1870 and 1880 censuses note that she cannot read or write.[20] Not only do the three documents fail to indicate her accurate age and relationship to "Thomas Merritt," but the censuses depict her as jobless, illiterate, and dependent on her younger family members. How could this seemingly incapable "Jane" stand up to pass the resolution for women's participation at conventions? Thanks to Reginald Pitts's recent discovery of her maiden name, Pointer, and her second marriage to Charles Ellis in Michigan, her life can be better illuminated. However, what can be found in public birth, marriage, and death records still keeps her life private.

If the census—the most official record of citizenry—does not offer details of Jane P. Merritt's life, Black women's local societies before 1849 may provide some clues about her life as a community activist. Because many antebellum Black women worked in groups for family and community needs, they served as organizers and constructive members who demonstrated what Black citizenry would look like.[21] For example, women members of Cincinnati's United Colored American Association took a prominent role in the public program, which Frederick Douglass singled out as a good example of women's leadership.[22] Through the Colored Ladies' Anti-Slavery Sewing Circle, the Daughters of Temperance, and countless bazaars and fairs, Black women raised funds for community services and protested the actions of Cincinnati's many male-dominated political and social organizations that could not dispense with these women's dedication.[23] However, a women's society without its alliance with organizations under male leadership rarely left records of its activities. In addition, even though we find some of their societies' names in Black periodicals, they tend not to give the names of elected women officers, because decision-making in female organizations was often by the consensus of the membership, placing less emphasis on individual leaders.[24]

Despite Black women's close work with male leaders at Colored Conventions, it is still questionable whether the leaders would successfully represent the women, who were frequently discouraged to speak for themselves. Given that the Pickaway County delegate, T. J. Merritt, was Jane's husband, her activism could have aligned with his participation in conventions. At the 1849 convention, he was appointed a delegate to the next national convention, held in Rochester, New York, in 1853, but he did not appear at it for an unknown reason.[25] Ohio African Americans' recognition of him as a local leader supports an assumption that he might have attended the Cleveland national convention in September 1848 as well. Accompanying him to Cleveland, Jane would have met well-known Black leaders including Frederick Douglass and Martin Delany. The convention proceedings remarked that all "colored persons present, delegates to this Convention, and they considered *women persons*," as the participants passed the resolution: "Whereas, we fully believe in the equality of the sexes, therefore, *Resolved*, That we hereby invite females hereafter to take part in our deliberations."[26] Jane P. Merritt must have felt hopeful about Black women's activism on equal ground with men's when she listened to the leaders' strong support for women's rights.

Unfortunately, Jane P. Merritt and other Black women's expectation for change would not have lasted long. That resolution was precipitated by Douglass's introduction to Rebecca Sanford, a newly wed white woman who had attended the Seneca Falls Convention with him a month earlier.[27] Her participation in the Cleveland convention raises the question of her quali- fication to represent Black women. It is not surprising that some historians mistakenly took her to be Black.[28] If Jane P. Merritt listened to Sanford's speech for women's right of property in the marriage covenant, she would have felt left out of the "women" whom Sanford presented to speak for.[29] In fact, Sanford's remarks on the women's condition had little relevance for most Black women's lives. Whereas her "women" were deprived of property rights that their husbands had, marriage for enslaved Blacks was never legal- ized because they themselves were "property," and most free Black women, like their male partners, worked outside of the home in low-paying jobs to support their families.[30] The lack of white women leaders' attention to Black women already appeared troubling to their contemporaries. For example, Parker Pillsbury once replied to Jane Swisshelm, a white woman who had led an 1850 women's convention at Worchester, Massachusetts: "[It may say] 'the Public are respectfully invited to attend.' But who ever dreamed that 'the public' meant anything colored? . . . Color was not discussed there—it need not have been. But it was needed that the declaration be made in regard to it. That ANY women have rights, will scarcely be believed; but that colored women have rights, would never have been thought of, without a specific declaration."[31] Jane P. Merritt would have responded to Sanford similarly to Pillsbury's critique of Swisshelm's neglect of Black women, especially the working class in free states. Sanford failed to address the concerns of Black women, who were not even allowed to speak at the convention, revealing the complex political terrain that they had to negotiate. Above all, Merritt and other Black women must have realized that they could not be represented by either Black male leaders or white women, even at the conventions where African Americans envisioned democracy based on equal citizenship.

The prevailing absence of Black women in records rather reveals the force that attempts to delete their presence, ironically making that absence too perceptible to ignore. Since Jane P. Merritt must have been a member of a local free Black community, as her leadership indicates, local meeting min- utes housed in the Ohio History Connection may include her name in the ag- gregate. However, not only did these minutes detail male members' names, but they also deliberately deleted female members' presence. For example, one page from the 1859 minutes of the Union Association of Colored Men of New Richmond meeting shows that the word "Daughters" was crossed out, as figure 9.1 shows. In the beginning the minutes proclaim, "Any male

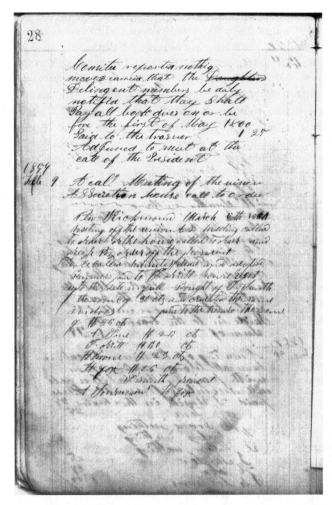

FIGURE 9.1. A page from the Minute Book of the Union Association
of Colored Men of New Richmond, Ohio, 1859. Courtesy of the Ohio
History Connection, African American Experience in Ohio.

person of color may become a member of this Association."[32] Certainly,
this exclusive male-centered statement does not seem to have discouraged
women from participating in the meeting. Later the minutes say, "Committee reported nothing move[d] [and] carried that the ~~Daughters~~ Delinquent
members be duly notified that they shall pay all back dues on or before the
first of May 1860."[33] There were women who gained the committee's attention, which the transcriber noted importantly, as the meeting was locked in
stalemate. Nevertheless, their female identity was deleted as if it should not
be remembered. Likewise, Jane P. Merritt vanished.

Although textual representation of Black women in the proceedings seems to fail, their namelessness and silence do not necessarily evince passivity that kept them in the margin or under strikeouts. Instead, the tension between the force to muffle them and their unwavering effort to engage in public affairs highlights Black women's exemplary dedication to achieving civil rights through communal works. The notorious Black Laws in Ohio discredited free Blacks' right to settle down in this "free" state. The participants at the state conventions of Ohio decried the laws as the biggest obstacle to Black people's political endeavor for citizenship. In particular, the 1849 convention ignited organized actions to successfully repeal the laws. The repeal lowered barriers to Black settlement and education in Ohio, which signaled an expansion of Black citizenship.[34] Discussing conventions in the post–Civil War South, Elsa Barkley Brown points out that African American women were hardly confined to a private sphere even without the franchise or elective office, because "it was their vision of freedom that granted them the right to assume the political responsibilities which neither the state nor some members of their own community acknowledged to be theirs."[35] This estimation illustrates what Jane P. Merritt and other Black women did to fight both the Black Laws that denied Blacks citizenship and the male-centered leadership that undervalued their contribution. While invited to be "auxiliary" help at the conventions, the women had a significant impact on male delegates' decision-making process because, regardless of limitations set by institutional authorities, they understood and exercised their freedom and responsibility.

Against the Black Laws, the state conventions suggested that African Americans "perform" civic virtue when their birth on American soil did not sanction their full citizenship. John Ernest argues that Colored Conventions per se were "collective performances designed to be a representative embodiment of an imagined African American community."[36] The 1849 state convention committees officially invited white citizens, as if the latter were supposed to observe the freed people's political movement in a form of histrionic display. Furthermore, the convention declared, "The resolutions are not placed in the order in which they were acted upon, but more according to the subjects contemplated in each."[37] This statement characterizes the convention as a theatrical stage for exhibiting to white audiences free Blacks' qualifications for legitimate membership in the United States rather than as an actual site for political enforcement. White audiences should witness and appreciate their fellow citizens' display of civic qualities because this spectatorship ultimately fostered connections between the Black body and humanity and between freedom and citizenship.

In the case of Black women, they had to perform their civic virtue not only to whites but also to Black men. The Black women's revolt at the 1849 convention perfectly illustrates the performativity of citizenship. Regardless of the lack of the records, the presence of Jane P. Merritt and other women provokes us to vividly imagine the scene at the Columbus convention. Merritt had a recognizable and performative way to compel the male members to record her action in print. She had carefully planned the revolt before the convention began. She gathered fellow women attendees who had also contributed to the convention by raising monies, cooking dinners, arranging flowers, singing songs, and cleaning the church. Jane P. Merritt and some of the other women must have urged their husbands and male family members to bring up the issue of women. At the same time, she—possibly through Lucie Ann Stanton, who was an Oberlin College senior and classmate with the convention chairman and her future husband, William Howard Day—persuaded Day to support Black women's rights. The Black women, who were invisible while the men proceeded with political issues, waited for their chance to come into their view until the last evening of the convention. We can picture the protest scene. They stood up and walked near to the podium in the center hall of Bethel Church. Most of the men looked at them in surprise and embarrassment. While Day read the resolution, these women, following Jane P. Merritt, theatrically exhibited their determination by standing behind him. Some male delegates such as Burnham and Reynolds denounced this resolution as unacceptable. But most of the men could see that without women's aid for foods, songs, ornaments, and seat arrangements, to name a few of their works, the convention meeting could not go smoothly. The men soon obeyed session chair John L. Watson's order to secure the women's equal ground for participation. By representing their needs and desires to their male counterparts, they became legitimate claimants to public considerations. Furthermore, their invitation of the men to the performance led the latter to see the former's legitimacy, which would urge the men to take action, because witnessing "brings with it responsibilities. When it involves other human beings, then it brings with it ethical, social, and political responsibilities."[38]

The textual character of the proceedings also reveals the performative aspect of the conventions. Pre– and post–Civil War Blacks in free states tried to demonstrate their civic virtue through the convention proceedings and minutes that antislavery and Black-owned periodicals published after the conventions took place. For Black women, printed material for public consumption, like the proceedings, functioned as a site where they should perform in silence. Even though both Black and white women were pilloried when they appeared to speak out in public, Black women were often slandered as "sexually promiscuous" more harshly than their white counterparts because of their race.[39] Therefore, "modesty, which I think so essential in your sex will naturally dispose you to be rather silent in company, especially in a large one. . . . One may take a share in conversation without uttering a syllable," an excerpt from "Hints to Young Ladies" in the *Colored American* insists.[40] Defying the prejudice against Black women through the omission of their voices, the proceedings allude that Black women are virtuous members within the ideological frame of nineteenth-century womanhood. As Peterson suggests, Black women such as Jane P. Merritt entered into the public arena "by consciously adopting a self-marginalization that became superimposed upon the already ascribed oppressions of race and gender and that paradoxically allowed empowerment."[41] Merritt had to compromise the dilemma of being a Black woman in a public space; that is, she knew that silence as womanly virtue would make her more favorable to her community, but she also realized that speaking for women at the risk of losing that virtue was inevitable. For this reason, she somewhat voluntarily let Day read the resolution instead of reading it herself, while keeping herself less visible but ensuring that her demand was recorded in the proceedings.[42] Without becoming a living spectacle of the Black woman's "degradation," Jane P. Merritt presented herself and other Black women as acceptable to broader audiences not only at the convention but also in free states where the minutes reached in print.

Aporia, or the "very present absence," can be interpreted as nineteenth-century Black women's conscious performance responding to exclusionary gestures of convention leadership, which resulted from not only sexism but also politics of class-based separatism. Highly educated Black women emerged as a notable group in Ohio because Oberlin College had admitted both Black and white students since its establishment in 1833.[43] Two of the best-known women at the state conventions are Sara Stanley and Frances Ellen Watkins. Stanley, who as a representative of the Delaware Ladies' Anti-Slavery Society submitted the speech at the 1856 state convention, was an Oberlin alumna. Watkins, as a famous poet and educator, was invited to deliver a speech at the 1858 state convention. Even though working-class women such as Jane P. Merritt—without, or with less, formal education—comprised most of the Black women population in the antebellum period, they were hardly welcome for a leading role at the conventions. As a matter of fact, leaders expressed apprehension over the lifestyles of working-class Blacks. For example, E. Smith, calling himself a "true Wesleyan" in Frederick Douglass's *North Star*, regarded urban Black people as low-skilled labor forces that would misrepresent the whole Black population as second-class citizens in the North: "[Blacks in the northern cities] engaged as waiters about hotels, barbers or boot-blacks, and the women washing white people's dirty clothes."[44] At the 1848 national convention, the committee including Douglass spoke in a similar manner that menial occupations "have been so long and universally filled by colored men, as to become a badge of degradation, in that it has established the conviction that colored men are only fit for such employments."[45] Paradoxically, the Black elite leaders' recognition of working-class men and women at the convention reveals that they significantly constituted the convention, not as mere onlookers but as active participants who could represent a wide spectrum of Black citizenship.

Jane P. Merritt remains quiet, but she firmly exists in historic moments. Despite the official admittance of women into the state and national conventions, the conventions failed to develop consistent policies that could foster Black women's leadership. To discover Jane P. Merritt, this essay depends on many fragments of archives and studies that are woven together by various speculations. How, then, do these fragments tell who Merritt was? The lack of recorded evidence about her may indicate her absence from history or less significance of her presence in that history. However, Mary Ann Shadd Cary, who served as a delegate at the national convention in Philadelphia in 1855, argues that "words, actions, events, and circumstances become important or trivial in proportion to the relations they sustain, or to the accidents of time and purpose inseparable from their real significance . . . [because] events, small in themselves, become the index to the most stupendous results."[46] The presence of forces that tried to silence Black women, deleted their voices, and blurred the image of their physical existence at the conventions appears indisputable.[47] At the same time, Black women in the margins of the proceedings and minutes performed to be recognized, heard, and recorded. Ernest claims that we should understand African American historiography through their engagement "in a dynamic mode of composition in which the act and conventions of writing—and the contingencies that shaped the performance of individual and collective identity."[48] Whereas these are the forces that promoted Black male and elite subjectivity as the representative Black citizenry, Jane P. Merritt and so many unnamed women reshaped the collective body of African Americans by keeping themselves recognizable through their reluctant quietness. Jane P. Merritt's absence from all other proceedings except the 1849 convention compels us to join her performance to mark Black women's place in history. Jane P. Merritt exists under the crossed-out mark on the indelible word "Daughters." And, most importantly, while looking for her, we cannot but perform the role of history making in an unconventional mode of identifying unrecorded women.

NOTES

This essay was written before Reginald Pitts discovered Mary Jane Pointer Ellis, who appeared as "Jane P. Merritt" at the 1849 convention, even though its revision heavily benefits from his study. Instead of detailing what he has found, this essay focuses on how to approach Black women activists whose names and voices were barely recorded. For the biographical information on Merritt, see "Mary Jane Pointer Merritt," in The "Conventions" of the Conventions: The Practices of Black Political Citizenship, by Carolyne King and Erica L. Ball, digital exhibit, Colored Conventions Project, https://coloredconventions.org/black-political-practices/womens-roles /mary-jane-pointer-merritt.

1. State Convention of the Colored Citizens of Ohio (1849: Columbus, OH), Minutes and Addresses of the State Convention of the Colored Citizens of Ohio, Convened at Columbus, January 10th, 11th, 12th, & 13th, 1849, Colored Conventions Project, http:// coloredconventions.org/items/show/247.

2. Because W. Hurst Burnham lived in Zanesville, Ohio, where Mary Jane Pointer grew up, he could have been acquainted with the Pointer family. He might be a businessman, as the Muskingum County Recorder indicates that he purchased nine lots on a business street on May 7, 1851. Muskingum County Recorder (database), accessed June 15, 2015, http://cotthosting.com/ohmuskingum/LandRecords/protected /SrchQuickName.aspx?rtn=True. According to the Sandusky Library Archive Research

Center, George J. Reynolds was a carriage maker and active Underground Railroad conductor in Sandusky, Ohio. The historian Wilbur Siebert depicts Reynolds as a skilled blacksmith "of mixed Negro and Indian blood." Reynolds also met with John Brown at the meeting in Chatham, Ontario, Canada, in May 1858 to discuss abolitionism. For more biography of George J. Reynolds, see "George J. Reynolds, Carriage Maker and Underground Railroad Conductor," *Sandusky History* (blog), February 7, 2008, http://sanduskyhistory.blogspot.com/2008/02/george-j-reynolds-carriage-maker -and.html.

3. James Oliver Horton and Stacy Flaherty, "Black Leadership in Antebellum Cincinnati," in *Race and the City: Work, Community, and Protest in Cincinnati, 1820–1970*, ed. Henry Louis Taylor Jr. (Urbana: University of Illinois Press, 1993), 80.

4. State Convention of the Colored Citizens of Ohio (1849), *Minutes and Addresses*. Emphases added.

5. State Convention of the Colored Citizens of Ohio (1850: Columbus, OH), *Minutes of the State Convention of the Colored Citizens of Ohio, Convened at Columbus, January 9th, 10th, 11th, and 12th, 1850*, Colored Conventions Project, http://coloredconventions .org/items/show/248. Emphasis mine.

6. According to Stacey Robertson, by 1850, most of the residents of Ohio, Indiana, and Illinois had been born in the West. Although western abolitionists sought to work collaboratively with their colleagues in eastern states, their movement was distinct in various ways. See Stacey Robertson, *Hearts Beating for Liberty: Women Abolitionists in the Old Northwest* (Chapel Hill: University of North Carolina Press, 2010), 5. While Robertson focuses on white midwesterners, Horton and Flaherty examine Black communities in Cincinnati, Ohio, which helps us see that the characteristics of Black midwesterners are different from Black easterners. At midcentury more than three-quarters of Blacks who took leadership in their communities were southern born, just two percentage points more than for Black Cincinnatians generally. Horton and Flaherty, "Black Leadership," 77.

7. "Convention of Colored People of Ohio," *Philanthropist* (New Richmond, OH), September 8, 1837, Colored Conventions Project, http://omeka.coloredconventions .org/items/show/1590. Kate Masur recently located these records.

8. "Colored Citizens of Ohio," *North Star* (Rochester, NY), June 29, 1849, 2, cols. 6, 7; William Cheek and Aimee Lee Cheek, *John Mercer Langston and the Fight for Black Freedom, 1829–65* (Urbana: University of Illinois Press, 1989), 133.

9. Derrick R. Spires, "Imagining a State of Fellow Citizens: Early African American Politics of Publicity in the Black State Conventions," in *Early African American Print Culture*, ed. Lara Langer Cohen and Jordan Alexander Stein (Philadelphia: University of Pennsylvania Press, 2012), 274, 279.

10. See John Ernest, *Liberation Historiography: African American Writers and the Challenge of History, 1794–1861* (Chapel Hill: University of North Carolina Press, 2004), 265; and John Ernest, *A Nation within a Nation: Organizing African-American Communities before the Civil War* (Chicago: Ivan R. Dee, 2011), 124. Patrick Rael also discusses the masculine discourse among Black elites in *Black Identity and Black Protest in the Antebellum North* (Chapel Hill: University of North Carolina Press, 2002), 33. In addition, see Benjamin Quarles, *Black Abolitionists* (New York: Oxford University Press, 1969), 26; and Ella Forbes, *African American Women during the Civil War* (New York: Garland, 1998), 211.

11. Hortense H. Spillers, "Introduction: Who Cuts the Border? Some Readings on 'America,'" in *Comparative American Identities: Race, Sex, and Nationality in the Modern Text*, ed. Hortense H. Spillers (New York: Routledge, 1991), 15, 25n29.

12. Saidiya Hartman, "Venus in Two Acts," *Small Axe*, no. 26 (June 2008): 9, 2.

13. Hartman, 13.

14. Eve Allegra Raimon, "Lost and Found: Making Claims on Archives," *Legacy* 27, no. 2 (2010): 257.

15. Carla Peterson, "Subject to Speculation: Assessing the Lives of African American Women in the Nineteenth Century," in *Women's Studies in Transition: The Pursuit of Interdisciplinarity*, ed. Kate Conway-Turner, Suzanne Cherrin, Jessica Schiffman, and Kathleen Doherty Turkel (Newark: University of Delaware Press, 1998), 115.

16. *British Banner* (London), November 20, 1855, 2, col. 3.

17. Colored Men's State Convention of New York (1855: Troy, NY), *Minutes of Colored Men's State Convention of New York, Troy, September 4, 1855*, Colored Conventions Project, http://coloredconventions.org/items/show/238.

18. State Convention of the Colored Citizens of Ohio (1850), *Minutes*.

19. Shirley Jo-ann Yee, "Black Women Abolitionists: A Study of Gender and Race in the American Antislavery Movement, 1828–1860" (PhD diss., Ohio State University, 1987), 52.

20. 1840 United States Census, Pickaway County, Ohio, digital image s.v. "Thomas Merritt," Ancestry.com; 1870 United States Census, Spring Valley Township, Greene County, Ohio, digital image s.v. "Jane Merritt," Ancestry.com; 1880 United States Census, Xenia, Greene County, Ohio, digital image s.v. "Jane Merritt," Ancestry.com; and 1900 United States Census, Xenia Township, Greene County, Ohio, digital image s.v. "Jane Merritt," Ancestry.com.

21. Carla Peterson, *"Doers of the Word": African-American Women Speakers and Writers in the North (1830–1880)* (New Brunswick, NJ: Rutgers University Press, 1995), 15–20. In this context, John Ernest (*Nation within a Nation*, 112) points out that the state conventions benefited from grassroots community activism.

22. Douglass emphasized the importance of Black women's organizations. One article in the *North Star* says, "We do not look up to the ladies of the American Antislavery Society, but should we desire assistance from any source, it will be mainly to the *colored* Anti-Slavery ladies we shall look for such leaders, the agenda of antislavery societies included the improvement of the free Black community as well as the commitment to end slavery" (August 14, 1848, 2, col. 3).

23. Horton and Flaherty, "Black Leadership," 73–74.

24. Horton and Flaherty, 74.

25. State Convention of the Colored Citizens of Ohio (1849), *Minutes and Addresses*. It is possible that he might have died suddenly when the cholera epidemic swept south Columbus and Cincinnati in late 1849. Cheek and Cheek, *John Mercer Langston*, 117.

26. Colored National Convention (1848: Cleveland, OH), *The Proceedings of the Colored National Convention, Held at Cleveland, Ohio, on Wednesday, September 6, 1848*, Colored Conventions Project, http://coloredconventions.org/items/show/280.

27. I wonder if he could have invited one of the Black women leaders, as an example of equality in sexes, to the 1848 convention instead of Rebecca Sanford, who omitted Black women from her speech. As Martha Jones suggests, "Indeed, Douglass's choice of Sanford as the sole female speaker left Black women's points of view indiscernible." Martha S. Jones, *All Bound Up Together: The Woman Question in African American Public Culture, 1830–1900* (Chapel Hill: University of North Carolina Press, 2007), 80.

28. Willie Mae Coleman calls Sanford "a lone Black woman," omitting her name while identifying her gender and (falsely assumed) race. Willie Mae Coleman, "Keeping the Faith and Disturbing the Peace, Black Women: From Anti-slavery to Women's Suffrage" (PhD diss., University of California, Irvine, 1982), 18. Yee ("Black Women Abolitionists," 338) also mentions "one Black woman" who joined with prominent male leaders at the convention.

29. Colored National Convention (1848), *Proceedings*.

30. Yee ("Black Women Abolitionists," 124) observes that economic necessity in most urban Black families required Black wives and daughters to contribute to the economic survival of the family while fulfilling their traditional domestic responsibilities. For instance, they took in boarders and extra laundry or worked as domestic

servants and dressmakers. See also Dorothy Sterling, *We Are Your Sisters: Black Women in the Nineteenth Century* (New York: W. W. Norton, 1984), 72, 95–96.

31. "From the Pittsburgh Visitor: Woman's Rights Convention and People of Color," *North Star*, December 5, 1850, 1, cols. 3, 4.

32. "Union Association of Colored Men of New Richmond, Ohio: Minute Book, 1859," 8, Ohio Historical Center Archives Library, Columbus, accessed April 20, 2015, http://dbs.ohiohistory.org/africanam/html/det69ab.html?ID=13903.

33. "Union Association of Colored Men," 33.

34. Nikki M. Taylor, *Frontiers of Freedom: Cincinnati's Black Community, 1802–1868* (Athens: Ohio University Press, 2005), 176.

35. Elsa Barkley Brown, "To Catch the Vision of Freedom: Reconstructing Southern Black Women's Political History, 1865–1880," in *African American Women and the Vote, 1837–1965*, ed. Ann D. Gordon, Bettye Collier-Thomas, John H. Bracey, Arlene Voski Avakian, and Joyce Avrech Berkman (Amherst: University of Massachusetts Press, 1997), 87.

36. Ernest, *Liberation Historiography*, 252.

37. State Convention of the Colored Citizens of Ohio (1849), *Minutes and Addresses*.

38. Kelly Oliver, *Witnessing: Beyond Recognition* (Minneapolis: University of Minnesota Press, 2001), 156–57.

39. Anne M. Boylan, "Benevolence and Antislavery Activity among African American Women in New York and Boston, 1820–1840," in *The Abolitionist Sisterhood: Women's Political Culture in Antebellum America*, ed. Jean Fagan Yellin and John C. Van Horne (Ithaca, NY: Cornell University Press, 1994), 120. See also Carol Lasser, "Enacting Emancipation: African American Women Abolitionists at Oberlin College and the Quest for Empowerment, Equality, and Respectability," in *Women's Rights and Transatlantic Antislavery in the Era of Emancipation*, ed. Kathryn Kish Sklar and James Brewer Stewart (New Haven, CT: Yale University Press, 2007), 324–25.

40. "From Gregory's Legacy to His Daughters, Hints to Young Ladies," *Colored American* (New York), September 15, 1838, 120, col. 2.

41. Peterson, *"Doers of the Word,"* 17.

42. In a similar manner, at the 1856 convention in Columbus, Ohio, Sara Stanley's speech was delivered by Mr. Harris. However, I cannot identity "Mr. Harris," as both W. D. Harris and J. H. Harris attended the convention.

43. Lasser's research on Black women at Oberlin suggests how they benefited from higher education and actively engaged in Colored Conventions. See Lasser, "Enacting Emancipation," 328.

44. "Selections," *North Star*, February 23, 1849, 1, col. 4. Recent study reveals that the working-class Blacks in Ohio, especially barbers, served as a central force to organize African American communities by promoting education, press publication, and aid societies. Jane's husband, T. J. Merritt, was also a barber. To understand the significant role of Black barbers in Black communities in Ohio, see Ann Clymer Bigelow, "Antebellum Ohio's Black Barbers in the Political Vanguard," *Ohio Valley History* 11, no. 2 (2011): 26–40.

45. "An Address to the Colored People of the United States," in Colored National Convention (1848), *Proceedings*.

46. Mary Ann Shadd Cary, "Trifles," *Anglo-African Magazine* 1 (1859): 55–56.

47. Patrick Rael (*Black Identity*, 6–7) suggests that the general absence of Black women in the records hints at a countervailing presence "that tended to silence women and that deeply conditioned the shape of Black public protest."

48. Ernest, *Liberation Historiography*, 6.

PART 3

OUT OF ABOLITION'S SHADOW

Print, Education, and the
Underground Railroad

THE ORGAN OF THE WHOLE

*Colored Conventions, the Black Press, and
the Question of National Authority*

Benjamin Fagan

By early January 1848, Frederick Douglass had lost patience with his sometimes ally and often rival Henry Highland Garnet. The two had been among the nearly seventy Black men who had met the previous October in Troy, New York, for the National Convention of Colored People. During the convention, Garnet had been appointed the head of the committee charged with preparing and distributing the meeting's minutes. The full convention report was published in Troy in 1847, but as the year turned to 1848, Douglass had still not received a copy. Douglass publicized his frustration in a January 14, 1848, editorial in the *North Star*, the newspaper he had founded just two months earlier. "We trust," the new editor remarked, "that no unworthy motive has withheld from us those proceedings; but would like to know the cause." "Perhaps," Douglass coyly suggested, "Mr. Garnet can explain."[1] The headline Douglass selected for his editorial points to one explanation for why he suspected Garnet of intentionally withholding the convention's minutes. Douglass titled his piece "Colored National Press." At the Troy convention Douglass and Garnet (along with a host of other delegates) had fiercely debated a proposal to create a "national" press that would print a range of publications, including a "national" newspaper. Douglass strongly opposed the idea, while Garnet argued in its favor. Garnet's position carried the day, and the convention delegates voted to pursue the project. During the debate Garnet had expressed mock surprise that the greatest objections to a national press "came from editors, who are, or are to be," and sarcastically concluded that "of course there was nothing of selfishness in all this."[2] Apparently still smarting from this charge, and correctly suspecting that it would make its way into the published minutes, Douglass turned to the pages of his new newspaper to defend himself.

Douglass used his January editorial to make his case against establishing a new Black newspaper and in doing so explored just what it might mean to designate any paper as a "national" publication. He agreed with the Troy convention on the necessity of "there being a printing press under the entire control of colored persons in this country" but asserted that, in the offices of the *North Star*, "such a press now exists." Douglass saw no need for a new journal, given the numerous Black newspapers already circulating across the country. "But to all this it may be answered," he admitted, "We not only want a press, but a 'National Press.'" Pointing to the uncertainty over the designation "national," Douglass asked, "What is the difference between a press and a national press?" Answering, in a way, his own question, the *North Star*'s editor contended that "that press, call it by what name you please,—Mystery, Ram's horn, Northern Star, or North Star, best sustained, most ably conducted, and thoroughly devoted to the rights and liberties of our enslaved and oppressed fellow-countrymen, will be the colored national press of this country, in every essential sense of the word."[3] Douglass argued that a newspaper's commitment to the cause of Black liberation, rather than the endorsement of a Colored Convention, is what made a newspaper "national" in the "essential sense."

Douglass's January 1848 editorial, written as an extension of the debates at the Troy convention held four months earlier, offers an especially clear instance of how Colored Conventions and Black newspapers engaged with one another. From the 1830s into the 1850s, Colored Conventions consistently took up the cause of the Black press in general and a Black "national" press in particular. Such discussions, as the debate in Troy and Douglass's subsequent editorial exemplify, reveal the ongoing fight over the meaning of the very term "national," a struggle that also necessarily involved any claims to authority that accompanied that designation. And just as the delegates to Colored Conventions argued over the definition and contours of a national Black press, Black newspaper editors and correspondents debated the merits and meaning of "national" Colored Conventions. Like the 1847 convention in Troy, which called itself a "National Convention of Colored People," numerous Colored Conventions claimed the moniker of "national" gatherings. In published minutes, delegates typically made no mention of the term "national" in reference to their own meetings, omissions that painted the conventions' claims to national authority as uncontested affairs. To be sure, Black audience participation, rules of order, and convention leaders' public engagement and recognition beyond the halls of the annual meetings could appear to validate the conventions' national authority. But commentary surrounding certain "national" conventions in the pages of Black newspapers tells a different story. The voices of those who felt unrepresented by national Colored Conventions may not have been heard in the churches and halls where such meetings took place or been recorded in their published minutes and reports. But, as Douglass's January 1848 editorial illustrates, Black newspapers offered an alternative venue for Black men and women to discuss and debate issues central to the Colored Convention movement and at times challenge a convention's claim to "national" authority.

In this essay, I read the minutes of Colored Conventions and the pages of Black newspapers together, exploring how these two crucial institutions of antebellum Black life and activism understood and imagined each other.

This comparative institutional analysis reveals, I argue, the importance of national authority for Colored Conventions and the Black press as well as the deeply contested nature of that authority for antebellum Black Americans. Delegates to national Colored Conventions used the meetings to explore the contours and consequences of an explicitly "national" Black community. As Eddie S. Glaude Jr. explains, the language of nation developed by these delegates represents "not so much a nationalist politics in the sense of a challenge to political power by a nation with an explicit and peculiar character as a commonly held sense of group distinctiveness—an ambiguously rich notion of 'we-ness.'"[4] And for Glaude, "efforts to generate a conversation among Black Americans about the problems facing them," of which Colored Conventions are a prime example, helped to create this sense of "we-ness."[5] Making a similar argument, John Ernest contends that Colored Conventions "created a national community to deal with national evils by transforming individuals into representatives" from Black communities scattered across the country.[6] Moreover, "since these meetings were as much attempts to create state and national networks as to convene representatives from networks already established," Ernest concludes that "those who attended the conventions played an important role in *defining* the community in whose name they gathered."[7] Building on the work of Glaude and Ernest, I explore how delegates to Colored Conventions defined not only the national community they were attempting to create but, more specifically, the qualities necessary for an individual or institution to claim the authority to speak for that nation.

The reports that Colored Conventions produced on the question of a national Black press, and the debates those reports engendered, provide a crucial account of the struggle over national authority within and among antebellum Black institutions. Delegates rarely questioned their own assumption of national authority but rather displaced such discussions onto the other Black institution dedicated to imagining and creating national community: the press. As scholars such as Frances Smith Foster, Elizabeth McHenry, and Eric Gardner have argued, Black newspapers before the Civil War sought to bring their readers together into a variety of kinds of communities.[8] And in their discussions of the Black press, delegates to Colored Conventions often lauded the power of Black newspapers to create decidedly national communities. By framing the Black press as an institution that, like the Colored Conventions movement, not only represented but also created a national body, these delegates anticipated Benedict Anderson's influential vision of the newspaper as an engine of nation formation. However, the debates over national authority that raged across Colored Conventions and Black newspapers in the 1840s and 1850s complicate Anderson's claim that, "regardless of the actual inequality and exploitation that may prevail in each, the nation is always conceived as a deep, horizontal comradeship."[9] Antebellum Black Americans understood that, in addition to "horizontal comradeship," vertical power relations shaped and defined national communities. Hence, the minutes of Colored Conventions and the pages of Black newspapers not only reveal how particular institutions and individuals attempted to assert their authority over other members of the nation but also record the resistance to such claims.

In this essay I focus in particular on the 1843, 1847, and 1854 conventions, all of which were not only designated as "national" gatherings but also produced lengthy and detailed reports that directly address the creation of a centralized Black press. In order to better understand how two of the primary institutions of antebellum Black activism engaged with each other, I place the minutes of these meetings into conversation with articles on national authority appearing in Black newspapers such as *Freedom's Journal*, the *Colored American*, the *North Star, Frederick Douglass' Paper*, and the *Provincial Freeman*. I begin by briefly tracing the ways in which Colored Conventions in the 1830s supported Black newspapers, before moving to the efforts of Colored Conventions in 1843 and 1847 to found and support an explicitly "national" Black press. I then take up the proposal by the 1854 National Emigration Convention to create a Black periodical that stretched beyond the borders of the United States to include Black voices located throughout the hemisphere, and consider how that plan challenged the boundaries of "national" identity. I conclude by briefly examining the ways in which Black newspapers covered the 1854 emigration convention, with a particular eye toward debates over whether that convention could claim the mantle of national authority and the potential limits of that designation. In my conclusion, I consider the potential for extending a comparative institutional approach to other antebellum Black organizations and point toward some possible avenues for future research.

Propositions for a National Press

Discussions of newspapers in general, and the Black press in particular, occupied delegates to some of the earliest Colored Conventions. Those attending the First Annual Convention of the People of Colour (which was in fact the second), held in Philadelphia in 1831, set aside time at the close of their meeting to address the power and necessity of newspapers that spoke for and to Black Americans. The "Convention would remind our brethren that knowledge is power," declared the published minutes, "and to that end, we call on you to sustain and support, by all honourable, energetic, and necessary means, those presses which are devoted to our instruction and elevation."[10] Four years later in 1835, delegates to the "Fifth Annual Convention, for the Improvement of the Free People of Colour in These United States," again meeting in Philadelphia, threw their support behind newspapers friendly to the cause of Black Americans. A committee "appointed to consider the claims of the presses in our favour" declared "that it is only through the instrumentality of that most potent reformer of public sentiment the public press, that any certain, speedy and radical change will be effected in the moral and political relation which we, as a people, hold in this country" and hence deemed it "obligatory upon every Christian, philanthropist, and patriot, of whatever hue or condition, to give his aid and support to those presses devoted to the great and holy cause of human rights."[11] The concluding convention address also pledged to "establish a press, and through it make known to the world our progress in the arts, science, and civilization."[12] The convention, as a body, failed to follow through on this promise, but at least one attendee took inspiration from its message. In 1837 Philip Bell, who had attended the 1835 convention as a delegate from New York City, founded the *Weekly Advocate* in his home city. The paper, whose name was quickly changed to the *Colored American*, operated until the end of 1841, and in the 1860s Bell would found the *Elevator* newspaper in San Francisco, California.[13] Bell offers a powerful illustration of how Colored Conventions spurred on the development of the Black press, though at times in ways not recorded in the minutes of the meetings.

During the 1830s, Colored Conventions repeatedly took up the cause of the press and at least indirectly inspired Black newspaper production in the following decade. Conventions in the 1840s took the next step to develop concrete plans for establishing a single Black newspaper that would, ideally, speak for and to all Black Americans. In 1843, delegates descended upon Buffalo for the National Convention of Colored Citizens.[14] Whereas the convention eight years earlier had considered the worth of sympathetic white newspapers, the Buffalo meeting focused its energies on the Black press. The convention underscored the importance of the Black press by creating a committee "to take measures to establish a press, to be the organ of the colored people in this country."[15] The convention packed the committee with experienced Black newspapermen. Samuel Cornish (editor of *Freedom's Journal* and the *Colored American*), Philip Bell, and Charles Ray (who had joined the staff of the *Colored American* in 1837 and edited it beginning in 1840) all served, as did Henry Highland Garnet, who would clash with Douglass later in the decade.

The 1843 committee produced a report that pointed to the two main tasks of a centralized Black newspaper. First, the committee reiterated the argument of the delegates to the 1835 convention regarding the power of the press in general to influence public opinion for good or ill. "The press takes hold of the public mind," they declared, "and gets at the public heart; its influence reaches the spot to form and influence public opinion; and to what do the disabilities of the colored people and the slavery of this country owe their existence, more than to public opinion?"[16] Hostile white newspapers did immense damage by circulating racist misrepresentations that turned "public opinion" against the cause of Black liberation, but a Black newspaper would allow Black Americans to refute and correct such accounts. In 1827, Samuel Cornish and his coeditor John Russwurm had offered the same rationale on the front page of the first issue of *Freedom's Journal*, the first Black newspaper published in the United States. "We wish to plead our own cause," they wrote. "Too long have others spoken for us. Too long has the publick been deceived by misrepresentations, in things which concern us dearly."[17] Sixteen years later Cornish and his fellow committee members underscored the power of the Black press to counter white attacks and as a result advance the cause of Black freedom. "If one class of the people ought to have a press absolutely under their control," they declared, "it is that class who are the proscribed, and whose rights are cloven down."[18] Echoing the opening editorial of *Freedom's Journal*, the 1843 convention understood the impact that Black newspapers could have on a white audience. By correcting the distortions peddled by white newspapers, the Black press could potentially turn white public opinion toward the cause of Black freedom.

In addition to influencing white attitudes, the 1843 committee trumpeted the power of a single, centralized Black newspaper to shape all Black Americans into a unified whole. First, though, a newspaper would introduce Black Americans to one another. "A paper emanating from, and circulating among us," wrote the 1843 committee, "will bring us almost as it were in contact; will make us better acquainted with each other, and with the doings of each other." The men who met in Buffalo had traveled from Maine, Massachusetts, New York, Ohio, Michigan, Illinois, Virginia, North Carolina, and Georgia. The delegates thus vividly understood the need for institutions to help bridge the vast distances between the Black communities located in these diverse places. Colored Conventions themselves served such a purpose, but a national Black newspaper could be even more effective by providing a cheap and frequent venue for Black men and women, most of whom would never meet face-to-face, to get to know one another. Samuel Cornish had made precisely this argument six years earlier when, as editor of the *Colored American*, he explained that Black Americans required a weekly newspaper "because our afflicted population in the free states, are scattered in handfulls [sic] over nearly 5000 towns, and can only be reached by the Press."[19] The overlapping arguments of the *Colored American* and the gathering in Buffalo, and the presence of Cornish as author of the 1837 editorial and a member of the 1843 committee, exemplify the reciprocal relationship between Black newspapers and Colored Conventions.

Beyond bringing Black men and women scattered across the United States into contact with one another, the 1843 committee contended, a centralized Black newspaper would help shape them into a unified Black community. The committee imagined that a single newspaper, read by Black Americans across the country, would "have the tendency to unite us in a stronger bond, by teaching us that our cause and our interests are one and common, and that what is for the interest of the one, or a point gained in our common cause in one section of the country, is for the interest of all, or a point gained by all." Crucially, the members of the committee did not expect a Black newspaper to simply comment on an already existing unified Black community but rather help create one by teaching Black Americans about their shared causes and concerns. At the same time that it created a unified Black community, though, the newspaper envisioned by the convention would display the achievements of that community to its members. The committee concluded that "being the organ of the whole," their planned newspaper "would necessarily chronicle the public measures of the whole, and thus become a medium to enable us to learn about, as well as from each other."[20] The 1843 convention hoped, then, to produce a Black newspaper that simultaneously formed and revealed the "whole" of Black America. In other words, the pages of a single Black newspaper, read and supported by all Black Americans, would become an environment where community formation and revelation mutually reinforced each other.

Despite the delegates' passion and planning, the 1843 convention failed to produce the desired result of a centralized Black newspaper. Four years later, in Troy, New York, the issue once again occupied the delegates to a Colored Convention.[21] The 1847 convention selected James McCune Smith to chair the committee it charged with reporting on a "National Press and Printing Establishment for the People of Color." Smith, a doctor from New York City, had extensive experience with the Black press. He had briefly co-edited the *Colored American* in the late 1830s and would contribute pieces to a variety of Black newspapers. Led by Smith, the Troy committee addressed many of the same issues as its Buffalo brethren, but this committee's plan was more ambitious. Like their predecessors in 1843, the 1847 committee members grounded their plan in the belief that the press "is the vehicle of thought—is a ruler of opinions."[22] But whereas the 1843 convention had focused on the creation of a Black newspaper, Smith and his collaborators envisioned a printing house that produced multiple publications. "Let there be, then, in these United States," they declared in their report, "a Printing Press, a copious supply of type, a full and complete establishment, wholly controlled by colored men; let the thinking writing-man, the compositors, pressman, printers' help, all, all be men of color;—then let there come from said establishment a weekly periodical and a quarterly periodical, edited as well as printed by colored men."[23] Here, the 1847 committee turned its attention to the conditions of production that made this "full and complete establishment" a national press. The primary requirement, according to the report, was that a Black man occupy every position in the chain of production. Only then could the press, and the publications it produced, claim to be the voice of a national community.

The multiple tasks that the 1847 report listed off in its discussion of production also pointed to the fact that no one person could create the publications they envisioned. Instead, the committee underscored how making and sustaining a national newspaper would necessarily be a collective effort. According to Smith and the other committee members, the story of the Black press in the United States demonstrated not only that Black Americans had the capacity to create a newspaper but also that no individual possessed the authority and ability to single-handedly operate a national press. Papers such as *Freedom's Journal* and the *Colored American* "abundantly prove that we have all the talent and industry requisite to conduct a paper such as we need; and they prove also, that among 500,000 free people of color no one man is yet set apart with a competence for the purpose of advocating with the pen our cause and the cause of our brethren in chains." A national press, operated as a collective enterprise, would take the burden of maintaining and sustaining a paper off of any single individual. "It is an imposition upon the noble-minded colored editors, it is a libel upon us as a free and think-ing people," the report concluded, "that we have hitherto made no effort to establish a Press on a foundation so broad and national that it may support one literary man of color and an office of colored compositors."[24] By focus-ing on collective production and "broad" support, Smith and his coauthors underscored that a "national" press could avoid the pitfalls that had doomed individually operated papers. Indeed, a key piece of their project's "national" character was its collective, collaborative foundation.

During the afternoon session on the first day of the Troy meeting, Smith delivered his committee's report and the convention debated its adoption. According to the convention's minutes, the basic plan for a printing press and publications controlled and staffed by Black men met little resistance, but numerous delegates balked at the implied scope and authority of a "na-tional" press. Thomas Van Rensselaer, for example, feared "that the under-taking was too great to be carried into successful operation," while Frederick Douglass "was in favor of a Press, but a National Press he was satisfied could not well be sustained."[25] Douglass also worried that, regardless of the re-port's emphasis on collective control, such a publication would allow a small group of men to claim to represent all Black Americans. He expressed con-cern that a "Paper started as a National organ, would soon dwindle down to be the organ of a clique."[26] By contrast James McCune Smith contended that rather than usurping the authority of local Black communities, a national press could address the issues and concerns of the many Black Americans who could not afford to produce their own paper. In support of this claim, Smith "instanced the fact, that in the recent struggle in Connecticut to ob-tain equal suffrage, the colored people of that State, were without the neces-sary means through which to make known and urge their claims,—whereas if this National Press were established—papers speaking forth our senti-ments, making known the wrongs we suffer, and demanding the rights due to manhood could then be issued by *thousands*, where now there is none."[27] Underscoring the fact that the press he supported would produce not a sin-gle newspaper but rather a host of Black periodicals, Smith again empha-sized the link between the national and multiple and the power inherent in that connection. No one Black newspaper could hope to be nimble enough to address all of the diverse concerns that occupied the Black communities scattered across the United States. But a national press, produced and sup-ported by the collective force of those communities, could unleash an array of publications upon the American landscape.

Ultimately, Smith's position carried the day, and the convention voted overwhelmingly to accept his committee's report. Like the efforts of earlier conventions, though, the enthusiasm of the delegates in Troy did not sustain the creation and maintenance of a press or a paper. But, as Douglass remarked in his January 1848 editorial, a host of local Black newspapers filled the void. These were not produced by the collectively operated and supported operation envisioned by Smith and his allies. Nevertheless, Douglass believed that the Black newspaper "best sustained, most ably conducted, and thoroughly devoted to the rights and liberties of our enslaved and oppressed fellow-countrymen, will be the colored national press of this country, in every essential sense of the word."[28] Douglass's formulation of what constituted a "national press" thoroughly revised the vision agreed upon at the 1847 convention. The report from the Committee on a National Press had drawn a clear distinction between the "press" and Black newspapers. In Douglass's definition, the newspaper and the press were one and the same. This conflation transformed the "national press" from a project for producing all kinds of Black printed materials into a designation that applied exclusively to a newspaper. Which newspaper in particular could claim that mantle would, according to Douglass, be determined not by Colored Conventions but rather by the laws of competition. The Black newspaper "most ably conducted" and "best sustained" would earn the title of "national press." This definition served Douglass well. For while he listed four possible candidates for the post, at the time he published his January 1848 editorial on the subject, the *Mystery* and the *Northern Star and Freeman's Advocate* had already folded. The *Ram's Horn* would sporadically appear into 1849, but editor Thomas Van Rensselaer struggled to keep his publication afloat.[29] Lest readers wonder which Black newspaper was "most ably conducted," Douglass routinely attacked the *Ram's Horn* as a publication filled with errors.[30] As Douglass's journals increasingly came to dominate the field of Black newspapers in the 1850s, his understanding of the "national press" as a single newspaper largely eclipsed the 1847 convention's notion of a centralized operation that produced multiple publications.

The Limits of National Authority

Seven years after the gathering in Troy, another Colored Convention took up the cause of a centralized, Black-owned and Black-operated publishing house. Meeting in Cleveland, Ohio, in August of 1854, delegates to the National Emigration Convention of Colored People focused most of their attention on the best destination for Black emigration out of the United States.[31] But they also formed a committee to consider "the Establishment of a Periodical, To be the Organ of the Black and Colored Race on the American Continent." As its very name suggests, the Cleveland committee, led by the Black poet James M. Whitfield, planned to create a publication far different from those envisioned by this committee's predecessors in Buffalo and Troy. Similar to opening statements from the committees at the earlier conventions, the report from the 1854 committee began by stating "that a well-conducted and well supported press, is a most potent instrument in the moral and intellectual culture, and elevation of any people."[32] But unlike earlier plans, which called for frequently published newspapers that could comment on current events, the Cleveland committee proposed a quarterly "literary periodical," provisionally named the *Africo-American Repository*. The *Repository* would be filled with writings "on the various branches of literature, science, art, mechanics, law, commerce, philosophy, theology, et cetera," and "all the articles shall be productions of colored men."[33] As a periodical devoted to showcasing Black writing, the *Repository* would thus "bring the evidences of progress before those who deny such progress, in a manner that it could not be disputed" and "present to colored men of ability an inducement to write, which they do not now possess."[34] By providing a venue for Black writers, the delegates to the 1854 convention expected the *Repository* to simultaneously cultivate Black literary talents and use such work to combat anti-Black racism. Black newspapers from *Freedom's Journal* to *Frederick Douglass' Paper* had included poems, fiction, and essays from Black writers in their pages, but the *Repository*'s exclusive focus on Black literary accomplishments signaled a new kind of Black periodical.[35]

In addition to being a literary quarterly rather than a weekly newspaper, the *Repository* would possess a different geographic scope than the publications proposed by earlier conventions. Sometimes directly, sometimes implicitly, the reports from the 1843 and 1847 conventions imagined papers that would speak for and to Black men and women in the United States. By contrast, the National Emigration Convention explicitly framed its periodical as the organ not of a U.S.-based Black population but rather of one located more broadly on the "American continent." For example, the committee's report proposed that "some of the ablest colored writers in both hemispheres should be engaged as its regular contributors" and explained that the quarterly could not be published more frequently in part because "a considerable portion of its patrons, as well as contributors, will probably be from other countries."[36] Unlike the publications proposed by earlier conventions or newspapers such as the *North Star*, the *Repository* made no effort to claim the mantle of "national press." Rather than being an act of modesty, this omission reveals the grand ambitions that the 1854 convention delegates had for their periodical. For, while some delegates to the 1847 convention worried that a "national" framework was too large a scale for a single newspaper, those who met in Cleveland seven years later believed that their periodical would speak for and to all Black Americans, within and without the United States, precisely because it would transcend national boundaries.

In an unfortunate echo of their predecessors in 1843 and 1847, the delegates in Cleveland were not able to put their plans for a literary magazine into action. But while the *Repository* never materialized in print, it profoundly influenced Black print culture by providing a blueprint for future Black periodicals. The *Anglo-African Magazine*, edited from 1859 to 1860 by the Black New Yorker Thomas Hamilton, echoed not only the *Repository*'s title but also its focus on Black literary contributions. Hamilton filled the *Anglo-African* with poetry, songs, fiction, sketches, histories, and scientific essays from many of the era's leading Black writers. Martin Delany, a leading force behind the 1854 convention in Cleveland, contributed a variety of pieces, including part of his serialized novel, *Blake; Or the Huts of America*. The *Anglo-African* did not feature writings from Black writers from across the hemisphere, but it did include numerous pieces that focused on Black American communities outside of the United States. James Theodore Holly's "Thoughts on Hayti," for example, advocated emigration from the United States to Haiti, while Delany's *Blake* imagined the Black revolutionary possibilities of Cuba.[37] The similarities between the outline of the *Repository* printed in the minutes of the 1854 National Emigration Convention and the *Anglo-African Magazine* that appeared five years later again suggest that while Colored Conventions may not have directly produced Black periodicals, the deliberations of such bodies deeply shaped the contours of the Black press.

The 1854 National Emigration Convention also offers a particularly vivid example of how the relationship between Black newspapers and Colored Conventions was not always one of mutual admiration and support. A year before the planned gathering, its main organizer, Martin Delany, asked Frederick Douglass (editor of *Frederick Douglass' Paper*) and William H. Day (editor of the *Aliened American*) to include the call for the convention in their papers. This was a common practice, and both men seemingly complied. But in a brief editorial that appeared in the same issue as the convention notice, Douglass clarified that "we have no sympathy with the call for this convention which we publish in another column" and pronounced the planned gathering "unwise, unfortunate, and premature."[38] Moreover, his paper apparently modified the call in a manner that undercut its authority. In an April 15, 1854, letter to the *Provincial Freeman*, a Canadian-based Black newspaper edited by Mary Ann Shadd, Delany thanked the paper for also publishing his convention's call. But the *Provincial Freeman* had copied its notice from *Frederick Douglass' Paper* (another common practice), and Delany asked Shadd "to *copy* the 'Call' from *the Aliened American*, as that is the *only* correct copy of it now being published in any of the papers."[39] The call that appeared in Douglass's paper, Delany explained, was "incorrect in ma[n]y particulars, even parts of sentences and paragraphs omitted, as well as a large part of the list of signers, from different States."[40] Such alleged changes made the idea for the Cleveland meeting appear to emerge from a small group of activists located in the same region and thereby weakened its claim to be a "national" convention. The convention retaliated against this and other slights by removing *Frederick Douglass' Paper* from the list of Black newspapers it recommended in its published minutes. While typically boosters of the Black press, Colored Conventions could also withhold their support from papers they considered hostile to their cause.

Frederick Douglass' Paper had, indeed, lobbed a series of attacks at the Cleveland convention before and after it met in August of 1854. Following the lead of its editor, the newspaper staunchly opposed any plan for Black emigration from the United States, but its primary objection to the convention seemed to stem from the gathering's claim to represent a "national" community. In a lengthy November 1854 letter to the newspaper reviewing the convention, and representative of the paper's general line of criticism, the Black attorney and professor George B. Vashon claimed that "nearly all of the delegates were from the same section of the country." Rather than a national convention, then, Vashon claimed that the meeting "seems to have been a Convention of Pittsburgers." Given the lack of geographic diversity among the convention's delegates, he concluded that "it would now be the part of wisdom for them to conclude, with the great majority of their brethren, that, in attempting to give a national character to their scheme, they made a false move."[41] In his 1848 editorial for the *North Star* Douglass had contended that a commitment to Black liberation could qualify a Black newspaper as a "national" endeavor. But six years later in the pages of *Frederick Douglass' Paper*, Vashon argued that a convention needed to represent a broad geographic area, rather than advance any particular politics, in order to claim a "national character." According to such logic, the 1854 gathering in Cleveland, if it in fact drew delegates from only a small region, did not qualify as a national gathering, and hence its arguments in favor of emigration could be dismissed as the ravings of a small minority of Black Americans.

Mary Ann Shadd's *Provincial Freeman* also weighed in on the "national character" of the 1854 convention. Shadd and her family had a long history of supporting Colored Conventions. Her father had been a delegate to the 1831 convention in Philadelphia, and she would (after much debate among the male delegates) join the 1855 Colored National Convention as a corresponding member.[42] Shadd had personally emigrated to Canada in 1851 and counted Martin Delany as a close friend and ally. But she also took issue with the "national" claims of the Cleveland convention, though from a very different point of view than Douglass and his correspondents. Vashon argued that the Cleveland convention was too geographically homogenous to claim a broad national mandate. By contrast, Shadd contended that the decision to mark the 1854 convention as a "national" gathering made it too small in scope to accommodate Black participants living outside of the United States. Like *Frederick Douglass' Paper*, the *Provincial Freeman* printed the call for the emigration convention. "It is not, however, to be understood," clarified Shadd in March of 1854, "that we consider the Call as intended to include Colored men resident in the Provinces."[43] "Had your Convention been a North American Convention the case would have been different," she explained to the convention's planners in an editorial a few weeks later, "but being a National affair, and we hailing from another nation, we may only hope for your 'arrival' on our shores in due time."[44] For Shadd, Colored Conventions that designated themselves as "national affairs" addressed and represented an exclusively U.S.-based Black population. From her vantage point in Canada, national authority was not something to be desired and fought over but instead a restrictive and exclusionary notion that ignored the presence of transnational Black American communities.

On the one hand, the fact that *Frederick Douglass' Paper* and the *Provincial Freeman* each critiqued the 1854 convention's "national" claims underscores the pride of place that national authority held for antebellum Black institutions. Over the course of three decades Colored Conventions developed plans for national newspapers. Such plans produced spirited debates precisely because of the assumption that a "national" designation would endow a newspaper with the authority to speak to and for all Black Americans. But as the coverage of national Colored Conventions in newspapers such as the *Provincial Freeman* reveals, Black Americans living beyond the boundaries of the United States used their own institutions to radically reframe the question of national authority.

Reading the minutes of Colored Conventions and the pages of Black newspapers together thus provides a nuanced account of how antebellum Black Americans took up, worked through, and challenged an individual's or institution's right to represent the Black men and women living within and without the United States. Such an account relies on a comparative approach that recognizes the deeply interwoven nature of antebellum Black institutions. Colored Conventions and the Black press shared key members, priorities, and strategies. Moreover, delegates to conventions saw the convention movement as an engine for the creation of Black periodicals, and their discussions at least indirectly sparked the creation of Black newspapers and magazines. In other words, Colored Conventions helped make the Black press, and a more thorough investigation of these two institutions could explore how Black newspapers similarly played a central role in the creation of Colored Conventions. This essay's focus on national authority represents only one lens through which to read the relationship between Colored Conventions and the Black press, and far more work remains to be done on the connections between these two pillars of antebellum Black America. Finally, it is my hope that this essay serves as a springboard for comparisons of other Black institutions.[45] For example, Black churches, schools, mutual benefit societies, banks, and militias represent other key nodes in the network of antebellum Black institutions, and we have only begun to explore and understand how these organizations, together, shaped Black life in the antebellum United States and beyond.

NOTES

1. [Frederick Douglass], "Colored National Press," *North Star* (Rochester, NY), January 14, 1848.

2. *Proceedings of the National Convention of Colored People, and Their Friends, Held in Troy, N.Y., on the 6th, 7th, 8th, and 9th October, 1847*, Colored Conventions Project, https://omeka.coloredconventions.org/items/show/279.

3. [Douglass], "Colored National Press."

4. Eddie S. Glaude Jr., *Exodus! Religion, Race, and Nation in Early Nineteenth-Century Black America* (Chicago: University of Chicago Press, 2000), 114.

5. Glaude, 114.

6. John Ernest, *A Nation within a Nation: Organizing African-American Communities before the Civil War* (Chicago: Ivan R. Dee, 2011), 111.

7. Ernest, 111. Emphasis in the original.

8. See Frances Smith Foster, "A Narrative of the Interesting Origins and (Somewhat) Surprising Developments of African-American Print Culture," *American Literary History* 17, no. 4 (Winter 2005): 714–40; Elizabeth McHenry, *Forgotten Readers: Recovering the Lost History of African American Literary Societies* (Durham, NC: Duke University Press, 2002), 84–140; and Eric Gardner, *Unexpected Places: Relocating Nineteenth-Century African American Literature* (Jackson: University Press of Mississippi, 2009). In her groundbreaking article, Foster focuses especially on the religious communities that Black printed materials, and especially newspapers, represented and created, while McHenry recovers the central role that Black newspapers played in making communities of Black readers. Gardner's book on the postbellum Black press in the midwestern and western United States explores how these geographies in particular shaped the communities imagined by Black newspapers. For more on the particular ways in which Black newspapers imagined and created different kinds of national communities see Ernest, *Nation within a Nation*, 164–90; and Benjamin Fagan, *The Black Newspaper and the Chosen Nation* (Athens: University of Georgia Press, 2016).

9. Benedict Anderson, *Imagined Communities: Reflections on the Origin and Spread of Nationalism*, rev. ed. (London: Verso, 2006), 7. For his discussion of the newspaper as a maker of national community, see Anderson, 33–36.

10. *Minutes and Proceedings of the First Annual Convention of the People of Colour, Held by Adjournments in the City of Philadelphia, from the Sixth to the Eleventh of June, Inclusive, 1831*, Colored Conventions Project, https://omeka.coloredconventions.org/items/show/72.

11. *Minutes and Proceedings of the Fifth Annual Convention, for the Improvement of the Free People of Colour in These United States, Held by Adjournments, in the Wesley Church, Philadelphia, from the First to the Fifth of June, Inclusive, 1835*, Colored Conventions Project, https://omeka.coloredconventions.org/items/show/277.

12. *Minutes and Proceedings of the Fifth Annual Convention.*

13. The final extant issue of the *Colored American* is dated December 25, 1841, though it is possible that the paper continued into early 1842. For more on Bell's life and work in New York City, see Carla Peterson, *Black Gotham: A Family History of African Americans in Nineteenth-Century New York City* (New Haven, CT: Yale University Press, 2011). For a discussion of Bell's editorship of the San Francisco–based *Elevator*, see Gardner, *Unexpected Places*, 92–132.

14. For a collaboratively created digital exhibit focused on the 1843 convention in general and the question of Black wealth in particular, see Sarah Patterson, *Prosperity and Politics: Taking Stock of Black Wealth and the 1843 Convention*, digital exhibit, Colored Conventions Project, https://coloredconventions.org/black-wealth/.

15. *Minutes of the National Convention of Colored Citizens: Held at Buffalo, on the 15th, 16th, 17th, 18th and 19th of August, 1843*, Colored Conventions Project, https://omeka.coloredconventions.org/items/show/278.

16. *Minutes of the National Convention.*

17. [Samuel Cornish and John Brown Russwurm], "To Our Patrons," *Freedom's Journal* (New York), March 16, 1827.

18. *Minutes of the National Convention.*

19. [Samuel Cornish], "Why We Should Have a Paper," *Colored American* (New York), March 4, 1837.

20. *Minutes of the National Convention.*

21. For a collaboratively created digital exhibit focused on the 1847 convention in general and its focus on the question of a national press in particular, see Ashley Durrance, Hannah Harkins, Nicholas Palombo, Leslie Rewis, Melanie Berry, Christy Hutcheson, Eli Jones, and Morgan Shaffer, *The Early Case for a National Black Press*, digital exhibit, Colored Conventions Project, https://coloredconventions.org/black -press/.

22. *Proceedings of the National Convention.*

23. *Proceedings of the National Convention.*

24. *Proceedings of the National Convention.*

25. *Proceedings of the National Convention.*

26. *Proceedings of the National Convention.*

27. *Proceedings of the National Convention.* Emphasis in the original.

28. [Douglass], "Colored National Press."

29. According to Frankie Hutton, the *Mystery*, edited by Martin Delany, ran from 1843 to 1847, while the *Northern Star and Freeman's Advocate*, edited by Stephen Myers, was only printed in 1842. Hutton lists the *Ram's Horn* as running from 1846 to 1848, but Douglass's references to the paper in the *North Star* suggest that it continued into 1849. See Frankie Hutton, *The Early Black Press in America, 1827 to 1860* (Westport, CT: Greenwood, 1993), 165–66.

30. In one editorial, for example, Douglass wrote that the "Ram's Horn states that we have taken the lecturing field for six months. This is a mistake, but one in keeping with those which that print makes when speaking of ourselves." Frederick Douglass, untitled editorial, *North Star*, March 9, 1849.

31. For a collaboratively created digital exhibit focused on the 1854 convention, see Ashley Durrance, Hannah Harkins, Nicholas Palombo, Leslie Rewis, Melanie Berry, Christy Hutcheson, Eli Jones, and Morgan Shaffer, *To Stay or to Go? The 1854 National Emigration Convention*, digital exhibit, Colored Conventions Project, https://colored conventions.org/emigration-debate.

32. *Proceedings of the National Emigration Convention of Colored People; Held at Cleveland, Ohio, on Thursday, Friday and Saturday, the 24th, 25th, and 26th of August, 1854*, Colored Conventions Project, https://omeka.coloredconventions.org/items/show/314.

33. *Proceedings of the National Emigration Convention.*

34. *Proceedings of the National Emigration Convention.*

35. In 1828, *Freedom's Journal* printed "Theresa—a Haytien Tale," perhaps the first published short story written by an African American. See Frances Smith Foster, "How Do You Solve a Problem Like Theresa?," *African American Review* 40, no. 4 (Winter 2006): 631–45. Commenting on Frederick Douglass's newspapers in the 1840s and 1850s, Elizabeth McHenry argues that "one of Douglass's literary goals in his newspapers was to claim artistic license for black literary arts and the work of black authors." See McHenry, *Forgotten Readers*, 116.

36. *Proceedings of the National Emigration Convention*, 30, 31.

37. For more on the *Anglo-African Magazine*, see Derrick R. Spires, *The Practice of Citizenship: Black Politics and Print Culture in the Early United States* (Philadelphia: University of Pennsylvania Press, 2019), 161–205; Erica Ball, *To Live an Antislavery Life: Personal Politics and the Antebellum Black Middle Class* (Athens: University of Georgia Press, 2012), 109–31; and Ivy Wilson, "The Brief Wondrous Life of the *Anglo-African Magazine*; or, Antebellum African American Editorial Practice and Its Afterlives," in *Publishing Blackness: Textual Constructions of Race Since 1850*, ed. George Hutchinson and John K. Young (Ann Arbor: University of Michigan Press, 2013), 18–38.

38. [Frederick Douglass], "The Emigration Convention," *Frederick Douglass' Paper* (Rochester, NY), August 26, 1853.

39. M[artin] R. Delany, "The Emigration Convention," *Provincial Freeman* (Toronto, Canada West), April 15, 1854; emphasis in the original. The *Provincial Freeman* never

altered the text of the convention call that it printed in its pages, and the issues of the *Aliened American* where the call would have appeared are not extant, so it is impossible to verify precisely what changes Douglass may have made.

40. Delany, "Emigration Convention."

41. G[eorge] B. V[ashon], "The Late Cleveland Convention," *Frederick Douglass' Paper*, November 17, 1854.

42. For more on Mary Ann Shadd's antebellum activities in particular, see esp. Carla Peterson, *"Doers of the Word": African-American Women Speakers and Writers in the North (1830–1880)* (New Brunswick, NJ: Rutgers University Press, 1995), 89–118; and Jane Rhodes, *Mary Ann Shadd Cary: The Black Press and Protest in the Nineteenth Century* (Bloomington: Indiana University Press, 1998), 1–41. For a collaboratively created digital exhibit focusing on the 1855 convention, see Jessica Conrad and Samantha deVera, *The Fight for Black Mobility: Traveling to Mid-century Conventions*, digital exhibit, Colored Conventions Project, https://coloredconventions.org/black-mobility.

43. [Mary Ann Shadd], "The Emigration Convention," *Provincial Freeman*, March 25, 1854.

44. [Mary Ann Shadd], "A Word about, and to Emigrationists," *Provincial Freeman*, April 15, 1854.

45. For a prime example of this sort of work, see Ernest, *Nation within a Nation*.

AS THE TRUE GUARDIANS OF OUR INTERESTS

The Ethos of Black Leadership and Demography
at Antebellum Colored Conventions

Sarah Lynn Patterson

With the most sympathizing and heartfelt commiseration, [we] show our
sense of obligation as the true guardians of our interests, by giving wholesome advice and good counsel.

—First Annual Convention of the People of Color, 1831

During the nineteenth century, the United States became increasingly reliant on public and private organizations to document its
ever-shifting population. Black-led forums carrying the moniker
"Colored Conventions" orchestrated information enterprises to study Black
communities' "moral and political condition as American citizens" at a time
when slavery in the South and racial discrimination in the North limited
Black Americans' access to citizenship rights and regularly threatened their
social, political, and economic well-being.[1] The 1843 National Colored Convention released the first comprehensive population reports since national
meetings began in 1830, believing the reports "sufficient . . . to wake up some
interest . . . upon this feature of [convention] business."[2] As a direct result,
statistical and sociological reports appeared in national and state convention proceedings throughout the antebellum and postbellum eras. The antecedents of W. E. B. Du Bois's and Booker T. Washington's turn-of-the-century
sociological analyses, including *The Philadelphia Negro* (1899) and *Up from
Slavery* (1901), Colored Conventions' population reports grant insight into
the interconnected relationship between Black activist-intellectuals' leadership ethos and the systems that supported their political agendas.

   This essay traces the organizational politics and challenges surrounding
Black convention demography between 1830 and 1843.[3] The reports undermined common perceptions about Black inferiority and legislative measures
that codified discrimination. Such measures promoted white Americans'
socioeconomic potential while reinforcing restrictions on Black Americans' personal and professional pursuits. Through the process of demography, Black delegations brokered real and imagined relationships between

leaders, participating communities, and public spectators. Accountability measures and belief systems associated with Colored Convention delegate positions impacted the creation of population reports. This essay seeks to illustrate the ways Black demography undergirded Black convention reformers' expressions of moral duty to represented communities, set contours for delegate roles, and provided Black communities with tools to resist inequality. Black convention demography established a key form of educational training that was grounded in American civic engagement.

Early Colored Conventions' population reports demarcate a uniquely *Black* public protest tradition among a host of contemporaneous abolitionist cohorts. Several white-run and Quaker organizations held political meetings that subsequently produced population reports advocating for Black rights and for the abolition of slavery.[4] For example, the Philadelphia-based Society of Friends, the 1840 Abolition State Convention held in Ohio, and the Pennsylvania Society for Promoting the Abolition of Slavery relied on demography. The latter reported having trouble articulating "the value of the colored people" in Philadelphia "when the census of the alms-house is made the criterion by which they are to be judged."[5] Despite the meaningful ways Colored Convention demography allowed Black leaders to stage protest apart from white organizations, their processes, designs, and outcomes remain at the margins of Black-led protest measures that are most frequently associated with Black reform cultures. Scholars often investigate convention cultures through the speech act and through iconic debates between celebrity delegates. William Banks in *Black Intellectuals: Race and Responsibility in American Life* (1996) argues that early Black congressional-style conventions reflect a passionate performance in democratic exercises often remembered for the oratorical genius of men such as Frederick Douglass and Henry Highland Garnet.[6] Banks argues, "Because no other venues were available, the conventions usually took on the air of tournaments, where orators competed with one another to enhance their reputations among their peers."[7] Distinguished and lesser-known intellectuals relied on convention-sponsored community assessments to grant greater context to issues raised on the floors of city hall buildings, churches, theaters, and other public spaces wherein Black delegations developed self-help practices apart from more popular, better-funded white-run abolitionist organizations.

Black demography reflects the ways united Black populations could build political power while educating public audiences. Black conventions participated in what John Ernest calls "the theatre of history" in the context of "the considerable illusions of white Americans": "African American historical writing . . . would need to identify the terms of its own existence— . . . defining the African American community both with and against the terms used by white Americans by which African Americans found themselves with common experiences set off from but fundamental to the white national story."[8] Not only did many Black convention leaders express commitment to the U.S. nation-state by pride of birthright and upbringing; they also laid claim to the New World's political apparatus. Known as "a pioneer in the use of statistics to combat pseudoscientific theories of racial inferiority," the New York delegate James McCune Smith expressed the value of strategic political organizing, proclaiming that "freedom has not made [free Blacks insane]; it has strengthened our minds by throwing us upon our own resources, and has bound us to American institutions with a tenacity which nothing but death can overcome."[9]

Statistical and qualitative reports helped justify the very existence of Colored Conventions. By the 1840s, America was on its way to becoming "one of the fastest growing and most heterogeneous populations in the world."[10] The 1843 numerical and qualitative analyses mirror a national trend toward data collection. Black-sponsored population data would have provided valuable information to Black readers. A Black entrepreneur seeking to launch a business in an urban center, an itinerant minister seeking a church home, a Black teacher hoping to join a school district, or a newspaper subscription agent searching for communities to serve would have found value in consulting population reports. The documents challenged economic exclusion and promoted local networks that could provide support systems for represented communities.

Statistical and qualitative reports gave represented communities a voice in convention proceedings while maintaining their anonymity. Parliamentary procedures limited the number of individuals who spoke or were documented as speaking at convention sessions. As a result, print proceedings discuss a relatively small number of individuals by name in comparison with the number of people who attended and who were represented. Population reports embedded in proceedings, however, rhetorically highlight a much larger number of participants (see fig.11.1). The reports define their participation in nation building as inhabitants, landowners, skilled workers, parents, and club and church members, among other categories. Moreover, convention leaders could include or omit information in order to shape the depiction of Black American life according to desirable outcomes. Given widespread racial violence during the 1840s, this style of reporting helped secure the safety of Black communities that elected representatives to advocate for their rights in the public sphere.

Data formatting in population reports reflects real boundaries of power. Antebellum convention demography and reporting were perpetually inchoate. This is evident in the fact that the 1843 population statistics do not follow the day's technical standards for the presentation of statistical information. As figures 11.2 and 11.3 show, by the 1850s and 1860s, national and state delegates had significantly enhanced the variety and formatting of data since 1843. The 1855 national delegation's report includes employment data to draw attention to desirable skills. It also includes unemployment data to draw attention to financial hardships. The 1865 California State Convention's report illustrates remarkable improvements to styles of itemization since 1843. It offers more details about goods, services, and educational opportunities

ALBANY, N. Y.

Colored inhabitants 700—real estate 70,000 dollars—mechanics and persons in mercantile business 28—churches 2, Baptist and Methodist, with 300 members inclusive—Sabbath-schools 2, with 100 members inclusive—common schools 2, with 90 members inclusive—literary societies 2, with 40 members inclusive; and one semi-monthly periodical.

BUFFALO, N. Y.

Colored inhabitants 700—churches 2, Methodist and Baptist—1 Sabbath-school, with 60 members—mechanics 20—merchants 2—1 common school with 80 members—1 total abstinence society, with upwards of 300 members.

ROCHESTER, N. Y.

Colored inhabitants 500—real estate 47.000 dollars—churches 2, Methodist, with about 200 members—1 Sabbath-school with 40 members—benevolent societies 3—1 debating society—mechanics 12—a district school with 40 members.

GENEVA, N. Y.

Colored inhabitants 311—real estate 10,000 dollars—common schools 1, with 50 scholars—1 female benevolent society—public property 1500 dollars.

LOCKPORT, N. Y.

Colored inhabitants 200—real estate $10,000, 1 common school, with 30 members—churches 1, Methodist, with 30 members—one Sabbath-school, with 20 members—mechanics 10.

NIAGARA FALLS, N. Y.

Colored inhabitants 50—professors of religion 20—real estate 300 dollars.

FIGURE 11.1. An excerpt from the report of the 1843 Committee on the Condition of Colored People, which included members Abner Francis, William Munro, Sampson Talbot, Theodore Wright, and William H. Yancy. The report appears in the minutes of the 1843 National Colored Convention at Buffalo, New York. Image courtesy of ColoredConventions.org.

created by and for Black consumers. Nonetheless, conventions' census-taking initiatives depended upon delegations' voluntary compliance with requests for population data even though most delegates held unpaid positions. Moreover, convention delegates lacked the political power to enact a vast majority of resolutions passed on behalf of Black communities. As such, Black population reports should be considered a reflection of delegations' *creative and intellectual direction* over political agendas.

Delegates' Notions of Moral Leadership at Early Colored Conventions

The movement's early Black tacticians lay several moral and organizational foundations that set the stage for demography as an educational, leadership endeavor. The African Methodist Episcopal (AME) Church and concurrent

NEW JERSEY.

Working at their Trades.

Blacksmith 1; House Carpenters 2; Dressmakers 5; Masons 1; Milliners 2; Cooper 1; Shingle Shavers 4; Patent Leather Manufacturers 2; Tinsmith 1; Engineers 2; Corsetmakers 2; Clergymen 2; Doctor 1; Teachers 3; Musicians 4; —Total 33.

Not working at their Trades.

House Carpenters 1; Machinists 1; Horse Shoers 1; Cooper 1;—Total 4.

PENNSYLVANIA.

Working at their Trades.

Boot and Shoemakers 37; Bakers 10; Ship Carpenters 42; Blacksmiths 15; Joiners 4; Sailmakers 14; Clergymen 35; Painters and Glaziers 5; Dyers and Hatters 4; Confectioners 35; Musicians 37; Dressmakers 125; Tailoresses 14; Physician 1; Doctors 7; Plain Seamstresses 40; Speculators in Merchandise 12; Land and Stock-jobber 1; Merchants 10; Milliners 7; Engineers 4; Saddle Treemakers 1; Paper Hangers 2; Turners 6; Ornamental Chairworkers 2; Teachers 20; Masons 4; Practical Farmers 37; Lumber Merchants 4; Several gentlemen of Fortune reputed for their good breed of cattle ;—Total 515.

Not working at their Trades.

Boot and Shoemakers 60; Ship Carpenters 2; Turners 7; Carpenters 30; Sailmakers 6; Painters and Glaziers 7; Musicians 15; Dressmakers 32; Tailoresses 4; Plain Seamstresses and Shirtmakers 10; Milliners 4; Horse Shoers 2; Machinists 2; Silver Plater 1; Mason and Bricklayers 4;— Total 186.

OHIO.

Working at their Trades.

House Carpenters 36; Blacksmiths 24; Ship Carpenter 1; Boot and Shoemakers 38; Dressmakers 49; Tailors 6; Carriagemakers 2; Horse Shoers 12; Machinists 4; Masons 12; Printers 2; Milliners 4; Painters 16; Composition Roofer 1;

FIGURE 11.2. An excerpt from the report of the 1855 Committee on Mechanical Branches among Colored People of the Free State, which Edward V. Clark chaired. Unlike the 1843 report, this one includes the number of unemployed workers by trade and numerical totals for each category. The report appears in the minutes of the 1855 National Colored Convention at Philadelphia, Pennsylvania. Image courtesy of ColoredConventions.org.

Common Institutions.

Public Day Schools.............. ...2
    Pupils................120
Public Night Schools........... 2
    Pupils.......... .....60 Adults.
Colored Children in Catholic Schools..10

Livingstone Institute.

Funds.... ....$3,000

Caulkers' Association.

Members................ 9

BUSINESS PURSUITS.

Mechanics, Manufacturers, etc.

Painters........ 4
House Carpenters....................3
Ship Carpenters.....................2
Caulkers.......................9
Boot Makers.....................4
Tailors.....................3
Brick Layers 2
Plasterers.... 2
Blacksmiths........ 4
Hose Makers....................1
Segar Makers.... 2
Tinners....................1
Upholsterers..... 2
Dress Makers.......... 10
Seamstresses....................5
Milliners....................3
Ladies Hair Dressers..................9
Tobacco Manufacturers... 4
Soap and Tallow Manufactory 1
Fancy Soap Manufactory.............1
Hair Restorative.....................1
Fancy Hair-workers............. ...2
Laundries...................10
Junk Stores....................2
Teamsters... 20
Real Estate Agents.............. 2
Barbers......

Liberal Professions.

Clergymen....................10
Editors.......................2

Total Wealth of City and County.$750,000

Sacramento County.

Number of Adults in City and County.470
Number that can read and write.....375
Number that cannot read or write.... 95
Number Children in City and County..150
Number attending school............ 49
Number not receiving instruction.....101
Sabbath Schools 2, membership of.... 44
Eight Teachers..two Superintendents. 10

A library belonging to each school, consisting of 350 volumes.

Number of Churches................2

A. M. E. Church, Rev. J. H. Hubbard, Pastor in charge, 32 members.

Baptist connection, Rev. Amos Johnson, 32 members.

Number of Mechanics......... 18
Farmers..... 10
Doctor....(............ 1

No person in the county supported by by the public, or benevolent societies.

Amount of Church and public property belonging to colored residents...$4,600

But one colored person in the County Hospital.

Amount of real estate and other property...................$137,245

Total amount of property represented by the people of color of this city and county, as far as can be ascertained............$141,845

Yolo, Colusa and Tehama Counties.

MADE BY BASIL CAMPBELL.

Adults ....16 Children.......5
    Total population....... 21
Number who can read and write.......15
Property owned in the county...$17,900
Farmers and Stock-raisers......... ...5
Stock-raisers without farms..........4
No school in the county.

As there are no delegates from the adjoining counties of Colusa and Tehama, I beg leave to report the condition of those counties, as far as I am acquainted. In the county of Colusa there are,
Adults...........8 Children.....13
    Total population.... 21
Number who can read and write.........5
Property owned in the county....$22,300
Farmers and Stock-raisers............5
Stock-raisers without farms... 2
No school in the county.

In the county of Tehama there are,
Adults............14 Children.... .17
    Total population.... 31
Number who can read and write.......15
Property owned in the county....$29,300
Farmers and Stock-raisers...... 7
Stock-raisers without farms............2
No school in the county.

Recapitulation of the three counties:
Adults............38 Children....35
    Total population.... 73
Number that can read and write.......35
Property owned.......... ......$69,500
Farmers and Stock-raisers........ ..17
Stock-raisers without farms............8

El Dorado County.

Male Adults.....................190
Female Adults..................... 75
Children.... 40

Total 305
Number that can read and write......223

Occupations.

Mechanics.....................4
Miners.......................50
Farmers.......................14
Hair Dressers.....................25
Laborers.......................40
Aggregate am'nt taxable property.$75,000
    One Church, owning two lots.
No school in the county.

FIGURE 11.3. An excerpt from the 1865 Committee on Statistics' report; the committee included members J. R. Starkey, Dr. Bryant, and M. L. Rogers. Unlike previous reports, this itemizes dollar amounts, institutions, and workers by trade. It also credits contributors and provides more specific details on populations, such as literacy rates. The report appears in the minutes of the 1865 California State Convention of Colored Citizens at Sacramento, California. Image courtesy of ColoredConventions.org.

temperance beliefs left imprints on convention delegates' concepts of community leadership during the 1830s. Held at popular AME edifices such as Mother Bethel in Philadelphia, early conventions provided educational training in public representation. The forums introduced delegates to processes of institution and constituent building that future delegates could use and amend for their own purposes. However, these conventions lacked consistent archival systems to preserve for long-term use convention literature such as population reports. Moreover, notable convention decisions created paradoxical frameworks in leadership and enumeration practices. Gender-based exclusion resulted in mostly male-only leadership cohorts despite Black women's ability to colead. And votes against using racial terminology in convention-sponsored literature also evidence the challenges that weakened the development of demography efforts leading up to the first population report that appeared in the proceedings of the 1843 National Colored Convention.

Early Black delegates collaborated to construe what self-determined community leadership would entail. Before he presided over the inaugural 1830 Colored Convention and a year after he founded the AME Church in 1816, Richard Allen and his Philadelphian peers, including James Forten, Absalom Jones, and Russell Parrott, outlined three leadership principles to combat "unmerited stigma attempted to be cast upon the reputation of the free people of color."[11] They believed a lack of literacy and civic education among Black people—"without arts, without science, without a proper knowledge of government"—diminished free people's ability to achieve full political rights.[12] Second, they believed it was important to "never separate ourselves voluntarily from the slave population in this country."[13] Third, they believed the disenfranchisement that Black Philadelphians experienced constituted an issue the majority of free Blacks confronted. As such, Black Philadelphians along with other Black Americans would share a desire "to participate in the blessings of [America's] luxuriant soil."[14] Such public meetings foreground the structures and philosophies exercised at 1830s Colored Conventions.

The Colored Convention delegate position was fashioned as a mode of representation that amplified community issues and visions for all of Black America. Public rather than religious calls to action empowered convention leadership within this framework. In the first instance where the role of delegate is explicitly defined, the 1834 national convention's minutes stipulate that delegate positions remain exclusive to Black men above twenty-one years of age who had maintained six months' residency in a U.S. "village, town, city, or county" or who represented a society or an institution that Black people facilitated.[15] In addition to attending convention sessions and working as liaisons between convention bodies and communities, elected delegates were expected to provide statistical and qualitative reports describing Black communities' characteristics, challenges, and successes. The 1834 delegation adopted a system for appointing delegates that was similar to the American congressional policy for elected representatives.[16] Like the congressional appointment and tax apportionment system, the proposed organization intended to calculate delegate representation according to represented populations' size and monetary contributions to the convention. By the end of the 1834 convention, a committee had collected twenty-five delegate reports. According to the convention, the reports suggested, "institutions for moral, religious and literary improvement throughout the non-slave holding states increased in numbers. . . . They have during the past year assumed a character of decided superiority."[17]

Even though religious organizations influenced conventions, religion was not the primary organizational framework at conventions. Five of the first seven national conventions took place in churches. These churches include Mother Bethel AME Church (1830), Wesley AME Zion Church (1831, 1835), Chatham Street Chapel (1834), and Park Presbyterian Church (1843).[18] According to Erica Armstrong Dunbar, "As the church became the nucleus for early black Philadelphia, . . . the church sanctuary and the homes of its members" were sites wherein "the experiences of African American men and women were most closely examined, nurtured and supervised."[19] The AME Church offered educational instruction in self-governance for free Black men interested in developing leadership skills through procedural-style activism. It supported Black leaders as they challenged oppressive, discriminatory practices that targeted free Black people. But while early nineteenth-century AME meetings provided moral, intellectual, and ceremonial blueprints for leadership, Colored Conventions operated as independent, distinctly public-facing forums beyond the AME Church's oversight. Early conventions' engagement with temperance beliefs as a basis for leadership philosophies also operated beyond the religious structures of the AME Church.

Temperance beliefs significantly impacted delegates' leadership ethos and their vision for delegate duties. As the 1833 convention would proclaim in a prominent font, "MORAL WORTH IS POWERFUL, AND WILL PREVAIL."[20] Conventions held during the 1830s placed intensive emphasis on a broader view of temperance ideology. Early delegations struggled to contend with the circumstances that undermined certain communities' ability to heed their interconnected uplift tenets: temperance, economy, and education.[21] Traditional nineteenth-century temperance supporters campaigned for abstinence from alcohol. In addition, the 1831 convention believed delegates' "obligation as the true guardians of our interests" included "giving wholesome advice and good counsel," thus expanding their temperance leadership to include denouncing a host of undesirable qualities such as amoral behavior, joblessness, and lack of education.[22] However, the 1831 Committee on the Condition of the Free People of Colour articulates the potential for tensions to arise out of faulty classifications of amoral behavior: "[The committee] would also respectfully submit to your wisdom, the necessity of your deliberate reflection on the dissolute, intemperate, and ignorant condition of a large portion of the coloured population of the United States. [The committee] would not, however, refer to their unfortunate circumstances to add degradation to objects already degraded and miserable; nor, with some others, improperly class the virtuous of our colour with the abandoned."[23] Vulnerable populations were often excluded as named offenders against the committee's notions of moral behavior. These groups included orphans, child laborers, imprisoned juveniles, the aged and infirm, and invalids and widowed parents who struggled with poverty, illiteracy, and unemployment, among other hardships.

As the passage suggests, intensive focus on highlighting and rooting out behaviors considered unbecoming of representative populations had the potential to strain relations between convention leadership and communities. Convention delegations' temperance rhetoric critiqued individuals who engaged in imbibing, gambling, "petty crimes," and raucous nighttime entertainment.[24] These groups were most obviously in need of traditional temperance training under the philosophy that "the destroyer, Intemperence [sic], directly counteracts the influence of . . . redeeming qualities, and what is worse, nurtures in their stead every thing loathsome," as the 1833 forum's Committee on the Subject of Temperance argued.[25] Instead, delegates wanted to attract populations in need of self-improvement and political support by advertising and encouraging the formation of local temperance and benevolent societies that focused on shaping individuals' moral character and lifestyle choices. In the 1831 and 1833 minutes, delegates' expression and practice of temperance leadership recognizes the limited power they hold over broader laws and social codes that contribute to Black people's disenfranchisement while also supporting a moral leadership ethos that framed Black communities' public profiles—whether positive or negative—as part of the larger movement's fight for equality.

Because early conventions failed to establish and publish in convention minutes ideal social classes for demography purposes, convention proceedings may have encouraged a sense of equality and unity across participating Black publics, including vulnerable populations. Hierarchical categories of social class may have grouped individuals into poor and lower classes, middle classes, and wealthy or elite classes. For instance, ideal standards for education, personal income, land and chattel ownership, and occupation would produce static metrics of success. On the other hand, the absence of metrics for social classes in antebellum convention minutes may also reflect a lack of understanding of the widely divergent classes of Black represented communities and a lack of trained statisticians and social scientists among early delegations' ranks. While antebellum convention records do not present a case for why social classes were not defined for enumeration purposes, the absence of such metrics likely contributed to a sense of unity among communities even as it reflects one of antebellum Colored Conventions' perennial struggles: articulating a standard set of categories for population reports and long-term positions dedicated to demography efforts. In another way, convention demography lacked a process for aggregating data given the varied hardships generational oppression, white obstructionist politics, and one's gender presented to the enumeration process. However, conventions increasingly demonstrated concerted efforts to incorporate demography as a leadership exercise alongside moral guidance.

Setting Contours for Delegate Roles: Practical Steps and Challenges in the Development of Colored Convention Demography

Because espousing temperance beliefs alone achieved uneven results in relation to political action plans, conventions held between 1830 and 1835 combined moral improvement messages with practical steps to support Black demography. The 1830 National Colored Convention set an important organizational standard for national convention record keeping. Its delegation outlined officers and committees to provide organizational consistency through the American Society of Free Persons of Colour, the intended parent society for all future conventions. The delegation designed positions to manage new cohorts of delegates, voting records, action plans, and population data. The recording secretary would maintain convention archives: "He shall be provided with a book, wherein shall be recorded the proceedings of the Society, of the Board of Managers, and of the Committees, or any persons entrusted with the care or concerns of the Society," as outlined in Article V.[26] Acting as a liaison between the American Society of Free Persons of Colour and all other societies, the Committee of Correspondence would "receive intelligence concerning the operations of the different societies throughout the United States, and from other persons aiming to improve the situation and condition of the people of colour; and also receive all essays on the subject."[27] In theory, the secretary and the Committee of Correspondence would have been extraordinarily instrumental in the work of predicting or affirming Black Americans' outlook and using such information to support political action. But along with frequent changes to the committee's membership and name over forthcoming years, subsequent proceedings do not articulate where and how its archive of literature would be stored.

By raising funds and proposing annual demography efforts, early Colored Conventions strived to achieve organizational permanence. The 1831 convention successfully proposed a "highly important" "general fund, to be denominated the CONVENTIONAL FUND, for . . . advancing . . . the public good."[28] Between 1833 and 1835, delegates purposed funds to circulate an estimated 10,000 copies of printed minutes to public readers in the United States.[29] While circulating minutes helped spur political momentum and attract new delegates, delegations directed more time and funds toward recording and printing proceedings than toward undertaking demography efforts and data aggregation. Despite this fact, the 1831 Committee on the Condition of the Free People of Colour built upon previous organizational structures for demography. Carrying a new name, the committee instituted "an inquiry in the condition of the people of colour throughout the United States . . . [to] report their views upon the subject at a subsequent meeting."[30] Members included Junius C. Morel, Abraham Shadd, William Duncan, Robert Cowley, Henry Sipkins, and Thomas Jennings, with these members representing states with significant Black communities in Pennsylvania, Delaware, Virginia, Maryland, and New York. The 1831 convention made a significant intervention by asking all individual delegates to supply demographic information for its represented communities and organizations. In turn, the newly initiated committee would oversee collection, organization, and dissemination of data reports. The committee anticipated the challenges that an undetermined annual national convention schedule would pose to producing politically advantageous, evidence-based depictions of Black America. So its second intervention strongly recommended that national delegations meet annually to improve the consistency of aggregated information. In doing so, the committee articulated a core goal connected to data collection at Colored Conventions: to develop a knowledgeable relationship between convention leaders and the larger Black U.S. populace. Nonetheless, an eight-year hiatus followed the 1835 national convention. Thereafter, the 1843 national convention realized early conveners' data collection goals by publishing the first comprehensive population report in its proceedings.

Outside of convention meetings, delegates' organizational activities and occupational labor further acquainted them with local politics affecting Black communities, which contributed to the vision for convention demography as a leadership-building strategy. Black delegates' experiences introduced them to communities' characteristics and political needs in ways that built expertise. This is especially true for communities in New York City and Philadelphia, which sent some of the largest delegations to early Colored Conventions. The 1843 forum included budding businessmen whose entrepreneurial acumen eventually led to trade and organizational ventures. The delegate and temperance activist William Whipper had been a secretary for the Philadelphia-based Reading Room Society for the Men of Color.[31] A member of the Committee on the Condition of the Free People of Colour, Abraham D. Shadd "inherited not only his father's occupation as shoemaker but also part of an estate estimated at $1,300" in 1819; he eventually became known as a dedicated Underground Railroad agent in Delaware.[32] By 1870, the 1831 convention's president, a tailor, John Bowers, had launched a Philadelphia-based secondhand clothing store, owned property estimated at $5,000, and had founded the Grand United Order of Odd Fellows to support networks of Black trade organizations.[33] Leslie Harris contends that, after the 1840s, "Black reformers shifted from moral perfectionism to examine labor as central to the black community's efforts at uplift," particularly as Black New York abolitionists, a dominating faction of convention delegations, realized that they "had to rely on the limited resources of blacks themselves."[34] However, this leadership philosophy took root sooner at 1830s national Colored Conventions, as delegates' labor enterprises suggest.

While often failing to consistently implement demography processes over the 1830s, delegates created an educational platform for Black leaders that prioritized morality, gainful employment, and community study as ways to achieve Black uplift.

Gender and Racial Markers: Challenges to Self-Assessment Efforts and Political Action at Antebellum Colored Conventions

Even while the "Colored Convention" moniker gained social value in the public sphere and enjoyed a level of public respectability among Black communities in the decades leading up to the American Civil War, conventions' internal parochial and patriarchal approaches to activism often disrupted enumeration exercises. Delegates claimed representative power to speak on behalf of communities and their interests, which served to debunk public perceptions that "supposes [Colored Convention leaders] indifferent to the state of things by which they are surrounded, and that they make little or no effort for their relief," as the Philadelphian commentator Joseph Willson posited.[35] From *Frederick Douglass' Paper* (1851–63) and the *New-York Tribune* (1841–1924) to book-length cultural commentary such as Willson's *The Elite of Our People: Joseph Willson's Sketches of Black Upper-Class Life in Antebellum Philadelphia* (1841), news and popular culture outlets carried reviews of convention-groomed intellectual cultures across free states, slave states, and territories throughout the United States and abroad in Canada and Great Britain. While fugitive slaves and entrepreneurs who struggled with unemployment and educational access regularly filled delegate ranks, conventions often sponsored an official brand that emphasized united delegations' intellectual aptitude and achievements. As a result, Black leadership practices reinforced the notion that the fight for freedom was to be won through Black men's civic empowerment and activist agendas. Because conventions were highly mediated by different interests, self-assessment efforts were often stalled, relaunched, and reframed according to a given delegation's leading values. Gender exclusion and debates about racial markers, for example, significantly impacted antebellum data collection and representation practices.

Black women had little stated involvement in structuring the national conventions' burgeoning enumeration processes beyond constituency. According to the 1830 federal census, Black women slightly outnumbered Black men.[36] Black women were certainly counted and recorded in population reports but held no stated leadership roles in designing, aggregating, or presenting reports for public consumption. Nonetheless, women connected to delegates as wives, daughters, sisters, and colleagues often embodied the ethos of conventions: a moral responsibility to learn more about Black communities and to engage in activism for Black social justice. Black women regularly attended national meetings, delivered public addresses, and held roles as newspaper correspondents and leaders of politically aligned organizations with temperance, benevolence, and religious foci. Free Black women were also financial and intellectual contributors to Black communities' progress through entrepreneurship and family rearing.

Still, all-male delegations implied that Black women were not fit to lead alongside Black men. On one hand, exclusionary practices on the basis of gender mirrored U.S. congressional leadership. An all-male delegation at assembly-style events was the day's modus operandi for large-scale political forums before the women's rights 1848 Seneca Falls Convention. Participating publics often considered single-sex delegations to be an acceptable approach to public leadership. Black men's leadership in public society represented the idea that Black women, families, and communities would gain social elevation by way of patriarchal systems of self-governance. On the other hand, conventions' recommendations for self-governance at the local level implicitly recognized that Black women *could* fulfill qualifications to become delegates. As early as the 1830 national convention, delegates promoted the creation of societies among participating communities: "Resolved, That this Convention enjoins and requires of each of its members to use their utmost influence in the formation of societies."[37] The 1833 national convention reiterated this call with a specific call to *women*: "We . . . recommend as powerfully tending to advance the Temperance reformation, the formation of Societies, in religious congregations; in each ward of large cities, and in each large village in the UNITED STATES. . . . We also recommend the organization of Female Societies."[38] Similar recommendations appeared in minutes in the 1840s, even as the tradition of mostly all-male delegations reigned until 1848. According to common practices and bylaws for delegate positions, leading a society or being elected by a society allowed one to become a convention delegate. However, 1843 national proceedings reflect a paradox of leadership wherein Black women may have met criteria to become delegates and to participate in the production of the first comprehensive population report but were excluded nonetheless.

The 1843 population report attends to and departs from Black women's underrepresentation at Colored Conventions. For example, the 1843 convention's sociological analysis collapses men's and women's identity markers—male and female, men and women—into a macroscale critical overview about communities. But the report lacks details about the gender dynamics of the populations described. However, the census-style report in the 1843 convention proceedings documents the existence of several women's societies. Whereas no division between genders is notated in categories on labor, property, and inhabitants, women are recognized in a category for societies. The listings include more than a dozen women's benevolent societies in Bath, Geneva, New York City, and Schenectady, New York, and in Cincinnati and Columbus, Ohio. The report rhetorically highlights gender inclusion, while the enumeration process that produced it remained exclusive to Black men.

Delegations passed conflicting resolutions at early Colored Conventions that illustrate key challenges to the efficacy of demography processes. In addition to gender exclusion, early delegations undermined self-assessment efforts through inconsistent data collection practices at the 1834 national convention and by recommending that racial markers (e.g., "colored") be discontinued in convention-sponsored political expression and printed materials at the 1835 national convention. Instead of one committee overseeing enumeration, as was stipulated by the 1831 national delegation, a number of committees at the 1834 meeting were deeply involved in collecting data on the condition of Black Americans. The minutes list several: a committee for Colored students of medicine; a committee on Colored mechanics; a committee on high schools open to Colored students; a committee on manual labor schools; a committee on Black American immigrants in Liberia; a committee on "the exclusion of our people in church privileges and travelling by steamboat";[39] a committee on the "actual number of coloured slave holders in the US"; and a committee to condense reports submitted by delegates.[40] Although the 1834 convention lacked a legible guiding philosophy that would impose consistency on its collection activities, the decision to quit the use of racial markers at the subsequent 1835 convention undermined 1834 delegates' vibrant investigative spirit toward community study.

Resolutions passed at the 1835 national convention effectively dismantled previous convention demography systems. The moral suasionist William Whipper successfully campaigned to establish an alternative organization outside of Colored Conventions. The organization was recognized as the American Moral Reform Society (established 1836) at the 1835 National Colored Convention held in Philadelphia. This move corroborated delegates' decision to alter the "logic of the conventions by shifting their focus away from reforming colored people" to "carrying out the moral duties of citizens and Christians," as Joan Bryant contends.[41] The organizational shake-up intended to make a firm declaration of intent toward encouraging Black people's assimilation into white society. As part of this new vision for moral leadership, the 1835 convention voted to excise the word "'colored,' when either speaking or writing concerning themselves; and especially to remove the title of African from their institutions."[42] The decision attempted to model a peaceable embrace of American identity without an emphasis on racial heritage. However, the decision left demography efforts unaccounted for, particularly in a moment when the 1835 convention had access to an influx of information managed by an assortment of committees from the previous year.

Moreover, a conflict arose between the resolution to strike racial markers from convention reports and a resolution to encourage petition exercises that 1835 delegates regarded as an instrumental political tool to improve Black communities' long-term outlook. Passing "after much discussion," delegates resolved to "recommend to the free people of colour throughout the U. States, the propriety of petitioning congress and their respective state legislatures to be admitted to the rights and privileges of American citizens, and that we be protected in the same."[43] In the passage, the delegation encourages Black people to demand citizenship rights by way of practicing the right to petition. In many cases, an endorsement of petitioning at the local level would reinforce an important correlation between enumeration practices and successful public protest in American politics. An activist's access to statistical and sociological information about certain types of communities strengthened his or her ability to describe grievances and make demands. Nonetheless, the vote against self-identifying race terminology in convention-related political literature, including demographic reports *and* petitions, undermined the convention's call for increased political engagement.

Taken together, the 1834 and 1835 conventions' enumeration practices and attitudes toward racial markers created a paradox that threatened to weaken reporting efforts in the future. The 1835 decision undermined the political usefulness of data on Black communities that the 1834 convention had collected. The decision also undermined a pivotal goal: to examine and better understand Black Americans as a politically divested group. And it threatened to stall future convention-based data collection. "Hegemonic ideologies of language," Jennifer Leeman argues, have shaped relationships between "language, race and national identity," particularly in the ways the federal census construed a sense of difference between individuals in America.[44] This has happened through "institutional practices and policies" that produced terminologies of race and ethnicity, which regularly favored white Americans and regularly created power differentials between white and nonwhite Americans.[45] Population reports had the potential to inform policy recommendations articulated in debates and resolutions appearing in the 1835 proceedings. The disuse of racial markers in enumeration exercises would render illegible Black people's accomplishments and social condition in comparison to white Americans and other racial groups.

The 1843 delegation disregarded the 1835 vote on racial markers because of a long temporal gap between national conventions and because of contemporaneous trends in demography, which the 1843 national convention's sociological and census-style reports illustrate. Specifically, the decision went against the grain of federal and state demography, which increasingly adopted additional categories to promote a better understanding of the American population. Additional details about populations that appeared in official government census reports reflect rising public interest in immigration, wage labor, and urban centers—leading topics of national discourse. Along with the appearance of the phrase "Colored Citizens" in the title of the 1843 proceedings, the 1843 statistical and sociological reports' use of racial markers indicates a firm rejection of the 1835 vote on racial markers. Importantly, the 1843 population reports allowed delegates and reading publics to assign value to certain geographical locations and types of labor and to the educational potential that convention literature held.

Readers and listening publics could benefit from the Black censuses and sociological reports in a variety of ways. Reports allowed Black readers to more effectively choose destinations for leisure, business, and political travel. They encouraged Black people to compare their circumstances with the conditions of other Black communities, with whom communications spanned from nonexistent to robust. Black leaders could inquire at newspapers or with named individuals in convention minutes to learn how such progress was achieved; they could mirror, transform, or supplement their own initiatives using that which was described in reports. The 1843 delegation seized an opportunity to counter circulating myths about Black economic stagnancy and social inferiority by including statistical and qualitative reports that could reframe readers' understanding of Black communities' progress. Subsequent population reports embedded in national and state minutes demonstrate increasing sophistication in content and format.

Antebellum Colored Convention Demography as Black Leadership Curricula

Colored Conventions' documentary records are sites of an understudied tradition in Black experimental writing production. For delegates, giving and receiving reports on the condition of Colored people was an accountability measure connected to roles associated with delegate positions and the larger ethos upholding convention cultures. While early national conventions struggled to permanently institutionalize demography, their pioneering concepts for public leadership and organizational structures for information exchange between leaders and communities influenced later conventions that practiced more sophisticated styles of self-assessment for political reasons (see figs. 11.1, 11.2, and 11.3). Published under the banner of an increasingly popular Black public protest platform, antebellum population reports appeared at a time when delegates were figuring out whether temperance and religious beliefs, civic duty, or militant abolitionism would dominate their approach to leadership. Examining the first thirteen years of conventions' understanding of delegate duties brings to bear the internal debates, intellectual ideals, and organizational processes that led to the first set of national-level census and sociological reports published in national convention minutes.

Demography efforts reflect delegates' interest in establishing organizational permanency in ever-shifting political environments. In one light, Black convention reports may be read as part of a curriculum in Black protest cultures and ideals. As learning materials, population reports helped public participants and spectators to understand a way by which Black leaders could conjoin representation systems with citizenship exercises in an age of pervasive disenfranchisement against Black American communities. Delegates' use of numerical and narrative formats within population reports resulted in more nuanced depictions of Black populations in comparison to government records. They also inherently remarked upon Black populations' fundamental contributions to American life and culture. Population reports presented an alternative method for endorsing Black empowerment alongside the speech act, debates between delegates, and resolutions. The reports made a case for Black citizenship by rhetorically positioning Black Americans within political formats resembling the U.S. government's census while also thematically engaging with two of the most popular antebellum forms of representational writing centered on Black subjects: the slave ledger and the slave narrative. Examining the organizational politics at antebellum conventions suggests that delegates' self-fashioned demography processes constituted a largely unstable political strategy that later national, state, and local delegations advanced in instrumental ways.

NOTES

1. This phrase appears on the title page of the minutes for the 1843 National Colored Convention. National Convention of Colored Citizens (1843: Buffalo, NY), *Minutes of the National Convention of Colored Citizens; Held at Buffalo; On the 15th, 16th, 17th, 18th, and 19th of August, 1843; For the Purpose of Considering Their Moral and Political Condition as American Citizens*, Colored Conventions Project, coloredconventions .org/items/show/278.

2. National Convention of Colored Citizens (1843), *Minutes*.

3. For much more information about Black population reports, see Sarah Lynn Patterson, *Prosperity and Politics: Taking Stock of Black Wealth and the 1843 Convention*, digital exhibit, Colored Conventions Project, http://coloredconventions.org/exhibits /show/exhibit-1843. Curated by Patterson in collaboration with undergraduate student researchers, the exhibit is a scholarly project hosted at ColoredConventions.org.

4. A gag rule (1836–44) allowed the House of Representatives to table a vast majority of petitions that argued against slavery in the South or requested its immediate dissolution.

5. Philip Foner and Ronald Lewis, eds., *The Black Worker: A Documentary History from Colonial Times to the Present* (Philadelphia: Temple University Press, 1978), 145.

6. William Banks, *Black Intellectuals: Race and Responsibility in American Life* (New York: W. W. Norton, 1998), 17.

7. Banks.

8. John Ernest, *Liberation Historiography: African American Writers and the Challenge of History, 1784–1861* (Chapel Hill: University of North Carolina Press, 2004), 40.

9. James McCune Smith, "Freedom and Slavery for Afric-Americans," *National Anti-Slavery Standard* (New York), February 8, 1844. (Reprinted from *New-York Tribune*.)

10. Margo J. Anderson, *The American Census: A Social History* (New Haven, CT: Yale University Press, 2015), 4.

11. "Philadelphia, January 1817," *Genius of Liberty* (Leesburg, VA), October 17, 1817.

12. "Philadelphia, January 1817."

13. "Philadelphia, January 1817."

14. "Philadelphia, January 1817."

15. Convention for the Improvement of the Free People of Color, Fourth Annual (1834: New York, NY), *Minutes of the Fourth Annual Convention for the Improvement of the Free People of Colour, in the United States; Held by Adjournments in the Asbury Church, New York, from the 2nd to the 12th of June, Inclusive, 1834*, 32, Colored Conventions Project, coloredconventions.org/items/show/276.

16. Convention for the Improvement of the Free People of Color, Fourth Annual (1834), 32.

17. Convention for the Improvement of the Free People of Color, Fourth Annual (1834), 25.

18. See "About the Colored Conventions," Colored Conventions Project, accessed March 20, 2017,coloredconventions.org/about-conventions.

19. Erica Armstrong Dunbar, *A Fragile Freedom: African American Women and Emancipation in the Antebellum City* (New Haven, CT: Yale University Press, 2008), 51.

20. Convention for the Improvement of the Free People of Color, Third Annual (1833: Philadelphia, PA), *Minutes and Proceedings of the Third Annual Convention, for the Improvement of the Free People of Colour in These United States, Held by Adjournments in the City of Philadelphia, from the 3d to the 13th of June Inclusive, 1833*, Colored Conventions Project, coloredconventions.org/items/show/275.

21. Convention of the People of Color, First Annual (1831: Philadelphia, PA), *Minutes and Proceedings of the First Annual Convention of the People of Colour, Held by Adjournments in the City of Philadelphia, from the Sixth to the Eleventh of June, Inclusive, 1831*, 4, Colored Conventions Project, coloredconventions.org/items/show/72.

22. Convention of the People of Color, First Annual (1831), 4.

23. Convention of the People of Color, First Annual (1831), 4.

24. Convention for the Improvement of the Free People of Color, Third Annual (1833), *Minutes and Proceedings*.

25. James Pennington led this committee. Convention for the Improvement of the Free People of Color, Third Annual (1833).

26. American Society of Free Persons of Colour (1830: Philadelphia, PA), *Constitution of the American Society of Free Persons of Colour, for Improving Their Condition in the United States; For Purchasing Lands; And for the Establishment of a Settlement in Upper Canada, also, the Proceedings of the Convention with Their Address to Free Persons of Colour in the United States*, Colored Conventions Project, coloredconventions.org/items/show/70.

27. American Society of Free Persons of Colour (1830).

28. Convention of the People of Color, First Annual (1831), *Minutes and Proceedings*, 4.

29. By the 1848 national convention, the estimated number of copies had climbed to well over 11,500. Convention for the Improvement of the Free People of Color, Third Annual (1833), *Minutes and Proceedings*, 28–29; Convention for the Improvement of the Free People of Color, Fourth Annual (1834), *Minutes*, 17; National Convention of Colored Citizens (1843), *Minutes*, 11; Colored National Convention (1848: Cleveland, OH), *Report of the Proceedings of the Colored National Convention Held at Cleveland, Ohio, on Wednesday, September 6, 1848*, 9, Colored Conventions Project, coloredconventions.org/items/show/280.

30. Convention of the People of Color, First Annual (1831), *Minutes and Proceedings*.

31. Richard P. McCormick, "William Whipper: Moral Reformer," *Pennsylvania History: A Journal of Mid-Atlantic Studies* 43, no. 1 (1976): 25.

32. John Silverman, "Mary Ann Shadd and the Search for Equality," in *A Nation of Immigrants: Women, Workers, and Communities in Canadian History, 1840s-1960s*, ed. Franca Iacovetta, with Paula Draper and Robert Ventesca (Toronto, ON: University of Toronto Press, 2002), 101.

33. "John C. Bowers," 1870 Federal Census. See the 1870 United States Federal Census at www.Ancestry.com.

34. Leslie Harris, *In the Shadows of Slavery: African-Americans in New York City, 1626–1863* (Chicago: University of Chicago Press, 2003), 218.

35. Joseph Willson, *The Elite of Our People: Joseph Willson's Sketches of Black Upper-Class Life in Antebellum Philadelphia*, ed. Julie Winch (University Park: Pennsylvania State University Press, 2000), 102.

36. According to the 1830 U.S. Census, Black women outnumbered Black men by 12,693 persons. *Fifth census; or, Enumeration of the Inhabitants of the United States. 1830; To Which is Prefixed, a Schedule of the Whole Number of Persons within the Several Districts of the United States, Taken According to the Acts of 1790, 1800, 1810, 1820*, pub. by authority of an act of Congress (Washington, DC: Duff Green, 1832), 163.

37. American Society of Free Persons of Colour (1830), *Constitution*, iii-iv. By the 1830 national convention's nominal standards for delegate positions, any person, including a woman representing an auxiliary or a society, could be a delegate: "Resolved, That the next General Convention shall be composed of delegates appointed by the Parent Society and its auxiliaries: provided always, that the number of delegates from each society, shall not exceed five, and all other places, where there are no auxiliaries, are hereby invited to send one delegate."

38. Convention for the Improvement of the Free People of Color, Third Annual (1833), *Minutes and Proceedings*, 19–20.

39. Convention for the Improvement of the Free People of Color, Fourth Annual (1834), *Minutes*, 11.

40. Convention for the Improvement of the Free People of Color, Fourth Annual (1834), 13.

41. See Joan L. Bryant's essay in this volume.

42. Convention for the Improvement of the Free People of Color, Fifth Annual (1835: Philadelphia, PA), *Minutes of the Fifth Annual Convention for the Improvement of the Free People of Colour in the United States; Held by Adjournments, in the Wesley Church, Philadelphia; From the First to the Fifth of June, Inclusive; 1835*, 14–15, Colored Conventions Project, coloredconventions.org/items/show/277.

43. Convention for the Improvement of the Free People of Color, Fifth Annual (1835), 9.

44. Jennifer Leeman, "Racializing Language: A History of Linguistic Ideologies in the US Census," *Journal of Language and Politics* 3, no. 3 (2004): 507.

45. Leeman, 507.

GENDER POLITICS AND THE MANUAL LABOR COLLEGE INITIATIVE AT NATIONAL COLORED CONVENTIONS IN ANTEBELLUM AMERICA

Kabria Baumgartner

I t was to be called the American Industrial School and located in north-western Pennsylvania near the city of Erie. Situated on over 200 acres, it was to feature new buildings, workshops, and a farm. The built environment mirrored the curriculum, which combined literary study with mechanical and agricultural training. The planners, led by African American abolitionist Frederick Douglass, identified two key rules to govern the institution: 1) an equal division of student time between schoolwork and craftwork and 2) the sale of school-made products. Douglass and his fellow planners envisioned a community wherein "the teachers [were] to be selected for, and pupils admitted into, the school without reference to sex or complexion."[1] This bold vision for a coeducational and interracial college would boast gender and racial diversity along with a strong curricular emphasis on economic independence. Yet, for all its boldness, this vision was never realized, as delegates at the 1855 national Colored Convention voted to reject it.

The American Industrial School was the last of four initiatives considered by the national Colored Conventions to establish a manual labor college in the pre–Civil War United States. Introduced by various African American male leaders and their allies, the first two initiatives, crafted in 1831 and 1847, made no provision to include African American women as prospective students, whereas the last two, in 1853 and 1854, did. Over a twenty-four-year period, conventioneers had swung from ignoring African American women as scholars to advocating greater acceptance of both coeducation and women's activism. Though the "woman question" was by no means settled in the 1850s, this shift reflects the ever-evolving nature of gender relations in free Black communities in the antebellum North. The 1853 and 1854 plans were thus the bellwether of a new era in African American higher education, one in which the quest for Black economic self-sufficiency depended on both men and women.

Education was a recurring subject at national Colored Conventions in the pre–Civil War era.[2] The African American struggle for education was rooted in the desire to bring about social and political equality and to defeat racial prejudice. Scholarly discussions, however, tend to read the specific educational plans introduced at national Colored Conventions, particularly the manual labor initiative, separately. In fact, the 1831 plan has become indicative of racial inequality and anti-Black violence in American higher education in the antebellum Northeast.[3] While it is true that, as historian James Anderson argues, African American leaders struggled to negotiate white racism in the antebellum North, there is more to the study of the manual labor college initiative than white opposition and virulent racism.[4] This essay broadens the scholarly discussion of the origins of African American higher education by examining the interplay between race, gender, and Black organizing.

The essay does this by beginning with a methodological intervention— namely, a process of serial reading, which locates and analyzes a particular theme, in this case education, within multiple sequential texts. Reading national Colored Convention reports in tandem and in sequence offers a fascinating bird's-eye view of the debates on gender and American higher education from the perspective of African American leaders. While African American men spearheaded the Colored Conventions, they were aware of the dominant trends in men's and women's higher education, and they were almost always in dialogue with African American women thinkers. Hence, the national Colored Convention reports reveal three key factors that help explain the evolution of manual labor college initiatives: the establishment of coeducational and interracial institutions of higher education; the contributions of African American women to these institutions and other activist organizations; and the emerging women's rights movement. Though the American Industrial School foundered, it did so not over the so-called woman question but rather over the question of resources and the idea of racial self-segregation.[5]

Manliness and the Manual Labor College

African American activists in the free states and territories of the United States believed that education was an engine of social mobility that would improve African American life. For instance, John Brown Russwurm and Samuel Cornish, African American editors of *Freedom's Journal*, the first weekly Black newspaper, published an editorial that touted education as "the principal mover to every other improvement."[6] Community leaders regularly encouraged African American youth, particularly boys, to acquire knowledge, attitudes, and skills with economic value. In doing so, these educated youth would embody respectability and virtue while also challenging the tenets that undergirded slavery and racial prejudice.[7] When African American abolitionist Maria Stewart spoke to an audience at the African Masonic Hall in Boston, Massachusetts, on February 27, 1832, for example, she stressed the "great necessity of turning your attention to knowledge."[8] African American men, women, and children had a responsibility to pursue that learning through any channel possible, from formal institutions to literary societies, churches, and even national Colored Conventions.

Local, state, and national Colored Conventions, from Philadelphia to Cincinnati, served as intellectual sites to strategize about African American higher education. At the first five national conventions, which were held consecutively from 1830 to 1835, most often in Philadelphia, delegates established "education, temperance, and economy" as the three pillars of progress.[9] Following earlier school-building initiatives by African American abolitionists James Easton, Samuel Cornish, and Peter Williams, six white abolitionists, including Simeon Jocelyn and William Lloyd Garrison, presented a plan to establish a manual labor college during the First Annual Convention of the Free People of Color at Wesleyan Church in June 1831.[10] At the proposed college, African American men from the United States, the "West Indies . . . in Mexico and South America" would study agriculture and the mechanical arts along with literary and scientific subjects.[11] Jocelyn, a white engraver by trade and a pastor from Connecticut, and his fellow boosters argued that the college would foster Black uplift. After a discussion about logistics, including an explanation of the proposed location of the college in New Haven, Connecticut, and the appointment of an educational committee and a fundraising agent, delegates unanimously adopted the proposal.

The 1831 proposed college followed the trend of the emerging manual labor school movement, which was making rapid progress at institutions of higher learning from New York to Ohio. George Washington Gale, a white Presbyterian minister from New York, pioneered this system of educational reform in the United States, envisioning it as a low-cost solution to educating more ministers in the wake of religious revivalism brought on by the Second Great Awakening. At institutions such as the Oneida Institute for Industry and Science in Whitesboro, New York, which Gale founded in 1827, the manual labor curriculum focused on agricultural labor, where students worked on a 115-acre farm, and the mechanical arts, where students worked in shops.[12] A group of reformers, including white philanthropist Lewis Tappan, soon organized the Society for Promoting Manual Labor in Literary Institutions in 1831 in New York City to advance the manual labor system throughout U.S. higher education.

The emphasis on increasing physical and mental strength, coupled with the potential for economic success, attracted radical abolitionists, both African American and white, to the manual labor system. For instance, white abolitionist Theodore Dwight Weld penned a report in 1831 on the advantages of a manual labor curriculum, liberally quoting leading national and international educators, including Christian Gotthilf Salzmann of Germany, who regarded the common, nonmanual labor model of education as a "grand source of bodily inactivity, voluptuous weakness, effeminacy."[13] At a time when African American men sought to fashion their lives anew and assert their manhood, the manual labor curriculum seemed especially fitting. Moreover, advocates contended that this curriculum prepared African American men specifically for skilled labor jobs. According to William Lloyd Garrison, the benefits multiplied: A trade would enable African American men to "accumulate money; money begets influence, and influence respectability. Influence, wealth, and character will certainly destroy those prejudices which now separate [African Americans] from society."[14] The manual labor model encouraged both mental and physical strength, which would ostensibly translate into economic self-sufficiency, self-reliance, and sociopolitical empowerment for African American men.

No plans were made, at least initially, to enroll African American women, and several factors might explain their omission.[15] First, it may have been the result of the very use of the term "college," which was generally equated at the time with institutions of higher education for white men.[16] Second, abolitionists suggested that educating African American men was paramount. A "Connecticut philanthropist" who backed the initiative argued that African American men were "needed in *our country pre-eminently*" (as opposed to being colonized in Africa) to campaign for Black civil rights.[17] Third, it is possible that Jocelyn and others aimed to introduce women as students at a later point. For instance, when John B. Johnson, an educator, planned to establish a high school that welcomed African American men in Logan County, Ohio, he made sure to note in his advertisement that "arrangements will be made as soon as practicable, for the instruction of females in those branches peculiar to a polite female education."[18] Nonetheless, formal educational opportunities for men usually preceded those for women.

The 1831 proposed college was poised to be the first Black college in the nation, let alone New England, and also the first sex-segregated college in African America. Sex segregation was the norm in U.S. higher education in the antebellum era. White men benefited from the growth of colleges and academies, while white women enjoyed the expansion of female seminaries and academies. Colleges in New England occasionally enrolled a few African American men just as female seminaries in the free states and territories occasionally enrolled a few African American women. Nevertheless, only twenty-eight African Americans had earned degrees from recognized colleges by 1860.[19] The most popular institution for African American men and women was Oberlin College. Founded in 1833 on coeducational principles, Oberlin opened its doors to African Americans in 1835 and operated on a manual labor system. Many African American conventioneers believed that, even more than in common schools, the proliferation of "colleges and high schools on the Manual Labor System" would "see the influence of prejudice decrease, and ourselves respected."[20]

White New Haven residents, however, bristled at the idea of an African American manual labor college. Residents argued that such a college promoted immediate emancipation, which interfered with the issue of slavery in southern states. Moreover, the very presence of African American men threatened the prosperity of Yale College. The mayor of New Haven, Dennis Kimberly, a Yale College graduate, called a city meeting where residents voted almost unanimously to reject the proposal and resist this plan.[21] Historian Hilary Moss finds that white middle-class and working-class New Haven residents objected to the proposed college partly because they worried about labor competition from African American men.[22] Some white residents, both elite and working class, denounced Black education altogether because it undermined the progress that had been made by the American Colonization Society, founded in 1816 to send African Americans to Africa. Still, even when opposition turned violent in New Haven, proponents did not abandon the initiative immediately. Rather, they redoubled their efforts, stressing the need to build manual labor institutions for Black uplift.[23]

Early national Colored Conventions addressed African American women's education, but they generally did so outside of the manual labor college initiative. For instance, Samuel Cornish established the Phoenix Society, which sponsored lectures, libraries, and reading rooms as well as a high school for young African American men and women in New York City. A convention resolution, passed unanimously, promoted the establishment of "Phoenix Societies in every State."[24] In 1833, Prudence Crandall, a white Quaker abolitionist, opened a seminary in Canterbury, Connecticut, for African American women, sparking controversy with white residents of the town. Delegates at the Fourth Annual Convention for the Improvement of the Free People of Colour passed a resolution "approv[ing] of . . . [Crandall's] truly philanthropic course."[25] While support for African American women's education surged after violence forced the closure of Crandall's seminary in 1834, it still did not herald the inclusion of African American women as prospective students at a Black manual labor college.

In 1833, the New England Anti-Slavery Society (NEAS) not only took over the manual labor initiative but also declared the proposed institution coeducational. Founded in January 1832, the NEAS was an interracial organization that championed the immediate abolition of slavery. Arnold Buffum, a white Quaker abolitionist from Rhode Island, served as president, with William Lloyd Garrison as corresponding secretary. The organization appointed a committee of five, which included Buffum and two African American barbers: James G. Barbadoes, who served as a delegate at the 1833 and 1834 national Colored Conventions, and John T. Hilton.[26] This committee decided to swap the name "seminary" for "college." For Buffum, calling the institution a college or seminary "was of no consequence." "It is the object," he argued, "which we would strive to accomplish."[27] The committee then proposed to open this institution to "colored youth of *both sexes*, where . . . the males are instructed in . . . agriculture and the mechanic arts, and the females in such domestic concerns."[28] A host of factors may have influenced this shift toward coeducation, including Maria Stewart's speeches on education, the recent establishment of African American women's literary societies, and the Garrisonian and Quaker belief in gender radicalism.[29] Whatever the reason, this all-male committee explicitly extended higher education to African American women by including the phrase "both sexes" in the revised proposal and outlining the general features of a gendered curriculum. Though African American conventioneers did not appear to campaign for a coeducational manual labor college, they did endorse the NEAS version.

While the manual labor college initiative stalled under NEAS leadership, factional disputes doomed the national Colored Conventions in the late 1830s, making the initiative collateral damage. While Garrison had raised $1,500 in England to support the initiative, some abolitionists expressed concern that building a college might "interfere with more direct exertions for the removal of slavery."[30] On the other hand, abolitionists such as William Whipper, an African American entrepreneur, still supported the initiative. Whipper sought to wrest control of it from the NEAS and position it under the aegis of his American Moral Reform Society, a national Black reform organization created at the 1835 national Colored Convention. A resolution passed by a vote of 10–9 to approve the American Moral Reform Society's control of the manual labor college initiative.[31] This close vote augured the split between African American leaders from Philadelphia and New York over the leadership and objectives of the national Colored Conventions.

Conflicts over strategies as well as questions about racial self-segregation and the role of women divided Black leaders across the free states and territories.[32] Even though no national Colored Conventions were held during an eight-year period, asserting Black masculinity remained a central focus for Black leaders who shared their opinions on education, labor, and republicanism in antislavery and Black newspapers. For instance, an ambivalent Charles Ray, editor of the *Colored American*, argued that a Black manual labor college was both good and bad—bad because a separate institution for African Americans reinscribed racial caste and good because it gave "young men" a classical, agricultural, and mechanical education, thus "render[ing] [them] competent members of society."[33] This notion of competence conformed to widespread republican beliefs in the antebellum North that yeoman farmers, artisans, and craftsmen were producers and hence independent and self-reliant.[34] In apprentice magazines and at mechanics' institutes, industry and economy were hailed as the two most important virtues engendering economic and social mobility for men, similar to the 1830s national Colored Conventions' trinity of education, temperance, and economy.[35]

Meanwhile, an ideology of female domesticity shaped African American male leaders' views on African American women's access to higher education. Charles Ray surmised that mothers should teach their daughters "all the principles of domestic economy" instead of sending them to school to study music.[36] An editorialist for the *Palladium of Liberty*, a weekly Black newspaper run by David Jenkins in Ohio, claimed that the "domestic circle" was the place where women had "the most powerful influence."[37] Some leaders who supported African American women's higher education often advocated a separate curriculum for young men and women at coeducational schools, just like the NEAS plan. Samuel Cornish surmised that women's education "shall fit them to become the wives of an enlightened mechanic, a storekeeper or clerk."[38] An educated mother could also encourage her sons to attend a manual labor school. Yet many free Black women in the North, including the working-class and even the elite, had to work outside of the home as servants, laundresses, or teachers, making the ideal of the domestic wife and mother rather elusive.

When the national Colored Conventions resumed in August 1843 in Buffalo, New York, the rhetoric of manliness infused resolutions regarding Black uplift. This particular meeting took on a more militant tone compared to earlier conventions, at least if Henry Highland Garnet's reading of his manifesto, "An Address to the Slaves of the United States of America," was any indication. "Brethen, arise, arise! Strike for your lives and liberties. Now is the day and the hour," Garnet roared. Garnet's words implicated the male slave as much as the free Black male, both of whom were called upon to embody self-reliance and self-determination. Even though the manual labor college initiative was not on the docket, the committees on agriculture and the mechanic arts encouraged free Black men to distinguish themselves as farmers and mechanics. "*Resolved*, That this Convention recommend and encourage agricultural pursuits among our people generally," the report reads, "as the surest and speadiest [*sic*] road to wealth, influence and respectability."[39] Like agriculture itself, Black emancipation and economic empowerment were collective goods to be cultivated through the work of African American men.

Furthermore, the possibility of becoming an economically independent African American male head of household depended on higher education. At least that is what some conventioneers surmised. At the 1847 National Convention of Colored People and Their Friends in Troy, New York, the Committee on Education reintroduced the Black manual labor college initiative. This committee comprised Alexander Crummell, who was familiar with manual labor curricula after having attended the Oneida Institute, and James McCune Smith and P. G. Smith, who were also well-educated African American activists.[40] Committee members argued that this initiative should be the "leading and most prominent object" of the convention since education was "a matter wound up in our very existence."[41] When African American abolitionist William Cooper Nell summarized the convention proceedings, he described the proposed institution as a "college for colored young men."[42] Since coeducation in U.S. higher education was fairly unusual in the antebellum era, it likely would have been mentioned had the conventioneers intended it.

The manual labor college initiative sparked debate among conventioneers, not about the woman question or even literary study versus manual training but rather about practicality. On one side, proponents such as James McCune Smith argued that a college would appeal to young African American men by providing direct training for employment. On the other side, skeptics such as Henry Highland Garnet did not see the "necessity" of such an undertaking, since colleges existed where "colored youth could be admitted," a valid point since some African Americans had graduated from colleges, academies, and seminaries.[43] Either way, however, far more opportunities existed for African American men to attend colleges and academies compared to African American women, who could count only a few institutions open to them. To skeptics, a college was "an extravagant and uncalled for measure" that actually furthered racial prejudice because it served African American men exclusively. The majority of delegates, however, supported the proposal, voting 26–17 to adopt it.[44] A committee of twenty-five men, including Charles Reason, Samuel Cornish, and Charles Ray, was charged with fundraising, though it appears the committee did not make much headway. The manual labor college plan fizzled once again, as did the possibility of imagining African American women as college students—that is, until the 1850s.

Coeducation and Black Economic Empowerment

When the manual labor college initiative reemerged at national Colored Conventions of the 1850s, delegates formally recognized African American women and women's higher education for the first time, marking a critical shift in the male-dominated discourse. The turning point can actually be traced to the 1848 meeting in Cleveland, Ohio, where male delegates affirmed women's rights. Concentrated discussions of women's social and political activism occurred at subsequent state, regional, and national Colored Conventions. African American male conventioneers began to include African American women in various national initiatives such as the manual labor college plan. In other words, the affirmation of women's rights in 1848 precipitated the inclusion of African American women as allies and co-benefactors of Black educational uplift by 1853.

Even though the subject of women's rights did not appear in the recorded proceedings of the 1847 national Colored Convention, African American activists had been wrestling with it. Historian Martha Jones argues that men and women, whites and African Americans, had nurtured alliances at antislavery organizations and church conventions throughout the 1840s. Arguably the ideology of female domesticity still shaped the views of many activists, but a growing sentiment had emerged among some activists who endorsed African American women's deep involvement in community uplift. For instance, African American abolitionists Martin Delany, Frederick Douglass, and William Cooper Nell maintained that African American women could help bring about Black emancipation and empowerment. Hence, Douglass's newspaper *North Star* featured essays championing women's rights, and Delany lectured at women's associational meetings. The year 1848 proved to be decisive, as African Americans participated in women's rights conventions at Seneca Falls and Rochester in New York.

Chaired by Douglass, the national Colored Convention in Cleveland, Ohio, in September 1848 brought the subject of women's rights to the fore of Black organizing. Douglass invited Rebecca Sanford, a white Quaker woman from Ann Arbor, Michigan, who had attended the women's rights convention at Rochester, to speak before the delegates at Cleveland. She invoked the theme of Christian women's regeneration, through the biblical Mary, to argue for women's suffrage and property rights. On the heels of this speech, Douglass and Delany proposed a resolution that read, "We fully believe in the equality of the sexes, therefore, Resolved, That we hereby invite females hereafter to take part in our deliberations."[45] Delegates affirmed it. This resolution not only impacted Black institutional culture, but it also set the tone for subsequent national and state Colored Conventions.

The Cleveland convention arguably motivated African American women to remain active in Ohio state conventions. In 1849, a group of African American women led by Mary Jane Pointer Merritt demanded formal acknowledgement and participation at the state convention in Columbus. Their demand was granted. Selina Scurry, wife of Giles O. Scurry, a farmer, penned a letter that was read by conventioneers at the 1850 convention. The following year, Selina Scurry, along with six other African American women—including Mary Jane Hopkins, a dressmaker; Lucinda Jenkins, the wife of David Jenkins, who served as a delegate at many state and national Colored Conventions; and Lucy Stanton, an Oberlin College graduate and likely the first African American woman to complete a collegiate course in the United States—pledged to fundraise to publish the convention proceedings of that year. African American women made sure that conventioneers formally acknowledged and recorded their contributions.

At the same time, free Black women began to matriculate at a few colleges and academies that had opened in the late 1840s and 1850s. Oberlin College was a leader in African American education. Before she participated in Ohio state conventions, Lucy Stanton delivered her powerful Oberlin commencement speech, "A Plea for the Oppressed," which denounced slavery as an institution that imprisoned the Black body and mind. Her activism took shape at Oberlin, where she met and later married William H. Day, also an Oberlin College graduate and delegate to national Colored Conventions. Other coeducational institutions were founded, such as the Union Literary Institute in Indiana (1846), the Allegheny Institute in Pennsylvania (1849), New-York Central College in New York (1849), and Albany Manual Labor University in Ohio (1853). These institutions received much attention from delegates at local, state, and national Colored Conventions, who were tacitly aware of coeducation as an emerging educational trend.

Despite this growth in educational opportunities, most free Black women still grappled with a myriad of challenges to educational access and employment. For most free Black women, higher education was a privilege they could not claim, and even if they did pursue it, there were no employment guarantees. Barbara Ann Steward, an activist and teacher whose father was African American abolitionist Austin Steward, lamented the lack of opportunities for African American women, who were too often confined to menial labor. She later reflected upon her own situation: "I have spent all my life in educating my head, and the brightest prospect I have today for the future, and the most advantageous offer I have ever had, is to sail for Monrovia on the coast of Africa, in October next."[46] For Steward, the African American pursuit of higher education ought to be linked with stronger employment prospects.

The subject of limited educational and employment opportunities commanded the attention of African American conventioneers who charted a path to Black uplift through economic empowerment. Over a three-day period in July 1853, approximately 140 delegates representing nine states met at the national Colored Convention in Rochester, New York, where they contemplated the subject of education and employment. In spite of virulent prejudice and the evil of American slavery, conventioneers praised the positive inroads that African Americans had made. The success of educated mechanics and teachers had far-reaching implications for Black communities, both enslaved and free. "The intelligent and upright free man of color," read the convention address, "is an unanswerable argument in favor of liberty, and a killing condemnation of American slavery."[47] Perseverance was vital. The convention appointed a committee, which included three African American educators, Charles Reason, George Vashon, and Charles Langston, to deliberate the planning and administration of a manual labor college.

An ideological orientation toward market culture and economic opportunity coupled with the rise of coeducational institutions informed the new version of the manual labor college plan. That Reason, Vashon, and Langston either attended or worked at coeducational institutions of higher education where they met African American women likely shaped their educational outlook. Vashon was the first Black graduate of Oberlin College, in 1844; Langston attended Oberlin College as well and taught in Ohio; and Reason, a mathematician, held a professorship at New-York Central College, making him the first African American professor at a predominantly white institution. In their committee report, Reason, Vashon, and Langston articulated a clear educational philosophy that supported the development of the "thinker and worker." Most educational institutions, they argued, lacked this congruity between intellectual improvement and practical employment and were thus one-dimensional. Hence, a college that combined the literary and the scientific was best adapted to prepare African American youth to create and produce. Young African American men could learn smithing and wheel wrighting while women could learn "weaving . . . [and] paper-box making" in the separate Department of Industry for Females. This curriculum and careful balance of working mind and body would, the report read, "develop *power*" for African Americans and their communities.[48]

Frederick Douglass endorsed the committee plan, though he altered it by favoring a more vocational, urban-oriented curricular model. Douglass claimed that African Americans in the United States experienced a "social disease" and the antidote was an educational philosophy that united body and mind.[49] A manual labor plan that emphasized farming was inopportune partly because African Americans appeared unwilling to migrate to rural areas. A vocational college made more sense because African Americans from urban areas could learn a trade that would teach them self-reliance. African American conventioneers then resolved to establish a manual labor school as a way to achieve "equality in political rights, and in civil and social privileges with the rest of the American people."[50] Douglass's ideas gained traction among some conventioneers, who suggested that the National Council of the Colored People, which was organized at the 1853 Rochester convention, appoint another committee to draft a specific plan for the school. For the very first time, a national Colored Convention extended education and occupational training to women and, in doing so, endorsed a coeducational college.

This new plan reflected ideological shifts among African American leaders, particularly with regard to gender and the idea of economic opportunity. The committee consisted of Douglass; John D. Peck, whose daughter, Louisa, attended Oberlin College; Amos G. Beman; John Jones; J. D. Bonner; and James McCune Smith. These leaders envisioned a new kind of institution, the American Industrial School, that would train "workmen [and] mechanics" who could participate in the marketplace.[51] This college would offer a curriculum that combined literary study and various branches of craftwork and mechanical trades. Some agricultural instruction would be offered, too. Students were to spend half of their time on craftwork so that they could produce "articles saleable for cash." Women were very much part of this plan. A special note in the industrial school proposal acknowledged that "methods and means" would be made available to prepare women for "an independent and honorable livelihood," which, given the school's curriculum and student body, included owning the means of production. In other words, the foundation of African American women's livelihood, at least, was not only marriage and motherhood but also practical knowledge and human capital.[52]

Almost all African American conventioneers championed Black educational uplift, but some raised serious concerns about the American Industrial School plan, ranging from costs and the school's racial self-segregation to its dogmatism. William H. Day was one of the first activists to dissent when he concluded that any funds procured for the school would be better spent elsewhere.[53] Defenders such as Charles Reason imbued the plan with great resonance: it would be a riposte to claims of Black inferiority; it would advance civilization; it would, apparently without the slightest bit of exaggeration, have global reach. "Intelligent young laborers," Reason wrote, would "enrich the world with necessary products."[54] At a meeting for the National Council of the Colored People in New York City in 1855, the plan, backed by

Douglass, engendered spirited debate among the thirteen African American delegates present. Edward V. Clark, a jeweler and prominent businessman, remained unconvinced that the school would be self-supporting, while George T. Downing, a caterer and businessman, and Philip Bell, a journalist, charged that the plan was "impracticable." Most critics identified other schemes to bring about Black uplift, such as associations and workshops for mechanics. In a close vote of 7–5, Douglass's plan for an industrial school was adopted.[55]

Abolitionists also raised concerns about the necessity of the proposed institution while slavery remained alive in the nation. An anonymously penned article published in the *National Anti-Slavery Standard* declared "all schemes of instruction, amelioration . . . delusive and cruel while slavery lasts."[56] Defenders countered this charge by embedding the objective of the proposed school within the ideology of Black uplift. James McCune Smith, writing under the pen name Communipaw, contextualized the project by detailing the long history of African American education, including the NEAS proposal from 1832. In the 1830s, establishing a manual labor school specifically and Black educational uplift more broadly was doubtless an abolitionist pledge. Smith argued that the rationale for a college was just as important then as it was in 1855, some twenty-three years later. In his criticism of white abolitionists, he queried, "Gentlemen, have you entirely abandoned . . . your solemn pledge?" Much had changed, however, as some abolitionists, Black and white, male and female, put the emancipation of the enslaved before all other goals.[57]

A few proponents praised the industrial school plan for providing a unique opportunity for free Black women. The American Industrial School promised not only to increase educational opportunities for African American women but also to expand their economic position. One African American male editorialist from Ohio believed that the American Industrial School could "furnish . . . our daughters with trades and respectable occupations instead of their being washerwomen, nurses, servant-girls, travelling servants, &c." "Respectable occupations" included teaching and dressmaking.[58] Speaking from experience, Barbara Ann Steward concurred: "A mere knowledge of books, without a trade of some kind is useless."[59] African Americans needed more than educational access; they needed a college and a curriculum that would prepare them for the American marketplace.

At the last pre–Civil War national Colored Convention, held in Philadelphia in October 1855, the industrial school initiative died because conventioneers were unconvinced by these arguments from Douglass, McCune Smith, and Steward, among others. The concerns raised at the 1847 and 1853 national Colored Conventions had resurfaced. The Philadelphia delegation submitted a report proposing to abandon the plan for five key reasons. First, the costs were too high to open the institution. Second, the curricular structure did not allow students to learn a trade effectively, which took upward of five years. Third, because the school, though not racially segregated, targeted African Americans, it did little to disrupt the preexisting racial hier-archy. Fourth, other educational institutions welcomed African Americans, a point made earlier that continued to elide African American women's ex-periences. Finally, the cost of attendance would preclude most poor African Americans from enrolling. Delegates such as McCune Smith tried in vain to save the plan.

Black educational uplift remained salient among the delegates, though a commitment to African American women's issues faltered. On the one hand, three women, Mary Ann Shadd Cary, Rachel Cliff, and Elizabeth Armstrong, served as delegates for the first time at the 1855 national Colored Convention. A "spirited debate," according to William Cooper Nell, accompanied the de-cision to seat Mary Ann Shadd Cary as a delegate. On the other hand, at least four resolutions relied on male-focused discourse to champion educa-tion as a path to equality and emancipation. African American (male) youth were still advised to pursue the mechanical arts, while the role of women was to encourage them! The Philadelphia delegation sought to replace the industrial school with a Bureau of Mechanic Arts, to be organized "amongst colored men." What bureaus and associations African American women might patronize were not to be found in the published minutes of the 1855 convention.[60]

Toward a New Era in Black Education

Over a twenty-four-year period, the evolution of gender politics in free Black community organizing was starkly depicted in the manual labor college initiatives proposed at national Colored Conventions in the pre–Civil War era. Reading the national Colored Convention reports serially reveals that the subject of African American higher education was always bound up with gender politics. At first, African American conventioneers and their al-lies tended to link African American men's pursuit of higher education on the manual labor platform to masculinity, economic prosperity, and racial equality. African American women were to play a distinctive role as support-ive wives and mothers. Some African American women did that and more, as they built social networks to participate in local, state, and national Colored Conventions, corresponded with African American male leaders in public forums, and studied at institutions of higher education. By the mid- to late nineteenth century, a growing sentiment among leaders to encourage Afri-can American women's community activism rivaled the ideology of female domesticity.

The American Industrial School plan implicated both African American men and women in the struggle for Black uplift. Instead of being confined to menial employment, African Americans had to become producers and skilled workers. What characterized Douglass's plan, then, was the potential for African American economic growth made possible by educating African American men and women to enter the marketplace. As the Civil War drew to a close, new colleges, academies, and institutes were established that borrowed some of the tenets of Douglass's plan such as coeducation and the industrial curricular model. A new era of African American higher education was born.

NOTES

1. "Plan for the American Industrial School," *Frederick Douglass' Paper* (Rochester, NY), March 24, 1854.

2. See, e.g., Howard Holman Bell, "A Survey of the Negro Convention Movement, 1830–1861" (PhD diss., Northwestern University, 1953); Bella Gross, "The First National Negro Convention," *Journal of Negro History* 31, no. 4 (1946): 435–43; Jane H. Pease and William H. Pease, "Negro Conventions and the Problem of Black Leadership," *Journal of Black Studies* 2, no. 1 (September 1971): 29–44; and R. J. Young, *Antebellum Black Activists: Race, Gender, and Self* (New York: Garland, 1996).

3. Hilary J. Moss, *Schooling Citizens: The Struggle for African American Education in Antebellum America* (Chicago: University of Chicago Press, 2009), 19.

4. James Anderson, "The Historical Development of Black Vocational Education," in *Work, Youth, and Schooling: Historical Perspectives on Vocationalism in American Education*, ed. Harvey Kantor and David B. Tyack (Stanford, CA: Stanford University Press, 1982), 183.

5. A digital exhibit on the Colored Conventions Project website accompanies this essay. See Sharla Fett and David Kim, *Working for Higher Education: Advancing Black Women's Rights in the 1850s*, digital exhibit, Colored Conventions Project, https://coloredconventions.org/women-higher-education.

6. "To Our Patrons," *Freedom's Journal* (New York), March 28, 1829.

7. Erica L. Ball, *To Live an Antislavery Life: Personal Politics and the Antebellum Black Middle Class* (Athens: University of Georgia Press, 2012), 36.

8. Maria Stewart, "An Address, Delivered at the African Masonic Hall, Boston, February 27, 1833," in *Meditations from the Pen of Mrs. Maria W. Stewart* (Washington, DC: Enterprise, 1879), 66.

9. *Minutes and Proceedings of the First Annual Convention of the People of Colour* [. . .] *June 1831* (Philadelphia: Published by Order of the Committee of Arrangements, 1831), 5.

10. The other four white abolitionists were Arthur Tappan, Benjamin Lundy, Thomas Shipley, and Charles Pierce.

11. Simeon S. Jocelyn, *College for Colored Youth: An Account of the New-Haven City Meetings and Resolutions* (New York: Committee, 1831), 10.

12. Milton C. Sernett, *Abolition's Axe: Beriah Green, Oneida Institute, and the Black Freedom Struggle* (Syracuse, NY: Syracuse University Press, 1986), 35.

13. Theodore D. Weld, *First Annual Report of the Society for Promoting Manual Labor in Literary Institutions* [. . .] (New York: S. W. Benedict, 1833), 22.

14. William Lloyd Garrison, *An Address Delivered before the Free People of Color, in Philadelphia, New York, and Other Cities, during the Month of June, 1831*, 3rd ed. (Boston: Stephen Foster, 1831), 10. I make a similar point in Kabria Baumgartner, "Towers of Intellect: The Struggle for African American Higher Education in Antebellum New England," in *Slavery and the University: Histories and Legacies*, ed. Leslie M. Harris, James T. Campbell, and Alfred L. Brophy (Athens: University of Georgia Press, 2019), 186.

15. In the letters I have examined about the manual labor initiative, there was no mention of admitting women. Still, discussions about admitting African American women may have occurred but did not end up in the published minutes.

16. Certainly, there were exceptions, but as scholar John R. Thelin points out, most

of the early institutions of higher education in the United States that welcomed women "were not originally called 'colleges' but rather went by such names as 'academy,' 'female institute,' or 'seminary for women.'" John Thelin, *A History of American Higher Education*, 2nd ed. (Baltimore: Johns Hopkins University Press, 2011), 56.

17. "College for the People of Color," *Liberator* (Boston), July 9, 1831.

18. "Miami High School, for Colored Youth" [advertisement], *Philanthropist* (New Richmond, OH), February 26, 1836.

19. Leon Litwack, *North of Slavery: The Negro in the Free States* (Chicago: University of Chicago Press, 1961), 139.

20. *Minutes and Proceedings of the Second Annual Convention, for the Improvement of the Free People of Color in these United States* [. . .] *June 1832* (Philadelphia: Martin and Boden, 1832), 34.

21. Jocelyn, *College for Colored Youth*, 5.

22. Moss, *Schooling Citizens*, 46.

23. This information on the New Haven incident appears in Baumgartner, "Towers of Intellect," 187; and Kabria Baumgartner, *In Pursuit of Knowledge: Black Women and Educational Activism in Antebellum America* (New York: New York University Press, 2019), 25.

24. *Proceedings of the Third Annual Convention, for the Improvement of the Free People of Colour in these United States* [. . .] *June 1833* (New York: Convention, 1833), 14.

25. *Minutes of the Fourth Annual Convention for the Improvement of the Free People of Colour* [. . .] *June 1834* (New York: Convention, 1834), 18.

26. The other committee members included Moses Thacher and Samuel E. Sewall. Both Barbadoes and Hilton were members of the General Colored Association, an abolitionist organization in Massachusetts, which merged with the NEAS in 1833.

27. Buffum to Rev. Simeon Jocelyn, January 11, 1832, African American Resources Collection, Connecticut Historical Society, Hartford, CT.

28. "School for Colored Youth," *Liberator*, September 29, 1832. Emphasis mine.

29. This assertion follows the work of historian Richard Newman, who demonstrates that Boston abolitionists embraced a more democratic perspective to their reform activity. See Richard S. Newman, *The Transformation of American Abolitionism: Fighting Slavery in the Early Republic* (Chapel Hill: University of North Carolina Press, 2002).

30. "Manual Labor School," *Liberator*, July 5, 1834.

31. *Minutes of the Fifth Annual Convention for the Improvement of the Free People of Colour in the United States* [. . .] *June 1835* (Philadelphia: William P. Gibbons, 1835), 10.

32. For an analysis of this split, see Leslie Harris, *In the Shadow of Slavery: African-Americans in New York City, 1825–1863* (Chicago: University of Chicago Press, 2003), 185; Margaret Hope Bacon, *But One Race: The Life of Robert Purvis* (Albany: State University of New York Press, 2007), 52–54; and Martha S. Jones, *All Bound Up Together: The Woman Question in African American Public Culture, 1830–1900* (Chapel Hill: University of North Carolina Press, 2007), 47–49. New research by Kate Masur has found that only a two-year hiatus existed between the last national Colored Convention in 1835 and the beginning of state conventions (which were previously thought to have started in New York in 1840 but actually began in Ohio in 1837).

33. "A Convention," *Colored American*, May 23, 1840.

34. These republican beliefs partly explained why African American leaders were not very concerned that a manual labor curriculum at a college or university might reinforce stereotypes about Black physicality and the condition of slavery. In the context of the "free labor" North, such learning would directly lead to self-determination and economic independence for African Americans.

35. Stephen Rice, "The Mechanics' Institute of the City of New-York and the Conception of Class Authority in Early Industrial America, 1830–1860," *New York History* 81, no. 3 (2000): 287.

36. Charles B. Ray, "Female Education," *Colored American*, March 18, 1837.

37. "Female Influence," *Palladium of Liberty* (Columbus, OH), April 3, 1844.

38. Samuel Cornish, "Female Education," *Colored American*, November 23, 1839.

39. *Minutes of the National Convention of Colored Citizens: Held at Buffalo* [. . .] *August 1843* (New York: Piercy and Reed, 1843), 16.

40. For an interesting study on Alexander Crummell, see Wilson Jeremiah Moses, *Alexander Crummell: A Study of Civilization and Discontent* (Oxford: Oxford University Press, 1989).

41. "Selections. The Colored Convention. Report of the Committee on Education," *North Star* (Rochester, NY), January 21, 1848.

42. William Cooper Nell, "Report of the Doings of the National Convention of Colored Americans and Their Friends, Held at Troy, NY, Oct. 6, 1847," *Liberator*, November 19, 1847.

43. *Minutes of the National Convention*, 9, 11.

44. *Proceedings of the National Convention of Colored People, and Their Friends, Held in Troy, NY* [. . .] *October 1847* (New York: J. C. Kneeland, 1847), 9.

45. Colored National Convention (1848: Cleveland, OH), *Report of the Proceedings of the Colored National Convention held at Cleveland, Ohio, on Wednesday, September 6, 1848*, Colored Conventions Project, accessed July 20, 2020, https://omeka.coloredconventions.org/items/show/280.

46. Barbara Ann Steward, "[Letter of Frederick Douglass], The Industrial School," *Frederick Douglass' Paper*, June 1, 1855.

47. *Proceedings of the Colored National Convention, Held in Rochester* [. . .] *June 1853* (Rochester, NY: Printed at the Office of *Frederick Douglass' Paper*, 1853), 17.

48. *Proceedings of the Colored National Convention, Held in Rochester*, 32.

49. *Proceedings of the Colored National Convention, Held in Rochester*, 34–35, 37.

50. *Proceedings of the Colored National Convention, Held in Rochester*, 40.

51. "An Effort, We Are Glad to Learn . . . ," *Frederick Douglass' Paper*, April 15, 1853.

52. "Plan for the American Industrial School," *Frederick Douglass' Paper*, March 24, 1854.

53. "Progress of Equality," *Liberator*, April 14, 1854.

54. Charles L. Reason, "Introduction (The Colored People's 'Industrial College')," in *Autographs for Freedom*, ed. Julia Griffiths (Auburn, NY: Alden, Beardsley, 1854), 14.

55. William Cooper Nell, "Colored National Council," *Liberator*, July 27, 1855. In New York, a group of African American activists met at the church of Reverend Hodges, where they resolved to reject "the establishment of proscriptive institutions."

56. *National Anti-Slavery Standard*, as reprinted and discussed in "The Testimonial to Mrs. Stowe, and What Shall be Done with It?," *Frederick Douglass' Paper*, May 27, 1853.

57. "Our Correspondents," *Frederick Douglass' Paper*, February 16, 1855. The rift between Garrison and Douglass no doubt played a role, as did ongoing debates between Boston and New York abolitionists. For more on this, see Benjamin Quarles, "The Breach between Douglass and Garrison," *Journal of Negro History* 23 (April 1938): 144–54.

58. Scioto, "For Frederick Douglass' Paper [letter from Scioto to Douglass, April 24, 1854]," *Frederick Douglass' Paper*, May 26, 1854.

59. Steward, "[Letter of Frederick Douglass]."

60. *Proceedings of the Colored National Convention, Held in Franklin Hall, Sixth Street, Below Arch, Philadelphia* [. . .] *October 1855* (Salem, NJ: National Standard Office, 1856), 12.

SECRETS WELL KEPT

Colored Conventioneers and
Underground Railroad Activism

Cheryl Janifer LaRoche

Introduction

In the pre–Civil War era, the names of Colored Convention attendees cut across activist organizations, zigzagging from antislavery meetings to vigilance committees, from Black church leadership to Freemason membership—all spaces of collective Black activism. Men—and a few women—representing various regions, states, and cities gathered at Colored Conventions organized for the purpose of improving the legal and political status for people of color. As we look with fresh eyes, membership rolls and rosters of attendees and delegates at these organizations read like a who's who of Underground Railroad activism.

Today, we gather from different disciplines and vantage points to redefine the broader cooperative meaning of the Colored Conventions movement. In providing access to transcribed minutes through technological advancements of the twenty-first century, the Colored Conventions Project captures the breadth of the movement, refocuses our attention, and expands understanding through linked data. By enabling multilayered scholarship and complex interpretations, the transcribed minutes and related documents highlight the range of pre- and post–Civil War issues demanding the attention and action of conventioneers across the country. But despite technological advances, establishing connections between leaders in the Colored Conventions movement and their dedication to ending slavery through abolitionism and the Underground Railroad movement remains one of the more difficult connections to recognize and document. Individual stories of activism in the Colored Conventions movement have not found their way into Underground Railroad literature. Widespread presence of Underground Railroad activism among convention members has eluded our interpretative grasp. For the past two centuries, the Underground Railroad has prompted ideas of lore, myth, and legend punctuated by outsized actions by Harriet Tubman or Levi Coffin, for example. Yet captives had been escaping slavery since the earliest days of enslavement. Escape was a diasporic response that began with the first landings of enslaved populations. Organized, assisted escapes became identified as and with the Underground Railroad beginning in the 1830s. Today's definition encompasses a broad interpretation of the Underground Railroad beyond the original focus on assisted escapes. Through the Network to Freedom Program, the National Park Service now defines the Underground Railroad as any escape, attempted or successful, assisted or otherwise, that occurred from the inception of this country to the end of the Civil War. To further complicate matters, slavery remained legal and enforced in the border states; the Emancipation Proclamation did not end the practice in Delaware, Maryland, West Virginia, Kentucky, or Missouri.[1] Supporters' demonstrated willingness to assist in escapes from slavery by whatever means necessary, whether labeled the Underground Railroad or not, is the reference point for this article.

Historical interpretations of the Underground Railroad left little room for consideration within scholarly debates. Here, I want to draw a distinction between abolitionism and the Underground Railroad. One could be overtly active in the abolitionist movement and have limited interest in physically coming to the aid of escapees. Yet as we clarify the topic of the Underground Railroad, political action is defined by a dedication to sounding the death knell for slavery by removing its unwilling captives. Just as the Underground Railroad has been historically trivialized, so too, until recently, has Black participation within the movement: the Underground Railroad narrative was full of frightened, shivering slaves and clever white heroes—often Quakers— outwitting would-be captors.[2] Individual stories of Black advocates assisting with escapes or working as Underground Railroad activists combined with a narrative of collective action reveal Black involvement in the Underground Railroad as both covert and collective: secret in its details, public in its existence, collective in its intent—both moral and illegal.

According to historian Craig Wilder, the linked ideologies of African American societies and cooperative institutions "tied every aspect of life to the destruction of slavery." I include Underground Railroad activism among such cooperative ideologies. Historian James Horton defines the national convention movement as calling for "continued antislavery agitation and stress[ing] the responsibility of Blacks who enjoyed the 'privilege' of freedom to take a stand against slavery at every public opportunity." Here, I lay the foundation for the argument that pre–Civil War Colored Conventions functioned as overt socially sanctioned, politically tolerated meeting spaces where public activists brought hidden agendas. Conventions were often held in churches that covertly served as stations on the Underground Railroad. Men of high moral caliber were bound together by a principled stand against slavery *and* were involved in the illegal operations of smuggling captives out of slavery, facilitating escapes, or hiding and aiding freedom seekers. When morality collided with injustice, they did whatever was expedient or required, all while separately conducting reputable businesses, leading church denominations, and establishing newspapers, schools, and moral reform societies. Convention activists practiced seemingly paradoxical ideologies at the intersection of moral duty and self-determined emancipation. More than a century later, presidential hopeful Barry Goldwater gave us two phrases that encapsulate the Colored Convention delegates' dedication: "extremism in the defense of liberty is no vice" and "moderation in the pursuit of justice is no virtue."[3]

Bringing an end to slavery, an explicit and implicit goal, entwined individual action with public political culture and magnified African American collective identity and commitment to political and social agendas. The secret actions of Blacks working through the Underground Railroad expose the work of Black leaders, free Blacks, and those held in bondage. They all negotiated two worlds—one hidden, where closely held efforts were critical to the success of the movement, and the other a public world of respectability and lawfulness.

Black activism fueled the inner workings of the Underground Railroad, as it operated across the expanse of Black institutional and communal life, in addition to its better-known interracial, transdenominational character. Colored Convention meetings fused fraternal organizations, activists, and free people of color together with childhood friends, relatives and schoolmates, and former, often self-emancipated captives, as well as with white abolitionists. Prominent participants representing Black churches or the Free and Accepted Masons routinely interacted with Underground Railroad operatives at Colored Conventions and major gatherings, providing information connecting Black activism to the larger world. The nation's prominent Black abolitionists and Underground Railroad activists maintained family ties to settlements across the country or had an acute understanding of what it took to escape from slavery. Several among them had gotten themselves out of captivity years earlier, and they vividly remembered the horrors of enslavement. Often their family members continued to be held in bondage.[4]

The Underground Railroad was in its ascendency as the Colored Conventions movement came into existence. In the accepted historical interpretation of the Underground Railroad movement, Black abolitionists and activists rarely played a decisive role. Uncovering the centrality of African American activism operating inside their own intersecting institutions in the cause of their own liberation is the work of this essay. It requires extensive knowledge of Underground Railroad operations, a detective's ability to research and decode the language of clandestine organizations, and a deep involvement with literature detailing the broad concerns and activism centered on slavery and its abolition. In the absence of conventioneers' outright declarations of their work on the Underground Railroad—with Jermaine Loguen, Charles B. Ray, Lewis Hayden, and Frederick Douglass among notable exceptions—if we study Colored Conventions without understanding the Underground Railroad or interrogate one facet of a conventioneer's life without understanding another, we likely will miss the deep interconnectedness of Black communal and organizational life. The important possibility of coordinated, albeit discrete, networks and intentions undergirds the early Colored Convention movement.

Although I emphasize the earlier pre–Civil War conventions, Underground Railroad activists' participation spans time, place, and region, as revealed by a general perusal of the list of state and national convention delegates. Editors Philip Foner and George Walker provide useful year-by-year reference notes in *Proceedings of the Black State Conventions, 1840–1865*, detailing information known at that time. The authors include Underground Railroad activities and aid rendered to freedom seekers by the convention's more obviously involved participants.[5] The references touch on the most recognizable Underground Railroad activists. The more difficult scholarship lies in recognizing and identifying lesser-known Underground Railroad operatives by state and region. Anyone well versed in the history of the Underground Railroad for a particular region or state can readily identify the names of operatives found on Colored Convention rosters vice versa.

This essay outlines the concept; deeper research will likely yield greater involvement of previously unrecognized Underground Railroad participants. Here I offer just two strategies. First, I explore well-known Underground Railroad sketches among the most conspicuous and active participants in the Colored Conventions movement. Second, across time and location, I surveyed and randomly selected convention participants not readily identified with Underground Railroad activity to determine if my premise held merit. I began to search the literature to determine whether these participants either had connections to Underground Railroad activities or had assisted freedom seekers in any capacity beyond the more famous examples. Therefore, several of the names and stories related to the Underground Railroad that appear in this article were unfamiliar to me at the outset of this research. The examples came to the fore as a result of researching Black convention participants' involvement with the Underground Railroad.

Tying Participants in the Colored Conventions Movement to the Underground Railroad

Leadership in Colored Conventions transected class, religious denominations, and Black institutions. Among convention leaders were the notable abolitionists Bishop Richard Allen, founder of the African Methodist Episcopal (AME) Church; wealthy sailmaker James Forten; Rev. Samuel E. Cornish, leader of the AME Zion Church; prosperous lumberman William Whipper; Rev. Peter Williams; William Hamilton; Robert Purvis; Frederick Douglass; and blacksmith J. W. C. Pennington, to name but a few. Dozens more would lead the Colored Conventions in the western states, collectively representing leadership and participants in a number of Black groups "united to protect their rights, and render aid to their unfortunate brethren driven into exile."[6]

Outward concern for the plight of the fugitive evinced in Colored Convention minutes matched the inner convictions expressed in the clandestine actions of leading conventioneers. Their names and influences weave through Underground Railroad narratives—so much so that space here will not permit the exposition of a fraction of their extraordinary undertakings in the cause of liberation. Directing our focus toward escape from slavery, rather than limiting scrutiny to a narrowly conceived "Underground Railroad," constitutes a critical first step in unraveling the mystery. Many participants in the Underground Railroad rarely used the term.

Until the issuance of the Emancipation Proclamation, particularly after the Fugitive Slave Act of 1850, escape from slavery was illegal, and offering assistance—often called abetting—was a serious, punishable crime. Abolitionists were much maligned and abolitionism much scorned. The romantic, often heroic ways in which this work is discussed in contemporaneous literature belies the dangerous, life-threatening, career- and reputation-ruining endeavor that it could be, particularly for Black leaders of high regard, social rank, or religious standing.

Richard Allen and Other Early Black Abolitionists

AME bishop Richard Allen brought the concept of the Colored Conventions to life by building upon the ideas of Hezekiah Grice. Allen was instrumental in the development and growth of several early nineteenth-century Black institutions. Not only did he and Absalom Jones lay the foundation for the Black Church, but their combined influence brought Freemasonry to Philadelphia by establishing the second lodge of the Free and Accepted Masons in the United States. Allen is widely known and revered for this institution building, yet his Underground Railroad involvement remains peripheral to the freedom-minded legacy he bequeathed to each of the organizations he instituted.

Although he was born in Philadelphia, Allen endured slavery in Delaware. Using monies he earned laboring during the American Revolution, he purchased his and his brother's freedom. His transcendent rise from slave to first bishop of the AME Church ensured that Allen maintained a profound understanding of what it meant to be held in slavery and what was required to get out. If we peer beyond the reverential aura of respectability that surrounded the AME bishop, we find a staunch opponent to slavery who, like so many of his fellow Colored Conventioneers, circumnavigated the legal dictates of the times to answer the call of higher moral law. Walter Proctor, Allen's contemporary and confidant of fifteen years, explained, "The house of Allen was a refuge for the oppressed."[7] Allen used his church—the same church that hosted early Colored Conventions—as an asylum from slavery. He and his wife, Sarah, tirelessly kept their Pennsylvania home open, using it to shelter anyone escaping slavery who came their way.

The first convention meeting Allen convened and held in Mother Bethel AME Church in Philadelphia focused on the problem of possible expatriation of Blacks from Cincinnati to Canada due to racial strife instigated by the city's white population, which was being confronted by job competition. Fierce clashes over work drove the Ohio legislature to pass restrictive laws that practically excluded Blacks from the city.[8] Education, mechanical and agricultural pursuits, and emigration to Canada ranked among the outward concerns that occupied the first convention. Certainly the title of the first convention, "American Society of Free Persons of Colour, for Improving their Condition in the United States; for Purchasing Lands; and for the Establishing of a Settlement in Upper Canada," bears that out. Many unspoken arrangements lay behind convention proceedings that mentioned "those forced to leave their homes" under a variety of unnamed circumstances.[9]

Austin Steward served as vice president of the first convention. Steward had escaped slavery in New York in 1814. He went on to play an important role both in helping escapees find freedom and in the abolitionist movement in the early 1830s. In his narrative, *Twenty-Two Years a Slave, and Forty Years a Freeman*, Steward described the racial difficulties he encountered during his travels to this first convention and his subsequent work on the Underground Railroad. Steward also served as president of the 1840 New York state convention, representing Rochester, New York. After he escaped to freedom, Steward developed a successful grocery business and meat market in Rochester, where he spent his profits helping other escapees find freedom through the Underground Railroad. The workers on the Underground Railroad prided themselves on being "quiet and undocumented," but Steward's store on the east bank of the Genesee River was "quite likely a place where," one historian reported, "those leading slaves to freedom might have gone for help."[10] The homes of Black abolitionists are often overlooked as Underground Railroad spaces. Steward says in his narrative, "My house has ever been open to the fugitive slaves; but more particularly when I resided in Rochester."[11]

When convention members sanctioned the establishment of the Wilberforce community in Canada in response to the brutal conditions Blacks faced in Cincinnati, Steward went on to become president of the Canadian Wilberforce Colony of free slaves. The Ontario colony functioned as a Canadian terminus of the Underground Railroad. Steadfast in his commitment to liberty, Steward was among the noteworthy convention participants who wrote influential narratives of their escape.[12]

William Whipper: Respectability and Black Activism

One of the most important books on the Underground Railroad, William Still's *Underground Railroad* provides extensive coverage of the Underground Railroad activities of one of the Colored Conventions' most prominent participants, William Whipper. For more than a half century, the moral reform activist worked to improve the conditions of his people. As the only delegate to have attended all of the first six Colored Conventions, Whipper was among the most influential men of his time.

In 1828, three years before the first Colored Convention was called to order, Whipper was living in Philadelphia and taking "an active part in the intellectual life of the Black community." At the height of Bishop Allen's ministry in the AME Church, Whipper had joined Allen by acting as the corresponding secretary for the short-lived American Society of Free Persons of Colour, for Improving their Condition; Allen served as president. When the two men recombined their efforts to form the First National Convention of the People of Color, Whipper again served as secretary to the convention. One chronicler at the time observed, "To the 'first annual Convention' certainly belongs the credit of having blown the first great blast, by which the people of color were awakened to the importance of their own united and energetic action, in removing their disabilities and securing equal rights with other men." Given that people of color "never let a subject of peculiar importance to them . . . pass without a public expression of their views and opinions," the state of free Blacks as well as the plight of freedom seekers was constantly on their minds.[13]

Whipper counted among his contemporaries the wealthy sailmaker James Forten and Forten's "magnetic" son-in-law, Robert Purvis—one of the reputed "presidents" of the Underground Railroad also featured in Still's lengthy exposé. Together these men fought the efforts of the Pennsylvania legislature to curb the freedom of free men of color. Such social and organizational networks offer clues to unraveling the concealed work of Black conventioneers in the Underground Railroad movement.

Historians of the Colored Conventions movement characterize William Whipper in the early 1830s "as an active part of the group that wrestled with the problems of education and possible expatriation to Canada" and by the latter part of the 1830s as "one of the leading exponents of the more theoretical moral reform ideas." Such a characterization would lead to a rather benign assessment of Whipper's efforts. By at least 1847, however, his thinking had radicalized to the extent that he was an active conductor on the Underground Railroad. He aided many escapees who came through Columbia, Pennsylvania. Situated on the eastern bank of the Susquehanna River, the northern boundary of the slaveholding states, "Columbia," Whipper observed, was "the great depot where the fugitives from Virginia and Maryland first landed."[14] A long bridge connecting Wrightsville to Columbia provided safe passage for successful escapees. Whipper's home was at the end of that bridge. Between 1847 and 1850, he operated an Underground Railroad station and was frequently called upon to take charge of the hundreds of "passengers"—sometimes as many as seventeen at one time—seeking immediate refuge on slavery's borderland.

Determined to exploit his responsible position as a wealthy lumber merchant, Whipper used his fleet of railroad cars and canal boats to ship escapees in Pennsylvania across the state on the main line of the Allegheny Portage Railroad. By his own account, he was responsible, directly or indirectly, for passing hundreds of slaves to the land of freedom. For five years, he contributed $1,000 annually to the cause. The complicity of his firm, Smith and Whipper, was whispered about in slaveholding regions. Indeed, on two occasions, attempts to set fire to the company's lumberyard were intended to punish the businessmen for their illicit acts.[15]

Whipper considered Canadian emigration another avenue of escape, explaining that he always persuaded anyone seeking their freedom "to go to Canada, as I had no faith in their being able to elude the grasp of the slave-hunters." Most of his immediate family relocated there. He taught his nephew James Whipper Purnell, who moved to Chatham, the outer workings of the lumber business as well as the inner workings of the Underground Railroad. Whipper's sister, Mary Ann, left Pennsylvania and came to Dresden, Ontario, where she met and married James Hollinsworth, also of Pennsylvania. Both Mary Ann and James were involved with Whipper in secreting escapees across the border on the Reading and Columbia Railroad.[16] Whipper declared in a revealing letter to William Still, "I am thankful for having had the glorious privilege of laboring with others for the redemption of my race from oppression and thralldom; and I would prefer to-day to be penniless in the streets, rather than to have withheld a single hour's labor or a dollar from the sacred cause of liberty, justice, and humanity."[17]

Expanding Underground Railroad Connections

Not only were the homes of Black abolitionists important sites of safety and refuge for men and women escaping slavery, but Black communities as a whole, in addition to their churches, functioned as sites of sanctuary. The life of Philadelphian Junius C. Morel, secretary to the first convention, is indicative of the life of commitment led by many of the delegates. Twenty years after that first convention, Morel emerged as an active part of the group that wrestled with the problems of education and possible expatriation to Canada in the Black community of Weeksville in Brooklyn, New York, as part of "A Committee of Thirteen." One of the committee's missions was to give aid—financial or otherwise—to escaping slaves.[18]

Add to these convention members the well-known Underground Railroad operatives J. W. C. Pennington, who wrote the seminal narrative *Fugitive Blacksmith*, and Abraham D. Shadd, both of whom served as delegates at the founding of the Colored Conventions movement. Newspaperwoman Mary Ann Shadd described her father, Abraham D. Shadd, as the chief brakeman on the Delaware Underground Railroad. This noted patriarch of his Underground Railroad family opened his home in Wilmington to those escaping slavery and continued his Underground Railroad work when he moved the family to a farm in West Chester, Pennsylvania. Abraham Shadd attended the first four national conventions and presided over the third in Philadelphia in 1833. Noted Underground Railroad operatives Robert Purvis, J. W. C.

Pennington, and David Ruggles were also present. The 1833 Colored Conventioneers formed a committee to "report whether any and how far encouragement ought to be given to the settlement in Upper Canada," where
Shadd eventually moved his family after the Fugitive Slave Act was passed
in 1850.[19]

Ruggles, one of New York's notable Underground Railroad operatives,
worked tirelessly with the Committee of Vigilance, a visible freedom institution dominated by African Americans. The committee championed suffrage,
education, and a range of community concerns. Whites preferred antislavery societies, while Blacks tended toward proactive vigilance committees.
Ruggles let it be known that his home was a source of information about the
kidnapping of Blacks in the city. In so doing, the Black abolitionist openly
and publicly disclosed that his home was a refuge for enslaved people seeking liberty and for families seeking help recovering their loved ones from
bondage. Ruggles's biographer, Graham Hodges, states directly that by 1838,
"Ruggles's home had become the city's central depot on the Underground
Railroad. Runaway slaves coming north already knew or quickly learned
that David Ruggles' house was the most welcoming place in New York."[20]
Frederick Douglass was guided there after his escape. Convention attendee
and escapee J. W. C. Pennington, who performed Douglass's marriage ceremony after his escape, was a close ally, and Ruggles maintained extensive
connections with Black abolitionists in Philadelphia. After John L. Smith
escaped, he came to New York looking for Ruggles with reference letter in
hand from Philadelphia. As Hodges points out, Ruggles used his wide network of contacts from Colored Conventions and other endeavors and organizations. When Basil Dorsey, a freedom seeker from Maryland, was arrested
in Doylestown, Pennsylvania, but later acquitted after a trial, it was Robert
Purvis who greeted Dorsey on the steps of the courthouse. Purvis and the
Pennsylvania Committee of Vigilance hurried the escapee by wagon to David
Ruggles's home. In turn, Ruggles sent Dorsey on to Northampton, Massachusetts. Black activism on the Underground Railroad was not confined to
physically spiriting escapees under the cover of night from one station to
another. Opening one's home to receiving escapees persisted as one of the
most important humanitarian acts of refuge and safety one could offer.

By 1843, delegates had revived the national convention movement after a
six-year hiatus, assembling for "The National Convention of Colored Citizens
Held at Buffalo for the Purpose of Considering Their Moral and Political
Condition as American Citizens." Antislavery was on the agenda alongside
a stance by a majority of delegates for radical political action and consideration of endorsement of physical violence in the overthrow of slavery. Henry
Highland Garnet first delivered his unyielding "Address to the Slaves of the
United States of America" at the Buffalo convention, advocating the use of
violence if necessary to bring an end to slavery. Historian Benjamin Quarles identified the speech as "the most forthright call for a slave uprising
ever heard in antebellum America."[21] Garnet sought a resolution to have the

speech adopted by the convention delegates, but it was suppressed by one vote; the speech was printed five years later with revised and softened language.[22] By Garnet's own admission in an April 1848 reprint, the document elicited more discussion than any previous paper ever brought before that or any other deliberative body of Colored persons and their friends.

Like so many delegates, Garnet had a realistic, firsthand confrontation with slavery. As a young boy, he and his entire family had escaped captivity in Maryland. Once settled in New York City years later, Garnet's family was hunted down by slave catchers and forced to flee again. Garnet's activism spilled over into the Underground Railroad. He was active with Black abolitionists Rev. Theodore S. Wright and Charles B. Ray of the New York Committee of Vigilance, claiming to have aided as many as 150 escapees in a single year. During the years he pastored the Liberty Street Presbyterian Church in Troy, from 1839 to 1846, the fiery abolitionist was active in the Underground Railroad in Rensselaer County, New York.[23]

Baptist minister Samuel H. Davis, chairman pro tem of the Buffalo national convention, set a militant tone when he delivered the keynote speech at the convention and stressed that Blacks were "determined no longer to submit tamely and silently to the galling yoke of oppression." His speech "hinted at using other than peaceful means to obtain rights long overdue."[24] Within a few years, Reverend Davis and his Buffalo congregation had amassed resources enough to construct Michigan Avenue Baptist Church, which served as a stop on the Underground Railroad in Buffalo. Escapees were hidden in the basement of the church before being ferried across the Niagara River to Canada. Davis moved on to Detroit to pastor Michigan's Second Baptist Church.

Baptist Underground Railroad activism in Detroit mirrored activism in Buffalo. Between 1836 and 1846, Rev. William Charles Monroe served as the first pastor of Second Baptist.[25] The church had deep involvement in both the Colored Convention movement and the Underground Railroad. Monroe had been part of the Colored Vigilant Committee of Detroit, which met in the basement of the church. With Monroe at the helm, leaders at Second Baptist associated with abolitionists John Brown and Frederick Douglass. With the Detroit River and the Canadian border a little more than 1,000 yards away, Second Baptist became a major stop on the Underground Railroad, hosting 500 freedom seekers over thirty years. The church is said to have had a room under the sanctuary where escapees remained until they could safely continue their freedom quest. Reverend Monroe presided over Michigan's First State Convention for Colored Citizens, which met at the church in October 1843; Martin Delany's first emigration convention met there in 1855; and John Brown's Canadian antislavery convention met in the church in 1858.[26] Through the participation of its ministers and lay leaders, the Black church silently collaborated with interracial organizations that claimed among their members activists, both discreet and fiery, with ties to the Underground Railroad.

Frederick Douglass

Of all the participants in the Colored Conventions, Frederick Douglass stands out as a prominent, widely acknowledged Underground Railroad operative. With his future wife, Anna Murray, to help accomplish his escape, Frederick Bailey's (as he was then known) flight is considered to have taken place on the Underground Railroad. When he finally arrived in New York City after his successful escape from Baltimore, Douglass was plugged into the Underground Railroad to move him safely across northern states. It was none other than David Ruggles who guided Douglass in his newfound freedom to New Bedford, Massachusetts. By 1838, the year of Douglass's escape, the Colored Conventions had been in operation for eight years. Douglass, like so many other participants, understood the deprivations of slavery and the many blessings of liberty.

Douglass's narrative of his escape, *Narrative of the Life of Frederick Douglass*, and his lectures brought him enough fame and fortune to purchase a substantial home in Rochester, seven miles from Lake Ontario and a steamboat ride to Canada. Since Douglass was frequently away traveling and lecturing, it was often left to his wife, Anna, to ensure the safety of the escapees who had made their way to their Rochester home. After the infamous Christiana riot in 1851, Douglass himself spirited William Parker, one of the two people implicated in the assault, to the steamboat bound for Canada.[27]

Time and again as Douglass grew in stature and prominence following his escape, the eloquent orator and searing writer fearlessly announced his Underground Railroad activity in his newspaper and other antislavery outlets. On January 8, 1858, Douglass wrote to the Ladies' Irish Anti-Slavery Association: "We have passed over our section of the underground railroad about forty within the last sixty days. Among them were two women, one of whom had escaped slavery 8 years prior has made several return trips at great risks and has brought out, since obtaining her own freedom, fifty others from the house of bondage. She has been spending a short time with us since the holidays." Douglass does not mention Harriet Tubman by name—she had yet to make a name for herself—but she was actively and very effectively working the Underground Railroad. The timing of the article—Tubman had escaped with eleven captives—plus his description of her "great courage and shrewdness" most certainly point to Tubman's work and strength of character. Kate Larson, Tubman's biographer, drew the same conclusion.[28]

Booker T. Washington, in his biography of Douglass, explains that the Underground Railroad activist could count on the cooperation of his friends and supporters, including Robert Purvis, Oliver Johnson, and Dr. James McCune Smith of New York City; Stephen A. Myers of Albany; William Rich of Troy; and Rev. J. W. Loguen of Syracuse. Many others actively assisted in the work, among them Charles Lennox Remond and William Whipper of Philadelphia; Thomas L. Dorsey, Rev. Henry Highland Garnet, and

Anthony Barrier of Brockport, New York; and Thomas Downing of New York City. Almost all of these names were associated with Colored Conventions at one point or another. Washington noted, "Douglass's home was always considered an asylum for runaways, and was constantly under the surveillance of the United States marshals; nevertheless, not a single fugitive, after reaching him, was ever apprehended and carried back."[29] As the Civil War drew nearer, conventioneers such as Douglass and "Underground Railroad king" and AME Zion bishop Jermain Loguen flaunted their Underground Railroad work.[30]

One final episode and two biographical sketches reinforce the connections between conventioneers and Underground Railroad activism. At the 1855 National Convention, Robert Purvis introduced three resolutions concerning the famous case of Passmore Williamson, a moral-minded Quaker being held in Moyamensing Prison as an accomplice in the escape of Jane Johnson and her two sons. Williamson served alongside William Still as a general member of the Philadelphia Vigilance Committee. Still and five Black porters had in fact rescued Johnson and her children, and the six liberators were on trial as Williamson languished in jail. Sympathy in Philadelphia for Williamson ran high and he received scores of visitors.

The first of Purvis's resolutions expressed the convention's "sincere admiration" of Williamson's fidelity to the convention's principles and of "his heroic devotion to the cause of freedom." The second resolved that Williamson was entitled to "the highest regard and the warmest admiration" for his "promptness . . . when called upon to fly to the aid of the slave when striving for his freedom." The third and final resolution appointed a committee of five—Robert Purvis of Pennsylvania, John S. Rock of Maryland and Massachusetts, George T. Downing of Rhode Island, Stephen Myers of New York, and Charles L. Remond of Massachusetts—to visit Williamson in jail and present "this expression of the National Convention." The delegates were in town attending the 1855 convention while the trial was taking place.[31] All five of the committee members were involved in the Underground Railroad.

Albany's Stephen Myers, a veteran of numerous state conventions, had been born into slavery in 1800 in Rensselaer County, New York, and was freed at the age of eighteen. Myers grew to become the most important leader of the local Albany Underground Railroad movement from the 1830s through the 1850s, by which time he called himself "Agent and Superintendent of the Underground Railroad."[32] It was Myers who looked after Harriet Tubman and her charges after she left Philadelphia with a party of escapees before they proceeded to New York by "steam railroad."[33]

While fellow committee member, lawyer, physician, and abolitionist John S. Rock lived in Philadelphia, he interacted with William Still, the father of the Underground Railroad. Rock migrated to Boston, joining the African American community in Beacon Hill, where he focused on his medical career. His mission of protecting and aiding freedom seekers took many shapes. Now practicing medicine rather than law, Rock worked through

Boston's vigilance committee to render medical services to ailing fugitives. He set up a practice in Boston, where many of his patients were people escaping slavery by fleeing to Canada through the Underground Railroad. Rock worked to send them off in good health.[34]

Conclusion

The Underground Railroad had no gathering spaces of its own, no meeting schedule for its members, and no delegates. Vigilance committees were the organizations whose members are most closely associated with the Underground Railroad. The individuals within the movement operated inside other organizations and denominations that routinely gathered at conventions and yearly meetings. Members from various parts of the country intermingled and possibly formulated strategies. Unlike Underground Railroad records, which often require painstaking research to uncover, the roster of officers, delegates, and participants at Colored Conventions offers a research treasure trove! Future study will determine whether a survey of Underground Railroad operatives yields similar interconnections. Is the W. Mitchell, for example, listed as a Fayette County delegate to the Ohio state convention of 1849 the prolific Underground Railroad conductor William S. Mitchell? How did Underground Railroad activists such as Moses Dickson, who operated in slave states such as Missouri, intersect with the Colored Conventions? Colored national and state conventions, in addition to religious conferences, were ideal, worthy, noble, and safe opportunities for Underground Railroad workers to be in one another's presence, affording the more radical participants convenient and justifiable access to one another.

The combination of membership rosters, issues tackled by the conventioneers, and cities and places where the meetings took place leaves an indispensable written record of achievement, cooperation, and collective action. Individual endeavors of acknowledged Underground Railroad workers and other Black abolitionists who helped captives escape constitute a distinct, seemingly unrelated record. Studying Black institutions separately masks the collective, cooperative, intertwined nature of the fight against slavery. Clashes erupted over the means to ending slavery, but commitment to bringing about the demise of the practice was universally shared across African American institutions. Whether each knew the extent of the others' various efforts in helping captives escape from slavery, either through the traditional Underground Railroad or through their individual efforts, I honestly cannot say—and we may never know. This essay outlines one fruitful approach for investigating the interrelated, complex components of nineteenth-century Black activism.

The sketches and stories provided here offer brief examples of the work of members of the Colored Conventions movement who were also active on the Underground Railroad or complicit in facilitating other avenues of escape from slavery. These Black activists leveraged personal networks that both encompassed and exceeded the conventions. Distinct lines of evidence sharpen the view of Black activism and advocacy for freedom. Colored Convention delegates, Underground Railroad activists, vigilance committees, or individuals acting on their own operated both above and in spite of the law in the ultimate cause of freedom.

NOTES

1. In June 1865, two and a half years after Abraham Lincoln issued the Emancipation Proclamation, Maj. Gen. Gordon Granger and Union troops landed at Galveston, Texas, bringing news that the war and slavery were over.

2. See, e.g., Levi Coffin, *Reminiscences of Levi Coffin, the Reputed President of the Underground Railroad* (Cincinnati, OH: Robert Clarke, 1880); R. C. Smedley, *History of the Underground Railroad in Chester and the Neighboring Counties of Pennsylvania* (Lancaster, PA: John A. Hiestand, 1883); and Larry Gara, *The Liberty Line: The Legend of the Underground Railroad* (Lexington: University Press of Kentucky, 1996).

3. Barry Goldwater, "Extremism in the Defense of Liberty Is No Vice," speech, Republican National Convention, San Francisco, July 16, 1964.

4. Cheryl Janifer LaRoche, *Free Black Communities and the Underground Railroad: The Geography of Resistance* (Urbana: University of Illinois Press, 2014).

5. Philip S. Foner and George E. Walker, eds., *Proceedings of the Black State Conventions, 1840–1865*, 2 vols. (Philadelphia: Temple University Press, 1979).

6. Bella Gross, "The First National Negro Convention," *Journal of Negro History* 31, no. 4 (1946): 435–43.

7. Daniel A. Payne, *History of the African Methodist Episcopal Church* (Nashville: Publishing House of the A.M.E. Sunday School Union, 1891), 84.

8. Gross, "First National Negro Convention," 435–43.

9. Howard Holman Bell, ed., *Minutes and Proceedings of the National Negro Conventions, 1830–1864* (New York: Arno, 1969).

10. "Newspaper Reports on the Convention of the Colored Inhabitants of the State of New York, August 18–20, 1840," Colored Conventions Project, http://colored conventions.org/items/show/230; C. Peter Ripley, ed., *The Black Abolitionist Papers*, vol. 2, *Canada, 1830–1865* (Chapel Hill: University of North Carolina Press, 1992); Laurel Wemett, "Austin Steward: A Forgotten Figure in the Abolitionist Movement," *Daily Messenger* (Canandaigua, NY), February 4, 2013, http://www.mpnnow.com /article/20130204/News/302049802; Austin Steward, *Twenty-Two Years a Slave, and Forty Years a Freeman: Embracing a Correspondence of Several Years, while President of Wilberforce Colony, London, Canada West* (Rochester, NY: William Alling, 1857).

11. Steward, *Twenty-Two Years*, 319.

12. Steward, 319. See also J. W. C. Pennington, *Fugitive Blacksmith; or, Events in the History of James W. C. Pennington, Pastor of a Presbyterian Church, New York, Formerly a Slave in the State of Maryland, United States* (London: Charles Gilpin, 1849), accessed July 23, 2020, https://docsouth.unc.edu/neh/penning49/menu.html; Richard Allen, *The Life, Experience, and Gospel Labours of the Rt. Rev. Richard Allen* (Philadelphia: Martin and Boden, 1833); Jermaine Loguen, *The Rev. J. W. Loguen, as a Slave and as a Freeman: A Narrative of Real Life* (Syracuse, NY: J. G. K. Truair, 1859); Frederick Douglass, *Narrative of the Life of Frederick Douglass, an American Slave* (Boston, 1845; reprint, New York: Penguin, 1982); Frederick Douglass, *Life and Times of Frederick Douglass: His Early Life as a Slave, His Escape from Bondage, and His Complete History to the Present Time* (New York: Bonanza Books, 1962); and Frederick Douglass, *My Bondage and My Freedom* (New York: Miller, Orton & Mulligan, 1855), accessed July 23, 2020, https://docsouth.unc.edu/neh/douglass55/douglass55.html.

13. Joseph Willson, *Sketches of the Higher Classes of Colored Society in Philadelphia* (Philadelphia: Merrihew and Thompson, 1841), 104–6.

14. Howard Holman Bell, *A Survey of the Negro Convention Movement, 1830–1861* (New York: Arno, 1969), iii; National Park Service, *Underground Railroad Special Resource Study* (Denver Service Center: U. S. Department of the Interior, 1995), 179.

15. William Still, *The Underground Railroad* (Philadelphia: Porter and Coates, 1872), 736, 740.

16. "The Whipper Family," Chatham-Kent Black Historical Society, Chatham, ON.

17. Still, *Underground Railroad*, 740.

18. LaRoche, *Free Black Communities;* Judith Wellman, *Brooklyn's Promised Land* (New York: New York University Press, 2014).

19. Bell, *Minutes*, 13. Abraham Shadd served Pennsylvania's 1841 and 1848 Colored Conventions.

20. Graham Russell Gao Hodges, *David Ruggles: A Radical Black Abolitionist and the Underground Railroad in New York City* (Chapel Hill: University of North Carolina Press, 2010), 109.

21. Benjamin Quarles, *Black Abolitionists* (New York: Oxford University Press, 1969; Cambridge, MA: Da Capo, 1991), 226.

22. Howard Holman Bell, "National Negro Conventions of the Middle 1840s: Moral Suasion vs Political Action," in *Blacks in the Abolitionist Movement*, ed. John H. Bracey Jr., August Meier, and Elliott Rudwick (Belmont, CA: Wadsworth, 1971).

23. Tom Calarco, *People of the Underground Railroad: A Biographical Dictionary* (Westport, CT: Greenwood, 2008).

24. Bell, "National Negro Conventions," 125.

25. Not to be confused with Rev. William C. Munroe. It is not clear whether these are two different men.

26. "Second Baptist Church of Detroit," National Park Service, accessed July 23, 2020, http://www.nps.gov/nr/travel/detroit/d13.htm; "Oldest African-American Church in Michigan Celebrates 175th Anniversary, Legacy of Activism," *Detroit Free Press*, February 5, 2011; Carol E. Mull, *The Underground Railroad in Michigan* (Jefferson, NC: McFarland, 2010); Karolyn Smardz Frost and Veta Smith Tucker, eds., *A Fluid Frontier: Slavery, Resistance, and the Underground Railroad in the Detroit River Borderland* (Detroit: Wayne State University Press, 2016).

27. Calarco, *People of the Underground Railroad*, 103.

28. *Anti-Slavery Reporter* 6, no. 6 (June 1, 1858): 144; Kate Clifford Larson, *Bound for the Promised Land: Harriet Tubman: Portrait of an American Hero (New York: Ballantine Books, 2004).*

29. Booker T. Washington, *Frederick Douglass* (London: Hodder and Stroughton, 1906). Washington interviewed Fannie Barrier Williams and her husband, Samuel, longtime family friends of Frederick Douglass.

30. *Weekly Anglo-African* (New York), May 5, 1860.

31. Quarles, *Black Abolitionists*, 164; *Proceedings of the Colored National Convention, Held in Franklin Hall, Sixth Street, Below Arch, Philadelphia, October 16th, 17th and 18th, 1855*, 24–25, Colored Conventions Project, https://omeka.coloredconventions.org/files/original/d37ab14f289ed66585da418df5c45099.pdf.

32. "Obituary (1800–February 13, 1870)," *Albany (NY) Evening Times*, February 14, 1870, evening edition; Charles Rosenberg, "Stephen A. Meyers," in *African American National Biography* (Oxford: Oxford University Press, 2013), accessed July 23, 2020, https://oxfordaasc.com/view/10.1093/acref/9780195301731.001.0001/acref-9780195301731-e-38986.

33. Larson, *Bound for the Promised Land*, 94.

34. James Oliver Horton, *Free People of Color: Inside the African American Community* (Washington, DC: Smithsonian Institution Press, 1993); Quarles, *Black Abolitionists*.

PART 4

LOCATING CONVENTIONS

*Black Activism's Wide Reach
and Unexpected Places*

SOCIAL NETWORKS OF THE
COLORED CONVENTIONS, 1830-1864

Jim Casey

olored Conventions resist neat narratives. There were conventions
held before the Civil War and after. There were national conventions
and state conventions, not to mention city, county, and regional
meetings. Over the span of seven decades, more than 5,000 people traveled
from forty different states to attend hundreds of conventions held in at least
thirty-one states. A few also sprang up in Canada, where delegates at some
of the earliest conventions debated emigrating. Later conventions opposed
emigration and took up many other questions around civil rights, labor, education, the press, and more. Those debates were never monolithic. Delegates
almost always had a range of ideas and opinions around which they formed
coalitions that arose and dispersed. It is a big history.

Many of the most basic historical questions about the Colored Conventions remain unanswered. How many conventions were held and where?
Who attended, and what did they talk about? The general shortage of information is partly due to the larger lack of attention and respect paid to the
long tradition of political activism by African Americans in the nineteenth
century. Before the advent of the civil rights movement in the twentieth century, this was the complete list of histories of the Colored Conventions: a
magazine article in 1859, an essay in 1904, a sketch in 1921, and a handful
of journal articles in the 1940s and 1950s.[1] Since then, a few dozen journal
articles and book chapters have taken up the Colored Conventions as a subject, but extended treatments remain scarce.[2] Unlike the press, churches,
or the military, among other institutions, where conventions as a part of
nineteenth-century African American life are concerned, the map lags far
behind the discovery of the territory.[3]

That is starting to change. Copies of the minutes and proceedings created
at each of the conventions do not exist in a single place. Rather, they survive
scattered across dozens of different archives, libraries, and other memory
institutions. Since April 2012, the Colored Conventions Project, begun at
the University of Delaware, has worked to identify conventions and locate
all existing minutes. At the start of this process, our sense of the conventions was based on four book collections of reprinted minutes of roughly

seventy conventions altogether.[4] Nobody knows how many convention minutes survive, but the estimates at the time of this writing put the number of conventions easily above 400. Identifying them all is slow and painstaking work, but every newly collected convention proceeding or related document is a new opportunity for studying, teaching, or learning about the Colored Conventions.

As those opportunities unfold, they raise a set of questions about how to locate a single convention among all of the others. Elsewhere in this volume, Carla Peterson observes that "a single convention may merely be one chapter of a longer narrative; we must then locate subsequent chapters in order to obtain a better sense of the larger story."[5] Many of the essays in this collection illustrate rich examples of longer narratives, from southern emigration conventions and debates on the Black press to Henry Highland Garnet's oratory and print activism. Those longer narratives show that the conventions can serve as a new means for mapping nineteenth-century African American history. But in that potential lies a provocation: How can we begin to grasp the relationships between so many conventions and so many people—and what can such narratives tell us?

In what follows, I map the social networks of the conventions from 1830 to 1864. By looking at co-attendance, or the conventions linked by a common delegate, I locate six distinct groups of conventions. Each group is a potential new narrative that serves to highlight the sheer scale and complex collective dynamics of the conventions. It is important to grasp those dynamics not just to recognize this important history but also to begin asking questions about the place of the Colored Conventions in the firmament of early nineteenth-century networks of Black organizing. After surveying those six groups, I expand the social network to regard the scarcity of connections in extant data between the Colored Conventions, the Underground Railroad, and antislavery groups. Tracing out these groups, this chapter offers what I consider to be a rough draft of a map of these complex, fascinating, and important social networks. It is my sincere hope that this draft will soon be rendered obsolete through critiques and improvements made by the growing community of researchers, students, and learners exploring this important chapter of American history. These analyses are steps toward expanding and enriching our sense of this expansive history.

The Process from Documents to Data

Visualizing the Colored Conventions requires assembling the relevant data. This assembly process has involved many hands and minds. The first collectors were the secretaries, compilers, and printers of the original minutes. Their names are only sometimes noted in the documents. Most minutes and proceedings are themselves actually collections of documents, including calls, resolutions, reports, correspondence, and rolls of delegates. During the twentieth century, a number of people worked to collect the minutes of the Colored Conventions, including Dorothy Porter, Howard Holman Bell, Philip Foner, and George E. Walker. Countless librarians and archivists have also spent time preserving, cataloguing, and sharing these materials in the dozens of archives, libraries, and memory institutions where they now exist.

In beginning to derive large amounts of information from the archives of the Colored Conventions, it is important to remember that these documents are not objective records of unmediated facts. As the essay by Derrick Spires in this volume shows, among many other examples, delegates were keenly aware of the stakes of the language they would or would not include in the published minutes and proceedings of their meetings. Careful attention to the language of their resolutions and addresses occupied a great deal of time at conventions, evincing their strong sense of the likely supportive or antagonistic public audiences for the texts they created together. I would submit that the minutes and proceedings of the Colored Conventions are best understood as collective self-expressions, resonating with the rhetorical and literary power of these collaborative, deliberative bodies. This essay's visualizations and analysis, then, are not an archeological study of what happened but a literary analysis of the sociability of the textual witnesses to the Colored Conventions.

Collecting

The advent of the Colored Conventions Project in 2012 brought together a group of scholars and librarians at the University of Delaware who began collecting digital surrogates of the minutes. We scanned books and microfilm and scoured online for any viable copies of convention minutes. Housed mainly as PDF files through the end of 2013, it became apparent that we needed to convert the minutes into texts that could be more easily searched, remixed, and shared. This insight led us to build Transcribe Minutes, an initiative to crowdsource the transcription of the minutes in partnership with the living Black communities that hosted so many of these conventions. Transcribe Minutes went live in February 2014 in partnership with the Lay Connectional of the national AME, facilitated by Denise Burgher and P. Gabrielle Foreman working closely with Pamela Tilley. In the first year and a few months, Transcribe Minutes created plain-text versions of more than 2,000 pages of minutes from ninety-one conventions. Our hundreds of dedicated transcribers deserve special recognition as well.

Indexing

Next, the minutes were ready to be translated into more structured forms of data. I adopted a two-pronged approach over a two-year period to collect the names of the delegates to all of the conventions for which we had obtained records. For transcribed conventions, I first ran the minutes through a software program called the Stanford Named Entity Recognizer (NER). The program used a classifier algorithm to make and tag educated guesses about what might be a name, organization, or place.[6] Then I began collating the names of the delegates tagged in each of the documents, including manually inspecting the output of the NER tool to make sure that all of the relevant names had been detected. The accuracy of the NER tool was enough to save some manual work, but many of the delegates' names presented problems with initials, typos in the original documents, and irregular formats. Remaining efforts were spent on manually typing up the names of the delegates in a comma-separated values (CSV) file or spreadsheet in the Convention Name Index (CNI).

Within a sense of the convention minutes as collective self-expressions, the CSV file is not a record of everyone who took part in a Colored Convention. Rather, the CSV file is an index of the names that appear as formally recognized delegates in the minutes of the Colored Conventions. This principle of organization embraces the arguments made by digital humanities scholars Katie Rawson and Trevor Muñoz for building humanities data sets as indices rather than as scalable databases that insist on totalizing and homogeneous data structures. As Rawson and Muñoz write, "An index is an information structure designed to serve as a system of pointers between two bodies of information, one of which is organized to provide access to concepts in the other." In this light, the CNI is an index because it provides several thousand pointers to hundreds of documents. Each record points to the appearance of a person's name in the minutes, a name written down as recognition of a person's legibility within a variety of regimes of personhood, citizenship, gender, status, and belonging in the nineteenth-century Colored Conventions.

Organizing

As the list of names of delegates began to grow, the increasing variety of the names required tinkering with the rows and columns of the CNI. Early drafts of the spreadsheet had columns for a person's full name, associated place (if any), leadership position (such as president, vice president, secretary, etc.), and the name of the convention attended. But exceptions came along, forcing me to rethink the organization of the data. Delegates came from Canada, so a column was added for country. Some names bore a suffix, so another column was added. A number of conventions listed the titles of the clergy in attendance, so another column was added for titles. When women broke into the ranks of the delegates, another column was added to infer gender. What bears elaborating here is that each of these columns reflected both a latent research question and my own particular observations about the convention minutes. Working with unstructured text, the challenge was to weigh the need for detailed information against the ability to have some consistency across different convention minutes. I could not ask after certain kinds of data at many conventions if I could not observe common values at those conventions. For example, early drafts of the CNI noted when delegates served on a particular committee. But because many of the conventions formed committees organically, reflecting the decentralized nature of the conventions themselves, a committee at one convention might have an entirely different name than a similar body at another meeting. The Business Committee at one occasion might overlap, or not, with the Rules Committee at another. Ultimately, I elected to forego noting committee memberships. It was not a lack of interest in the committees but a decision to focus on the delegates to the conventions as a narrower and comprehensive, if limited, category of information. This thinking also determined the decision to abandon early attempts to index all names that appeared in the conventions. I chose to index only the names of the delegates formally listed, knowing that this data would provide a strong starting place. Those early editorial decisions do not foreclose the option to expand the scope of the data.

Refining

With a narrowed focus on the names and associated places of the delegates, I moved into the delicate process of refining the data. The goal of refining the data was to make it possible to find matches of names across multiple conventions, to provide what archivists and librarians refer to as access points.[7] Finding those matches is a mix of data wrangling and historical research. The range of obstacles to finding those matches is large, including the use of abbreviations, typographical errors, spelling errors, and the potential for false positive matches. Using a tool called OpenRefine, I worked through the CNI to find any potential matches that appeared in slightly varied forms in the source documents. This process is a precarious one, with the potential to erase someone from the history of the conventions quite literally, at the level of the CSV file. I set the threshold for deciding that two names matched at three corresponding data points. One person whose name varied quite a bit was Henry Highland Garnet. The variety of spellings of his name is an instructive example on the potential and perils of refining this data. The minutes for the 1840 state convention at Albany name a delegate as "H. Highland Garnet" from Troy, New York. The minutes for the 1844 state convention at Schenectady name a delegate as "Henry H. Garnet" from Troy. Then the minutes for the 1843 national convention at Buffalo name a delegate as "H. H. Garnit" from Troy. I established these as the same person based on the common place listed (Troy) and the consistency of the initials and last name. That makes for three corresponding data points. These were not to be confused with the Reverend George Garnet, also from Troy, listed in the minutes of 1840. As this example shows, this process is not perfect. But the painstaking nature of the process is paramount, because drawing a match between two names risks erasing one if the match is not accurate. To draw a match between certain names, just because they match spellings or have some fuzzy resemblance, would remove a person from being recognized in the data. That goes against the basic impetus of this recovery work, so I erred on the conservative side during the data refining process. Likely many more matches exist in the CNI but those matches will require further research to corroborate.

Is It a Social Network?

After the collecting, transcribing, extricating, and refining process began to progress, I conducted a preliminary series of experiments with the data in a social networking software program called Gephi.[8] Gephi offers a suite of tools for visualizing and analyzing network graphs. As with the construction of the data set, my early experiments in Gephi produced a mixed set of results that required exploration and fine tuning. The full graph of antebellum conventions includes 1,751 nodes (unique names and conventions) and 2,306 links (lines that express attendance at a particular convention). See figure 14.1, which includes all of the antebellum conventions and delegates.

Even without labels, this graph suggests several things about the network of the conventions. First, one-fifth of the nodes account for nearly half of the links. This fits with a principle called "scale-free networks" coined by Albert-László Barabási in 1999. Barabási and his colleagues coined the principle of scale-free networks after building a map of links on the early World Wide Web and discovering that a very small number of websites accounted for most of the links. We can expect to find that a scale-free network will distribute the number of links according to a power law, meaning that 80 percent of the links involve only 20 percent of the nodes. Attendances at antebellum conventions roughly follow a power law: only 20 percent (301) of delegates ever attended more than one convention. While that offers a strong caution against speaking of the conventions as a single, homogenous group, it does show that the antebellum Colored Conventions constitute a social network in ways that can reward further analysis.

Does It Tell Us Anything New?

Identifying a historical movement as a social network only opens a set of questions; it remains to determine whether the tools of social network analysis can help raise any productive questions or arrive at any meaningful conclusions. Unfortunately, very few historians have ever weighed in on the contours of the Colored Conventions as a distinct set of events and people. One of the few was Howard Holman Bell. Bell's work in the middle of the twentieth century offers several rich theses that can serve as useful test cases for understanding the conventions as a social network. Perhaps the most relevant is his argument that the national convention of 1843 was a turning point in the movement. Earlier national conventions, during the 1830s, had relied on the language of moral suasion, or the appeals to morality, in support of the cause for Black freedom and civil rights. Starting in 1843, Bell argues, a younger generation of delegates pushed to make political action the object of the conventions. This juncture fundamentally altered the tone and discourse of the Colored Conventions.

Bell's argument suggests that in viewing the conventions as a network we should be able to see two distinct communities among the delegates

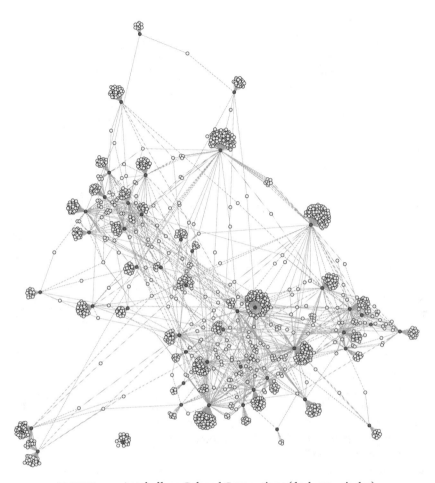

FIGURE 14.1. Antebellum Colored Conventions (dark gray circles)
and their delegates (light gray circles).

from before and after the 1843 convention. In this period, there were twelve
national conventions attended by 532 delegates. Given that Bell's argument
describes relations between conventions, rather than between individuals,
it is helpful to draw the antebellum network in those terms. This change
in terms of analysis introduces the perspective of co-attendance, or links
between two conventions created by a person who attends both meetings.

Co-attendance is demonstrated in figures 14.2 and 14.3. Figure 14.2 shows
Amos Beman linked with two of the national conventions he attended in
1843 and 1853. Figure 14.3 shows the projected links between those meetings to indicate Beman's shared attendance. By making those projections
for delegates at all of the national conventions, it is possible to draw links

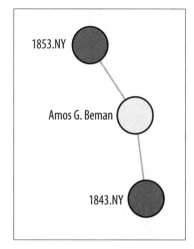
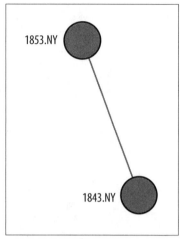

FIGURE 14.2. (*left*) Delegate network. Amos G. Beman attended
the 1843 and 1853 national Colored Conventions.

FIGURE 14.3. (*right*) Co-attendance link projected via Amos G. Beman
between the 1843 and 1853 national Colored Conventions.

between every national meeting in this period. Figure 14.4 shows the results
of that process. Next, we can identify groupings within this graph by using a
metric from social networks analysis called modularity. Modularity identi-
fies clusters within a graph. Clusters, or communities, are defined as a group
of entities that are more likely to be linked to one another than to any other
entities in the graph.[9]

Calculating modularity for the network of national convention co-
attendees reveals that they are divided among the early national meetings
(1830–35) and the later ones that begin in 1843. In other words, a graph of
co-attendance at the national conventions concurs with Bell's thesis about
the 1843 convention as a moment of change. Replicating Bell's findings with
this preliminary analysis shows the validity of viewing the Colored Conventions as a social network. This relatively basic perspective (links of delegate
attendance) makes it possible to ask larger questions about the dynamics of
this sprawling history.

By using this analysis, I can map the social networks of the antebellum
conventions. The process of establishing links between conventions and
then clustering those links by modularity reveals that the antebellum Colored Conventions fit into six discrete communities. The six communities
correspond roughly with specific regions. Meetings took place in Pennsylvania, the border states, California, Maryland, northeastern states, and
transnationally, spanning the United States and Canada. While a small
number of people bridged those six communities, the regionally distinctive

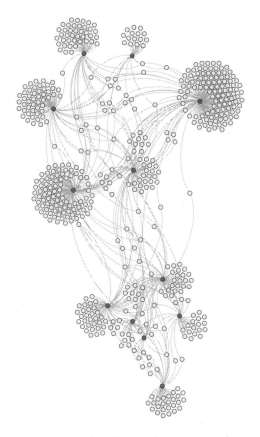

FIGURE 14.4. National Colored Conventions (dark
gray circles) and delegates (light gray circles).

communities offer a caution against thinking about the conventions as a
singular, linear movement. Instead, the six communities described below
are an invitation to further study the dynamics of the regional communities
that thought nationally and worked regionally to advance the cause of Black
freedom and civil rights.

The Six Groups of Conventions by Common Delegates

Group 1: The Pennsylvania Conventions

The first group amounts to a history of the antebellum conventions in Pennsylvania. This component includes the first six national conventions (1830–35)
and the only two antebellum Pennsylvania state conventions (1841, 1848). No
person attended all eight conventions, but about 15 percent attended more

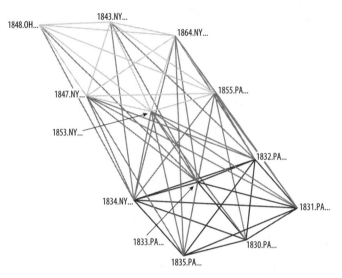

FIGURE 14.5. National Colored Conventions, by co-attendance and modularity. The two different line widths indicate the two groups determined by modularity scores.

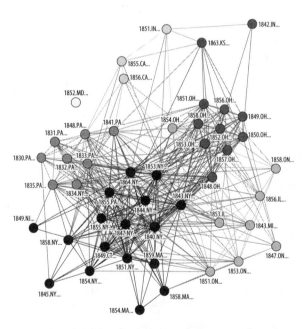

FIGURE 14.6. Antebellum state and national Colored Conventions grouped by co-attendance and shaded by modularity. The groups are Pennsylvania conventions (center, left); border state conventions (upper right); California conventions (upper left); the slave state convention (detached in upper left); the northeastern conventions (center), and the transnational conventions (lower left).

than one convention (51 of 349 delegates). Only six men (2 percent) went to more than half of the conventions in this group: William Whipper, Abraham D. Shadd, John Peck, Frederick A. Hinton, John C. Bowers, and Peter Gardiner. Within this group, the 1834 convention in New York may appear to be an outlier, but Pennsylvania sent nearly as many delegates as the home state, and New York City apparently never hosted another state or national convention.

Evidence of a strong community throughout Pennsylvania comes as no surprise, given the state's robust community of activists, religious leaders, entrepreneurs, educators, and print agents. But the temporal stretch from the early national conventions to the 1841 and 1848 state conventions suggests that any scholarship interested in the early Philadelphia conventions might find it worthwhile to consider a longer history of these conventions through the retrenchment of legal rights in the state in the ensuing decades. Sixteen men, and undoubtedly just as many women, went to conventions in both decades, and their long-standing collective work links the debates over emigration and anti-Black laws in the 1830s with the debates over suffrage in the late 1840s.[10]

Group 2: The Border State Conventions

The next group includes thirteen conventions held in cities that bordered slave states, including Ohio, Indiana, Illinois, and Kansas. More than at any other set of conventions, delegates at the nearly annual meetings in Ohio from 1848 to 1858 formed a discrete and consistent cohort.[11] At least eight of them attended more than a handful of conventions together, including John Booker, William Hurst Burnham, William Howard Day, John I. Gaines, David Jenkins, Charles H. Langston, John Mercer Langston, and L. D. Taylor.[12] Despite any number of debates and disagreements among them, the consistency of their cohort over time stands as one of the richest histories of collective activism illuminated by the framework of the Colored Conventions. Most of that cohort did leave Ohio after the Civil War, yet their departures do not mean that the conventions were a failed or ephemeral endeavor. Taking what they had learned and honed at the conventions, Ohio's delegates went on to accomplish a great many things. John Mercer Langston helped found Howard University's law school. In 1890, he was one of the earliest Black citizens elected to Congress. David Jenkins was elected to the state legislature of Mississippi. Many others went on to prominent careers in business, education, and the churches. The many illustrious subsequent careers in public life show just how much the antebellum border state conventions were a crucible for postbellum Black national and international leaders. The border state conventions pose a stark challenge, then, to the traditional ways of organizing nineteenth-century African American history divided by the Civil War. Colored Conventions did not just hold debates and pursue goals; they created leaders.

The presence of only one of the two Indiana state conventions in this group manifests a number of features of the distributed, larger network of the Colored Conventions. No minutes survive for the 1842 state convention in Indiana, so the list of delegates is projected from all of the names that appear in the "Circular" published in the *Indiana State Sentinel* newspaper. The actual statewide meeting in 1842 was likely much larger in number, but the names in the circular establish few connections with any other Colored Conventions. The only person who attended conventions in Indiana and in other states was N. Morgan (first name unknown). The only person who attended both Indiana conventions was John G. Britton, a barber, Freemason, and self-freed man who moved to Indianapolis, married Cheney Lively, and became an important leader of the state's several thousand free Black citizens.[13] As Cheryl LaRoche's work shows, there was a dynamic Black community in Indiana in this period, but inquiries into the social networks of the conventions can extend no further than the limits of the archives.[14]

Group 3: The California Conventions

The group of conventions in California shows some of the limits of ending this network analysis at the end of the Civil War. At first glance, the annual state conventions in California from 1855 to 1857 have few delegates in common with any other conventions.[15] The only other convention that shares multiple delegates with the California group is the 1843 national convention in Buffalo, connected through Jonas H. Townsend and David Lewis. Frederick G. Barbadoes's father, James G. Barbadoes, had attended several early national conventions (1833–34), but the general lack of connections to other state or national meetings underscores the organic, decentralized, and frequently idiosyncratic growth of the conventions. The Civil War brought a tidal change to the ranks of the delegates to eastern state and national conventions, but in California there was a much higher degree of continuity. Only four men attended all three conventions: J. J. Moore, William H. Harper, Henry M. Collins, and Frederick G. Barbadoes. But fourteen of them (12 percent) went to conventions before and after the war, representing nearly a tenth of the total number of the 180 transbellum delegates. Even conceding the small sample size, no other state's conventions can match that rate of consistent attendance.

The continuity of the California conventions indicates another manner in which the Civil War presented a different set of social effects than in the eastern states. The California conventions and their delegates experienced these events at some geographic and social remove. Yet a number of them attended postbellum southern national conventions. Their wide travels suggest a triangular pattern of mobility observable in the conventions from the Northeast to the West and then the South. That pattern is exemplified by Mifflin W. Gibbs, Frederick G. Barbadoes, and others but merits further research before any concrete conclusions can be drawn about the power of latent links that connected delegates across regions or periods.

Group 4: The Slave State Convention

Networks can also be shaped by racist mob violence. Amid thousands of connections in this network, one convention stands apart: the 1852 state convention of Maryland. It was the only Colored Convention held in a slave state before the Civil War. The meeting was to start in Baltimore on a Monday, but a white mob attacked the delegates to the convention, wounding many and possibly killing at least one person, Walter Sparks. The assembly did start the next day, but many had gone home. A few of them wrote back to request their names be removed from the rolls of delegates. As *Frederick Douglass' Paper* reported that week, "A large police force prevented any riot."[16] They met for another few days, passing resolutions in favor of Liberian emigration and pledging to meet again the following November in Baltimore. It is not clear whether they ever did.

This sole antebellum slave state convention remains a mystery in part because none of the delegates attended any other conventions. That may be for several reasons, including the oppressive Black Laws passed in Maryland restricting the movement of people of color across state lines. The year 1852 saw an increase in the harsh jailing of Black sailors who arrived into the massive port of Baltimore. Although the convention was covered extensively in the press, particularly by *Frederick Douglass' Paper*, it may have also lacked some legitimacy among the population it proposed to represent. A letter published in a number of white abolitionist newspapers by Philip Scott and James Gray, two African American residents of Baltimore, claimed that "nine-tenths of the coloured people [of the state] knew nothing of what was being done in their name." Whether it was a lack of legal mobility, carceral surveillance, or controversy, this convention is simultaneously absent and present in the social networks of the Colored Conventions. This convention deserves much more research. Not only was it a remarkable collective act in a city and state driven by the legal ownership of Black people, but the event of a Colored Convention in an antebellum slave state adds a layer of complexity to any conclusions we might reach about what Colored Conventions were and where they occurred.

Group 5: The Northeastern Conventions

By far the largest group in the social network of the antebellum Colored Conventions is the cluster of northeastern conventions in New York and surrounding states. Most historical scholarship on the conventions engages with the meetings in this group, including those attended by the most widely known delegates.[17] There is a distinct group of conventions held in Massachusetts (1854, 1858, and 1859). Loosely affiliated are the smaller state's conventions held in 1849 in New Jersey and Connecticut. Most notable, however, are the five national conventions (1843, 1847, 1853, 1855, and 1864) and seven New York state conventions (1840–58). Altogether, 692 delegates attended these conventions, with 128 (or 18 percent) attending more than one. Some of the most widely known participants in the Colored Conventions attended many of the meetings in this group. While many of them undoubtedly knew and encountered one another outside of the conventions, a few people played key roles by bridging multiple communities.

The centrality of Stephen Myers in this group offers a few insights about both the northeastern group and the wider social network of the Colored Conventions. His place in the network helps bridge multiple communities of delegates otherwise only loosely connected. This status in the network is registered by calculating a value in a network graph called "betweenness centrality." Betweenness centrality is a number calculated in a graph by first taking every node and counting the number of steps required to move from that node to any other node in the network. After calculating that number of steps for every node, the algorithm looks to find the shortest path between any two nodes taken at random. A node will have a higher betweenness centrality if it is more likely than not to be on that shortest path. In other words, betweenness centrality refers to the person who connects the highest number of otherwise unconnected people.

By connecting many otherwise unconnected people, Myers opens up a new set of possible questions to ask about the centrality of certain figures as both a personal effort and a collaborative enterprise with associated women. While Myers did not attend the vital national convention in 1843 in Buffalo, he attended every subsequent national gathering until his death in 1870. In his efforts for temperance, against slavery, and on the Underground Railroad, Myers worked constantly with many of his fellow convention goers. He also served as editor and agent for at least five different Black newspapers. Just as significantly, all of his public work was done in a close partnership with his wife, Harriet Myers. She worked alongside her husband on many of those newspapers and was a constant presence in the Colored Conventions and temperance societies. Her organizing acumen would have played a significant role in her husband's ability to bridge those communities. Stephen and Harriet Myers's activism has been relatively well documented, but the two of them show the central role of women who worked alongside some of the delegates who bridged multiple communities. Harriet Myers, Mary Ann Shadd, Julia Griffiths, Frances Harper, and Sarah Mapps Douglass are only a few of the women who played influential, if invisible, roles in linking these communities across the network of the conventions. They show one of the primary wayfinding capacities of the graphs of the social network of the antebellum Colored Conventions: using these tools, it is possible to identify those whose work to connect different collective bodies would have depended on partnerships with women. Most textual records of the conventions exclude women, but these network values suggest that men with high betweenness centralities would have worked closely with a diverse array of people across multiple social groups. Calculating these values across the entire antebellum network, then, returns a number of people who attended conventions in several of the groups outlined in this chapter, such as William Charles Munroe, who attended northeastern, border state, and transnational conventions. This example shows some of the potential for using these social network graphs to experiment with different criteria for centrality in the networks of the conventions.

Group 6: The Transnational Conventions

The final group to survey is the transnational conventions. Along with meetings in Michigan, Ohio, and Illinois, this group includes a quartet of conventions held in what was then known as Canada West. Some of the conventions in the United States in this group were explicitly organized around emigration, such as the massive gathering in Cleveland, Ohio, in 1854. The conventions held in Detroit and Chicago are a stark reminder that Black activists moved across the U.S.-Canadian border constantly, even as oppressive laws to the south made passage more perilous. From Detroit, the distance to Ontario cities such as Chatham or Amherstburgh was only a few short miles. The meetings in Drummondville (today Niagara Falls, Ontario) and Toronto were less than a single day's boat ride from such strongholds of Black activism as Buffalo and Rochester. The graph bears these geographies out. At least two key Black leaders of Detroit, William Charles Munroe and William Lambert, attended three conventions together in this transnational group: in Detroit (1843), Cleveland (1854), and Chatham (1858). Israel Campbell became another central figure in this group after he crossed the Detroit River into freedom in 1849.[18] Conventions held by these leaders unfolded on both sides of the border.

The four conventions in Canada West spanned a heterogeneous community knit only by weak links. Involving both established and fledgling Black communities, the meetings brought Black people together who had come to the area from throughout the United States. None of the 142 total delegates went to all four of the conventions held between 1847 and 1858. Josiah Henson attended three.[19] Eight men attended two of the conventions, including Henry Bibb, E. B. Dunlop, Thomas Smallwood, Richard Warren, J. Anderson, Israel Campbell, George Cary, and M. F. Bailey. Only two of these running delegates in Canada West—Bibb and Dunlop—had any prior experience with conventions in the United States. This lack of strong ties to U.S. conventions shows that these four meetings were not simply exported versions but novel formations convened to meet the needs of a population fighting to build a new life and culture in Canada West. It is yet another reminder of the decentralized growth of the social network of the antebellum Colored Conventions.[20] This transnational group of conventions offers powerful evidence of the ways that the social network could simultaneously observe and transcend political geography.

Across Networks: Colored Conventions,
the Underground Railroad, and Abolition

These six groups frame thousands of relationships between nineteenth-century African Americans, relationships that seemingly did not extend in equal numbers into the white-led groups clustered around the Underground Railroad or antislavery societies. No convention happened in a vacuum, but the lack of apparent links between Black-led and white-led movements can locate the Colored Conventions in the world of antebellum efforts for racial justice in more precise ways than assuming any gaps. Along with the growing information about the Colored Conventions, a great deal of data is available about the Underground Railroad and antislavery groups. All of this data is vexed, shaped by centuries of decisions based on racial hierarchies about what to record, store, and reproduce. But some of the data can be useful.[21]

Data is available about the Underground Railroad through the work of Wilbur Siebert. Siebert, a white historian, published a book in 1898 called *The Underground Railroad from Slavery to Freedom* with an appendix titled "Directory of the Names of Underground Railroad Operators." The appendix lists nearly 3,000 names. Siebert gathered them from a wide variety of sources, including interviews with surviving operators and the work of earlier historians such as William Still.[22] Owing to the secrecy of the Underground Railroad and the elapsed time, the appendix is far from comprehensive. Unequal racial coverage in the appendix is only one of many problems with Siebert's data.[23] Keeping these deficits in mind, I follow after the work of Cheryl LaRoche and others who find the 1898 appendix nevertheless useful for engaging with the larger patterns of the Underground Railroad.[24] Even incomplete data can help generate useful questions.

Large-scale data about antislavery circuits has only recently become available. The Boston Public Library has digitized its Anti-Slavery Collection and made it freely accessible on the Internet Archive. The Anti-Slavery Collection contains about 40,000 total items, including the personal papers and correspondence of many of the most notable white abolitionists and antislavery societies of the nineteenth century. A model for access, the Boston Public Library has uploaded nearly 10,000 documents in high-quality images, replete with metadata and cataloguer notes. Like Siebert's data, the Anti-Slavery Collection has an unequal coverage of white and Black people. But the coverage is not so uneven that we cannot bring the Boston Public Library's metadata into conversation with the Colored Conventions to ask questions about networks over space and time.[25]

Those networked conversations raise as many questions as answers. Weaving these three data sets together as a network raises more questions than conclusions. The three communities altogether amount to 5,676 entities with 6,375 links. Filtering out the entities in this graph with only a single link reduces the messiness of the network quite a bit. Only 459 (8 percent) of the entities link to at least two of the data sets, and only nine men (0.1

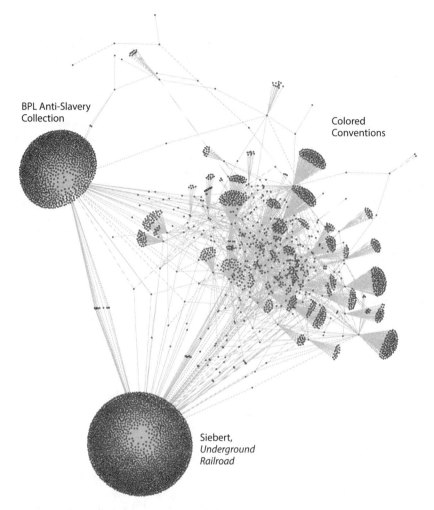

FIGURE 14.7. Network of data sets of the Colored Conventions, Siebert's *Underground Railroad*, and the Boston Public Library's Anti-Slavery Collection.

percent) appear in all three components. The resulting graph (fig. 14.7) is useful for browsing and exploration, but this interorganizational graph needs to be projected into similar terms as the co-attendance graph (see fig. 14.6) to enable any meaningful comparisons. As before, I can project the network by considering organizational bodies (conventions, the Underground Railroad, or the antislavery node) linked if they share connections to a given person.

This transformation produces a comembership graph that, surprisingly, yields very little change to the groups in the network save for the emergence of a new group. Most of the groups by co-attendance remain the same. The new group includes the Underground Railroad, the antislavery node, and nine conventions that had previously appeared in the transnational and border state groups, including meetings in Illinois, Indiana, Michigan, Ohio, and Canada West. Their move into a new group expresses their loose connection to the conventions as much as the strength of their ties to the Underground Railroad or abolition. Moreover, the emergent group in the comembership network shows that different communities of African American leaders across North America had different kinds of relationships with white philanthropists and abolitionists. That analysis may be fairly obvious at the outset, but the framework opens up room to compare the ways that different communities of African American leaders across different geographic areas interacted with white-led groups. The possibilities for this analysis are yet another reminder of the ways that data visualization is a useful tool for generating new questions, far more so than for generating any finite answers.

Next Steps

These are only a few of the possibilities for mapping the broader networks of the Colored Conventions. A view of the attendance network provides a first draft, but only that—a draft that can and needs to be picked apart and enriched. But while the broader scope can remain a valuable perspective on the big history of the Colored Conventions, there is much more to include. Women's crucial roles are just starting to be recognized more adequately in chapters in this volume, such as those by Psyche Forson-Williams, Eric Gardner, and Jewon Woo, and in online exhibits created by the Colored Conventions Project. But these are just the start. Including women's roles in the conventions will require rethinking the ontology of the data set used in this chapter in ways that will help us more fully understand the ubiquity of Black women's activism in the nineteenth century.

Part of that work will require expanding the focus of this chapter to account for the many contemporary, overlapping social organizations led and populated by men and women. There were many robust nineteenth-century Black networks, including mutual aid societies, vigilance committees, Freemason lodges, schools, literary societies, fundraising groups, churches, and periodicals. Each of these groups represents an opportunity to thicken the social networks in ways that will fill in more of the map of the enormous history of early Black networks.

I want to conclude by pointing out one last basic feature of this network graph that I find compelling: the entire movement has an extremely high degree of resiliency. It is a resilient network. No group in the network depends on only a single connection to the rest of the people and gatherings. The conventions as a movement responded to each challenge that arose in the nineteenth century with a convention. When confronted with countless episodes of a deeply white supremacist culture, racist legal codes, lack of access to educational opportunities, the loss of voting rights, the Fugitive Slave Act, the promises and failures of Reconstruction, among others, the conventions arose in response to all of these, on many occasions, in so many places. Even when racial violence prevented one meeting, others quickly arose. Remarkably, in dozens of states across six decades, the conventions were a movement that could not be stopped.

NOTES

1. For early accounts, see "The First Colored Conventions," *Anglo-African Magazine* 1, no. 10 (1859): 308; John W. Cromwell, *The Early Negro Convention Movement*, Occasional Papers 9 (Washington, DC: American Negro Academy, 1904); and Ruth A. Gallaher, "A Colored Convention," *Palimpsest* 2, no. 6 (1921): 178–81. Among others, see Howard Holman Bell, "Free Negroes of the North 1830–1835: A Study in National Cooperation," *Journal of Negro Education* 26, no. 4 (1957): 447–55; and Howard Holman Bell, "National Negro Conventions of the Middle 1840's: Moral Suasion vs. Political Action," *Journal of Negro History* 42, no. 4 (1957): 247–60. Bell also published work in *Phylon* in 1960 and 1967 on the state conventions. Also valuable but less well known are Bella Gross's writings; see Bella Gross, "The First National Negro Convention," *Journal of Negro History* 31, no. 4 (1946): 435–43; and Bella Gross, *Clarion Call: The History and Development of the Negro People's Convention Movement in the United States from 1817 to 1840* (New York: printed by the author, 1947).

2. For the complete list, see the bibliography at Colored Conventions Project, coloredconventions.org/bibliography.

3. See the Colored Conventions Project bibliography for the most recent studies on conventions. Those that focus specifically on the conventions qua conventions are Harry Atwood Reed, *Platform for Change: The Foundations of the Northern Free Black Community, 1775–1865* (East Lansing: Michigan State University Press, 1994), and the indispensable works by John Ernest, *Liberation Historiography: African-American Writers and the Challenges of History, 1794–1861* (Chapel Hill: University of North Carolina Press, 2004) and *A Nation Within a Nation: Organizing African-American Communities before the Civil War* (Chicago: Ivan R. Dee, 2011).

4. Howard Holman Bell, ed., *Minutes and Proceedings of the National Negro Conventions, 1830–1864* (New York: Arno, 1969); Philip S. Foner and George E. Walker, eds., *Proceedings of the Black State Conventions: 1840—1865*, 2 vols. (Philadelphia: Temple University Press, 1979); Philip S. Foner and George E. Walker, eds., *Proceedings of the Black National and State Conventions, 1865–1900* (Philadelphia: Temple University Press, 1986).

5. See Carla L. Peterson's essay in this volume.

6. There are other classifiers available, but my use of the Stanford NER required only the basic classifier. See Jenny Rose Finkel, Trond Grenager, and Christopher Manning, "Incorporating Non-local Information into Information Extraction Systems by Gibbs Sampling," *43nd Annual Meeting of the Association for Computational Linguistics: Proceedings of the Conference* (New Brunswick, NJ: Association for Computational Linguistics, 2005), 363–70, http://nlp.stanford.edu/~manning/papers/gibbs crf3.pdf.

7. Richard Pearce-Moses, *A Glossary of Archival and Records Terminology* (Chicago: Society of American Archivists, 2005), s.v. "access point," http://www2.archivists.org /glossary/terms/a/access-point.

8. Mathieu Bastian, Sebastien Heymann, and Mathieu Jacomy, "Gephi: An Open Source Software for Exploring and Manipulating Networks," *Proceedings of the Third International AAAI Conference on Weblogs and Social Media* (2009): 361–62.

9. M. E. J. Newman, "Modularity and Community Structure in Networks," *Proceedings of the National Academy of Sciences* 103, no. 23 (June 6, 2006): 8577–82, doi.org/10.1073/pnas.0601602103.

10. The sixteen men are John Peck, John C. Bowers, Robert Purvis, Stephen Smith, Samuel Van Brakle, William Whipper, John B. Vashon, William Lewis, Robert Brown, Joshua P. B. Eddy, Richard Johnson, Abraham D. Shadd, James Bird, Frederick A. Hinton, Samuel Johnson, and George Richardson.

11. We have uncovered another two Ohio state conventions, held in Columbus in 1843 and 1844. The only known accounts are brief articles published in the *Cincinnati Weekly Herald and Philanthropist* (October 18, 1843) and the Columbus *Palladium of Liberty* (November 13, 1844). Neither account provides the names of delegates, but the few mentioned indicate that they likely would fall within the group who attended the border state conventions. The 1844 meeting lists about a dozen people central to the conventions, including those named in this section, along with Alphonso M. Sumner, John L. Watson, and others.

12. There are a number of other people who played pivotal roles in the wider range of conventions but were less central in this particular group of conventions, including Peter H. Clark, John Malvin, H. Ford Douglass, John L. Watson, and Charles A. Yancy.

13. Another potential expansion to this work would be to consider the symbiotic relationship between the Colored Conventions and African American Freemasons. Anecdotal evidence suggests links in Massachusetts, Indiana, and California, but I imagine there are much broader patterns to map out supported by the excellent records kept by many of the lodges.

14. Cheryl Janifer LaRoche, *Free Black Communities and the Underground Railroad: The Geography of Resistance* (Urbana: University of Illinois Press, 2014).

15. The convention in 1857 was held in San Francisco and no minutes appear to have survived. I include the 1857 convention here because the few names that do appear also show up in earlier and later minutes. The article on the 1857 convention in the *San Francisco Chronicle* also mentions the *Mirror of the Times*, a newspaper edited and published by a collaborative group that was central to the state's Colored Conventions, including W. H. Newby, Jonas H. Townsend, and William H. Hall.

16. "Baltimore, July 27," *Frederick Douglass' Paper* (Rochester, NY), June 30, 1852.

17. Frederick Douglass, Stephen Myers, William Rich, Amos G. Beman, Charles B. Ray, William H. Topp, William J. Wilson, William Wells Brown, Henry Highland Garnet, James McCune Smith, Jermain Wesley Loguen, James W. C. Pennington, George T. Downing, William Cooper Nell, and many more.

18. Israel Campbell, *An Autobiography: Bond and Free; or, Yearnings for Freedom, from My Green Brier House; Being the Story of My Life in Bondage, and My Life in Freedom* (Philadelphia: C. E. P. Brinckloe, 1861; Documenting the American South, 2001), 210, http://docsouth.unc.edu/neh/campbell/campbell.html.

19. Josiah Henson, author of a popular narrative and widely known as the basis for the main character of Harriet Beecher Stowe's *Uncle Tom's Cabin*, had lived in the British territory since 1830.

20. Black leaders in Toronto and other communities in Canada West did hold other kinds of events. People connected to the Refugee Home Society, the Dawn Settlement, and the *Provincial Freeman* all organized public meetings filled with debates. None of those meetings seem to have adopted the parliamentary procedures or nomenclature of the U.S.-based Colored Conventions, for reasons that remain to be determined.

21. Questions surrounding the process of constructing data to represent records of nineteenth-century African American history and culture are far too complex to unpack fully in this space. In addition to interventions on archival gaps and silences,

most notably in the work of Frances Foster, Saidiya Hartman, Eric Gardner, Lois Brown, and many more, the theoretical complications of data that deals with race are just beginning to enjoy greater, much-needed conversations. Some of the voices that inform this chapter include Jessica Marie Johnson, Johanna Drucker, Miriam Posner, and Tim Sheratt, along with the many members of the Colored Conventions Project, including Denise Burgher, Labanya Mookerjee, Sarah Patterson, David Kim, Gabrielle Foreman, Carol Rudisell, Curtis Small, and many others.

22. See William Still, *The Underground Railroad : A Record of Facts, Authentic Narratives, Letters, &c.* (Philadelphia: Porter and Coates, 1872). Still's history offers an interesting means of enriching Siebert's data. See Wilbur Henry Siebert, *The Underground Railroad from Slavery to Freedom* (New York: Macmillan, 1898). Where Siebert (in an appendix) lists those who did the assisting, Still lists those who made the passage to freedom. Still's data is structured in short chapter headings and could raise new theoretical possibilities around data to represent slavery, self-emancipation, and the Colored Conventions movement.

23. Siebert notes at the start of the appendix that "the names of colored operators are marked with a †." Revealingly, Siebert assumes the default race of Underground Railroad operators is white. The distribution of operators by race registers his perspective, with only 5 percent (151) of the operators marked as Black. That obviously does not reflect the reality of the thousands of people of color who assisted refugees from the South.

24. LaRoche's geography of the Underground Railroad in Indiana is a compelling model for potential future work mapping the Colored Conventions. Most minutes of conventions provided locations that were associated with each delegate. That information makes it possible to ask many questions about the large-scale patterns of mobility for Black activists in the nineteenth century through the lens of the conventions.

25. The data deployed in this chapter about the Anti-Slavery Collection comes from Caleb McDaniel, "Data Mining the Internet Archive," *Programming Historian* 3 (2014), programminghistorian.org/lessons/data-mining-the-internet-archive.

THE EMIGRATION DEBATE AND THE SOUTHERN COLORED CONVENTIONS MOVEMENT

Selena R. Sanderfer

At the turn of the twenty-first century, innovative approaches began to interrogate the dynamics of Black social movements. The combined use of historical methodology and social movement theory has afforded the academy a better understanding of how variables such as collective resources or burgeoning political and economic opportunities have interacted to influence participation in the Great Migration and the modern civil rights movement.[1] While these theories have dominated academic discourse, research on Black Nationalism by political theorists has begun to revisit the most basic organizing component of collective action: a shared grievance among participants.[2]

The positive effect that grievances or social strains have on movement emergence is observable in movements for territorial separatism, specifically the emigration movements among the Black lower class in the South during the latter half of the nineteenth century.[3] As social strains on southern Blacks increased, usually in the form of severe violent economic and/or political repression, their support for territorial separatism—a form of Black Nationalism whereby participants sought to relocate, separating themselves from white authority—increased as well.[4] Black separatism traditionally includes the formation of a separate nation; however, it is not inherently nationalistic. It can also entail an economic, social, political, cultural, or partial statist separation from whites, such as the formation of an all-Black state or town, a condition that would allow advocates a degree of autonomy while maintaining a tangential connection to white society.[5]

The resolutions passed by southern Black conventions either advocating or condemning separatist movements to Liberia, Kansas, or all-Black communities in the South reflect the ebb and flow of emigration movements taking place after the Civil War. Immediately after the war, southern Black leaders first recognized the potential for meaningful social change, particularly Black landownership, and thus support for emigration movements at southern Colored Conventions was generally low or nonexistent. However, as racialized violence in the South surged and the prospects of landed proprietorship diminished, Black southerners retreated from racial conciliation and turned to emigration in increasing numbers. In response, Black leadership gradually began to condone emigration as a resistance and uplift strategy.

The emancipation of over 4 million enslaved Blacks ushered in a new era for Colored Conventions. With the exception of the 1852 Maryland Free Colored Peoples Convention, the prohibition of Black political activity during the antebellum era had almost entirely deterred southern Black leaders from organizing racial conventions until 1865. Thereafter, in the tradition of their northern brethren, Black southern conventions began efforts to reform education, suffrage, and various civil rights laws.[6] In comparing pre–Civil War northern and post–Civil War southern convention movements, the most significant difference was their postures with respect to emigration. Only one or two generations removed from Africa, during the early republic period Black northern elites such as Paul Cuffee of Rhode Island, James Forten and Richard Allen of Pennsylvania, Perry Lockes and Prince Saunders of Massachusetts, and Abraham Thompson and Peter Williams Jr. of New York forwarded the cause of African emigration to counter growing discrimination in the United States. Their views were overwhelmingly rejected by Black residents, who were optimistic that abolition in the North foreshadowed more progressive racial policies and thus vehemently defended their claims to American citizenship.[7] Although a few northern Black Nationalists such as Mary Ann Shadd Cary, who supported emigration to Canada, and James Theodore Holly, who advocated emigration to Haiti, trumpeted self-removal during the antebellum period, they simultaneously condemned immigration to Africa and chastised Black southerners for working with white colonization agencies such as the American Colonization Society.[8] Likewise, economic initiatives promoting landownership found some support in northern conventions and among leaders such as Lewis Woodson, Henry Bibb, Martin Delany, and Henry Highland Garnet. However, Black northerners were mostly what historians James and Lois Horton called an "urban poor people," and often, such as in the case of Haiti, farming communities founded by northern emigrants faltered in part because of their lack of experience.[9] Southern residents on the other hand never deviated from their objective of becoming landed proprietors, and southern conventions eventually acquiesced to the growing tide of Black emigrants, who chose separatism as an acceptable option for achieving this goal and with it improving one's livelihood.

The promise of landownership was a fundamental objective for Black southern separatists, who in both the antebellum and postbellum periods were most often employed as agriculturalists. Of the approximately 15,000 American Blacks who emigrated to Liberia from 1822 to 1904, nearly 80 percent were from the southern states.[10] Formerly enslaved farmworkers and poor free Blacks wished to obtain for themselves the independent yeoman culture observed among southern whites by applying the novel idea of emigration to attain economic and political self-determination. A sample ship manifest to Liberia from the 1860s provides fragmentary evidence of this demographic trend. Previously residing in Georgia, South Carolina, Virginia, Maryland, and Pennsylvania, forty-eight of the seventy-eight working-age men who embarked for Liberia on May 30, 1867, were farmers, making it the most frequently listed occupation.[11] Researchers of twentieth-century social movements have documented how movements composed predominantly of one social class generally possess class-centered goals.[12] The same argument can also be applied to movements of the nineteenth century. Most southern Black separatists were farmers who belonged to the southern laboring class; consequently land acquisition and economic independence were two key movement objectives.[13]

In the nineteenth century, formerly enslaved Black Nationalists in the South advanced a racial uplift strategy of landownership and emigration to Africa that was distinct from the Eurocentric moral and civilizing missions espoused by some branches of northern leadership with regard to African emigration.[14] Free Black activists such as Alexander Crummell, an Episcopalian priest, and Daniel Payne, bishop of the African Methodist Episcopal (AME) Church, had resided in the North for decades before the start of the Civil War and had evinced views of Africa far different from poor southern Blacks. Crummell clearly stated that his interest in Africa was twofold: 1) as a place to express "the temporal, material interests of adventurous, enterprising, colored men" and 2) as it "pertains to the best and most abiding interests of the million masses of heathen on this continent—I mean their evangelization."[15] For him, Africa was a place where Black Americans could exercise superior positions in government and society while proselytizing the indigenous people.[16] Payne, on the other hand, voiced reservations about Black American activity on the continent and cautioned freed people "that Africa cannot be regarded as an asylum, from the White man's oppression nor the White man's power."[17] Their advocacy for or adversity toward African emigration spoke to a cohort of freeborn, educated, middle- and upper-class Black Americans, who in more cases than not resided in the North. Lower-class southern Black Americans did not prioritize these same concerns or dismiss proposed advantages when assessing emigration. When the possibility of emigration was discussed at southern Black conventions after the Civil War, little if any consideration was given to native African peoples. Rather, Black southern representatives emphasized the potential for Black American uplift through economic enterprise, social equality, and political sovereignty in Africa.[18]

In 1865, the Colored People's Convention of the State of South Carolina succinctly outlined the shared desires of the nation's Black citizens: "That we shall be recognized as men; that we have no obstructions placed in our way; that the same laws that govern White men shall direct colored men; that we have the right of trial by jury of our peers, that schools be open and established for our children." However, one aspiration, "that we be permitted to acquire homesteads for ourselves and children," distinguished their calls for redress from those at similar conventions.[19] Like previously emancipated people throughout the diaspora, formerly enslaved Blacks in the South formed a protopeasantry by seeking to achieve racial, political, and economic autonomy through landownership.[20] Throughout the country, Blacks sought equal access in education, the courts, suffrage laws, and social accommodations; nevertheless, the unwavering insistence on land acquisition and economic independence as a basic human right clearly distinguished Black southern nationalists.

Most southern Blacks before and after the Civil War were employed in agricultural work and lived a largely subsistence-based existence. Their desire to become independent landowners and to resist subjugation was in part influenced by this background. Delegates to the Convention of the Colored People of Virginia of 1865 showed their commitment to agricultural livelihoods when they resolved that "the surest guarantee for the independence and ultimate elevation of the colored people will be found in their becoming the owners of the soil on which they live and labor."[21] That same year, the State Convention of Colored Men of the State of Tennessee advised Black residents, "Agriculture is one of the elements of wealth, we desire you to purchase or rent lands, and commence cultivating them." Representatives assertively questioned white residents: "Why can we not till them [lands] independently, there by acquiring a portion of the power in Tennessee?"[22] Perhaps delegates inadvertently answered their own question, as landownership was linked to wealth and political power within the state. For southern Blacks, landownership was the ultimate symbol of social and economic achievement. For freedmen, it represented the antithesis to their enslavement and could effectively preserve their liberty, making them and their progeny perpetually independent.[23] Contrary to future hopes, the precariousness in their lives continued, as their newly empowered citizenship and motivation to acquire land instigated white southerners to commit thousands of murders and outrages against them in order to maintain white supremacy.

Although Black southerners believed they deserved to be landowners, such repressive measures meant that they had to be tactful while asserting their rights in order to lessen white aggression. Members of the 1867 Alabama state convention were concerned about procuring land but also sought to allay white fears of Black political power by declaring that their assembly "did not dream of, or intend the organization of a colored man's party."[24] Their calls for reform, however, included a new sense of confidence reinforced by their present status as freemen, and they cautioned white citizens "that if the employers of colored men carry out their threats to discharge them because of political differences, and to otherwise torment them by the denial of their rights before the law, they [Black citizens] will, as loyal Republican citizens carry out, with united voice, for the presence of a standing army, ask for additional legislation by Congress looking to the punishment of treason, and even to the confiscation of the property of the guilty."[25] Only a couple of years after the Civil War, Black residents in Alabama wished to promote interracial accord while exercising their rights yet simultaneously declared their power as loyal American citizens to potentially usurp white landownership in the region and create for themselves an independent economic base. Ultimately, the convention chose not to antagonize racial tension by laying claim to the land held by ex-Confederates and Confederate sympathizers, "unless the future conduct on the part of the late rebels should point to it as an imperious necessity."[26] Yet landownership remained a goal among recently freed men and women in the South; however, another means of obtaining it would have to be procured.

Since most emigrants were farmers, it was not surprising that the lack of landownership opportunities after the Civil War was the most compelling reason for increased participation in territorial separatism. Black landownership in the South was both an act of westernization and resistance.[27] Blacks embraced southern yeoman values of subsistence farming in order to resist economic exploitation. By the late 1860s, the failure to achieve economic independence had devastated lower-class aspirations for any degree of equality—political, social, or otherwise—in the South and led the region's Black residents to advocate territorial separatism in considerable numbers.

For many, emigration to any foreign country or U.S. territory willing to accept Black emigrants and pledge avenues to landownership was preferable to tenancy in the South. In 1875 after the African Emigration Committee of the Philadelphia Annual Conference of the AME Church recommended adopting a resolution advising the Black population of the South against African emigration, the controversial Bishop Henry McNeil Turner, the first bishop of the AME Church elected in the South and the convention's lone dissenter, proposed debating the topic further. Established leaders in the church characterized African emigration as "a speculative movement of thoughtless men" to which "the solid thinkers of our race were opposed." Rev. James Crawford Embry argued that African emigration was contrary to the evolution of modern man. He posited that "history and geography show that all intelligent races inhabit the temperate and not the torrid zone" and hinted that emigration was a conspiracy when he made the remark that "the White race could not get rid of the colored race in this country; for here we expect to live and die." Rev. J. W. Scott, presiding elder of the Florida conference, continued the denouncement and cited the "injurious effects in the South unsettling the industrial pursuits among the colored people." He concluded by ridiculing movement participants who did not possess "five dollars in their pockets but were ready to emigrate to Africa." As Bishop Turner was also derided and dismissed, reporters observed how he poignantly "strove to justify his actions, and those with whom he is identified in the emigration movement," and accused the opposition of being akin to race traitors with his final comment that "the agitators were not in his ranks, but they were on the other side."[28] Turner reflected the desires of his southern constituents to consider territorial separatism as a means to achieving economic and political self-determination, while Scott and Embry wholeheartedly rejected the strategy. Different strategies for Black uplift across regions and classes became more pronounced after the conclusion of the Civil War, as impoverished southern Blacks began to view their plight as being inherently different from that of their relatively more advantaged northern brethren. Now, for the first time both groups were able to debate in public their respective visions for the newly freed population.

The diverging sentiments on emigration between 1865 and 1879 resulted from the emphasis southern Blacks placed on land acquisition as the most practical tool for achieving independence. Although largely absent from northern Colored Conventions' agendas, landownership remained a pressing objective for southern conventions throughout Reconstruction. Unlike Bishop Turner, however, many of the northern leaders of the AME Church failed to appreciate why the masses of formerly enslaved Blacks living in the South prioritized landownership. A. Jackson of Tallahassee, Florida, was a young man who was accustomed to farming and disagreed with anti-emigrationist views. In a letter to the *Christian Recorder*, Jackson reasoned that southern Blacks should "cultivate the soil that will yield the most" and therefore it was necessary that they relocate "into richer sections of the country where they will be better paid for their labor."[29] Leaders such as Bishop Turner were the exception. They recognized the merits of Jackson's strategy and those of other poor southern Blacks in similar circumstances. During the antebellum era, Turner had been a member of the poor free Black community in Charleston, South Carolina. He grew up in the context of slavery and the cotton economy and thus, after the Civil War, comprehended southern Black prioritization of landownership and the strategy of territorial separatism to resist racial exploitation.

Farmers such as Jackson understood the disconnection between Black leaders and the formerly enslaved population in the South. Jackson declared that if the bishops of the AME Church were truly concerned about their people being defrauded by emigration schemes, they should "advise the leading and representative men of our race to go among our people, more than they do, and instruct them how to manage, so as to prevent so much fraud, and that those of them who have means, invest it in the purchase of land."[30] Other Black farmers also perceived a growing disparity between the ideals promulgated by Black leaders and the needs of a rural population.

During the Exoduster movement to Kansas in the late 1870s and early 1880s, an anonymous farmer wrote the *Christian Recorder* regarding this tension: "Right here is where all the anti-emigrationists have erred. They forget that all these emigrants are practical farmers and that the tastes and necessities of a people are not cheaply, but more adequately, supplied on the farm, and particularly one of their own, than elsewhere."[31] A farm "of their own" would end the cycle of dependency and uncertainty that the burgeoning sharecrop and crop lien systems placed on Black farmers. Similar to the yeoman ideal in the antebellum era, freed people sought to be self-sufficient farmers who supplemented their staples with the sale of cash crops for market. Gradually, more and more of the Black leadership acknowledged Black farmers' calls and began to echo the philosophies and strategies of the southern masses.

The promise of political and economic self-determination influenced the relative lack of support for emigration movements in the years immediately following the Civil War. Southern Black leadership expected to enjoy such rights, but initially following the conciliatory posture of white leadership, they took a measured approach when claiming them. At the 1865 South Carolina Convention of Colored Men, Dr. Moses G. Camplin, a Black delegate from Charleston who would eventually become an advocate of emigration to Liberia, initially believed that "the future was more bright and promising than some anticipated, and that after a while, when time had effaced some of the bitter memories of the late conflict, the White man and the Black man would consent to be friends and brothers, and live together in peace and harmony." Although he used the rhetoric of racial harmony, Camplin emphasized individual responsibility to his Black audience in an attempt to counter the racial stereotype of Black indolence and the white fear of Black dependency after the war.[32] Many early Black leaders shared his views, and although sympathetic to discrimination, they did not aggressively push for economic policies that could best meet the needs of their mostly rural constituents.

Most southern whites, even those espousing support for Black uplift, still held paternalistic views that did not sufficiently address the needs of the masses of freed men and women. Reverend Pell, an invited speaker to the 1866 Freedmen's Convention held in Raleigh, North Carolina, recounted how he "had always cherished a warm feeling towards the colored people" and believed that "if the people of both races would work as they ought, and they will shortly have to, North Carolina will become a giant state."[33] Ex-governor William W. Holden held similar views and advised Black North Carolinians that their first concern should be "to procure homes, no matter how cheap or small," and that "the true interest of the colored race was to cultivate the friendship of the Whites." He assured them that they were "entitled to all their civil rights, and would have them," but ultimately advised them "for the present to keep out of politics. It was a 'weariness to the flesh' among the White people. They [Blacks] had not yet demonstrated their capacity for self-government, and would not until the Union was restored and our liberties consolidated."[34] Holden and Pell reasoned that they were aiding Blacks, but through their and other white southern leaders' unwavering commitment to white supremacy, they ensured that no policies aiming to increase the status of poor Blacks would be seriously considered by state legislatures. Many southern Blacks did not agree with all of the advice of white sympathizers, yet they respectfully and strategically resigned themselves to wait to exercise civil liberties for the sake of cultivating amicable race relations.

While some Blacks made political compromises with whites, delayed approaches to economic self-determination could not satisfy the masses of freedmen for very long. New leaders, previously held in bondage, became more vocal and expressed a growing discontent and an unwillingness to adhere to appeasing political protest etiquette. At the same 1866 Freedmen's Convention in North Carolina, former governor William A. Graham, who was invited to speak at the convention, evinced an air of paternalism in the letter he sent to be read in his absence. In it, he stressed frugality, industriousness, and honest living to the freedmen so that they could generally "advance in the scale of life."[35] After the usual beatitudes and calls for racial improvement, delegate Calvin MacCray of Richmond County radically changed the mood of the proceedings by describing how, in the presence of invited white speakers, Black people residing in his region of the state were "most shamefully treated by the Whites. Their money and firearms are taken from them under the pretext that it is an order issued for them to take these things away, and colored laborers are most cruelly whipped on plantations." Other delegates tried to steer the direction of the proceedings back to more palatable experiences. Edmund Bird of Alamance County countered that "prejudice existing against the Negro is only entertained by the lower and ignorant class of Whites." J. A. Green of Gages County supported this point and spoke highly of the whites in his region, as did representatives Henry Powell and William Leak of Anson County, who described a "spirit of harmony and kindly feeling existing between the Whites and Blacks."[36]

However, it was not long before other Black representatives began to gain confidence, cease with pleasantries, and instead relay the much more tense and violent state of race relations in the South. Representative Hubbard Little of Montgomery County generally spoke well of whites but expressed how he was pained to hear that "a colored man was shot and instantly killed for trespassing on the premises of a White person"; he further stated that "his people are in a most deplorable condition, they having no colored church nor school house."[37] Little was supported by representatives Charles Harrel of Bertie County, who described how local "colored men were cheated out of their labor; children were taken and bound without the consent or consultation of their parents," and Charles Carter of Sampson County, who reported that "these matters are known to agents of the Freedmen's Bureau, but they take no steps to arrest the evil in its onward march."[38] After invited speakers Reverend Pell and the superintendent of North Carolina schools F. A. Fiske concluded their speeches, more accommodating Black leaders tried to return the racially harmonious decorum. Delegate Harmon Unthanks of Guilford County informed the meeting that "the great feeling of love and unity existed between both races in his county," and Thomas A. Sykes of Pasquotank firmly insisted that the intention of local whites was "to assist the colored people in their onward march to education and intelligence."[39] Despite closing on a positive note, new leaders had planted the seeds of incongruence; this somewhat tame exchange foreshadowed more heated meetings, where lower-class Blacks would voice their support for emigration and dissatisfaction with Black leadership's seemingly antiquated strategies for uplift.

Black southern conventions emphasized land acquisition but initially vehemently opposed achieving it through territorial separatism or any other collective action that could be interpreted as aggressively autonomous and thus incur the wrath of whites. The representatives to Tennessee's 1865 convention advised the Colored residents of the state, "We must exercise forbearance and endure as far as practicable, the many petty differences between us and the Whites, or between ourselves. The scheme of colonization is impracticable, and we must relax no effort to continue our habitation in this country in full enjoyment of all rights and privileges exercised by any other class of citizens."[40] During the Civil War, President Abraham Lincoln contemplated various colonization endeavors to places in Latin America and the Caribbean as possible solutions to the perceived problem of emancipating 4 million Blacks.[41] Black leaders defended their claims to American citizenship and emphasized their contribution to the country to counter proponents of deportation.

Leaders did not want to seem too oriented toward Africa for fear that whites would assume that they all desired to live there or simply naturally belonged there. The 1865 South Carolina Colored Convention in an "Address to the Colored Citizens of the State" declared, "We are Americans by birth, and we assure you that we are Americans in feeling." Delegates optimistically addressed whites "not as enemies but as friends and fellow countrymen, who desire to dwell among you in peace, and whose destinies are interwoven, and linked with those of the American people."[42] Although most bondsmen and bondswomen in the South were freed by the Emancipation Proclamation, the legitimacy of their status as American citizens was often called into question. Succumbing to fears of racial amalgamation and social equality, Abraham Lincoln tied Black emancipation to removal and as late as 1864 investigated the feasibility of Black colonization in Mexico, Haiti, and Central America.[43] In 1865 Black North Carolinians resolved to offer official recognition to the nations of Haiti and Liberia; however, fearing national support may be construed as support for colonization, James Walker Hood, the convention president and an elder in the AME Church, implored his fellow delegates to "live here with the White people; all talk of exportation, expatriation, colonization and the like was simple non sense."[44] Hood's dismissal of territorial separatism as a legitimate uplift strategy was not uncommon during the years immediately following the Civil War.

When defending their American status, delegates often appealed to the spiritual character and military achievements of Blacks. Appeals to white morality and claims of providence were made at the 1865 Convention of Colored Citizens of the State of Arkansas: "Our future is sure—God has marked it out with his finer; here we have lived, suffered, fought, bled, and many have died. We will not leave the graves of our fathers."[45] While many exhortations reflected a genuine spirituality among constituents, Blacks understood how they could use religious references to humanize and increase, however slightly, whites' endearment toward them. Black soldiers' contributions were also a dominant motif in claims to American citizenship, and Black conventions heralded them across the South. At the Kentucky First Convention of Colored Men in 1866 delegates affirmed, "We are 'native and to the manner born'; we are part and parcel of the Great American body politic; we love our country her institutions; we are proud of her greatness and glory in her might; we are *intensely Americans*, allied to the free institutions of our country by the sacrifices, the deaths and slumbering ashes of our sons, our brothers and our fathers whose patriotism, whose daring and devotion, led them to pledge their lives, their property and their sacred honor, to the maintenance of her freedom, and the majesty of her laws."[46] Masters of diplomacy, Black southerners utilized patriotism, religiosity, paternalism, and above all racial civility to become independent landowners and exercise political rights while keeping white repression at bay. They tapered assertive calls for civil rights with those of interracial harmony and sanguinity. Despite such displays, Black southern hopefulness began to subside as the drive to solidify white supremacy after the Civil War intensified. Black delegates, once optimistic, became cynical about the prospect of achieving racial harmony and equal rights in the South. As the denial of political and economic rights was compounded by Black southerners' desperate need for basic physical protection, more and more of them began to support emigration as a feasible option to end their injustices and, consequently, Black southern conventions followed suit.

For Black southerners, territorial separatism was often a philosophy of last resort. They wanted to remain in their ancestral homes in the American South but were ultimately unwilling to sacrifice their racial manhood and citizenship for that right. At the close of the 1866 State Convention of the Colored People of Georgia, Capt. J. E. Bryant, the white elected president, idealistically dismissed the threats of disgruntled white southerners while he made a plea for their support of Black empowerment:

Nor can we close this memorial without calling your attention to the often repeated threat which we hear in various parts of the State, leading us to believe there must be a contemplated plot in reserve for our general extermination. This we infer from being frequently told; "When the Yankees all leave, you had better leave with them or you will wish you had;" and other remarks too numerous to mention. True, the better informed of us have but little fears; but there are thousands who are kept in unsettled suspense from such remarks, and we think this greatly militates against the contract system. But give us laws just and equal in their protective bearing, and these fears will be banished, and ill-designing men will be utterly powerless.[47]

Three years later Bryant's worst fears were realized. In 1869, Georgia State Colored Convention representatives wrote more with an air of powerlessness than of confidence when they described listening "with horror to the harrowing details of the most unparalleled outrages perpetuated upon colored laboring men, consistently in fraud, violence and murder, committed under the most atrocious circumstances, and with the most hellish cold-bloodedness." The Georgia convention showed immense bravery in the face of overwhelming persecution when it resolved that its only defense was to "publish these facts to mankind and invoke the aid of all the liberty-loving people of the world, all the friends of law and order in our country," and to "advise our people to the extent of their power, to defend themselves against any and all of these outrages."[48] Following the Civil War, a climate of violence coupled with political and economic turmoil induced more than 700 Black Georgians to leave the state and remove themselves to Liberia. Over 300 would leave in the year 1868, the same year that political redemption began in Georgia as Democrats refused to allow elected Black legislators to be seated and murdered over a dozen Black Republicans.[49] Black leaders gradually, in response to freedmen's increased participation in separatist movements, began to understand emigration as an act of defense.

Episodic violence also circumscribed the Tennessee State Convention of Colored Men in 1866 and 1876, where Black representatives debated emigration to Africa and Kansas, respectively. White violence directed toward Blacks was particularly intense during this period as whites murdered more than 179 Black residents. These violent conditions, in part, compelled over 200 Black Tennesseans to immigrate to Liberia from 1866 to 1869 and nearly 4,000 to Kansas from 1870 to 1880. Faced with such circumstances, Black convention representatives shifted their stance on emigration. Regarding the Exodusters' emigration to Kansas, delegates at the 1876 convention proclaimed, "We are not going to tear our shirts about it."[50] No longer emphasizing calls for patience regarding race relations in the South, they now gave passive support to Tennessee's emigrants.

By 1879, the year of the "Exoduster fever," thousands of Blacks left the South to form all-Black towns such as Nicodemus and Dunlap in Kansas. The National Conference of Colored Men was finally catching up to the general idea that emigration "should be encouraged and kept in motion until those who remain are accorded every right and privilege guaranteed by the Constitution and laws."[51] Delegates espousing rhetoric to promote peace, tolerance, and patience between the two races no longer characterized the mood at Black conventions. Calls for territorial separatism became much more insistent and dogmatic as the national conference also resolved "that unless White friends take immediate steps to guarantee such rights, there will be an immediate emergency for an entire exodus of the race from the states in order to ameliorate their condition."[52] Southern conventions' support for emigration, however, was not uniform and was usually reserved for movements within the United States and its territories.

As disillusionment for achieving a livelihood in the South ran high, so, too, did support for emigration among Black convention leaders, who followed the lead of their constituents in publicly advocating the formation of Black towns. The change in Black leaders' emigration position was a direct result of the masses' unwavering advocacy for and use of territorial separatism as a strategy to counter racial subjugation. P. B. S. Pinchback, then a Louisiana state senator, remarked on this reversal and attested to the rural Black strategy of emigration commonly called "voting by one's feet" when he spoke at the 1879 National Conference of Colored Men hosted in Nashville, Tennessee: "I will take the opportunity to make this suggestion, that in considering this matter [emigration] you should bear in mind that the South being the home of the Colored people, they being adapted to its climate, its soil—have been born and raised there—we should not advise them to leave there unless they have very good reason to do so. On the other hand, we should not advise them to remain where they are not treated well. [Applause]."[53] Black leaders could no longer dismiss the motivations of Black southern emigrants. Their acquiescence turned to approval, which began to be heralded by others. In the view of Fredrick Douglass, the cause of Black southern emigration was primarily harassment by whites, and he insisted that Blacks would only abandon their beloved homes under extreme pressure.[54] Such sentiment was shared by other elites such as James C. Napier of Nashville, who upheld that "it is the sense of this conference that the great current migration which has, within the past few weeks, taken thousands of our people from our midst, and which is daily carrying hundreds from the extreme Southern States, should be encouraged and kept in motion until those who are left are awarded every right and privilege."[55] Gradually, Napier and other Black leaders ceased to emphasize idealism in race relations and Black uplift and began to sanction the more feasible strategies, such as separation, already employed by Black southerners.

While most Black southerners agreed to prioritize landownership, it was not until the occurrence of racial pogroms, continued political injustices, and widespread economic despair that Black leadership began to voice support for emigration. At the end of Reconstruction in 1876 and with the removal of federal troops, whites inflicted a reign of terror on Blacks in the South, and for the first time state Colored Conventions publicly endorsed emigration movements. Postwar optimism and strategic cooperation no longer moderated demands for self-determination. Rather than hope for interracial accord, Black southerners pragmatically asserted themselves by removing their labor and capital. Most supported movements to separate communities within the United States; still others recommended emigration to any hospitable territory where landownership could be realized.

Formerly enslaved Black southerners rationalized landownership through territorial separatism as an effective means of achieving self-determination and survival. Although adverse to any emigration movements immediately following the Civil War, southern Colored Conventions during the 1870s eventually came to reverse their views after witnessing systematic repression and widespread disenchantment with the progress of race relations.

Research that focuses too narrowly on Black elites diminishes the force, collective action, and power of once enslaved and impoverished Blacks whose own ideology and strategies for uplift ultimately inspired the shift on emigration from denunciation to encouragement among Black leadership. Their contribution complicates the narrative of Black Nationalism and offers a much needed supplement to the discourse on the Black protest tradition and Colored Conventions movement.

NOTES

1. Aldon Morris, *The Origins of the Civil Rights Movement* (New York: Free Press, 1986); Doug McAdam, *Political Process and the Development of Black Insurgency, 1930–1970* (Chicago: University of Chicago Press, 1999); Belinda Robnett, *How Long? How Long? African-American Women in the Struggle for Civil Rights* (London: Oxford University Press, 2000); Stewart E. Tolnay and E. M. Beck, *A Festival of Violence: An Analysis of Southern Lynchings, 1882–1930* (Urbana: University of Illinois Press, 1995); William J. Collins, "When the Tide Turned: Immigration and the Delay of the Great Black Migration," *Journal of Economic History* 57, no. 3 (September 1997): 607–32; William J. Collins, "Race, Roosevelt, and Wartime Production: Fair Employment in World War II Labor Markets," *American Economic Review* 91 no. 1 (March 2001): 272–86; David S. Meyer and Debra C. Minkoff, "Conceptualizing Political Opportunity," *Social Forces* 82, no. 4 (June 2004): 1457–92.

2. Tommie Shelby, "Two Conceptions of Black Nationalism: Martin Delany on the Meaning of Black Political Solidarity," *Political Theory* 31, no. 5 (October 2003): 664–92; Tommie Shelby, "Foundations of Black Solidarity: Collective Identity or Common Oppression?," *Ethics* 112, no. 2 (January 2002): 231–66; Tommie Shelby, *We Who Are Dark: The Philosophical Foundations of Black Solidarity* (Cambridge, MA: Harvard University Press, 2005); Ray Block Jr., "What About Disillusionment: Exploring Pathways to Black Nationalism," *Political Behavior* 33, no. 1 (2011): 27–51; Ray Block Jr., "Disillusionment with American Race Relations and Support for Black Nationalism: An Endogeneity Problem" (paper presented at the Midwest Political Science Association, Chicago, IL, April 2004).

3. In societies that are not well integrated, social strains such as political or economic disruptions can increase discontentment and induce collective action. Steven Buecheler, "Social Strain, Structural Breakdown, Political Opportunities and Collective Action," *Sociology Compass* 2, no. 3 (May 2008): 1031–44; David A. Snow, Daniel M. Cress, Liam Downey, and Andrew W. Jones, "Disrupting the 'Quotidian': Reconceptualizing the Relationship between Breakdown and the Emergence of Collective Action," *Mobilization* 3, no. 1 (March 1998): 1–22.

4. Black Nationalism can be broadly defined as an ideology that encourages the formation of racial solidarity and self-determination. Claude Andrew Clegg defines Black Nationalism as "a general template of ideologies, programs, and political visions geared toward encouraging racial pride, collective action, and group autonomy among people of African descent." Claude Andrew Clegg, *Africa and the African American Imagination* (Ann Arbor, MI: ProQuest Information and Learning, 2006), 24. Scholars have also bifurcated Black Nationalism into philosophies broadly emphasizing a shared cultural identity and ones supporting Black political and economic sovereignty. Shelby, "Two Conceptions," 667, 676; Robert A. Brown and Todd C. Shaw, "Separate Nations: Two Attitudinal Dimensions of Black Nationalism," *Journal of Politics* 64, no. 1 (February 2002): 22–44.

5. Raymond Hall, *Black Separatism in the United States* (Hanover, NH: University Press of New England, 1974), 3; Michael C. Dawson, *Black Visions: The Roots of Con-*

temporary African-American Political Ideologies (Chicago: University of Chicago Press, 2001), 21.

6. For more on Black southern conventions, see also Blake J. Wintry, "African-American Legislators in the Arkansas General Assembly, 1868–1893," *Arkansas Historical Quarterly* 65, no. 4 (Winter 2006): 385–434; Bobby L. Lovett, "African Americans, Civil War, and Aftermath in Arkansas," *Arkansas Historical Quarterly* 54, no. 3 (Autumn 1995): 304–58; Elsie M. Lewis, "The Political Mind of the Negro, 1865–1900," *Journal of Southern History* 21, no. 2 (May 1955): 189–202; Judy Bussell LeForge, "State Colored Conventions of Tennessee, 1865–1866," *Tennessee Historical Quarterly* 65, no. 3 (Fall 2006): 230–53; Judy Bussell LeForge, "Alabama's Colored Conventions and the Exodus Movement, 1871–1879," *Alabama Review* 63, no. 1 (January 2010): 3–29; John Cimprich, "The Beginning of the Black Suffrage Movement in Tennessee, 1864–65," *Journal of Negro History* 65, no. 3 (Summer 1980): 185–95; Herbert Aptheker, "South Carolina Negro Conventions, 1865," *Journal of Negro History* 31, no. 1 (January 1946): 91–97; Martin Abbott, "Freedom's Cry: Negroes and Their Meetings in South Carolina, 1865–1869," *Phylon Quarterly* 20, no. 3 (Third Quarter 1959): 263–72; and A. A. Taylor, "The Convention of 1868," *Journal of Negro History* 9, no. 4 (October 1924): 381–408.

7. James Oliver Horton and Lois E. Horton, *In Hope of Liberty: Culture, Community and Protest among Northern Free Blacks* (Oxford: Oxford University Press, 1997), 171–202.

8. Floyd J. Miller, *The Search for a Black Nationality: Black Emigration and Colonization 1787–1863* (Urbana: University of Illinois Press, 1975), 93–133; Ousmane K. Power-Greene, *Against Wind and Tide: The African American Struggle against the Colonization Movement* (New York: New York University Press, 2014).

9. Horton and Horton, *In Hope of Liberty*, 194; Howard Holman Bell, *A Survey of the Negro Convention Movement, 1830–1861* (New York: Arno, 1969); Howard Holman Bell, *Minutes of the Proceedings of the National Negro Conventions, 1830–1864* (New York: Arno, 1969); Philip S. Foner and George E. Walker, eds., *Proceedings of the Black State Conventions, 1840–1865*, 2 vols. (Philadelphia: Temple University Press, 1979); Miller, *Search*, 93–133.

10. This number is derived from Eric Burin, *Slavery and the Peculiar Solution* (Gainesville: University of Florida Press, 2005); Tom W. Schick, *Emigrants to Liberia, 1820–1843* (Newark: University of Delaware Press, 1971); Robert T. Brown, *Immigrants to Liberia, 1843–1865: An Alphabetical Listing* (Philadelphia: Institute for Liberia Studies, 1980); and Peter J. Murzda, *Emigrants to Liberia, 1865–1904: An Alphabetical Listing* (Newark, DE: Liberian Studies Association of America, 1975).

11. "List of Emigrants from Liberia by the Ship Golconda," *African Repository* 43, no. 7 (July 1867): 7–15. Other occupations included two coopers, four carpenters, five laborers, one minister, four engineers, two cooks, two shoemakers, one druggist, one stonecutter, two plasterers, one upholsterer, one clerk, three waiters, one barber, one blacksmith, one cabinet maker, one butcher, three painters, and five bricklayers.

12. H. Svi Shapiro, "Radical Movements, Ideology, and the Sociology of Educational Ideas," *Social Praxis* 6, no. 3–4 (1979): 193–94; W. E. B. Du Bois, *Black Reconstruction in America* (New York: Harcourt, Brace, 1935), 145–48, 248.

13. Rosalie Hooper, Selena Sanderfer, and Eileen Moscoso, *Stake Claim or Take Flight: The Birth of Southern Conventions after the Civil War*, digital exhibit, Colored Conventions Project, http://coloredconventions.org/southern-conventions.

14. For more on northern philosophies toward Black Nationalism, see also Tunde Adeleke, *UnAfrican Americans: Nineteenth-Century Black Nationalists and the Civilizing Mission* (Lexington: University Press of Kentucky, 1998); Tunde Adeleke, "Black Americans, Africa and History: A Reassessment of the Pan-African and Identity Paradigms," *Western Journal of Black Studies* 22, no. 3 (Fall 1998): 182–94; Wilson Jeremiah Moses, *The Golden Age of Black Nationalism 1850–1925* (Hamden, CT: Archon Books, 1978); and Patrick Rael, *Black Identity and Black Protest in the Antebellum North* (Chapel Hill: University of North Carolina Press, 2002). Information on southern

separatist movements can be found in Selena Ronshaye Sanderfer, "For Land and Liberty: Black Territorial Separatism in the South, 1776–1904" (PhD diss., Vanderbilt University, 2010); Kenneth C. Barnes, *The Journey of Hope: The Back-to-Africa Movement in Arkansas in the Late 1800s* (Chapel Hill: University of North Carolina Press, 2004); Claude Andrew Clegg, *The Price of Liberty: African Americans and the Making of Liberia* (Chapel Hill: University of North Carolina Press, 2004); Edwin Redkey, *Black Exodus: Black Nationalist and Back-to-Africa Movements, 1890–1910* (New Haven, CT: Yale University Press, 1969); Steven Hahn, *A Nation under Our Feet: Black Political Struggles in the Rural South from Slavery to the Great Migration* (Cambridge, MA: Harvard University Press, 2003); and Nell Irvin Painter, *Exodusters: Black Migration to Kansas after Reconstruction* (New York: Alfred A. Knopf, 1976).

15. Alexander Crummell, *The Relations and Duties of Free Colored Men in America to Africa: A Letter to Charles B. Dunbar, M.D., Esq., of New York City* (Hartford, CT: Case, Lockwood, 1861), 9.

16. Wilson J. Moses, *Alexander Crummell: A Story of Civilization and Discontent* (New York: Oxford University Press, 1989); Elizabeth J. West, "Of Providence and Rhetoric: The Failure of Alexander Crummell's Anglo-African Nationalism," *Journal of Colonialism and Colonial History* 5, no. 3 (Winter 2004); Walter L. Williams, *Black American Attitudes toward Emigration to Africa* (Chapel Hill: University of North Carolina Press, 1977).

17. Daniel Payne, "African Emigration: Colored Americans and Africa Colored Americans and America—Bishop Payne's Second Letter," *Christian Recorder* (Philadelphia), August 8, 1878.

18. For the purposes of this study, the terms "delegate" and "representative" are used interchangeably when referring to convention participants.

19. *Proceedings of the Colored People's Convention of the State of South Carolina, Held in Zion Church, Charleston, November, 1865: Together with the Declaration of Rights and Wrongs; An Address to the People; A Petition to the Legislature, and a Memorial to Congress* (Charleston: South Carolina Leader Office, 1865), 25.

20. Sidney Mintz, *Caribbean Transformations* (Chicago: Aldine, 1974), 135.

21. *Proceedings of the Convention of the Colored People of Virginia held in the City of Alexandria, August 2, 3, 4, 5, 1865*, in *Proceedings of the Black National and State Conventions, 1865–1900*, ed. Philip S. Foner and George E. Walker (Philadelphia: Temple University Press, 1980), 268.

22. *Proceedings of the State Convention of Colored Men of the State of Tennessee: With the Address of the Convention to the White Loyal Citizens of Tennessee, and the Colored Citizens of Tennessee; Held at Nashville, Tenn., August 7th, 8th, 9th and 10th, 1865* (Nashville: Daily Press and the Times Job Office, 1865), 25–26.

23. Christopher Fyfe, *"Our Children Free and Happy": Letters from Black Settlers in Africa in the 1790s* (Edinburgh, UK: Edinburgh University Press, 1991), 1, 3; Douglas R. Egerton, *Death or Liberty: Africans Americans and Revolutionary America* (New York: Oxford University Press, 2009), 218.

24. *State Convention of the Colored Men of Alabama, 1867*, in Foner and Walker, *Proceedings of the Black National and State Conventions*, 303.

25. *State Convention of the Colored Men of Alabama*, 303.

26. *State Convention of the Colored Men of Alabama*, 303.

27. Mintz, *Caribbean Transformations*, 135.

28. "A Lively Discussion. African Emigration at a Discount. A Bishop and an Elder Rebuked. Logic, Wit and Laughter. Philadelphia Conference Speaks Out against the South Carolina Scheme. The Manager Speaks for Himself and Associates," *Christian Recorder*, May 23, 1878.

29. A. Jackson, "Emigration. Mr. Editor," *Christian Recorder*, April 1, 1875.

30. Jackson.

31. A Farmer, "Things in the West," *Christian Recorder*, February 5, 1880.

32. *Proceedings of the Colored People's Convention of the State of South Carolina*, 19.

33. *Minutes of the Freedmen's Convention, Held in the City of Raleigh, on the 2nd, 3rd, 4th, and 5th of October, 1866* (Raleigh, NC: Standard Book and Job Office, 1866), 21.

34. *Minutes of the Freedmen's Convention*, 25.

35. *Minutes of the Freedmen's Convention*, 10.

36. *Minutes of the Freedmen's Convention*, 17–18.

37. *Minutes of the Freedmen's Convention*, 17–18.

38. *Minutes of the Freedmen's Convention*, 21.

39. *Minutes of the Freedmen's Convention*, 21.

40. *Proceedings of the State Convention of Colored Men of the State of Tennessee*, 25.

41. James D. Lockett, "Abraham Lincoln and Colonization: An Episode That Ends in Tragedy at L'Ile a Vache, Haiti, 1863–1864," *Journal of Black Studies* 21, no. 4 (June 1991): 428–44; Phillip W. Magness and Sebastian N. Page, *Colonization after Emancipation: Lincoln and the Movement for Black Resettlement* (Columbia: University of Missouri Press, 2011); Michael Vorenberg, "Abraham Lincoln and the Politics of Black Colonization," *Journal of Abraham Lincoln* 14, no. 2 (Summer 1993): 22–45; Eric Foner, *The Fiery Trial: Abraham Lincoln and American Slavery* (New York: W. W. Norton, 2011).

42. *Proceedings of the Colored People's Convention of the State of South Carolina*, 24.

43. Lockett, "Abraham Lincoln and Colonization," 428–44; Richard Blackett, "Lincoln and Colonization," *OAH Magazine of History* 21, no. 4 (October 2007): 19–22; Thomas Schoonover, "Misconstrued Mission: Expansionism and Black Colonization in Mexico and Central America during the Civil War," *Pacific Historical Review* 49, no. 4 (November 1980): 607–20.

44. *State Convention of the Colored People of North Carolina, Raleigh, September 29, 1865*, in Foner and Walker, *Proceedings of the Black National and State Conventions*, 180–81.

45. *Proceedings of the Convention of Colored Citizens of the State of Arkansas, Held in Little Rock, Thursday, Friday and Saturday, November 30, December 1 and 2, 1865*, in Foner and Walker, *Proceedings of the Black National and State Conventions*, 188.

46. *Proceedings of the First Convention of Colored Men of Kentucky Held in Lexington March the 22nd, 23d, 24th, and 26th, 1866 with the Constitution of the Kentucky State Benevolent Association* (Louisville, KY: Civil and Calvert, 1866), 23.

47. *State Convention of the Colored People of Georgia, Augusta, January 10, 1866*, in Foner and Walker, *Proceedings of the Black National and State Conventions*, 235.

48. *Georgia State Colored Convention, Macon, November 1869*, in Foner and Walker, *Proceedings of the Black National and State Conventions*, 413.

49. Sanderfer, "For Land and Liberty," 184; Lee W. Formwalt, "The Camilla Massacre of 1868: Racial Violence as Political Propaganda," *Georgia Historical Quarterly* 71 no. 3 (Fall 1987): 399–426.

50. Alrutheus A. Taylor, *The Negro in Tennessee, 1865–1880* (Washington, DC: Associated Publishing, 1941), 106–7; "The Black States," *Christian Recorder*, August 21, 1873; Walter Fleming, "Pap Singleton, the Moses of the Colored Exodus," *American Journal of Sociology* 15 (July 1909): 73–75; William Cohen, *At Freedom's Edge: Black Mobility and the Southern White Quest for Racial Control, 1861–1915* (Baton Rouge: Louisiana State University Press, 1991), 170. Representatives at the 1876 convention were quoting Abraham Lincoln when he referred to the independent Black nation of Haiti.

51. *Proceedings of the National Conference of Colored Men of the United States, Held in the State Capitol at Nashville Tennessee, May 6, 7, 8 and 9, 1879* (Washington, DC: R. H. Darby, 1879), 9.

52. *Proceedings of the National Conference*, 9.

53. *Proceedings of the National Conference*, 4–5.

54. Fredrick Douglass, "The Negro Exodus from the Gulf States," *Frank Leslie's Popular Monthly*, January 1880, 39–48, 42–43.

55. *Proceedings of the National Conference*, 27.

FURTHER SILENCE UPON OUR PART WOULD BE AN OUTRAGE

Bishop Henry McNeal Turner and the
Colored Conventions Movement

Andre E. Johnson

In August of 1893, African Methodist Episcopal (AME) Church bishop Henry McNeal Turner (1834–1915) issued a call to convene a Black national convention. At the time of his call, Turner had established himself as a leader within the African American community. Known as a powerful orator, Turner preached integrated revivals; commanded audiences with senators, congressional leaders, and presidents; and became a favorite correspondent for the *Christian Recorder* newspaper. He was the first African American chaplain in the U.S. Armed Forces, an agent for the Freedmen's Bureau, a Georgia state constitutional delegate, and a state representative. His oratorical powers had a lot to do with him becoming the presiding elder of Georgia and later the twelfth bishop and one of the "four horsemen" of the AME Church.

Along with these accomplishments, Turner was the first African American postmaster general (Georgia). He offered bills in the Georgia House of Representatives giving all women the right to vote and creating an eight-hour workday, was his church's publication manager (1876–80), ordained the first woman as an elder in the AME Church (an ordination that the other bishops later rescinded), and motivated hundreds, if not thousands, of African Americans to emigrate to Africa. While Marcus Garvey has the distinction of being the leader of the "Back to Africa" movement, Garvey merely talked about going to Africa—Turner had some success at actually persuading people to go.

Moreover, Turner found time to start three newspapers—the *Southern Recorder* (1887–89), the *Voice of Missions* (1893–1900), and the *Voice of the People* (1901–4)—and served as editor of all three. He took four trips to Africa himself, established the AME Church there, wrote numerous articles and essays for various newspapers, wrote several introductions to books, and preached all over the United States. With Frederick Douglass near the end of his public career at the time of the 1893 convention (he would die less than two years later), many believed Turner was ready to assume the mantle of leadership.[1]

Turner's call for a national convention was not anything out of the ordinary, because Colored national conventions had been held since 1830. Tradition has it that Hezekiel (Hezekiah) Grice provided the impetus for the first national convention when he wondered aloud if African Americans should emigrate to Canada after Ohio reactivated its Black Codes and forced upward of 1,000 Black residents, who migrated to Canada, out of the state. Grice wrote several Black leaders proposing a national convention to discuss the issue. The leaders liked the idea, and after tensions between New York and Philadelphia leaders about who would host the convention, on September 15, 1830, in Philadelphia, Pennsylvania, at Mother Bethel AME Church, forty Black delegates from nine states attended the convention, which lasted ten days.[2]

It was at these conventions that African Americans could voice their opinions and concerns about the issues and problems many faced daily. According to historian Howard Holman Bell, delegates at these conventions "made specific demands for the elimination of slavery and chided the American Anti-Slavery Society for its unwillingness to champion social equality."[3] Delegates also promoted ideas of equal treatment under the law, suffrage, temperance, education, and moral reforms. Bell argued that the conventions not only "mirrored progress, but influenced Negro opinion, and demonstrated to the American public that the man [person] of color was ready to assume the full responsibilities of citizenship."[4]

While Colored Conventions were ubiquitous during the nineteenth century, two things made Turner's call special. First, it had been four years since the last national African American convention of any kind, and second, among the items delegates typically discussed—racism, equality, fair treatment, and better accommodations—there would be one more. The delegates were to again consider the merits of emigration, either to Africa or somewhere else. For Bishop Turner, the time had come for Black Americans to seriously reconsider moving away from America.

In this chapter, I examine Turner's role in the Colored Conventions movement. As I demonstrate, Turner had always been part of and played significant roles in national, state, and local conventions. The 1893 National Colored Convention held in Cincinnati from November 28 to December 2 is one of the very last, if not the last, to claim that title. I examine Turner's role as the president of the convention, analyze his keynote address, and posit why Turner believed that a national Colored Convention would be the best medium to again advocate for emigration.

Turner and the Colored Conventions

Turner was a prime mover in the postbellum Colored Conventions movement on the national, state, and local levels. One of the first he attended was the Contraband Convention in Washington, DC, during the Civil War. Held at different churches throughout the city, the weekly convention gatherings aimed to help formerly enslaved people with food, clothing, and any other necessities. Turner wrote about one of those meetings in which the delegates decided to raise money for a hospital. "The colored convention met at Zion Wesley Church, on Tuesday night last, and resolved upon the erection, as soon as possible of a hospital for the sick, afflicted, and destitute. They resolved that each delegate should advance ten dollars, as a beginning, to the sum of $5,000, which they think will be required to complete the object in contemplation."[5]

However, plans for the hospital fell through, as Turner noted in a follow-up letter to the editor published in the *Christian Recorder* on February 21, 1863. "I am sorry to inform you that the convention for the erection of a hospital has come to no decisive point. I was informed that a residentiary question had staggered its contemplated measures. But I think the indifference of the members to the call of the President, Mr. Wm. Slade has done more harm than the question of residence, though I regard the entire residential question as foolishness, unless, they are going to build the hospital, and generally such agitators give the least."[6]

On November 7, 1865, Turner received orders to report to Augusta, Georgia, and continue to serve as a chaplain in the army. But Turner had other plans. In a letter published December 30, 1865, in the *Recorder*, Turner wrote that "by the time I had arrived at Augusta, however, I had made up my mind to resign the chaplaincy." He cited as his reason his need to attend to church affairs. Settling in Augusta, Turner joined others there in a Freedmen's Convention ten days later. Chairman James Porter asked Turner to offer the opening prayer, and even though Turner was not yet a full resident of Georgia, the convention requested that he, along with J. E. Bryant and Aaron A. Bradley, participate fully in the proceedings.[7]

Turner made his presence known throughout the convention, advocating for the masses of new delegates, many of them recently freed. When Bradley suggested that *Cushing's Manual* "be the rules which should govern the deliberations of the Convention," Turner objected, because many of the participants were not used to the formal conventions of conventions; Turner thought that a few simple rules instead would suffice. After much discussion, his suggestion prevailed when the convention decided to appoint a committee to offer rules for the proceedings; Turner served on this committee.[8]

It was out of this convention that delegates created the Georgia Equal Rights Association. Though Turner did not serve in any leadership capacity at the association's convention that met in April 1866, the convention's president, J. E. Bryant, named Turner, along with a white man, Rev. H. F. Edes, as one of the editors of the association's organ, the *Loyal Georgian*. The selection was Bryant's attempt at racial reconciliation, as he also selected one Black man (C. H. Prince) and one white man (Thomas Beard) as financial agents for the Freedman's Saving Bank. The convention also named Turner as its delegate to Congress.

Later, in October 1866, at the Convention of the Equal Rights and Educational Association of Georgia, delegates appointed Turner to a committee responsible for conferring with the rival Union League and "uniting all the friends of equal rights in one convention." Turner also served on the Committee on Address and Condition of the Colored People in the State. The convention again selected him to serve as the official Washington delegate on behalf of African Americans in Georgia, and he recommended that the leaders of the convention publish the proceedings from the meeting.[9]

Writing weeks later in the *Recorder*, Turner praised the work of the African American delegates. "The convention of colored men from all parts of the State, which was held here a few weeks since did honor to our race and exhibited a degree of progress intellectually, and highly commendable, in a people so recently freed. There was marked ability developed in their entire proceedings, the idea that colored men could not govern themselves, if permitted, is all a hoax. The addresses which they prepared and memorialized the legislature with, will stand as a monument of colored ability in Georgia for centuries."[10]

In 1868, Georgia voters elected Turner and thirty-one other African Americans to serve in the state legislature. After the white representatives voted to remove the Black representatives from office on September 3, 1868, Turner issued a call for another state convention, published in the *Hartford Daily Courant* on September 24, 1868. After listing grievances and naming the reasons for such action, Turner concluded:

> In view of this state of things, we call upon the colored men of every county in this state to send delegates to a state convention of colored citizens, to be held in the city of Macon, on the first Tuesday in October, 1868, for the purpose of taking into consideration our condition, and determining upon the best course for the future. There can be no doubt that our personal liberty is in as great danger as our civil and political rights. The same power which would override the constitution in one thing will do it in another. It is, therefore, a solemn duty which every colored man owes to himself, his family, and his country, to maintain his manhood and his right of citizenship.[11]

In December 1868, Turner testified before a congressional hearing on the Reconstruction efforts in the state of Georgia. He acknowledged that he not only was a member of that convention but also served as its president. When George Boutwell of Massachusetts asked, "Did the convention represent the Negro population of the State pretty extensively[?]" Turner responded:

> Very extensively. There were not members from all the counties. The poverty of our people was so great that in some instances two counties joined together and sent one man to represent them both. *One hundred and eighty delegates* were present from all parts of the State. What is known in Georgia as "the negro belt" was well represented; I mean the middle and southern parts of the State. Several of our delegates had to

walk 50 or 60 miles; and one man, I think, walked 105 miles to get to the convention, owing to the fact that neither he nor his constituents were able to pay his fare there by railroad.[12]

Turner further noted that the convention appointed a special committee on "murder and outrages," and every member submitted a report. "A synopsis of the report was made by the committee," Turner continued, "which I would be glad to place in the hands of this committee if they will allow me." Turner added, "If I had known that I would be called upon by the committee to make a statement in regard to the condition of the colored people, being president of the Civil Rights Association, and receiving letters and reports from all parts of the state, I could have laid before you an immense mass of documents on that subject."[13]

Turner attended the Georgia State Colored Convention in Macon in November 1869. According to reports, "it numbered 236 delegates, representing 56 counties," and resulted in the formation of labor associations for both men and women. Concerned about fair labor practices and equity of pay, delegates adopted resolutions that "declared that capital could only be safe when the laborer is protected," that "capital could have no advantage over united labor," and "that there were no advantages between the two when justice was done." Also, delegates named Turner to serve as editor of a newspaper to support the movement.[14]

In January 1871, Turner called for African Americans to hold another state convention in Atlanta starting February 1, 1871, to address the results of recent elections in which Democrats took control of the Georgia state house. "Whatever is done," wrote Turner in the pages of the *Recorder*, "must, in order to be effective, be the work of mature deliberation, where all the statesmanship, experience, and intellectual sagacity in our possession can be brought into requisition." Turner also was not opposed to attendees from outside of Georgia coming to the convention:

> Representative Colored gentlemen from other States, who may deign to visit us, may expect the courteous usual from those whose interest and destiny are identical. The people are requested to send the most intelligent men in their counties as Delegates, and supply them with means to meet their board and traveling expenses, and to furnish them with all the documentary information possible relative to the late Election, School Organization, Labor Movements, Administration of Justice, Emigration Feeling, Acquisition of Property, and the general condition of our people, etc. Delegates are expected to remain at least three days in session or till their work is completed.[15]

Apparently, due to the issues and concerns the convention attempted to address, there was a need for "more practical understanding and mutual cooperation." Delegates concluded that a "more thorough union of effort, action, and organization" was needed to address what were the beginning stages of dismantling hard-fought Reconstruction victories. Therefore, on February 3, 1871, the convention adopted a preamble and resolution that authorized Turner, as the president of the Georgia state convention, to issue a call in the name of the convention "to be held at such time and place as he and those whom he may advise, shall determine best." Turner issued it, calling for the convention to meet in Columbia, South Carolina, on October 18, 1871. At noon on that day, Turner called the convention to order. After a motion to appoint a Committee on Credentials, delegates elected the permanent organization: president A. J. Ransier, who was then lieutenant governor of South Carolina; secretaries John H. Devereaux of Georgia and Henry E. Hayne of South Carolina; and treasurer Edwin Belcher of Georgia.[16]

About two weeks later, on November 3, 1871, Turner again found himself before Congress testifying about the conditions of African Americans. His testimony gave him an opportunity to talk about the Southern States Convention recently held in Columbia, South Carolina, in 1871. When asked about how many murders had been committed in the state since the spring of 1868, Turner responded: "We held a Southern States convention week before last in Columbia, South Carolina, at which place there were delegates from all the Southern States. We meet together at the request of the committee on murders and outrages, and according to the best of our knowledge and belief, it was estimated that since reconstruction between fifteen hundred and sixteen hundred had been perpetrated."[17]

When his interlocutor asked whether it was "in the South," Turner answered, "No, in the State of Georgia." When pressed on how many murders have happened in all the southern states since 1868, Turner responded that it had not been "less than twenty thousand." That number, Turner noted, was what delegates had agreed upon based on the reporting that each delegate made to the Murder and Outrages Committee. When the congressman asked whether they had published the proceedings from the convention, Turner responded, "They are now in press for publication. I will say, however, that it was thought best not to insert it in our proceedings this estimate. While it was put in our report, *it was stricken out afterward, that particular feature will not appear when our proceedings* come to be published. The report was curtailed to a small document from what it was originally."[18]

On October 7, 1875, fifty delegates held a convention in Augusta, Georgia, for "refuting charges that Negroes intended an insurrection and to determine what course was best for the colored race to pursue." Turner took a more active role in this convention. In a speech delivered at the convention, Turner critiqued the government for its oppression of African Americans. This led Turner to promote the idea of African emigration. He argued that if African Americans emigrated, they would succeed at obtaining rights in Africa that they could not get in America. Reportedly, the speech did not go over well. The Jackson, Mississippi, *Daily Clarion* reported that Turner's

"proposition did not meet with very cordial approval." Other delegates acknowledged that while the "American frying pan might be hot, the African
fire was considerably hotter." After some more debate, the delegates decided
to postpone the emigration question until a future occasion.[19]

Turner and the
1893 National Colored Convention

Eight years later, after the gains made during Reconstruction began to wane
and the Colored Conventions movement was transforming into new shapes
and forms, Turner insisted that the conventions were still important. Writing in the *Christian Recorder* in February 1883, Turner reminded his audience of the importance of Colored Conventions.

> I think it was a great mistake to abolish colored conventions, if it was
> done at the bidding of Mr. (Frederick) Douglas, that prince of Negroes. A
> national colored convention has been greatly needed for the last several
> years. If the Northern Negro is satisfied with matters and things, we of
> the South are far from being. Indeed I have been thinking of calling one
> for the last twelve months; not political but a civil and moral conven-
> tion. Gov. (Pinckney Benton Stewart) Pinchback said to me, a few years
> ago, that the colored people should hold a national convention every
> three or four years if they could to have grievances and complaints.
> Such a convention is needed more, yes far more needed, than any mere
> self-improvised committees.[20]

Ten years later, Turner would call for a national convention with the hope
of offering a significant emigration plan that delegates could support. Despite negative views of emigration from most African American leaders,
Turner, in the *Voice of Missions*, issued the initial call:

> I do not believe that there is any manhood future in this country for the
> Negro and that his future existence, to say nothing of his future happi-
> ness, will depend upon his nationalization. . . . But knowing that thou-
> sands and tens of thousands see our present conditions and our future
> about as I do, and after waiting for four years or more for some of our
> colored statesmen or leaders to call a national convention or to propose
> some plan of speaking to the nation or to the world, or to project some
> measure that will remedy our condition, or will even suggest a remedy,
> and finding no one among the anti-emigrational party or anti-Negro na-
> tionalization party disposed to do so, and believing that further silence
> is not only a disgrace but a crime, I have resolved to issue a call in the
> near future for a national convention to be held in the city of Cincinnati,
> where a spacious edifice is at our disposal, to meet sometime in No-
> vember, for the friends of African repatriation or Negro nationalization

elsewhere, to assemble and adopt such measures for our actions as may commend themselves to our better judgment.[21]

To build interest, Turner followed the initial call in the *Voice of Missions* with another one two months later in the same newspaper reminding people of the importance of the convention. Turner issued a call to action to African Americans in response to the "reign of mobs, lynchers, midnight and midday assassins" that continually terrorized Black people. He also wanted to meet because he argued it was time for African Americans to say and do something for themselves. Turner wrote, "At all events, while other people are saying so much about us and doing so much affecting our destiny, we as a free and distinct race should meet in council and say or do something ourselves; otherwise, mankind will rightly decide that we are not only an inferior race but hopelessly ignorant, woefully degraded and a set of such human brutes that we are not fit to be the vassals of cannibals. Further silence upon our part would be an outrage upon our posterity and a scandalous shame upon our race is now living."[22]

The response was overwhelming. Turner wrote in the *Voice of Missions* that over "three-hundred responsible Negroes" had endorsed the call and that "delegates from all over the world would attend." Even though Turner called for a "Black National Convention," the convention itself became known as "Turner's Convention." He was the leader, the architect, and the convener.[23]

On November 28, 1893, Turner called the convention to order. According to reports in the *Austin Weekly Statesman*, the *Morning Call*, the *Rock Island Daily Argus*, the *Arizona Republican*, and the *Coconino Weekly Sun*, convention attendance was better than many originally expected, with the list of delegates reaching over "five hundred with more to come." The subject of discussion for the convention was the "general welfare of Afro-Americans." The convention named W. H. Council temporary chairman, and J. H. Willis served as temporary secretary. Later the delegates named Turner as the convention's president. Earlier in the day, C. H. J. Taylor, the U.S. minister to Liberia, delivered an address in which he called for the country to pay the heirs of any lynched person $10,000, but many of the delegates came to hear Turner's opening address later that evening.[24] Many knew that Turner favored emigration and knew it was to be the central point of his speech. However, although Turner did address emigration, he spent the majority of his speech addressing lynching and offering a wholesale critique of America.[25]

The subject of lynching took up almost half the speech and provided a good place for Turner to begin a series of critiques against society. Turner joined other Black leaders in trying to explain the widespread assertion that there was an uptick in Black sexual violence, white propaganda that Ida B. Wells would soon upend. Turner argued that "if" Black men raped white women, it was because whites were degrading African Americans. After mentioning that there was only one account of rape involving a Black man in the West Indian Islands, Turner stated:

> It may be, however, due to the fact that there the laws and institutions recognize the black man as a full-fledged citizen and a gentleman and his pride of character and sense of dignity are not degraded and self-respect imparts a higher prompting and gentlemanly bearing to his manhood, and makes him a better citizen and inspires him with more gallantry and nobler principles. For like begets like. While in this country we are degraded by the public press, degraded by class legislation, degraded on the railroads after purchasing first class tickets, degraded at hotels and barbershops, degraded in many states at the ballot box, degraded in most large cities by being compelled to rent houses in alleys and the most disreputable streets. Thus we are degraded in so many respects that all the starch of respectability is taken out of the manhood of millions of our people, and as degradation begets degradation, it is very possible that in many instances we are guilty of doing a series of infamous things that we would not be guilty of, if our environments were different.[26]

Turner reasoned that even if Blacks were guilty of raping white women, lynch law was still unjustified. "Under the genius and theory of civilization throughout the world, no man is guilty of a crime, whatever, until he is arrested, tried by an impartial process of the law and deliberately convicted. . . . Lynching a man is an act of barbarism and cannot be justified by even what a distinguished bishop terms 'emotional insanity.' For even insanity has no authority to intrude its maddened vengeance upon the law and order of the public."[27]

After sharing his concerns about lynching, Turner turns his attention to a scathing critique of the country. The critique comes in two parts—first, in a prophetic warning to the nation and, second, in judgment that America does not have any desire to include African Americans in the covenantal promises.

Turner's convention warning sounds an apocalyptic note that future Black writers and activists, from James Baldwin and Malcolm X to Fannie Lou Hamer and Ta-Nehisi Coates, would resound. "Unless this nation," Turner warned, "awakes from its slumber and calls a halt to the reign of blood and carnage in the land, its dissolution, and utter extermination is only a question of a short time." Turner lists other countries—Egypt, Greece, Babylon, Nineveh, and Rome—that were "numerically stronger than the United States," and he prophetically foresaw the time when America will also *go down* unless it changes its ways.[28]

Sensing that America would not "change its ways," however, Turner offered a bitter and robust critique against the nation. When speaking about the lack of protection that African Americans have in the United States, Turner stated:

The truth is, the nation as such, has no power or disposition to give us manhood protection anyway. Congress had the constitutional power to pursue a runaway slave by legislation into any state and punish the man who would dare conceal him and the Supreme Court of the United States sustained its legislation as long as slavery existed. Now the same Supreme Court has the power to declare that the Negro has no civil rights under the general government that will protect his citizenship, and authorize the states to legislate upon and for us, as they may like; and they are passing special acts to degrade the Negro by authority of the said tribunal, and Congress proposes no remedy by legislation or by such a constitutional amendment as will give us the status of citizenship in the nation that is presumed we are to love and to sacrifice our lives, if need be, in the defense of.[29]

To emphasize his point, Turner highlighted the hypocrisy of the nation.

Yet Congress can legislate for the protection of the fish in the sea and the seals that gambol in our waters, and obligate its men, its money, its navy, its army and its flag to protect, but the 8,000,000 or 10,000,000 of its black men and women, made in the image of God, possessing $265,000,000 worth of taxable property, with all their culture, refinement in many cases, and noble bearing, must be turned off to become the prey of violence, and when we appeal to the general government for protection and recognition, Justice, so-called, drops her scales and says, away with you.[30]

Turner acknowledged those who expressed a hope for "better times for the Negro in this country." However, he saw "no signs of a reformation" in the condition of African Americans. "To the contrary," he argued, "we are being more and more degraded by legislative enactments and judicial decisions." While acknowledging that promoting education and erecting some schools has helped, Turner lamented, "A hundred things have been done to crush out the last vestige of self-respect and to avalanche us with contempt." He then offered a solution. "My remedy," Turner declared, "without a change, is, as it would be folly to attempt resistance and our appeals for better conditions are being unheeded, for that portion of us, at least who feel we are self-reliant to seek other quarters."[31]

Turner's call was for a plan of action that would help relieve the suffering of African Americans, and one way he advocated this position was to proclaim that America owed African Americans "billions of dollars" for slavery. His position would make Turner one of the first to advocate for reparations as a leader in front of such a large audience. In making his case, Turner argued: "This nation justly, rightly, and divinely owes us work for services rendered, billions of dollars, and if we cannot be treated as American people, we should ask for five hundred million dollars, at least, to begin an emigration somewhere, for it will cost, sooner or later, far more than that amount to keep the Negro down unless they re-establish slavery itself. Freedom and perpetual degradation are not in the economy of human events. It is against reason, against nature, against precedent, and against God."[32]

The audience shouted and cheered throughout the speech and erupted in applause at the end.[33] However, by the end of the convention, it was clear that the overwhelming majority of delegates was not in favor of emigration anywhere. Instead of an emigration plan, delegates offered modest proposals and recommendations. For example, there was a four-part resolution passed by the delegates that called for the convention "One—To give the United States courts jurisdiction over all cases of mobs attended with loss of life. Two—empower United States courts to offer rewards for the arrest of offenders. Three—To empower United States marshals to employ detectives to hunt down such offenders. Four—To collect all costs of such prosecution from convicted dependents, or in case one or more defendants are paupers, to make collection from the counties in which they reside."[34]

When the subject of relocation came up for debate on November 30, the committee on emigration produced a lengthy report. According to the *St. Paul Daily Globe*, the session did not start until "dusk of the evening" with its "sole business" on hearing and debating the report. The report "recited the ills of the Afro-American and favored emigration to Africa as the most certain and feasible mode of escape from their ills." One noticeable shift in the report's language was that instead of using the term "colored," committee members used the terms "Negro" or "Afro-American" when referring to Black people.[35]

Even though the report was unanimous in committee, when it came time for the delegates to discuss the plan, only Turner spoke up for it. Turner again reminded the delegates that the "United States was indebted to the Negro" for $40 billion for unrequited labor in slavery." He also suggested that he knew that "2,000,000 negroes in the United States were anxious to emigrate to Africa, and that he could, on short notice, fill 500 ships with them."[36]

As much as Turner talked about the merits of emigration, other speakers "vehemently opposed the report," favoring remaining in the United States and "patiently trusting in God and the future to secure them equality before the law." Seeing delegates not inclined to vote in favor of any emigration plan, Turner adjourned the meeting without any action taken on the subject. After the failure of the emigration report, the convention took up another action, which was to establish an Equal Rights Council with Turner acting as chancellor and to continue to appeal to Congress, governors, and the American people for fair and equal justice.[37]

According to the December 1893 edition of the *Voice of Missions*, the convention remained in "session over four days and nights" and "between seven and eight hundred delegates" took part. It was an "orderly convention, and when a speaker had the floor, no man interrupted." The writer wrote that "it was the largest convention ever held by colored people in the history of the country," and they pledged to raise "at least one hundred thousand dollars" to right the wrongs done to African Americans.[38]

For Turner, however, this was not enough. In an article published after the convention, he sarcastically asked, "What under heaven would [I] want with a national convention of over seven hundred delegates to endorse African emigration, when at least two million colored people here in the South are ready to start to Africa at any moment, if we had a line of steamers running to and fro?" Indeed, Turner had created interest in emigration, but without the funds for transportation, it was just a dream on the part of Turner and his supporters.[39]

Conclusion

When Bishop Henry McNeal Turner thought the time was right and ripe for African Americans to seriously consider emigration, he decided to call a national Colored Convention to discuss the matter. His reasoning was probably threefold. First, Turner saw the conventions as spaces and places to share innovative ideas. Turner knew that emigration was a tough sell, but the conventions had always been a place for delegates to lift, debate, and sometimes celebrate such nontraditional ideas. Second, African Americans ran and operated the conventions. The convention movement demonstrated to Turner and others that Blacks could organize and produce good and effective work if given a chance. However, finally, the reason why Turner harkened back to the convention movement was that while others saw brighter days ahead for African Americans, Turner saw something else. He saw that despite the rhetoric of racial uplift, despite numerous announcements of how much success African Americans achieved, Black folk still suffered in mass numbers. Lynchings went unabated, violence was a daily threat to any African American, and too many lived under the threat of terror every single day. Thus, Turner suggested that what Black folk needed was a national convention to discuss what it means to live unprotected and randomly facing violence every single day of your life. In the end, and despite not getting the support he imagined for his emigration plan, Turner envisioned the Colored Conventions as the place where friends and foes alike could come, talk, disagree, and reason together.

NOTES

1. For more on Bishop Turner, see Andre E. Johnson, *No Future in this Country: The Prophetic Pessimism of Bishop Henry McNeal Turner* (Jackson, MS: University Press of Mississippi, 2020) and *The Forgotten Prophet: Bishop Henry McNeal Turner and the African American Prophetic Tradition* (Lanham, MD: Lexington Books, 2012); and Stephen Ward Angell, *Bishop Henry McNeal Turner and the African American Church in the South* (Knoxville: University of Tennessee Press, 1992).

2. Howard Holman Bell, *A Survey of the Negro Convention Movement: 1830–1861* (New York: Arno, 1969), 13–14.

3. Bell, 2.

4. Bell, 4.

5. Henry McNeal Turner, "Washington Correspondence," *Christian Recorder* (Philadelphia), January 10, 1863, The #HMTProject, http://www.thehenrymcnealturner project.org/2017/05/washington-correspondence-january-10.html.

6. Henry McNeal Turner, "Washington Correspondent," *Christian Recorder*, February 21, 1863, The #HMTProject, http://www.thehenrymcnealturnerproject.org/2017/05 /washington-correspondent-february-21.html.

7. Freedmen's Convention of Georgia (1863: Augusta, GA), *Proceedings of the Freedmen's Convention of Georgia: Assembled at Augusta, January 10th, 1866, Containing the Speeches of Gen'l Tillson, Capt. J. E. Bryant, and Others*, 3, Colored Conventions Project, http://coloredconventions.org/items/show/524.

8. Freedmen's Convention of Georgia (1863), 4–5.

9. Georgia Equal Rights Association (1866: Augusta, GA), *Proceedings of the Council of the Georgia Equal Rights Association: Assembled at Augusta, Ga., April 4th, 1866: Containing the Address of the President, Captain J. E. Bryant, and Resolutions Adopted by the Council*, 4–5, Colored Conventions Project, http://coloredconventions.org/items /show/1193; Convention of the Equal Rights and Educational Association of Georgia (1866: Macon, GA), *Proceedings of the Convention of the Equal Rights and Educational Association of Georgia: Assembled at Macon, October 29th, 1866; Containing the Annual Address of the President, Captain J. E. Bryant*, 2–3, Colored Conventions Project, http:// coloredconventions.org/items/show/525.

10. Henry McNeal Turner, "Letter from Henry McNeal Turner," *Christian Recorder*, November 24, 1866, The #HMTProject, http://www.thehenrymcnealturnerproject .org/2017/10/letter-from-henry-m-turner-november-24.html.

11. Henry McNeal Turner and James Porter, "H. M. Turner; James Porter," *Hartford (CT) Daily Courant*, September 24, 1868, The #HMTProject, http://www.thehenry mcnealturnerproject.org/2017/10/h-m-turner-james-porter-september-24.html.

12. "Testimony from Henry McNeal Turner," in *The Miscellaneous Documents of the House of Representatives for the Third Session of the Fortieth Congress Committee on Reconstruction Relative to the Affairs in Georgia, 1868–69* (Washington, DC: Government Printing Office, 1868), The #HMTProject, http://www.thehenrymcnealturner project.org/2017/10/testimony-from-henry-m.html.

13. "Testimony from Henry McNeal Turner."

14. Georgia State Colored Convention (1869: Macon, GA), *Georgia State Colored Convention, Macon, November 1869*, Colored Conventions Project, http://coloredconventions .org/items/show/569.

15. Henry McNeal Turner and Others, "State Convention of Colored Men," *Christian Recorder*, January 28, 1871, The #HMTProject, http://www.thehenrymcnealturner project.org/2017/10/state-convention-of-colored-men.html.

16. "Call for a Southern States Convention," *Semi-weekly Louisianian* (New Orleans), October 8, 1871, *Chronicling America: Historic American Newspapers*, Library of Congress, http://chroniclingamerica.loc.gov/lccn/sn83016631/1871-10-08/ed-1/seq-3/; The Colored Convention," *Charleston (SC) Daily News*, October 19, 1871, *Chronicling America: Historic American Newspapers*, Library of Congress, http://chroniclingamerica .loc.gov/lccn/sn84026994/1871-10-19/ed-1/seq-1.

17. "Testimony of Henry McNeal Turner," in *Testimony Taken by the Joint Select Committee to Inquire into the Condition of Affairs the Late Insurrectionary States*, vol. 7, *Georgia* (Washington, DC: Government Printing Office, 1871), para. 126, The #HMTProject, http://www.thehenrymcnealturnerproject.org/2017/10/testimony-of-henry -m-turner-november-3.html.

18. "Testimony of Henry McNeal Turner," para. 132.

19. *Dallas (TX) Daily Herald*, October 9, 1875, *Chronicling America: Historic American*

Newspapers, Library of Congress, http://chroniclingamerica.loc.gov/lccn/sn83025733 /1875-10-09/ed-1/seq-1; *Daily Clarion* (Jackson, MS), October 15, 1875, *Chronicling America: Historic American Newspapers*, Library of Congress, http://chroniclingamerica .loc.gov/lccn/sn83045232/1875-10-15/ed-1/seq-2; *Weekly Clarion* (Jackson, MS), October 20, 1875, *Chronicling America: Historic American Newspapers*, Library of Congress, http://chroniclingamerica.loc.gov/lccn/sn83016926/1875-10-20/ed-1/seq-4.

20. Henry McNeal Turner, "The African Question," *Christian Recorder*, February 22, 1883, para. 15, The #HMTProject, http://www.thehenrymcnealturnerproject.org/2017 /05/the-african-question-february-22-1883.html.

21. Henry McNeal Turner, "A Colored National Convention," *Voice of Missions* (Atlanta), August 1, 1893.

22. Henry McNeal Turner, "Colored National Convention Called," *Voice of Missions*, October 1, 1893.

23. Henry McNeal Turner, "Colored National Convention Called," *Voice of Missions*, November 28, 1893.

24. "Oh! Let My People Go," *Austin (TX) Weekly Statesman*, November 30, 1893; "Colored Convention," *Morning Call* (San Francisco), November 29, 1893; "Colored Men in Conference," *Rock Island (IL) Daily Argus*, November 29, 1893; "Asking for Back Pay," *Arizona Republican* (Phoenix), November 29, 1893; "Colored Convention," *Coconino Weekly Sun* (Flagstaff, AZ), December 7, 1893.

25. For more on Turner's speech, see Johnson, *Forgotten Prophet*, chap. 3.

26. Henry McNeal Turner, "Speech of Bishop H. M. Turner before the National Council of Colored Men," *Voice of Missions*, December 1893.

27. Turner.

28. Turner.

29. Turner.

30. Turner.

31. Turner.

32. Turner.

33. Edwin Redkey, *Black Exodus: Black Nationalist and Back-to-Africa Movements, 1890–1910* (New Haven, CT: Yale University Press, 1969), 187.

34. *Morning Call*, November 30, 1893, *Chronicling America: Historic American Newspapers*, Library of Congress, http://chroniclingamerica.loc.gov/lccn/sn94052989/1893 -11-30/ed-1/seq-2.

35. *St. Paul (MN) Daily Globe*, December 1, 1893, *Chronicling America: Historic American Newspapers*, Library of Congress, http://chroniclingamerica.loc.gov/lccn /sn90059522/1893-12-01/ed-1/seq-5.

36. *St. Paul (MN) Daily Globe*, December 1, 1893.

37. *St. Paul (MN) Daily Globe*, December 1, 1893; *Wheeling (WV) Daily Intelligencer*, December 2, 1893, *Chronicling America: Historic American Newspapers*, Library of Congress, http://chroniclingamerica.loc.gov/lccn/sn84026844/1893-12-02/ed-1/seq-1; "A Great Colored Convention," *Voice of Missions*, December 1, 1893.

38. "Great Colored Convention."

39. Johnson, *Forgotten Prophet*, 91.

A CONVENTION OF GRUMBLERS!

Creating Black Texans and
Reproducing Heteropatriarchy

Daina Ramey Berry and
Jermaine Thibodeaux

I n the Sunday edition of the *Brenham Daily Banner*, the local central Texas newspaper reported that a "large number of colored men met at the city hall and elected delegates to the State convention of colored men to be held at Austin on the 10th" of July. Of those assembled at the Brenham government building, "forty-five delegates were elected" to attend the 1883 State Convention of Colored Men of Texas some ninety miles away. And while in Austin, the assembled convention participants would eventually "elect delegates to the national colored convention which [would] meet in Washington, D.C., in November next." As had been customary since the first Colored Convention held in the state in 1866, this new class of chosen delegates contained proven, civic-minded community leaders that hailed from a broad cross-section of Black Texas society. Many of the men selected at the Brenham city hall were well-known "preachers, school teachers, farmers, mechanics" from the surrounding community. By highlighting the presumed respectability of these chosen Black delegates, the *Daily Banner* invoked prevalent racial stereotypes by casually reminding its readers that the Brenham "meeting was composed exclusively of colored men" and, notwithstanding this particular fact, surprisingly, the gathering "was quiet, orderly, and businesslike."[1] Undoubtedly, what transpired in Brenham on that muggy summer day was in keeping with the well-choreographed performances that played out in numerous Texas towns and cities on the eve of the 1883 Colored Men's Convention. Black men across the state gathered to choose the best among their ranks to participate in the important upcoming statewide convention.

When the Austin-based Colored Men's Convention commenced on July 10, 1883, several dozen Black men from across the state filed into the state capitol building and assumed their places in a cordoned-off hallway. There, they vigorously debated some of the hot-button issues afflicting their various communities. Though underwhelming, the official meeting space for the convention confirmed the harsh realities of Jim Crow Texas, yet it did not distract the delegates from pursuing the important business they came to address. First, Rev. M. Henson led the convention delegates and visitors in a series of devotional exercises in an effort to set a solemn tone for the three-day event. Shortly thereafter, those in attendance elected Rev. Abraham Grant, a prominent African Methodist Episcopal Church minister and Florida native, as temporary president of the convention and Rev. Isaiah Benjamin Scott as its secretary.[2] Hoping for both accurate and widely disseminated reporting of the proceedings, the convention officers granted "reporters of the city and State papers" floor seats to record the convention sessions for the general public and the historical record. In all, there were four Colored Texas newspapers in attendance: the *Austin Citizen*, the Paris *People's Informer*, the Dallas *Christian Star*, and the Marshall *Baptist Journal*.[3]

Accurate attendance proved difficult to calculate and slowed down some of the early business of the Committee on Credentials. The chair expressed his frustration with the lack of accessible attendance information, especially since he hoped to assign a member from each congressional district to the committee. Despite the challenge of "not having a roll of the Convention" on hand, the chair received the delegates' approval to organize a committee of eleven members.[4] After this small hiccup, the delegates moved to more pressing matters and "in a very strong light" began to articulate the "grievances of the colored people in the State of Texas."[5]

Although the State Convention of Colored Men met in Austin in the summer of 1883, Black Texans were already in the center of a brewing political storm and ever-changing racial dynamics across the state. Historian Alwyn Barr notes that the "end of Reconstruction did not halt Black political participation in Texas, though it resulted in a lessening of Negro involvement and influence."[6] The once vanquished Democratic Party "solidified its control of the state administration in the mid-1870s by eliminating the integrated State Police and militia" and used the full weight and force of the state to roll back many of the hard-won gains Black Texans had achieved in the aftermath of the Civil War.[7] Thus, not only did Black men in Texas lose valuable social and economic standing with their expulsion from these two law enforcement bodies, but they also suffered a notable decline in valuable political capital at the state level. In fact, Black Texans witnessed dwindling representation in the state legislature and in various local governments. Moreover, Blacks' waning political power, economic misfortune, and a surge in racial violence throughout the state bestowed a heightened significance to the 1883 Colored Men's Convention, especially during a decade in which four statewide Colored conventions were already held. This Austin meeting, though, came at a prime moment, one that Black Texans proved eager to assess. They knew that in order to battle the shifting social and political climate in the state, an effective, well-articulated plan of attack was needed. The time had come to improve the overall quality of life for Black Texans. For many, the Colored Men's Convention was a reasonable place to begin this serious and necessary work. Surprisingly, a convention aimed at uncovering and resolving many of the ills plaguing Black Texans did not see the need for Black women's participation in the three-day meeting.

The Black male delegates at the Austin Colored Men's Convention believed it both practical and justifiable to address a host of issues that affected *all* Black Texans, yet at the same time they excluded Black women from attending the July convention. By marginalizing and even silencing Black women, delegates, in effect, showed their support for decades of sex discrimination and gender disenfranchisement, long threads in American history. The confounding actions of the assembled male delegates were a slap in the face to the many women activists who had been involved in political activism and protests in Texas for decades. And when considering the overall organization and execution of the 1883 Colored Men's Convention, is it not too farfetched to ask if these men were nothing more than anxious patriarchs seeking to reclaim their political authority in state and local politics, as so many had done during Reconstruction? Or, were they simply responding to a gradual shift away from the community- and family-centered political discourse and practice that thrived during slavery? Perhaps the convention's Black male delegates realized that an individualistic and even heteropatriarchal brand of Black Texas politics would become the new normal in Texas politics. Clearly, the 1883 Colored Men's Convention marked a noticeable change in the trajectory and character of African American politics in the Lone Star State. Gender became a roadblock for Black women activists, yet it served as the force that allowed Black men to reassert themselves in state matters at a time when Black political power was on the decline.

Following the passage of the Fifteenth Amendment (1870), Black men in Texas and across the nation began to exercise their citizenship rights by voting and participating in the legislative process. By contrast, Black women, nonetheless, did not merely disappear into the background, because their lives changed as well. They witnessed a shift in both intra- and interracial politics, namely as their male counterparts received the right to vote and they did not. Notwithstanding entrenched racial and gender constraints of the times, Black women remained politically engaged in both the public and private spheres. In fact, they shunned apolitical labels and continued to serve as outspoken activists within the confines of their homes and their broader communities. Historian Elsa Barkley Brown notes that on the eve of emancipation, "a vision of citizenship and freedom also inspired" both Black men and women to make the most sense of their newfound status. This "vision" informed both their interracial and intraracial politics, which were mainly "gender and class-inclusive." In what would become new freedmen's towns and Black neighborhoods scattered throughout the South, "all people were assumed to have a stake in and therefore a voice in the issues affecting the community, and decisions were reached only after debate and discussion among all."[8] Consequently, as longtime political agents themselves and as valued voices within their communities since slavery, Black women did not necessarily internalize the denial of national suffrage, for example, as an absolute foreclosure on their political potential. If anything, such a gendered exclusion amplified their voice. Far away from Texas in the nation's capital, Mary Ann Shadd Cary, the first woman to enroll in the Howard University School of Law, after she served as the first Black woman newspaper editor in North America, was one of many Black women who advocated for Black women's suffrage alongside recently conferred universal male suffrage. According to historian Paula Giddings, Shadd Cary noted that the "Fourteenth and Fifteenth Amendments said that all Blacks were citizens with the right to vote," and she labored to have the word "'male' be taken out of the Constitution," insisting that the emphasis, instead, should fall on the notion of citizen, a category to which *both* Black men and women belonged at this juncture.[9] Moreover, many Black women long realized that access to the ballot or a seat in a legislative body were not the only ways to affect political and social change in their worlds; they found other ways to "negotiate and transform" the nation's highly racialized and gendered political terrain. Many of their ideologies and political strategies grew out of a realization of the Black community's collective power and did not rest on a singular individual's or a single sex's ability to do all of the advocating and pushing for change.

The passage of the Civil Rights Act of 1875, which guaranteed African Americans equal treatment in various aspects of public life, emboldened one Black Texas woman, Milly Anderson, to deploy the political and legal means available to her in pursuit of justice and equality. Anderson filed a lawsuit in federal district court against the Houston and Central Railroads for denying her admission to the first-class "ladies car," a space typically reserved for white women. Because Anderson had paid the first-class fare for her seat, federal judge Thomas H. Duval issued the following opinion: "That every citizen of the United States, male or female, native born or naturalized, white or black, who pays to the carrier the fare demanded for the best accommodations, is entitled to the best provided for the different sexes."[10] Though she was unable to vote or hold elected office, Anderson refused to be silenced or rendered altogether invisible by a largely male and white justice system. As a self-proclaimed "lady," she sought the same treatment as her white counterparts, but she quickly realized that not even money or class would spare her from the day-to-day predations experienced by countless Black women in Texas and across the South. For Anderson and other Black women, the mundaneness of southern racial and gender discrimination was not enough to halt steadfast challenges to the status quo. In fact, Anderson's demonstrated political savvy and her activist spirit proved too tenacious for that goliath ultimately known as Jim Crow. And through her determination and astute use of the law, Anderson prevailed—not only for herself but for all Black women in Texas. Anderson's turn to the courts further underscored Black women's ability to imagine a version of freedom and citizenship in which they were already stakeholders, even when consistently pushed to the margins, discounted, or muted by overwhelming patriarchal forces—both Black and white.

Black women pushed forward even outside of the formal channels of political power. In the thick of the sweltering mid-July Texas heat in 1877, Black Galveston-area domestic servants and laundresses went on strike. Unsatisfied with their wages and working conditions, these women withheld their services and demanded a wage increase to $1.50 per day or $9.00 per week. The pay increase they sought was an expression of how they valued themselves and how they chose to assert their right to collectively bargain for what they believed were fair wages. Some lost their livelihoods because of their labor protest, but the defiant political statement they made by advocating for an equitable wage surely resonated with the Texas public. Within days, news of the strike made it onto the pages of various state newspapers and the laundry strike became a subject of everyday conversation throughout the state.

Surprisingly, though, no record exists that shows if white employers ever met the laundresses' demands. Nonetheless, the act of organizing a labor strike during an era in which women, and especially Black women, had little formal political clout further spotlights the long history of Black Texas women recognizing their agency and the totality of their worth both as laborers and entrepreneurs. Together, these two separate events, Milly Anderson's federal lawsuit and the Galveston laundresses' strike, also reveal that Black women in Texas cultivated and practiced a form of politics outside and even within striking proximity to male-dominated political spaces, and not necessarily because they wanted to but because they had to. And in some respects, Black women in Texas were ahead of their time in terms of their dogged, public activism.[11] Black Texas women evinced a political adeptness and an awareness of their individual and collective power long before the emergence of a robust Black clubwomen's movement in the state and across the nation. Thus their glaring absence from the nearly four-decades-long Colored Men's Convention movement in the Lone Star State is a gross erasure that should encourage scholars to consider a sustained exploration and recovery of Black women's political and intellectual history.

Black Texans began to organize and hold their own conventions in the state during Reconstruction. The last Colored men's convention took place in Houston in 1895 at the United Brothers Friendship Hall, and there the delegates tackled a wide range of topics—from politics to the surge of anti-Black violence and lynchings.[12] Before Black men organized their own conventions, they eagerly participated in the state's Reconstruction constitutional conventions from as early as 1869. Black women did not attend these gatherings, yet they found other ways to organize and encourage political engagement among their menfolk. In fact, the historical record of Texas is replete with examples of Black women organizing "in churches, in schoolhouses, and in town meetings to express their concerns and act upon their grievances." And when they could, some Black women proved themselves as such dedicated political activists that the Houston press, for example, reported in June 1869 that "80 negro women and 150 negro men were present" at a local meeting of Radical Republicans.[13] Over time, the 1869 Republican Convention would be the exception rather than the rule that describes the extent to which some Black Texas women would go to be heard and included in statewide political discussions.

Though usually separated by sex at various political functions throughout the nineteenth century, all Black Texans addressed the deplorable conditions they encountered in towns and cities across the state. Between 1870 and the 1890, life in the Lone Star State mirrored patterns of Black existence in all other southern and many northern states. Specifically, racial discrimination, state and extralegal violence, and varied forms of gender and even class oppression remained hardcore daily realities for Black Texans.

From 1870 to 1899, the forty-two Black men who served in the Texas legislature fought tirelessly to ameliorate these conditions and through their service "continued to address the needs of women and Blacks."[14] Moreover, in the formal political space of the Texas legislature, Black women's needs were seemingly tended to, but in no way did Black legislators allow women's issues to dominate their political agendas; nor did these men permit or welcome Black Texan women to do their own bidding within the halls of these exclusive spaces. In these corridors of power, Black women were certainly thought of and spoken for, but once more, male politicians refused to invite them to the table as full political agents in the fight for change in the state. Furthermore, this particular pattern of political engagement also later informed how Black Texans would organize and conduct their business at the various Colored Conventions throughout the 1880s and 1890s.

When that group of prominent Black Texas men met in convention at Austin in July of 1883, their proceedings undoubtedly covered the pressing topic of civil rights, but their meeting also planned to address the quickly deteriorating social and economic conditions affecting Blacks across the state. Historian Alwyn Barr maintains that "African Americans held four conventions from 1883 to 1889" and, each time, "they expressed a high level of concern about shrinking political clout, decreased economic opportunity, and increased racial violence and discrimination."[15] Just as the conventions' agendas proved rather predictable so too did the long-standing tradition of all-male convention delegations; women were to be discussed but not invited to join the male delegates in crafting an inclusive agenda that took seriously women's voices and experiences. Not a single woman appeared in the 1883 convention notes, and even the janitor that the convention secretary was "authorized to employ" was most likely a man.[16] Thus, it is safe to assume that the wives of convention delegates were also barred from entering the convention space, if they traveled with their husbands at all, since they are not referenced in speech transcripts or the convention minutes.

At the start of the 1883 Austin convention, delegates roundly criticized a recent Supreme Court decision that declared the 1875 Civil Rights Act unconstitutional.[17] For Black Texans in general and Black women in particular, the high court's decision represented a regrettable step backward in the long fight to ensure social parity between Blacks and whites in the aftermath of emancipation. After all, it was the particular 1875 Civil Rights Act that allowed Milly Anderson to sue and win her case for the denial of her rightful seat in the "ladies car" on a Texas train that same year. The Austin convention delegates wanted to hear from high-ranking state officials, so they invited the governor into their space. Texas governor John Ireland, a Democrat and noted secessionist, spoke at the nonpartisan Austin convention on day two of the proceedings. Ireland made it known that he would not dabble too much in the divisive racial politics of the day during his remarks. The convention proceedings noted the governor's "plain and direct address," and then afterward, the delegates assured Governor Ireland that "nothing would be done with the intention of severing the races" during the convention, "as their interests are one," for they are all Texans. Even after reassuring the governor that their intentions were not necessarily to further divide the races, these Black men wanted to foreground their concerns about the constant indignities visited upon Black Texas women. And while they welcomed Ireland's compliments of the good work being done at the Prairie View State Normal School and were generally respectful during the governor's talk, many of the convention delegates believed the governor's remarks simply fell short of genuinely acknowledging the growing adversities faced by Black Texans. Once Abraham Grant, the convention president, took to the podium following the governor's speech, he reiterated the delegates' pledge to steer clear of divisive political rhetoric in the presence of the governor, but he reminded Governor Ireland to great applause, "As long as the railroads sell us and our wives and daughters first-class tickets and defraud us by compelling us to ride in the second-class cars, where there is smoking, chewing, drinking and swearing, so long will colored men continue to agitate the question of railroad grievances."[18] From Grant's remarks, one could recognize that the assembled men felt compelled, because of their race and sex, to protect the women in their lives from wanton de facto and de jure discrimination. Surprisingly absent from Grant's remarks, however, was any suggestion of sons or other male relatives needing the same protection despite the all-too-common lynchings and vigilante violence directed at Black men throughout the state. It was obvious that the convention delegates believed Black men and boys could presumably fend for themselves in ways that Black women and girls could not. Thus, even in their attempt to address widespread Black oppression, which certainly affected Black women as well, convention delegates were seemingly unable to advocate for racial equality and justice without clinging to gender stereotypes, hegemonic notions of paternalism, and, of course, entrenched patriarchy.

Holding true to their pledge to avoid deeply political topics while the governor was present, the delegates decided to focus their energies on the seemingly safer social and economic issues plaguing the Black community. These issues included temperance, homesteading rights, and, more important, education reform and a repeal of slavery-era miscegenation statutes.

The latter two issues were unquestionably political and as germane to Black women's lives as they were to the room of gathered Black male attendees. Together, both topics consumed a great deal of debate time on the convention floor and further reflected how racial concerns were intimately bound to gender conventions of the times.

Even though Black women did not physically attend the 1883 Colored Men's Convention, their invisible presence, or the very thought of Black women, helped shape the contours of most of the deliberations that unfolded during the meeting. Even in the midst of their physical occlusion, matters explicitly concerning Black women took up tremendous space during the convention. Though physically absent, their voices, namely the cross-gender conversations the men brought to Austin with them, resonated loudly as the principled, moralizing guides for much of the convention's debates. A care and concern for Black women and, arguably, a sense of manly obligation guided both what appeared on the convention's agenda and how the delegates of the Austin Colored Convention tackled many of those topics.

Again, as Black Texas men met throughout the 1880s to discuss issues that affected their status as voters and taxpaying citizens with standing in their own communities, these homosocial gatherings "did on some occasions [directly] address issues related to women and gender roles."[19] Not surprisingly, convention delegates offered strong gendered and class-based admonitions to Black Texas women whenever afforded the opportunity. One resolution proffered at the 1883 convention "urged women to be responsible mothers and wives, especially in raising children."[20] Ironically, there was neither a discussion of the values of fatherhood nor a public scolding of Black men to act as responsible parents or husbands to balance the debate. The delegates' advice to Black women seems to suggest that the strength and survival of the Black family and the Black community rested largely, if not exclusively, on the shoulders of women. Moreover, in many ways, these gendered and class-based instructions reeked of paternalism and further reinforced the specter of heteropatriarchy present at the convention and within the Black Texas community writ large.[21] This overtly masculine tone characterized the political ethos of much of the 1883 Colored Men's Convention and, frankly, *all* of the subsequent Texas Colored Conventions.

Throughout successive convention meetings during the 1880s, including the 1883 Austin convention, male delegates publicly chided Black women for straying outside of the bounds of respectability politics.[22] Recent scholarship by African American women historians has added to our understanding of respectability. There is a confirmed push against the very notion of respectable women and the value of Black respectability in an unapologetic white supremacist society.[23] So it should not be surprising that the 1883 Colored Men's Convention actually contained a Committee on the Moral Advancement of the People, which tackled a broad range of issues from anti-gambling crusades to education reforms and, most notably, "the immorality of colored women."[24] Men, it seemed, were rarely the explicit targets of this committee or of the convention delegates as a whole. Rather, Black women's actions, words, and movements were closely scrutinized and policed not only by white Texans but also by the Black men in their lives and certainly by those who attended these Colored Men's Conventions. And since convention delegates were often members of the Black elite, namely the clergy, their elevated social position imbued their words and moralizing with a certain heft and irreproachability. In fact, ministers frequently presided over convention proceedings, and a plurality of convention delegates "ranked as good examples of the growing Black middle class in the state."[25] Moreover, one could argue that a gathering of Black men preaching *at* Black women also signaled to white male elites that *this* group of Black men had *their* women under control and therefore were equally worthy patriarchs in a state and region where rigid gender, like racial, conventions also mattered. As many of these convention delegates, according to Alwyn Barr, "had established themselves as community leaders engaged in a variety of activities that sustained" Black Texas, their selections as delegates to these Colored Conventions were indeed public acknowledgments of their roles as race and moral leaders. Additionally, their presence at and participation in these Colored Men's Conventions also served as an open endorsement of a particular brand of Black respectability politics, which undeniably centered maleness. These chosen delegates' communally conferred status as the "best men" of the race could be deployed to convince prejudiced white Texans that Blacks were indeed worthy of better opportunities and more respectful treatment in their quotidian affairs.[26]

Collectively, the delegates at the 1883 Austin Colored Men's Convention found antebellum miscegenation statutes "more controversial than the subject of equal accommodations," and "many believed the deeply-held conviction by whites of the social inferiority of blacks . . . derived from the social attitudes inherent in the laws against intermarriage between the races."[27] Starting with an 1858 law and for many years after Reconstruction, Texas lawmakers forbade cohabitation and intermarriage between whites and Blacks but said nothing of casual sexual relations across the color line. Between 1879 and 1882, legal authorities only punished whites who married Blacks and even went as far as to publish in the press "reported cases of intermarriage or even rumors of one that came to their attention."[28] And while intermarriage received a bulk of the courts' attention in these types of matters, interracial sex or cohabitation, on the other hand, often went unpunished or was ignored altogether by white power brokers, according to frustrated convention delegates. Specifically, white Texas men could and did engage in casual sex with Black women or Black sex workers without legal sanction, but when an interracial relationship evolved into legitimate marriage, the newly wedded couple would face stiff felony charges for violating the antimiscegenation statutes. This double standard infuriated many Black Texas men, especially since they did not claim, if they so chose, the same unchecked access to white women's bodies during this time. After all, the myth of the Black rapist and the fragile white lady continued to haunt the southern imagination long after Reconstruction, and this particular trope undoubtedly shaped the contours of southern social relations well into the twentieth century.

Moreover, the Austin Colored Men's Convention delegates lamented the fact that white men typically enjoyed unfettered access to Black women's bodies and their sexuality just as they had during slavery. They also decried the fact that the problematic law "impose[d] an insignificant fine only for the same persons to live together in unlawful wedlock, or have carnal intercourse with each other without being married." And in cases of cross-racial cohabitation, "ninety-nine cases in one hundred" are "not even reported, or if reported not punished."[29] Delegates at the 1883 Austin convention wanted the latest version of the state's miscegenation law repealed. In 1877, the Texas legislature invalidated the 1858 statute, citing it as a slavery-era law that technically viewed Blacks as property. By 1882, the state adopted a new miscegenation code, which forbade interracial marriage *and* sexual relations.[30] This latest iteration of the law, from the convention delegates' perspective, constituted both moral and legal hypocrisy and had the most debilitating effect on Black women in particular and especially those women already at the margins of Black society. The newly revised yet highly questionable 1882 miscegenation law, according to convention delegates, "makes pretensions to preserving public morals, common decency and chastity" yet does little to protect the "most promising" Black women from white aggressors and, unfortunately, "increase[s] immorality in the lower classes of both races to an alarming extent."[31] As the chosen "best men" from their respective communities, the assembled delegates at the Austin Colored Men's Convention deemed it a matter of most pressing urgency to highlight the problematic miscegenation law and fight for its repeal. And once more, it was Black men alone who raised their distinct objections to the antimiscegenation law during convention proceedings. Nevertheless, one can only imagine how the physical presence of Black women at the convention may have enriched those conversations and added a layer of nuance that stemmed directly from Black women's lived experiences. That the convention delegates spoke *of* and *for* both Black men and women on this issue can be read simply as men assuming they knew better and therefore did not need actual women's testimonies and input to craft a statement in opposition to the antimiscegenation law. If anything, this shameless sex chauvinism was on full display right alongside the patently racist antimiscegenation statutes the male delegates spent hours decrying.

And while the delegates' worries about the uneven legal consequences of interracial sex appeared mostly genuine, their general heteropatriarchal posture and lack of inclusivity during much of the convention arguably weakened many of their racial concerns. For one, these convention delegates assumed the roles of protectors and guardians of Black women and simultaneously advocated a particularly wholesome brand of morality and sexuality within the Black community. Their charge was not to defend merely *all* Black women but to save those especially deemed "most promising," or less sullied and certainly heterosexual, from the transgressions of white male predators. Neither the law nor the convention delegates presumed the possibility of authentic, organic interracial or even same-sex relations within the Black community. Instead, such myopic thinking foreclosed the realization or even the possibility of a range of Black sexual experiences and couplings. Furthermore, the effort and the assumed need to defend Black women from this unjust miscegenation statute merely reinforced heteropatriarchy in the name of racial uplift, and to some degree, the convention's delegates, perhaps unwittingly, denied Black women the agency to act as authorities over their own sexuality. The men set the parameters of what good, wholesome Black sexuality would look like, again, without consulting Black women. While the men's intentions may have been grounded in the spirit of community preservation and protection, one could also argue that not only did convention delegates buy into hegemonic notions of southern manhood and Black masculinity, but their insistence on policing Black women's bodies, hearts, and minds also avails their actions to closer scrutiny and highlights just how pervasive gender and even class politics were at the 1883 Colored Men's Convention. Again, though Black women were not physically present in this space, the very *thought* of them and the actual (in)visibility of their bodies prompted a great deal of male-centered discussion and action about and for them and presumably on their behalf. Sadly, however, most of those discussions were couched in blatantly problematic gendered, political, and classed terms, and unfortunately, Black women themselves were not present at the Austin convention to offer any rebuttal.

Like the controversial issue of miscegenation, statewide efforts to reform education also consumed the agenda during the 1883 Colored Men's Convention. Ultimately, a close reading of the convention's proceedings reveals again how elements of racial paternalism and heteropatriarchy shaped the delegates' response to the growing education crisis in the state. Higher education for Black Texans began immediately after Reconstruction. Some of the first Black schools were private institutions founded primarily by white religious groups, and most of the state's Black colleges were founded as co-educational institutions.[32] Tillotson Institute in Austin was one of the first institutions of higher education established for Black Texans and the first college in Austin. The University of Texas at Austin was founded in 1881 and opened its doors in 1883. Though many of the private institutions such as Tillotson Institute "struggled to overcome their extremely modest beginnings," they still served as vital centers of education and social uplift within Black communities.[33] Students at Tillotson, for example, were constantly reminded that their presence on campus stemmed primarily from the school's belief that they, like the delegates of the Colored Conventions, constituted the "elect of their race."[34] Chartered in 1877 by the American Missionary Society, Tillotson opened its doors for the first time on January 17, 1881. In its inaugural class of 250 students, school administrators advised incoming college women to bring "one sheet, pillow slip, dress, skirt, pair drawers, under vest, night gown, apron, two towels, pair hose, shirt waist, four handkerchiefs."[35] School officials also discouraged new pupils from participating in activities that appeared in conflict with the school's Christian mission, so from the very beginning, Tillotson officials attempted to police students' dress and social habits. Namely, the school dictated a respectable dress code and discouraged college women from traveling on the Sabbath and from wearing garments too "elaborately trimmed."[36] Tillotson's president, W. E. Brooks, who was described by the American Missionary Society as "a gentleman of evident Christian piety, an accomplished scholar, and a man thoroughly impressed with the dignity and importance of his trust," was present at the 1883 Colored Men's Convention, though the specifics of his remarks there remain elusive.[37] The recorded proceedings simply note, "On invitation, he made a few remarks, which were well-received."[38] Though the convention's delegates tackled funding disparities for the state's public schools, it can be inferred that Brooks was present to urge for additional support of the few Black colleges in the state.

By the 1880s, Black Texas public officials and citizens duly noted the declining conditions at many Black colleges and lamented the state's failure to do its part to ensure the adequate and fair funding of both free schools and state colleges. At the 1883 Colored Men's Convention, assembled delegates wanted federal funds to build more schools for Black youth, and some even called for the state legislature to appropriate additional money to expand a recently founded college for African Americans. Convention delegates also demanded that the state exercise more oversight of municipal authorities and how they dispersed funding for Black schools in particular. Noting that many local cities "make shameful discrimination" in the matter of school funding because they simply "refuse to give colored schools the same provisions as to character of buildings, furniture, number and grade of teachers as required by law," convention delegates were careful to direct blame at "some of the local authorities" and not at "the provisions made by the Legislature."[39] Casting blame away from the powerful elected officials in Austin was a learned strategy throughout the convention movement in the state. That is not to say that this was a uniform or universal practice, as there were many moments when convention delegates called to task state politicians for their lack of gravitas on Black issues or statewide concerns that adversely affected Black Texans at a disproportionate rate. It was deemed more productive and albeit safer to castigate local political officials or members of the Black community than Austin's mighty power brokers.

When it came time to request more funding and state attention to institutions of higher education, convention delegates held up Prairie View A&M University as a jewel in the public education system. However, at the same time, the university came to symbolize how the 1883 Colored Men's Convention delegates wielded their gendered power in ways that proved limiting to

Black women. Established in 1876, Prairie View A&M University was in dire need of financial resources by the time the Colored Men's Convention met in the early 1880s. Convention delegates viewed Prairie View as both an affordable and sustainable educational option for the state's Black population. And many delegates sought to exploit the school's growing female enrollment by compelling school administrators to craft a curriculum in which the enrolled women would learn how "to take care of the home" and make it "pleasing and attractive" for their husbands and children.[40] Armed with their educations in home economics and teacher training, freshly graduated Prairie View women would then go out into the world and presumably do little to interfere with the deeply entrenched political world crafted and dominated by men. It is notable that Black Texas colleges produced a majority of the state's teachers and educated citizens. In particular, Black women college graduates over time "returned to their communities in greater numbers to teach, to lead, and to serve as role models in churches, clubs, community organizations and institutions."[41] Black women saw education as a vehicle to reaching both personal and larger communal goals. Education, they believed, would, in many respects, liberate them and the whole of society from a litany of social and ethical ailments, particularly since women were barred from numerous professions despite possessing "the energies and talents" to "serve the children and parents in their neighborhoods and communities."[42] For Black women, educational attainment provided a stepping stone to greater possibilities not just for themselves but for the entirety of the race. Yet upon closer examination, the fact that Black women were the most educated and produced most of the state's Black educated citizens troubles the ironic exclusion of many of these women from a significant gathering such as a Colored Convention.

Furthermore, the influential delegates at the 1883 Austin Colored Men's Convention and subsequent Colored Conventions worked diligently to shape the educational outcomes for Black Texas women, all with the hope that the men's vision of education, and perhaps freedom, for Black women would keep them a subordinate sex in most areas of life. The convention delegates' dabbling in the inner workings of higher education—from funding to curriculum—also demonstrated both their sense of male privilege and, again, a growing anxiety at a time when both the social and political ground was shifting slowly toward women's liberation more generally and away from Black male leadership in Texas politics writ large.

Ultimately, the 1883 Colored Men's Convention reflected a gradual turning point and eventual crisis in Black Texas politics and gender relations. While male delegates met in convention at several junctures throughout the 1880s, their articulated concerns revealed a move away from a more inclusive, collective racial politics to one predicated on male power and racial paternalism. Seemingly gone were the days in which Black men and women debated together and pushed for social and political change that would benefit all and not merely advantage some. Thus, by precluding women from these single-sex gatherings, the assembled male delegates made it possible to speak *at* and *for* Black women rather than speak with them. And in so doing, the delegates at the Colored Men's Convention reproduced, to some extent, the terms of heteropatriarchy and individual liberalism that lived quite comfortably within the political spaces, both formal and informal, of the white mainstream. So while the *Brenham Daily Banner* mocked the 1883 meeting as a "convention of grumblers," noting that those in attendance complained unfairly about the lack of "social equality" for Blacks and worked to further bring about "an antagonism between the races," the Texas newspaper took a page from the 1883 convention's playbook. The *Banner* reminded its readers that "so long as the colored people behave themselves they will be kindly treated by the whites and in every way opportunity will be given them to advance themselves."[43] Interestingly, the Texas press placed an emphasis on Blacks modifying their behavior as a condition for peaceful and improved social relations in the state rather than on addressing systemic factors that perpetuated inequality and anti-Black racism. In several ways, this was the same tactic deployed by the delegates of the 1883 Colored Convention. By vowing not to wade too deeply into politics, the Colored Convention turned the mirror mostly on Black Texas and criticized and chastised while leaving state politicians largely unscathed. Black women, however, were not so fortunate. More than all others, they found themselves on the receiving end of most of the convention's haughty moralizing and palpable heteropatriarchy.

By the 1890s and the turn of the twentieth century, women across the color line began to agitate for more rights and recognition in both the public and private spheres. Without surprise, Black Texas women made their presence known by attending subsequent Colored Conventions in the state and even by participating in meeting proceedings. Though heteropatriarchy shaped the contours of Black Texas politics of the 1880s, its stay was arguably rather brief. Black women knew better and Black men aspired to do better, as both sexes had to work together to later battle Jim and Jane Crow. Furthermore, Black Texans quickly realized that they would have to join forces to agitate and attack all future threats to their survival and coexistence in the racially hostile Lone Star State. By the dawning of the twentieth century, Black Texans—men and women—flexed their political muscles by becoming influential voices in the Grange movement and the future People's Party. The lessons learned at and after Austin also gave Black Texans the organizing strategy and experience needed when it was time to champion antilynching or eradicate the all-white primaries in 1944. If anything, the Colored Conventions movement, both in Texas and nationwide, taught future generations to envision their newfound freedom in bold and certainly intersectional ways. Gender was unquestionably a part of the larger Black freedom struggle and therefore needed to be fully included in all matters of importance to the race.

NOTES

1. *Brenham (TX) Daily Banner*, July 1, 1883.

2. *Austin (TX) Weekly Statesman*, July 12, 1883.

3. *Proceedings of the State Convention of Colored Men of Texas* (Houston: Smallwood and Gray, 1883), 7.

4. *Proceedings*, 1.

5. *Proceedings*, 2.

6. Alwyn Barr, *Black Texans: A History of African Americans in Texas, 1528–1995* (Norman: University of Oklahoma Press, 1996), 70.

7. Barr, 85.

8. Elsa Barkley Brown, "To Catch the Vision of Freedom: Reconstructing Southern Black Women's Political History, 1865–1880," in *African American Women and the Vote, 1837–1960*, ed. Ann Gordon, Bettye Collier-Thomas, John H. Bracey, Arlene Avakian, and Joyce Berkman (Amherst: University of Massachusetts Press, 1997), 66–99. See also Rosalyn Terborg-Penn, *African American Women and the Struggle for the Vote, 1850–1920* (Bloomington: Indiana University Press, 1998).

9. Paula Giddings, *When and Where I Enter: The Impact of Black Women on Race and Sex in America* (New York: Bantam Books, 1984), 70–71.

10. United States v. Dodge, 25 F. Cas. 882 (W.D. Tex. 1877).

11. Another example of a well-documented Black women's labor strike can be found in Tera Hunter's *To 'Joy My Freedom: Southern Black Women's Lives and Labors after the Civil War* (Cambridge, MA: Harvard University Press, 1998). Hunter examines how these Black Atlanta women were propelled by the optimism of emancipation and their newfound rights to fight for greater economic and social equality.

12. Alwyn Barr, "Early Organizing in the Search for Equality: African American Conventions in Late Nineteenth-Century Texas," in *Seeking Inalienable Rights: Texans and their Quests for Justice*, ed. Debra A. Reid (College Station: Texas A &M University Press, 2009), 9.

13. Ruthe Winegarten, *Black Texas Women: 150 Years of Trial and Triumph* (Austin: University of Texas Press, 1995), 66.

14. Weingarten, 66.

15. Alwyn Barr, "Early Organizing," 8.

16. *Proceedings*, 4.

17. The Supreme Court invalidated the 1875 Civil Rights Act in a series of cases that came before the Court and known collectively as the Civil Rights Cases. The Court's main contention was that the law was unconstitutional since it regulated not state action but actions by private entities such as private companies operating hotels or theaters, for example. For more information about the Civil Rights Cases and the fall of the 1875 Civil Rights Act, see John Hope Franklin, "The Enforcement of the Civil Rights Act of 1875," in *Race and History: Selected Essays 1938–1968* (Baton Rouge: Louisiana State University Press, 1989); and Kenneth W. Mack, "Law, Society, Identity, and the Making of the Jim Crow South: Travel and Segregation on Tennessee Railroads, 1875–1905." *Law and Social Inquiry* 24, no. 2 (1999): 377–410.

18. *Proceedings*, 5.

19. Alwyn Barr, "Early Organizing," 10.

20. Barr, 10.

21. By "heteropatriarchy," we simply mean the dominance of heterosexual males in society. We deploy the term in this context because the delegates at the 1883 Colored Men's Convention, and, quite frankly, at all of the others, concerned themselves with matters beyond the political realm. In many cases, the assembled delegates used these gatherings to reinforce conventional gender expectations and to comment on and police Black women's sexuality. For these reasons, the term "patriarchy" alone does not suffice. Few scholars have written about heteropatriarchy in particular,

but a key starting point is Andrea Smith, "Heteropatriarchy and the Three Pillars of White Supremacy: Rethinking Women of Color Organizing," in *Color of Violence: The INCITE! Anthology*, ed. INCITE! Women of Color against Violence (Durham, NC: Duke University Press, 2016), 66–73.

22. For a thorough discussion of "respectability politics," see Evelyn Brooks Higginbotham, *Righteous Discontent: The Women's Movement in the Black Baptist Church, 1880–1920* (Cambridge, MA: Harvard University Press, 1993); Victoria W. Wolcott, *Remaking Respectability: African-American Women in Interwar Detroit* (Chapel Hill: University of North Carolina Press, 2001); E. Frances White, *Dark Continent of Our Bodies: Black Feminism and the Politics of Respectability* (Philadelphia: Temple University Press, 2001); and Frederick C. Harris, "The Rise of Respectability Politics," *Dissent*, Winter 2014.

23. For more recent critiques of the notion of respectability politics, see Brittney C. Cooper, *Beyond Respectability: The Intellectual Thought of Race Women* (Urbana: University of Illinois Press, 2017); and Treva B. Lindsay, *Colored No More: Reinventing Black Womanhood in Washington, D.C.* (Urbana: University of Illinois Press, 2017).

24. *Proceedings*, 9.

25. Barr, "Early Organizing," 11.

26. Interestingly, though, the Colored Convention delegates were not in staunch opposition to the wave of segregation that swept through the state long before *Plessy v. Ferguson* (1896). There were some areas, such as in education, where the Black delegates found comfort in truly separate *yet* equal educational accommodations, for they appreciated Black Texans controlling their educational destinies, especially at the local level.

27. Lawrence D. Rice, *The Negro in Texas, 1874–1900* (Baton Rouge: Louisiana State University Press, 1971), 148; Donald R. Walker, "Penology for Profit: A History of the Texas Prison System, 1867–1912" (PhD diss., Texas Tech University, 1983), 318.

28. Rice, *Negro in Texas*, 150.

29. *Proceedings*, 13. For a history of antimiscegenation statutes in Texas and the greater Southwest and larger United States, see Martha Menchacha, "The Anti-Miscegenation History of the American Southwest, 1837 to 1970," *Cultural Dynamics* 20, no. 3 (November): 279–318.

30. Barr, *Black Texans*, 83.

31. *Proceedings*, 13.

32. Ruthe Winegarten, *Black Texas Women: A Sourcebook* (Austin: University of Texas Press, 1996), 106.

33. Winegarten, 105.

34. "About HT," Houston-Tillotson University History, accessed March 12, 2015, http://htu.edu/about/history.

35. Winegarten, *Black Texas Women*, 105.

36. Winegarten, 105.

37. "Tillotson Institute," *American Missionary* 35 (January 1881): 242.

38. *Proceedings*, 7.

39. *Proceedings*, 14.

40. Winegarten, *Black Texas Women*, 111.

41. Winegarten, 105.

42. Winegarten, 105–6.

43. *Brenham (TX) Daily Banner*, July 14, 1883.

NONE BUT COLORED TESTIMONY AGAINST HIM

*The California Colored Convention of 1855
and the Origins of the First Civil Rights
Movement in California*

Jean Pfaelzer

In 1850, Pennsylvania abolitionist Mifflin Wistar Gibbs sailed for California. As soon as he reached San Francisco, Gibbs rushed up to the goldfields in the Sierra foothills, but like most Black miners, he faced brutality and, discouraged, soon came down from the mountains. With his friend Peter Lester, Gibbs opened the Emporium for Fine Boots and Shoes in San Francisco—one of the largest shoe stores in the West. The business thrived. But Gibbs and Lester were outraged that the city required them to pay the "poll tax" but would not allow them to vote, and in an act of passive resistance, the partners announced that they would no longer pay the tax, even if the tax collector "lugged off twenty or thirty dollars' worth of goods, in 'payment.'" Indeed, city agents then seized all the shoes from the store and put them up for sale. At the auction, Gibbs and Lester's white friends urged the crowd to give these shoes a "terrible letting alone," and the city had to return them to the emporium.

Perhaps provoked by Gibbs and Lester's victory, in 1851 two white men entered the boot emporium and turned on Lester. Recalled Gibbs: "With vile epithets, using a heavy cane, again and again [they] assaulted my partner, who was compelled to tamely submit, for had he raised his hand he would have been shot, and no redress. *'I would not have been allowed to attest to the "deep damnation."'*" Greatly shamed by his inability to save his partner and by the fact that he was banned from testifying—"attest[ing] to" the brutal assault he had witnessed in his store—Gibbs found himself "ostracized, assaulted without redress, disenfranchised and denied [his] oath in a court of justice."[1] Lester also decried his inability to testify about the assault: "There are many who, ever since this unjust enactment, have taken every opportunity to wrong us, both civilly and criminally, and . . . they remain sheltered under these unjust statutes." A proslavery minority in California, wrote Lester, had created a "political complexion more resembling a country under the servile and humiliating circumstances of slavery than as one of the sovereign and independent States of a free and enlightened people."[2]

Just a few months earlier, in December 1850 in Sacramento, California, Sarah Carroll, a nineteen-year-old prostitute and a free woman of color, brought a charge of grand larceny against William Potter, a freeman of color, for stealing $700 of her property. Carroll declared that Potter had spent the night in her room, took a key she kept hidden in a pocket of her skirt, opened her trunk, and stole one white stone breastpin, one heart set with a diamond, six chemise buttons, one blue shawl decorated with white flowers, several gold coins, and ten dollars in gold nuggets. Then, she charged, Potter hid her things in his luggage on board the steamship *New World*. Carroll swore to her complaint by marking her name with an *X*, and a justice of the peace ordered Potter to be arrested and his baggage searched. Potter claimed that he was, in fact, white and therefore Carroll could not testify against him. Two days later the justice released Potter from jail, "he proving himself a white man & none but Colored testimony against him." Because Carroll, as a Black woman, could not bear witness as to the race of the man found with her belongings, the police arrested her for bringing false charges.[3]

For African Americans who arrived in California soon after the discovery of gold, the ban on testimony by Blacks was a formidable barricade to freedom. The constitutional doctrine of states' rights enunciated in the Tenth Amendment made it easy for California to turn to its own legislature to do the work of legitimizing the racist beliefs that would allow bondage to endure. The California Constitution of 1849 and the criminal and civil codes that set up the judicial system in California (1850) banned testimony by Indians, Blacks, and, later, Chinese migrants from testifying or introducing evidence against a white person in a court of law or before a justice of the peace. The call for equal access to the judicial system drove a unique coalition of enslaved and free Blacks to launch petition drives, rallies, lawsuits, and three Colored Conventions and forged the first civil rights movement in the Golden State—a coordinated and mass effort to create access to justice by focusing, for the moment, on one law.

In 1850 California entered the United States as the most racially diverse state in the union. It also entered the union with a brutal history of slavery and ethnic cleansing. And it also entered the union with a legacy of abolition. Just two years earlier, California had been a possession of Mexico, which in 1829 had outlawed slavery in all of its territories. In 1848 the Treaty of Guadalupe Hidalgo marked the U.S. victory in the U.S.-Mexico War and the seizure of the top third of its land; it included the pledge that Mexico's abolition law of 1829 would forever endure in California. In practice, after Mexico had won independence from Spain in 1821 and gained control of California, Blacks and Indians in the state had the right to live as free people under the cover of the Mexican constitution.[4] But this was a false promise.

The Missouri Compromise of 1820 had balanced the admission into the

United States of slave states and free states and had preordained that California would be free. Yet this agreement would quickly unravel in a conflu-
ence of precarious events. Until Mexico began to disband them in 1836, the
twenty-one Franciscan missions still held thousands of California natives
as captive laborers. As Mexico quickly distributed miles of mission lands
to wealthy ranchos and former Spanish soldiers, many California Indians
remained unfree peons on the lands of their ancestors. In 1848, forty Blacks
from the United States, mostly men, lived in California—servants to U.S.
soldiers, sailors who deserted impressment on ships, and Black Mexicans
brought by the Spanish as slaves to work the land and oversee Indian "neo-
phytes," or converts held at the Franciscan missions.[5]

On January 24, 1848, gold was discovered on land owned by John Sutter,
an early settler who kept 500 Indian slaves on his cattle ranch. News of California's shiny wealth traveled across the U.S. South and lured miners from
China, Mexico, Chile, Argentina, Panama, and Australia. With illusions of
plucking golden nuggets from California's cold rivers and with hopes of
extending slavery onto its fertile land, unemployed veterans from the U.S.-
Mexico War returned to the West. Plantation owners and hired "traffick-
ers," first from Mississippi, Kentucky, and Missouri, quickly forced 2,000
enslaved Blacks to trek across the plains, walking alongside carts or driving
oxen in wagon trains, to mine for their owners. California soon had more
enslaved African Americans than any state or territory west of Texas.[6] Labor
was scarce and wages were high in California, and white merchants and free
Blacks traveled west, convinced that huge profits awaited them for supply-
ing, transporting, and banking the gold rush.[7]

Enslaved George Dennis sailed south with his owner to the mouth of the
Chagres River, hauled his master's gambling tent on his back through the
hot jungles of the isthmus of Panama, and finally sailed up to San Francisco.
Dennis pitched the tent, swept the ground, and kept the coins dropped on
the ground, and he used this money to buy his freedom and then purchase
his mother out of slavery. Together they set up their own gambling tent,
opened boardinghouses, and donated thousands of dollars to the abolition
movement in California. The transport of enslaved African Americans to
California unsettles a north/south history of slavery in the United States.

At first Frederick Douglass feared that California would align with the
plans of "emigrationists" and pull Blacks from the cause of freedom. The
lure of gold, he believed, would disrupt the antislavery movement. In November 1849, however, Douglass announced, "The wealth of California is, as
it should be, shared by colored as well as white men."[8] Gold would deliver a
new state with free labor, free will, and money to purchase families out of
slavery. For free Blacks, California promised a respite from unemployment,
poverty, and the Fugitive Slave Law of 1850. Here, they hoped, Black farmers
could claim land from the vast holdings of the Franciscan missions. Black
entrepreneurs could open saloons, laundries, and restaurants. Black sailors jumped ship in San Francisco Bay and rushed to the Sierra foothills on

horseback, by riverboat, and on foot. As the emigration debate raged in the East, 5,000 Blacks moved to California by 1855.[9]

Apparently few slaves fled to California—it was far away and uncharted and the Black community was new. Free Blacks with long ties to abolition, such as Mifflin Wistar Gibbs, Mary Ellen Pleasant, William Newby, and Peter and Nancy Lester, presumed that California would offer legal sanctuary. California was under pressure to write a constitution and join the Union. In 1849, forty white delegates—mostly southerners, miners, and slave owners— and eight Latino delegates (seated at a separate table) met in the old Mexican capital of Monterrey. Slaves forcibly transported to California should have already been free under the terms of the Missouri Compromise. But the delegates also faced demands by white miners who did not want to compete with enslaved miners. Unlike Ohio and Indiana, which, respectively, entered the union in 1803 and 1816, California did not free any slaves, Native or Black, already in the state. The California Senate ratified the constitution—just three months before Sarah Carroll would file charges against William Potter—and in September 1850 California entered the union as a free state with a constitution that declared "neither slavery nor involuntary servitude, unless for the punishment of crimes, shall ever be tolerated in this state." (This language would be echoed in the Thirteenth Amendment, ratified by Congress on December 6, 1865, but not by California until December 18, when it was already the law of the land.)

In fact, California remained a slave state. Its constitution was a fraudulent ticket to the civic and military benefits of statehood. With most eyes turned to the "Gold Mountain," southerners won control of the governor's mansion and the legislature.[10] In January 1849 proslavery governor Peter Burnett called for an all-white California, and the new legislature nearly passed a bill to ban slaves, former slaves, and "Free Negroes and Persons of Color" from entering the state.[11] Anyone who transported African Americans into California would face arrest. This bill would have legalized the bondage of slaves already in the state, forced their removal after a year, and allowed masters to beat a slave who was "lazy, disorderly, [or] guilty of misbehavior."[12] California was dreaming of a white future.

The California legislature quickly passed a series of acts to encode Burnett's vision and undermine the promise of a free state. The Act for the Governance and Protection of Indians legalized the kidnapping and sale of California's Native people.[13] The Foreign Miners Tax (1851) required foreign migrants to pay a back-breaking tax, and many miners from Mexico, Argentina, Chile, and China fled the state. Nevertheless, this ethnic tax would soon provide 50 percent of the state's budget.[14]

California quickly passed the Civil and Criminal Procedures Acts to set up the new judicial system: neither Blacks, mulattos, nor Indians could testify, give evidence, serve on a jury, or be a witness in any action in which a white person was a party, even if a white person corroborated their testimony. A person whose "blood" was 50 percent Negro was legally Black in civil actions;

one-eighth Negro was considered Black in criminal actions. In civil cases, slaves maintained their character as property; property can't speak. In criminal cases, slaves were considered human beings; human beings are capable of making moral choices and can be held culpable.[15] As Saidiya Hartman notes, testimony laws created slaves as part property and part human.[16]

In 1852 California passed its own Fugitive Slave Law. It already had three such laws at its back—the U.S. Constitution, the Fugitive Slave Law of 1793, and the federal Fugitive Slave Act of 1850, a piece of the "Compromise of 1850" that allowed slave hunters to capture a fugitive slave in any territory or state just by orally "confirming" that the captured person was a runaway slave. If a U.S. marshal failed to arrest and return a runaway, he faced a fine of $1,000. Any person who aided a fugitive slave faced six months in jail. Any Black person could be turned over to any claimant who simply swore that he owned him. Rewards for captured runaways prompted the kidnapping of free Blacks. Testifying—the ability to speak in a court of law—establishes legal access and verifies humanness. Yet neither a fugitive nor a free Black could testify on his or her own behalf in California, as in many other states, which was a direct threat to their citizenship.[17] In state and national Colored Conventions, African Americans would coalesce around this prohibition.

By 1852, 3,000 Blacks had moved to the new state. Thousands more followed. Half arrived free; half arrived enslaved. Most hurried to the goldfields, but about 900 stayed in San Francisco and Sacramento—nearly all men. At first, few Black women crossed the country, unwilling to bring children to an unknown land with few Blacks and a 92 percent male population.[18] Yet when word reached the East that female servants, laundresses, and cooks were earning thirteen dollars a week plus board in California, compared to $1.00 to $2.10 a week in the South or six to seven dollars a week in New York City, free Black women journeyed west.[19]

Free and enslaved Blacks panned for gold right next to one another, waist deep in freezing water. They lived side by side in tent camps and worked alongside one another in boardinghouses and restaurants. They shared segregated neighborhoods in the cities. And by 1850 they could share the news that all African Americans in California were free. For Blacks who came to California as free people, born free or manumitted, their safety hinged on proving this status. For Blacks who entered enslaved, their safety hinged on proving that they entered after the state constitution was passed. Together, this unique Black community faced the ban on testifying and together forged the struggle to overturn it—in the legislature, in courtrooms, and in three Colored Conventions that would meet before the Civil War.

Many Blacks who had been forcibly transported to California as slaves were sometimes unaware of their new legal status as free people, and tried to escape in the vast and raw state. Flight was easy in the redwood forests or on ships bound for Mexico, Panama, British Columbia, or lumber towns along the coast. Many sailors, ship stewards, and cooks were free Blacks, ready to help. Without a plantation economy, at first California lacked slave

catchers. As soon as Philadelphia abolitionists Peter and Nancy Lester settled in San Francisco in 1850, they turned their home into a meeting site for
newly arrived Blacks and explained that all were now free under California's
constitution. Newly arrived free Blacks, such as Mifflin Wistar Gibbs, Peter
Lester, Nancy Lester, and Mary Ellen "Mammy" Pleasant, informed enslaved
Blacks that they were legally free and offered transportation, safe houses,
legal advice, and money for an Underground Railroad growing in the West.[20]

In 1850 Lester wrote to the *Pennsylvania Freeman*, "I thought when I got
here I would have no anti-slavery work to do, but I find as much to do here as
I did with you. I find slaveholders are here with their slaves from all the slave
States in the Union. We had two in our little domicile last evening. I asked
them how much they made a week! '$14' was the reply. We then wished to
know who got it. 'Master' of course. . . . When they left we had them strong
in the spirit of freedom." And, Lester added, "They are leaving every day."[21]

Some southern owners brought slaves to California, planning to strike it
rich and quickly return with them to the South. But once in California, many
decided to stay; they staked gold claims, bought land, and relied on the eastern tradition of "sojourner clauses" that allowed them to travel with slaves
into free states if they could prove they "intended" to leave. How long were
they going to get away with calling themselves "temporary" and retaining
their slaves? These southern slaveholders were not tourists and not just passing through. To escape the terms of freedom in California's constitution,
some had forced sham contracts or indentures on their slaves before they
set out. Others promised manumission after a fixed period of slave labor. In
1851, Peter Brown wrote his wife from diggings on the Cosumnes River that
he was paying eighty dollars per month for his freedom, and within a year
he had "cleared" $300 to purchase his son. His fellow slaves were earning
four dollars per day for their owners. Brown wrote that he expected to return
home within the year as a freeman. He described "immense sums . . . paid to
their owners by the colored men who have come here as slaves, and who by
a course of honest industry have paid for . . . their freedom."[22]

In 1851 Governor Burnett told the legislature that slaves had been manumitted and brought to California "bound to service for a limited period
as hirelings" and concluded that "we have thus . . . practical slavery in our
midst."[23] African Americans who had been brought out as slaves when California was still a Mexican territory needed to establish their new status as
free people, and they needed to claim their rights under the state constitution if California were to copy northern "sojourner laws" that protected
plantation owners who brought slaves to work with them at the cotton ex-
changes in New York or to serve them at resorts in Niagara Falls.[24] The new
constitution stated it would not "tolerate" slavery—"tolerate" was not a legal
standard.[25]

African Americans in California faced enduring risk. Amid advertisements for suction pumps, Havana cigars, and tobacco wrapped in foil, in
1851 a notice appeared in the *Sacramento Union*: "$100 reward for the delivery

of a certain slave named SAMPS. Said boy is 23–25 years old; a light mulatto; spare made; well favored and about five feet ten or eleven inches high. He was a slave in Alabama and brought to California by me in 1849, and left me on the Mokelumine River [sic], about the 1st of July, 1850." His owner would pay for Samps to be returned to a miner's boardinghouse seven miles from Jackson Creek in Calaveras County.[26]

Brutal as it was, the Fugitive Slave Act of 1850 did not apply in California where fugitives did not cross a state line to enter a free state. Samps fled *within* a free state, where slave owners had "voluntarily" brought their slaves. And so, in 1852, California passed its own Fugitive Slave Act to close this loophole and have the machinery of the new police and courts enforce slavery in the free state. To pull this off, California reached back to its brief pre-statehood moment and falsely claimed that it had been a U.S. "territory" and thereby had the right to hold slaves. Under the new law, slaveholders kept the right to "travel" in California with their slaves. Any person who had arrived enslaved before statehood became an immediate "fugitive from labor." If a man or woman "held to labor in any state" escaped *inside* California, then the owner could hire a bounty hunter to seize his "fugitive." Anyone who rescued, hid, or helped a fugitive faced jail.[27] Finally, California's Fugitive Slave Act reaffirmed the ban on testimony by Blacks. Just eighteen months after its constitution promised freedom, in April 1852, California reinstated humans as property.[28]

Hovering over enslaved and free Blacks was the early California Supreme Court case *In re Perkins* (1852). In June 1849, Charles Perkins left his humid Mississippi plantation for California's gold mines, taking with him Robert Perkins, Carter Perkins, and Sandy Jones—three of his father's slaves. Not realizing that they were now free, the enslaved men mined for Perkins. After three months Charles Perkins realized he would make more money if he rented out the men, kept their salaries for himself, and mined on his own. After a few weeks he'd had enough and told the men they had fulfilled their obligations and were free. Disillusioned and tired, Perkins returned to the South, and the three Black men returned to the goldfields and thrived. Once back in Mississippi, Charles Perkins discovered that slaves were selling for $1,000 apiece. Regretting his decision, he hired vigilantes to seize the men and their gold dust and have them arrested as runaways under the new law. A local judge refused to let the men testify that they had bought their freedom and were wrongfully held. Quickly, the Black community raised the first of many defense funds and launched a movement against the new law.

Five years before the *Dred Scott* decision, the California Supreme Court justices—all from slave states—decided *In re Perkins*.[29] A slave brought into the free state did not "become ipso facto free." "People of the United States" had the right to immigrate to California "with every species of property they had" and enjoy "everything inherent with *its* use and possession." Slaves were a species of property. Not only did the court declare that California's Fugitive Slave Law was constitutional; it added that it had maintained slavery in order to "obliterate" Blacks from California.[30] The court ignored the core issue—these three men were residing in a free state—and it ordered that they be shipped back to Mississippi. Apparently en route, they escaped in Panama. Had the three men been allowed to testify that first night, Blacks in California would not have faced this dangerous precedent.[31]

Across the country, the politics of Black abolition were shifting; Frederick Douglass now declared that "the only way to make the Fugitive Slave Law a dead letter is to make half a dozen or more dead kidnappers."[32] Blacks in California were turning to organizing tactics from Black abolition in the East. Mifflin Wistar Gibbs had served on the Board of Managers of the State Convention of Colored Citizens of Pennsylvania in 1848 and had traveled the lecture circuit with Frederick Douglass.[33] In California, he saw that the need to testify would unite free and enslaved Blacks, from former slaves who had purchased their bodies or worked for their manumission to free Blacks who were kidnapped into bondage. Both free and enslaved Blacks needed to testify that when disillusioned masters returned to the South, they had willingly abandoned or freed their slaves in California.[34] A Black woman who was raped by a white man without a white witness to corroborate the assault needed to testify on her own behalf.[35] Free Black Stephen Hill was kidnapped from his prosperous ranch and, unable to testify, lost his land.[36]

In 1851 Mifflin Gibbs, William Newby, William Hall, and Jonas Townsend —all experienced Black abolitionists—launched the first Franchise League in San Francisco. Copying an East Coast tactic, they circulated petitions demanding the right for free Blacks to testify.[37] In response, the state legislature copied Congress's "gag rule" for antislavery demands and refused even to receive or debate the petitions (one member moved to burn them).[38]

At the center of Black activism in California was Mifflin Wistar Gibbs. As a free child of color, Gibbs had worked in cotton fields and had seen "drivers with their scourging whip in hand" threaten gangs of slaves, and he became determined to "kill anybody that would make me a slave."[39] After his family moved to Philadelphia, Gibbs used his job on the omnibus cars to rescue and transport fugitives, such as the daring Ellen Crafts, who escaped by dressing as a man while her husband, William, posed as her slave. Gibbs reported that it was he who had opened the wooden crate when William "Box" Brown shipped himself to Philadelphia from Virginia.[40] By 1849 Gibbs had moved to Rochester and lectured with Douglass. There he met returning gold seekers dazzled by good fortune.

The California Colored Conventions and the Ban on Testimony of African Americans

Gibbs determined to use "all moral means to secure legal claim to all the rights and privileges of American citizens."[41] The petition movement for the right to testify grew, uniting enslaved and free Blacks. Protest meetings arose in the scattered Black communities across California. Journalist

Jonas Townsend joined Gibbs and Lester in the Franchise League—what Gibbs called "the first pronouncement of the colored people from the state . . . against a continuous series of outrages, injustices and unmitigated wrongs."[42] The African American presence in California was less than five years old when the league published a call in the *Sacramento Daily Union* for the first California Colored Convention, to meet in Sacramento on November 20, 1855, to demand the right to testify.[43] The right to be a witness signified freedom, and in the first civil rights movement in California, the demand for a legal voice became the path to civic belonging.[44]

The strategy of the California Colored Conventions of 1855, '56, and '57 was to create a defiant Black communal voice—through the convention itself, through the movement it would spawn, and through a challenge to only one law.[45] In 1855, forty-nine Black delegates traveled from eleven counties to meet at the Colored Methodist Episcopal, or African Methodist Episcopal (AME), church in Sacramento—the first Black church west of Texas, just a few blocks from the state capitol where the Fugitive Slave Law had been passed.[46] There were no railroads, few roads, and few riverboats to bring the eager delegates to the state capital from hundreds of miles away.

The convention of 1855 opened with the declaration that the delegates had come together "for the purpose of taking into consideration the propriety of petitioning the Legislature of California for a change in the law relating to the testimony of colored people."[47] Although the delegates declared that this pressing subject "interests all classes—interests both races," the convention never referred to Chinese or Native residents. Despite a vow to tolerate dissent, the convention quickly became fractious over the politics of Black identity and the "propriety" of its demands in what historian Howard Holman Bell calls a "violent altercation."[48] William Yates argued that the convention should "acknowledge that in form, appearance and education the African cannot compete with the Caucasian race, yet his sympathies are as warm and his feelings as human. He can be grateful for kindness shown, and is as ready to forgive the injuries done him."[49] William Newby declared that Blacks were entitled to testify because "our social, moral, religious, intellectual and financial condition . . . compare[s] favorably with any class in the community." The Reverend J. J. Moore observed, "Do not let those who deny us possession of intellect and soul" see that "we cannot govern our passions. . . . Let us rather prove to them that we have . . . to plan a work of moral regeneration."[50] The Reverend Darius P. Stokes announced that the Colored population of California owned $3.5 million in businesses and property. God, he claimed, had intervened and delivered prosperity in order to show that the effects of slavery were "mutable."[51] Others argued that Blacks in California were now "fit" for freedom and could be trusted to tell the truth.

A year later, the convention of 1856 split over the move toward militant change. William Newby objected to a resolution that hailed "with delight [the nation's] onward progress" and announced he would "welcome a foreign army" if it would bring freedom to Black Americans, and, as Howard

Holman Bell, one of the few scholars of the Colored Conventions movement, observed, the resolution was barely defeated, by a vote of 29–27.[52] Cultural historian Derrick Spires has observed that delegates at national Colored Conventions sought to "manufacture" the citizenship from which they had been excluded.[53] But in Sacramento, these delegates sought to manufacture their entitlement to citizenship.

Immediately Gibbs called statements that justified civil rights based on Blacks' respectability "undignified and untrue"; the ban on Blacks' testimony was due to "prejudice against them and not ignorance of their general condition."[54] J. H. Townsend called Stokes's justification for civil rights based on Blacks' financial worth "crouching," and he argued instead for a "manly" appeal for "what is simply just."[55] Delegate David Lewis believed the "'oath' would make people careful how they act before us." Others argued that whites would see the right to testify as an intervention of God; evidence of Christian redemption would sway the white legislature.

The Colored Convention of 1855 ultimately declared that California's ban on testimony was "unjust in itself, and oppressive to every class in the community; that this was intended to protect white persons from a class whose intellectual and social condition was supposed to be so low as to justify the depriving them of their testimony." Any "test [of] race, color, creed or country" was both "unwise and unjust." The convention of 1856 endorsed this version, for the right to testify was "as valuable as the right to self-defense."[56]

Critic John Ernest reminds us how the rhetoric and the widely dispersed minutes of the Colored Conventions contributed to the possibility of reenvisioning and transforming contemporary Black politics.[57] The 1855 California convention believed that it could speak and write the community into political existence and, hence, into legal access. Although grounded in the vocabulary of "moral suasion" and sentimental transcendence, the convention leaders gave petitions to each delegate with the assignment to gather signatures demanding the right to testify.

Over the next two years the delegates delivered 8,000 signatures to the legislature, seeking to overturn the ban on Black testimony. The very fact of the conventions confirms that Blacks sought to remain in California, challenging competing drives for Black emigration to Canada or the Caribbean by the American Colonization Society that Frederick Douglass so despised. The California Colored Conventions barely alluded to slavery, did not profess abolition, and appointed no women delegates. Only one woman, Priscilla Stewart, who had served on the Business Committee of the antislavery convention held in Philadelphia in 1848, offered comments, but these were not recorded in the minutes.[58]

The Colored Convention of 1855 was the first civil rights meeting in California.[59] Blacks in California held four conventions, which in the decade that spanned the Civil War launched churches, schools, and two Black newspapers, the *Mirror of the Times* and the *Pacific Appeal*. Although only two editions of the *Mirror of the Times* now remain, the 1855 convention would not disband until it launched the editorial board and arranged for its funding. The *Mirror*, first edited by J. H. Townsend, was lasting evidence of the convention's desire for a voice through Black journalism, and it appeared before the next convention of 1856.[60] Thus the conventions stitched together the larger Black communities in San Francisco, Sacramento, and Stockton with scattered smaller communities—from the timber county of Humboldt and the mining towns of Marysville and Nevada City down to Los Angeles. The convention of 1855 urged Black parents to get educations for their children, and it created an executive committee that worked with J. B. Sanderson to desegregate schools. It set up the network, led in part by Mary Ellen Pleasant, that raised thousands of dollars to defend fugitive slaves. Frederick Douglass called the California Colored Convention "the presentation of an industrious, enterprising, thrifty, and intelligent free Black population."[61]

In the most interracial state in the nation, the delegates did not mention the recent 1854 California Supreme Court decision that would profoundly impact them all: In the trial of *People v. Hall*, the conviction of a white man hinged on the testimony of a Chinese man. In its bizarre ruling, the court held that the Chinese were Mongolians. Thousands of years ago, Mongolians had crossed the Bering Strait, migrated south, and became American Indians; hence, the Chinese were Indians, and Indians could not testify. So, neither could the Chinese. In the era of brutal genocide against and legal kidnapping and sale of Native people, particularly women and children, and the seizure, forced transport, and public sale of young Chinese prostitutes displayed in cages along Jackson Street in San Francisco, the California conventions did not explicitly declare that the free state had become a slave state, but they began to take down the legal scaffolding of African American slavery in California.

The Black Community, Archy Lee, and the Right to Testify

The Colored Conventions did not immediately win African Americans the right to testify in California. Nor did they immediately end the state's Fugitive Slave Act. Long past the peak of the gold rush, slave owners continued to move to California with their slaves. These related wrongs came to a head in 1858. In 1857, Mississippi slave owner Charles V. Stovall had crossed the plains with a small herd of cattle and his father's enslaved cook, Archy Lee. Archy Lee left behind his enslaved mother, two brothers, and a sister, whom he inevitably viewed as Stovall's hostages. Finally reaching the eastern slopes of the Sierras, Stovall bought a farm and pastured his emaciated cattle. Then, he made his way to Sacramento where he rented a room and ran ads in the *Union* newspaper for students who would pay him five dollars per month to attend his school.[62] Desperate for cash, after just two months Stovall "hired out" Archy Lee for thirty dollars per month but kept his wages. In Sacramento, Lee met free Blacks who told him that he was living in a free state. Stovall began to worry that he would lose his valuable chattel property, and, besides, his school was failing; in January 1858, he decided to return to Mississippi. Lee refused to be taken back and fled, hiding in the Hotel Hackett, a Black-owned residence that housed many abolitionists and reformers. Stovall's scouts quickly seized the fugitive from this obvious hiding place, and Archy Lee spent the next months in jail, on trial, or in flight, aided by members of the Executive Committee of the Colored Convention of 1857.[63]

The legal issues remained: Could Charles Stovall persuade the California Supreme Court, a bench where southerners outnumbered northerners two to one, that he was just traveling through the state with his slave? Did a Black man, free under the state constitution, have the right to remain in California? The Black community, many of whom had attended the conventions, closely watched Lee's trials.[64] Stovall's attorney argued that the state's ban on slavery was "inoperative" because there was no law that had "enabled" the state constitution. And nothing in the national constitution banned slavery. The status of "slave" could follow Archy Lee wherever he dwelled. Besides, the federal Bill of Rights guaranteed the right to property, and Archy Lee was property. Finally, turning to the recent *Dred Scott* decision (1857), Stovall's lawyer asserted that Stovall had come to California only for his health and had no intention of remaining—despite the fact that he had a ranch and school.

Even as the community coalesced around his case, Archy Lee was unable to testify to the fact that he was now a freeman. He was able, however, to escape prison, and his flights, captures, and trials made headlines. To keep Stovall from taking Archy Lee back to Mississippi, Lee's lawyers, hired and paid by the Black community, obtained a series of writs of habeas corpus that required the state to "produce" him. They hoped to use his case to unravel the finding in *Perkins* that a slave, transported onto free soil, was not automatically free and argue that "the master's control over a slave" stops in California where any slave "becomes virtually free." The recent *Dred Scott* decision of 1857, they said, did not apply to Archy Lee because his owner had "voluntarily" brought him into California; Lee had not fled from Stovall *to* California.[65] The verdict was bizarre. Justice Peter Burnett, the former governor, described California's natural beauty and climate and predicted that many southern "travelers" would soon come to California "for health and pleasure," and they were "accustomed" to their enslaved servants, whom they viewed as "part of the family." California should not prevent slave owners from enjoying the sights without the help of their "domestics."[66] Stovall prevailed, and Archy Lee was returned to him chained in heavy manacles.

As they waited for a ship to return them to the South, Stovall kept Archy Lee hidden away. But the Committee of One Hundred, drawn from a united Black community, had found a low-level commissioner, James Riker, an African American ship's steward, who prepared another writ of habeas corpus ordering Stovall to "produce" Archy. Riker then issued a warrant for Stovall's arrest and charged him with kidnapping. Blacks across California patrolled wharves and docks, searching outbound ships for Stovall and Lee.

Delegates to the Colored Conventions were cooks, waiters, and deckhands on the small steamboats that delivered mail and food to lumber and fishing towns up and down the coast; they were the eyes and ears of Black neighborhoods. When the ship *Orizaba*, bound for Mississippi, sailed from San Francisco's Vallejo Street wharf on March 5, 1858, James Pleasant, Mary Ellen Pleasant's husband, had been hired on as a cook. Likely it was he who leaked word that the *Orizaba* was sailing toward a secret rendezvous in the middle of San Francisco Bay. Bearing Riker's warrant for Stovall's arrest, the sheriff and two officers quietly boarded the *Orizaba* as it prepared to lift anchor. All were now on the lookout for a little boat sailing from Angel Island where Stovall and Archy Lee had spent the night in a hidden cove. George Dennis, Mary Ellen Pleasant, and members of the Colored Conventions' Executive Committees rented a police tugboat for the unconscionable sum of $3,050 to follow the *Orizaba*, and they arrived just as the ship met Stovall's rowboat. The police immediately took Archy Lee into custody for his own protection.

Archy Lee's fourth and most costly hearing again turned on the right of Blacks to testify. Stovall argued that the writ that took Lee from the *Orizaba* was invalid because it had been signed by Riker, a free Black man who could not testify against a white man in court. Invoking the federal Fugitive Slave Act, the judge returned Lee to Stovall, while masses of Black San Francisco residents protested in the streets. At last, as Stovall again prepared to transport Archy Lee back to the South, the Black leadership located a federal commissioner who finally agreed to hear Lee's testimony; this was perhaps the first major testimony of a Black man against a white man in California. First, Lee asserted that once he'd arrived in California he was no longer a slave. He then offered evidence that Stovall intended to become a permanent resident of California, in which case he could not retain a slave. Finally, he argued that Stovall had never produced evidence that Lee was in fact a fugitive from Mississippi. With this the commissioner ruled that Archy Lee was not a fugitive slave. Critic and historian Edlie Wong points out that for Blacks to sue for *wrongful* enslavement, they paradoxically had to assent to the idea that there was *rightful* bondage, and hence, she argues, such rulings were conservative.[67] Nonetheless, Charles Stovall, now facing charges of perjury, slipped out of town and was ferried to the middle of San Francisco Bay, where he boarded the mail steamer *Sonora* and began his journey back to the South. Archy Lee was free.

The struggle for abolition in California continued. Three Colored Conventions met in California before the Civil War—in 1855, 1856, and 1857—increasingly stitching California into the national struggle over freedom for Black Americans. Mary Ellen Pleasant, once a fugitive slave, invested in banks, laundries, brothels, and boardinghouses in California, which were soon known as "safe houses" for runaways. She hired attorneys for fugitive slave cases and raised $10,000 for John Brown's raid. Former fugitive Biddy Mason refused to leave California with the man who claimed ownership over her, established Los Angeles's historic FAME church, the first of the AME churches in Southern California that hosted the conventions in Sacramento, and found refuge for fugitives in Southern California.[68] Flights from slavery in California established what Paul Gilroy terms the "mnemonic function" of shared experience; violence shaped the shared consciousness of Blacks in California and prompted the petitions and conventions that, in turn, renewed Blacks' communal identity in a strange land. By invoking the ideals— if not the practice—of the American legal system, slavery in California ruptured the system that provoked the gatherings in the first place. Historian Eddie Glaude sees that the cultural solidarity of the Colored Conventions brought belonging to Blacks in California: in spite of using the national rhetoric, the particular conditions of violence, suffering, and death "differentiated the moral identity [of] Black and White America in real terms."[69] Derrick Spires goes further and sees that Colored Conventions were "unofficial modes of participatory politics" and a "viable, visible, and a potentially revolutionary mode of direct intervention."[70]

Wrote William Newby to Frederick Douglass, "A change has come over the spirit of our dreams." The transport of enslaved African Americans had ended with the gold rush, and in 1855 California's Fugitive Slave Law was not renewed. Faced with the petition drives, in 1858 the legislature let the ban on Black testimony die. The right to testify, Newby predicted, would mark a step toward freedom and "impel us to renewed efforts in defense of our bleeding country."[71] The communal praxis of the California Colored Conventions had indeed, in the words of John Ernest, "collected the scattered bones" of a dispersed people to create a new political and communal body in the West.[72]

Exodus

Even as San Francisco celebrated the release of Archy Lee, Mifflin Wistar Gibbs saw the long shadows of the *Perkins* decision, the *Dred Scott* case, and the legal costs and dire risks of saving Lee. In 1858 Gibbs sailed north to assess the possibilities for a new settlement for Black Californians in British Columbia. In Vancouver, Gibbs made a deal with James Douglass, the mulatto governor, who was seeking a stable population for the new colony. Gibbs, perhaps reluctant to return, sent James Nagle, a ship captain, back to San Francisco, and at a celebration for Archy Lee at the AME church, he announced the terms: free or enslaved, California's Blacks who moved to British Columbia would receive the vote, the right for Black children to attend public schools, and twenty acres of land. Within a week, Archy Lee and thirty-five free and enslaved Blacks boldly boarded the steamship *Commodore* and sailed for British Columbia, while 700 other African Americans began the long trek from California to Victoria; some stopped at secure sites on California's Underground Railroad, others hiked or caught steamships, and some drove their cattle 1,000 miles north.

Among these was teacher Priscilla Stewart. Once she reached Canada on the *Commodore*, she wrote "'A Voice from the Oppressed to the Friends of Humanity' Composed by One of the Suffering Class" and printed a few copies of her poem, which she distributed to "California Pioneers" to raise money.[73] In the poem, Stewart writes of flight and the unsettling fear of yet another dislocation. She marks with irony how quickly Blacks had to leave their sanctuary in California.[74] Yet she still claims California as her rightful and native land, as she cries out that her homeland has betrayed her. She has suffered the real and mental dungeons of a home that wrapped enslaved African Americans in the "chains of hell." Finally, the poet turns to Black readers and urges them to redeem this "native land" where "tyrant slavery" entered this "sweet home" that was theirs by right.

> Look and behold our sad despair
>   Our hopes and prospect fled;
> The tyrant slavery entered here,
>   And laid us all for dead.
>
> Sweet home! When shall we find a home?
> If the tyrant says that we must go
>   The love of gain the reason,
> And if humanity dare say "No."
>   Then they are tried for treason. . . .
>
> Far better breathe Canadian air
>   Where all are free and well,
> Than live in slavery's atmosphere
>   And wear the chains of hell.
>
> Farewell to our native land,
>   We must wave the parting hand,
> Never to see thee any more,
>   But seek a foreign land. . . .
>
> May God inspire your hearts,
>   A Marion raise your hands;
> Never desert your principles
>   Until you've redeemed your land.

Redemption in California was a civic duty. Although the "tyrant slavery had entered here," within eight years, from 1850 to 1858, Blacks in California had torn down the legal scaffolding that had been assembled to recreate bondage in the Golden State. An underground railroad of homes, hotels, and ships that transported and hid fugitive slaves quickly formed. AME churches emerged across the state, where people gathered to pray and organize. Black merchants continued to resist the violence hurled at their shops; most prospered and donated thousands of dollars to sustain legal challenges to segregated education, bans on landownership, and the state's Fugitive Slave Law, which the legislature let lapse in April 1855—seven months before the first convention met. In 1863, 100 years ahead of Rosa Parks, Charlotte Brown, a young free woman of color, deliberately sat in the white section of San

Francisco's segregated trolleys, was ejected twice, and was seized by the conductor when she made the historic statement, "I said I would seek redress." Charlotte Brown went to trial twice, sued the Omnibus Railroad Company, won $500 in damages, and opened public transportation to Black riders.[75] The three Colored Conventions in the 1850s generated 8,000 petitions to the California legislature and made possible the renowned victory of Archy Lee, which hinged on his being able to speak in court to his status as a freeman. In 1858 the new state did not renew the ban on the testimony of African Americans.

Witness: a person; a truth; a theological and political action.

NOTES

1. Elizabeth Parker and James Abajian, *A Walking Tour of the Black Presence in San Francisco during the Nineteenth Century* (San Francisco: San Francisco African American Historical and Cultural Society, 1974), 9–10. See also Mifflin Wistar Gibbs, *Shadow and Light: An Autobiography with Reminiscences of the Last and Present Century* (Washington, DC, 1902).

2. Peter Anderson et al., "The Mirror of the Times," *Black Abolitionist Papers Editorial*, Black Abolitionist Papers 8431, pp. 25626, 25627, 25628, http://bap.chadwyck.com. udel.idm.oclc.org/home/home.do.

3. State of California, Sacramento County, "People vs W H Potter," December 12, 1850.

4. Rudolph Lapp, *Blacks in Gold Rush California* (New Haven, CT: Yale University Press, 1995), 8, 25.

5. Donna R. Mooney, "The Search for a Legal Presumption of Employment Duration or Custom of Arbitrary Dismissal in California, 1848–1872," *Berkeley Journal of Employment and Labor Law* 21, no. 633 (2000): 7, 31, 51; Lapp, *Blacks in Gold Rush California*, 1, 8, 25.

6. Quintard Taylor, *In Search of the Racial Frontier: African Americans in the American West, 1528–1990* (New York: W. W. Norton, 1998), 78.

7. Lapp, *Blacks in Gold Rush California*, 42; Mooney, "Search," 8, 51.

8. Frederick Douglass, *North Star*, November 30, 1849.

9. *Minutes of the Negro State Colored Convention, California, 1855*, in *A Survey of the Negro Convention Movement, 1830–1861*, ed. Howard Holman Bell (New York: Arno Press, 1969), 137. See Bell, *Survey* (214) for the debate over the political equivalency of the moves to Africa and California. Bell argues that "there was no tendency in 1858 for the established abolitionist leaders to favor emigration under any circumstances."

10. Peter Burnett had been instrumental in the ban on Black migration to Oregon. See Archives of the Oregon Historical Society, in Quintard Taylor, "The History of African Americans in the West," 13, accessed July 22, 2020, http://quintardtaylor.com /courses/history-313-history-african-americans-west.

11. Leonard L. Richards, *The California Gold Rush and the Coming of the Civil War* (New York: Alfred A. Knopf, 2007), 67, 242n7.

12. California State Assembly, Assembly Bill 145, "A Bill for an Act Prohibiting the Immigration of Free Negroes and Persons of Colour to this State," April 15, 1850, *California State Assembly Journals*, 1849–50 Session, Sacramento, https://clerk.assembly .ca.gov/archive-list. See also Stacy Smith, *Freedom's Frontiers: California and the Struggle over Unfree Labor, Emancipation, and Reconstruction* (Chapel Hill: University of North Carolina Press, 2013), 62, 63, 262nn33–34.

13. Mooney, "Search," 7, 8, 51. For recent discussions, see Benjamin Madley, *An American Genocide: The United States and the California Indian Catastrophe, 1846–1873*

(New Haven, CT: Yale University Press, 2016); and Andrés Reséndez, *The Other Slavery: The Uncovered Story of Indian Enslavement in America* (New York: Houghton Mifflin Harcourt, 2016).

14. Jean Pfaelzer, *Driven Out: The Forgotten War against Chinese Americans* (New York: Random House, 2007; Berkeley: University of California Press, 2008), 22–23, 31–33, 42–43, 142.

15. Edlie Wong, *Neither Fugitive nor Free: Atlantic Slavery, Freedom Suits, and the Legal Culture of Travel* (New York: New York University Press, 2009), 4, quoting James Kent, *Commentaries on American Law, 1826–1830*.

16. Saidiya Hartman, *Scenes of Subjection: Terror, Slavery, and Self-Making in Nineteenth-Century America* (New York: Oxford University Press, 1997), 7–8.

17. "Fugitive Slave Act 1850," National Center, accessed July 21, 2020, http://www.nationalcenter.org/FugitiveSlaveAct.html. Note also that the national Fugitive Slave Act of 1850 explicitly extended to territories as well as states. No Black person had the right to testify or the right to a defense. "In no trial or hearing . . . shall the testimony of the alleged fugitive be admitted into evidence." It followed that alleged fugitives did not have the right to a jury trial. "Fugitive Slave Act of 1850," § 6.

18. For a reliable biography of Mary Ellen Pleasant and an astute analysis of the opportunities for Black women in this liminal state, see Lynn M. Hudson, *The Making of Mammy Pleasant: A Black Entrepreneur in Nineteenth-Century San Francisco* (2003; repr., Urbana: University of Illinois Press, 2008), 32–33.

19. Hudson, 32.

20. During the 1830s Peter Lester had studied at Clarkson Hall, an abolitionist school. In the 1840s he joined the abolitionist movement and in 1849 served on the Committee of the Pennsylvania Anti-Slavery Society and attended several Colored Conventions.

21. Peter Lester, "Letter from California," *Pennsylvania Freeman* (Philadelphia), December 5, 1850. The letter was written in San Francisco on October 13, 1850. Biographical information also from Lester to William Still, November 30, 1859, *Weekly Anglo-African* (New York), May 12, 1860, Black Abolitionist Papers.

22. Peter Brown to Mrs. Ally Brown, December 1, 1851, Amoureux-Bolduc Papers, Missouri Historical Society, St. Louis, MO, cited in Taylor, "History of African Americans," 18.

23. Paul Finkelman, "The Law of Slavery and Freedom in California: 1848–1860," *California Western Law Review* 17, no. 3 (1981): 451.

24. Wong, *Neither Fugitive nor Free*, 2, 79, and passim.

25. *Journals of California Legislature*, 1851, Sacramento, California.

26. Advertisement, *Sacramento (CA) Daily Union*, October 30, 1851.

27. *Laws of the State of California*, 1853, Sacramento, California, citation 94.

28. Stacey Smith, "Pacific Bound: California's 1852 Fugitive Slave Law," *BlackPast*, January 6, 2014, http://www.Blackpast.org/perspectives/pacific-bound-california-s-1852-fugitive-slave-law#sthash.NSTO0FiT.dpuf.

29. In re Perkins, 2 Cal. 438 (1852); Dred Scott v. Sandford, 60 U.S. 393 (1857).

30. *Perkins*, 2 Cal. at 424, 455 (J. Anderson concurring).

31. Finkelman, "Law of Slavery," 444; *Perkins*, 2 Cal. at 424, 455 (J. Anderson concurring). See also Smith, "Pacific Bound"; George Tinkham, *A History of Stockton from Its Organization to the Present Time* (San Francisco, 1880), 128; and Harry L. Wells, *History of Butte County, California in Two Volumes* (San Francisco, 1882), 119.

32. James Oliver Horton and Lois E. Horton, *Slavery and the Making of America* (New York: Oxford University Press), 193.

33. *Minutes of the State Convention of Colored Citizens of Pennsylvania, Convened at Harrisburg, December 13–14, 1848* (Philadelphia, PA: Merrihew and Thompson, 1849), http://udspace.udel.edu/handle/19716/17268.

34. Gibbs, *Shadow and Light*, 46–47.

35. Lapp, *Blacks in Gold Rush*, 5–16.

36. Carlo M. de Ferrari, *The Gold Spring Diary: The Journal of John Jolly with a Brief History of Stephen Spencer Hill* (Sonora, CA: Tuolumne Historical Society, 1966), 125–42; "Wood Tucker vs. Stephen Hill, et al. County Court, Tuolumne County. Petition for writ of injunction filed by O. R. Rozier on behalf of Wood tucker on August 12, 1854," *Daily Alta California* (San Francisco), September 1, 1854; *Daily Alta California*, April 9, 1858. See also Lapp, *Blacks in Gold Rush*, 140–41.

37. "William Hall," *Pacific Appeal* (San Francisco), August 23, 1863. In the East, Hall and Gibbs had worked closely with abolitionists Dr. James McCune Smith and Revs. Theodore Wright and Alexander Crummell to organize petition drives demanding that free Blacks have the right to testify.

38. *California Journal of the Assembly*, 1853, *California State Assembly Journals*, 1853 Session. See California Legislature, Fourth Session, Assembly, March 12, 1853; *Sacramento (CA) Daily Union*, March 15, 1853; and *California Journal of the Assembly*, 1854, 259–61. *California State Assembly Journals*, 1854 Session. The 1853 petition, suggested assemblyman George Carhart, should be thrown out the window. Alternatively, proposed his colleague A. G. McCandless, it should be burned.

39. Gibbs, *Shadow and Light*, 21.

40. Gibbs, 26.

41. See James Fisher, "The Struggle for Negro Testimony in California," *Southern California Quarterly* 51, no. 4 (December 1969): 313–24; and *California Journal of the Assembly*, 1852, *California State Assembly Journals*, 1852 Session, 395.

42. Gibbs, *Shadow and Light*, 47.

43. "The Convention of 1855," *Sacramento Daily Union* and *Pacific Appeal*, April 12, 1862.

44. De Ferrari, *Gold Spring Diary*, 125–42; "Wood Tucker vs. Stephen Hill"; *Daily Alta California*, April 9, 1858. See also Lapp, *Blacks in Gold Rush*, 140–41.

45. *Proceedings of the First State Convention of the Colored Citizens of the State of California* (Sacramento: Democratic State Journal Print, 1855), 16. See also *Proceedings of the Second Annual Convention of the Colored Citizens of the State of California* (San Francisco: J. H. Udell and W. Randall, 1856); and *Proceedings of the State Convention of Colored Citizens* (San Francisco: Printed at the Office of the *Elevator*, 1865).

46. Herbert G. Ruffin II, "The Conventions of Colored Citizens of the State of California (1855–1865)," *BlackPast*, February 4, 2009, https://www.blackpast.org/african -american-history/conventions-colored-citizens-state-california-1855-1865. See more at http://www.Blackpast.org/1851-2#sthash.q8VfP1mv.dpuf.

47. *Minutes of Negro State Colored Convention*, 3.

48. Bell, *Survey*, 119.

49. *Minutes of Negro State Colored Convention*, 5.

50. *Minutes of Negro State Colored Convention*, 5.

51. *Minutes of Negro State Colored Convention*, 12–13.

52. Bell, *Survey*, 119; *Minutes of Negro State Colored Convention*, 10–13.

53. Derrick R. Spires, "Imagining a State of Fellow Citizens: Early African American Politics of Publicity in the Black State Conventions," in *Early African American Print Culture*, ed. Lara Langer Cohen and Jordan Alexander Stein (Philadelphia: University of Pennsylvania Press, 2014), 274.

54. *Minutes of Negro State Colored Convention*, 11.

55. *Minutes of Negro State Colored Convention*, 10.

56. *Minutes of Negro State Colored Convention*, 14.

57. John Ernest, *Liberation Historiography: African American Writers and the Challenge of History, 1794–1861* (Chapel Hill: University of North Carolina Press, 2004), 223.

58. "Proceedings of the Anti-slavery Convention Held in Philadelphia," *North Star* (Rochester, NY), November 10, 1848.

59. Only the *Grass Valley Telegraph* sent a reporter to the convention, and he noted

only that Blacks came together to "compare notes, communicate information as to the general condition of things among themselves, and if possible fix upon some common plan for the intellectual, moral, and social improvement of their condition as a class in this State." The paper stated that racist southerners in California were as irrelevant, as "the ultra abolitionists of the North are among the Northern men . . . these good folks only are desirous to see the condition of the colored people in our midst improved, by means of proper educational and social privileges, to the end they may become intelligent, law abiding and useful." Quoted in *Minutes of Negro State Colored Convention*.

60. Bell, *Survey*, 203.

61. Carter G. Woodson, ed., *The Mind of the Negro as Reflected in Letters Written during the Crisis, 1800–1860* (Westport, CT: Greenwood, 1969), 654. Quoted in David Brion Davis, *The Problem of Slavery in the Age of Emancipation* (New York: Alfred A. Knopf, 2014), 193.

62. Lapp, *Blacks in Gold Rush*, 10.

63. Delilah Beasley, *The Negro Trail Blazers of California*, reprint of author's ed. (Los Angeles, 1919; New York: Macmillan, 1997), 78.

64. "Case of 'Archy,'" *Sacramento (CA) Daily Union*, January 9, 1858.

65. *Dred Scott*, 60 U.S. at 393.

66. Archy, *supra* note 60, at 167. See also Finkelman, "Law of Slavery," 461.

67. Wong, *Neither Fugitive nor Free*, 7.

68. Hudson, *Making of Mammy Pleasant*, 33.

69. Eddie S. Glaude Jr., *Exodus! Religion, Race, and Nation in Early Nineteenth-Century Black America* (Chicago: University of Chicago Press, 2000).

70. Spires, "Imagining," 275.

71. [William?] Nubia [Newby] to Douglass, *Frederick Douglass' Paper* (Rochester, NY), June 1, 1855.

72. Ernest, *Liberation Historiography*, 263.

73. Hallie Q. Brown, *Homespun Heroines and Other Women of Distinction* (Xenia, OH: Aldine Publishing Company, 1926), 241. Stewart returned to San Francisco and resumed teaching with Reverend Sanderson after the Emancipation Proclamation. See also Beasley, *Negro Trail Blazers*; and Nicholas Patrick Beck, "The Other Children: Minority Education in California Public Schools from Statehood to 1890" (EdD diss., University of California, Los Angeles, 1975).

74. See Ernest, *Liberation Historiography*, 263, on how the communal praxis of the Colored Conventions collected the scattered bones of a people unmoored.

75. Charlotte Brown v. Omnibus Railroad Company (12th Dist. San Francisco 1863).

CONTRIBUTORS

Erica L. Ball is professor of history and Black studies at Occidental College.

Kabria Baumgartner is associate professor of American studies and core faculty in Women's studies at the University of New Hampshire.

Joan L. Bryant is associate professor of African American studies at Syracuse University.

Jim Casey is assistant professor of African American studies, history, and English at Pennsylvania State University.

Benjamin Fagan is associate professor of English at Auburn University.

P. Gabrielle Foreman is professor of English, African American studies, and history at Penn State University, where she holds the Paterno Family Chair of Liberal Arts. She is an affiliate professor at Penn State University Libraries and at the University of Delaware's Departments of English, History, and Africana Studies.

Eric Gardner is professor of English at Saginaw Valley State University.

Andre E. Johnson is associate professor of communication at the University of Memphis.

Cheryl Janifer LaRoche is an archeologist and historian in the anthropology department at the University of Maryland, College Park.

Sarah Lynn Patterson is assistant professor of African American literature and culture in the Department of English at the University of Massachusetts, Amherst.

Carla L. Peterson is professor emerita in the Department of English at the University of Maryland, College Park.

Jean Pfaelzer is professor of English, women and gender studies, and Asian studies at the University of Delaware.

Daina Ramey Berry is chair of the Department of History and the Oliver H. Radkey Professor at the University of Texas at Austin.

Selena R. Sanderfer is associate professor in the history department at Western Kentucky University.

Derrick R. Spires is associate professor of English at Cornell University and an affiliate faculty member of American studies, media studies, and visual studies.

Jermaine Thibodeaux is assistant professor in the Clara Luper Department of African and African American Studies at the University of Oklahoma, Norman.

Psyche Williams-Forson is chair and associate professor of American studies at the University of Maryland, College Park, and an affiliate faculty member of anthropology, African American studies, theater, dance and performing studies, women's studies, and the Consortium on Race, Gender, and Ethnicity.

Jewon Woo is associate professor of English at Lorain County Community College, Ohio.

INDEX

Page numbers in italics refer to illustrations.